STUDY GUIDE TO ACCOMPANY

WONNACOTT AND WONNACOTT:
ECONOMICS

STUDY GUIDE TO ACCOMPANY

WONNACOTT AND WONNACOTT: ECONOMICS

THIRD EDITION

PAUL WONNACOTT
University of Maryland

RONALD WONNACOTT
University of Western Ontario

PETER HOWITT
University of Western Ontario

McGRAW-HILL BOOK COMPANY

New York St. Louis San Francisco Auckland Bogotá Hamburg Johannesburg
London Madrid Mexico Montreal New Delhi Panama Paris
São Paulo Singapore Sydney Tokyo Toronto

Study Guide
to Accompany Wonnacott and Wonnacott:
ECONOMICS

1 2 3 4 5 6 7 8 9 0 WEBWEB 8 9 8 7 6

ISBN 0-07-071661-7

This book was set in Caledonia by Better Graphics.
The editors were Alison Meersschaert and Paul V. Short;
the production supervisor was Joe Campanella.
New drawings were done by J & R Services, Inc.
Webcrafters, Inc., was printer and binder.

CONTENTS

PART FIVE
MICROECONOMICS: IS OUR OUTPUT PRODUCED EFFICIENTLY?   151

PART SIX
ECONOMIC EFFICIENCY: ISSUES OF OUR TIME   207

PART SEVEN
MICROECONOMICS: HOW INCOME IS DISTRIBUTED   257

ANSWERS TO CROSSWORD PUZZLES   307

PREFACE

This study guide is intended to help the student who is taking an introductory economics course using the textbook *Economics* by Paul Wonnacott and Ronald Wonnacott. It makes no attempt to be self-contained: it can be used as a supplement to, not as a substitute for, the textbook.

Each chapter is designed for you to read and work through after reading the corresponding chapter in the textbook. Each study-guide chapter contains seven sections:

1. *Major purpose.* This section sets out very briefly the basic ideas that will be developed in the chapter.

2. *Learning objectives.* This section consists of a list of tasks that you should be able to accomplish after you have studied the chapter in the textbook and in the study guide. The purpose of this section is twofold. First, it should help to give you direction and purpose while studying the rest of the chapter. Second, it should serve as a checklist to test your comprehension after reading the chapter.

3. *Highlights of chapter.* This section contains a summary of the important points of the chapter. Its purpose is mainly to reinforce the textbook by going over these main points from a somewhat different perspective and adding illustrative examples. To a student learning a subject for the first time, everything is likely to appear equally important. This section should help sort out the more important from the less by focusing more narrowly than the text and by drawing attention to the particularly important material.

4. *Important terms: Match the columns.* This section sets out the important concepts along with the definition of each. Your task is to match each term with its definition. One of the best ways of doing this is to write out your own definition first; this provides the most effective form of review.

5. *True-false questions.*

6. *Multiple-choice questions.*

7. *Exercises.*

These three sections are meant to help you learn by doing. Besides providing reinforcement through repetition, many of the questions and exercises are designed to guide you toward discovering ideas that will be explicitly introduced only later in the textbook. Spend a few minutes going over the true-false and multiple-choice questions as a self-test, even if you believe you understand the textbook chapter well enough to proceed without using the study guide in any other way. Answers to questions in these sections are provided at the end of each chapter.

8. *Essay questions.* This section is designed to help you apply important concepts that have been developed in the text, as well as to stimulate your imagination. No answers have been provided for this section. Thus the questions may be used as material for classroom discussion.

9. *Crossword puzzles.* Every second chapter includes one of these puzzles. Our hope is that you will find them entertaining, whether or not you are a crossword puzzle enthusiast. Each puzzle, of course, draws heavily on the terms introduced in the related chapter.

This third edition of the study guide has a number of new chapters, corresponding to the new chapters of the Wonnacotts' textbook. In addition, each of the old chapters has been reworked with a view to improving the clarity of exposition, and all the old true-false and multiple-choice questions have been replaced or reworked.

As the two new authors of this edition, we should like to thank Peter Howitt for his efforts in writing the original first edition, and bringing this guide so successfully through the second edition as well. Those familiar with the previous editions will clearly see the mark of his substantial contributions to this edition. At the same time we should like to point out the many contributions he has made to the textbook itself. It has been a personal and professional pleasure to be associated in this joint effort with so discerning and distinguished a colleague.

Paul Wonnacott
Ronald J. Wonnacott

SPECIAL NOTE FOR THOSE STUDYING ONLY THE SOFT-COVER VOLUME
"AN INTRODUCTION TO MICROECONOMICS"

For students studying the microeconomics soft-cover volume, use the first six chapters of this study guide and then skip to Chapter 20, which corresponds to Chapter 7 in the soft-cover volume. The key for the balance of both books is as shown in the following chart.

Numbers referred to in this study guide	Numbering in microeconomics soft-cover volume	Key
Chapter 20, Figure 20-1, 20-2, etc.	Chapter 7, Figure 7-1, 7-2, etc.	Subtract 13 from any chapter number in this study guide. Similarly, treat any figure, appendix, box, or table number in the same way.
Parts 5, 6, and 7	Parts 2, 3, and 4	Subtract 3 from Part number in this study guide.

A FASTER WAY TO STUDY ECONOMICS

MICRO STUDY GUIDE: Computerized Interactive Study Guide to accompany
Wonnacott/Wonnacott: ECONOMICS, 3/e

Micro Study Guide is a new computer program for the Apple II and IIe and the IBM PC computers, keyed directly to your textbook and study guide for faster understanding and learning of economics.

Chapter by chapter, in a tutorial fashion, Micro Study Guide allows you to check yourself on how much you have learned in the exercises provided: fill-in-the-blanks, multiple-choice, and matching. With interactive practice and self-testing, your understanding and learning of economics will be enhanced.

Micro Study Guide is easy to use. Three simple keystrokes are all you need to get started.

If you don't own a computer, ask your professor where you may use one on campus.

To order, complete and mail the order form. Be sure to indicate the type of computer you have and your method of payment.

ORDER FORM (Micro Study Guide to accompany Wonnacott/Wonnacott, ECONOMICS, 3/e)

Mail to:

Soft Productions, Inc.
100 Center - Professional Building
Mishawaka, IN 46544

Name _____

School _____

Address _____

City _____

State _____ Zip _____

Please send me Micro Study Guide

for _____

by _____

_____ Apple $12.95   _____ IBM $12.95

Other machines you would like

Software for _____
                (Brand name)

Computer I use _____

Year in College ____ SR   JR   SO   FR
                        (Circle one)

My Major _____

Please indicate method of payment

_____ Personal Check _____ Visa _____ MasterCard

Account # _____

Expiration Date _____

Signature _____
             (Required on all charges)

PART ONE

BASIC ECONOMIC CONCEPTS

CHAPTER 1

ECONOMIC PROBLEMS AND ECONOMIC GOALS

MAJOR PURPOSE

The major purpose of this chapter is to provide a broad overview of *economic developments* and *economic objectives*, as a background for the more detailed topics of the following chapters. Five major economic objectives are discussed: *high employment*, a *stable average level of prices*, *efficiency*, *equity*, and *growth*. You should gain some understanding of the problems which have arisen in the U.S. economy, and why it is not always easy to solve these problems. In particular, it may be difficult to deal with problems when the government has a number of goals, some of which are *in conflict*. That is, solving one problem may make others more difficult to solve.

Learning Objectives

After you have studied this chapter in the textbook and study guide, you should be able to:

List five major economic goals

Describe, in broad terms, what has happened to U.S. unemployment, inflation, growth, and the distribution of income in recent decades

Distinguish the views of Adam Smith and J. M. Keynes with respect to the proper role of the government

Define terms such as inflation, deflation, recession, and efficiency

Distinguish between allocative efficiency and technological efficiency

Describe briefly how changes in relative prices may contribute to allocative efficiency

Explain why it is harder to identify the problems created by inflation than those created by unemployment

Explain the distinction between equity and equality

Explain how some goals may be *complementary*, while others are in *conflict*

If you have studied the appendix to Chapter 1 in the textbook, you should also be able to:

Describe some of the ways in which people may be misled by graphs

Explain the advantage of using a ratio (or logarithmic) scale

Explain the difference between a nominal and a real measure

HIGHLIGHTS OF CHAPTER

Economics is one of the social sciences—it involves the systematic study of human behavior. The aspect of behavior which interests economists is how people earn a living, and the problems which may make it difficult for them to do so. In the words of Alfred Marshall, economics is the study of people "in the ordinary business of life."

The objective of *economic theory* is to discover and explain the basic principles and laws that govern economic life. Economic theory helps us to understand questions such as: Why are some prices higher than others? Why does the average level of prices rise? Why are some people richer than others? What causes large-scale unemployment?

Economic policy addresses such questions as: How can the government reduce inflation? How can it reduce the unemployment rate? What steps can individuals take to increase their incomes, or reduce the risks of unemployment? How does a business increase its profits?

Economic theory and economic policy go hand-in-hand. Just as a physician needs to know how the human body works in order to heal patients, so the economic policymaker needs to understand economic theory in order to prescribe economic policies that will be successful. Scientific studies of how things work are often inspired by a policy motive—to do something about problems. Thus, scientists strive to unlock the mysteries of the human cell in order to find out why cancer occurs, and ultimately to be able to cure cancer. Similarly, studies of how the economy works are often motivated by the desire to solve economic problems, such as recession and large-scale unemployment.

Perhaps the most hotly contested issue in all of economics is the question of how much the government should intervene in the economy. Many of those in government are motivated by the desire to promote the public welfare. After all, the policies that they promote will be their monument in history. But well-meaning policymakers do not always adopt policies that work in practice. Furthermore, the government may be used to benefit individuals or groups at the expense of the public as a whole.

Adam Smith attacked many governmental interventions in the economy as being contrary to the public interest. Even though tariffs benefited the protected sectors of the economy, they inflicted higher costs on consumers, and acted as a drag on efficiency. Smith conceived of the private economy as a self-regulating mechanism. By pursuing their own interests, individuals would regularly contribute to the common good. There was no need for extensive government interference to ensure that things would come out all right.

A century and a half later, J. M. Keynes was skeptical of Smith's message of laissez faire. Things were not coming out all right. The economy was in a deep depression, with many people out of work. It was the responsibility of the government, said Keynes, to do something about this tragic situation. He recommended government spending on roads and other public works as a way to provide jobs.

Full employment is one of the major economic objectives. Four others are also described in this chapter: a *stable average level of prices, efficiency,* an *equitable distribution of income,* and economic *growth.* Other goals might be added to this list, for example, economic freedom, economic security, and the control of pollution.

The first two goals—full employment and stable prices—come under the heading of maintaining a stable *equilibrium* in the economy. There has in fact been considerable instability in the U.S. economy. The most notable disturbance occurred during the Great Depression of the 1930s, when output and employment dropped sharply, and remained at very low levels for a full decade. During World War II, there was an effort to produce as many munitions as possible. Unemployment ceased to be a significant problem, but prices began to rise substantially. Since the end of World War II in 1945, we have avoided severe disturbances comparable to those from 1929 to 1945. However, there have been periodic recessions, with rising unemployment. Inflation was severe during the later 1940s and the 1970s. During the decade of the 1970s, the average level of prices doubled.

Of the major economic problems, unemployment is perhaps the most obvious. When employment declines, we have less output to enjoy. We not only forego the output which might have been produced, but we also must face the demoralization that comes with unemployment.

The problems with inflation are less obvious. When people buy goods, they obviously dislike higher and higher prices. But there are two sides to every transaction—the buyer's side and the seller's. With widespread inflation, not only do the prices of what we buy increase. Wage rates also go up, as well as the prices of what we sell. It is not so clear whether individuals are net gainers or net losers.

However, there are certain segments of the population who do lose. Those who have pensions set in money terms lose: As prices rise, their pensions buy less. (However, some pensions, including the Social Security pensions paid by the government, are increased to compensate for inflation.) Those who own government bonds or other interest-bearing securities lose. Through the years, they receive payments whose value becomes smaller and smaller as prices rise. On the other hand, people who have borrowed can benefit: They repay their loans in money whose value has declined.

Inflation generates a feeling that the economic system is unfair. There are arbitrary redistributions of income and wealth, such as the gains to debtors and losses to bond owners. Inflation can also make it more difficult to make wise and well-informed decisions. *Prices* provide an important source of information to the business executive and consumer. During periods of rapid inflation, when all prices are rising at a brisk pace, the message carried by prices may be obscured. It becomes more difficult to make good decisions.

If inflation accelerates to very high rates—such as 1,000% per year—it becomes known as *hyperinflation*. Money is losing its value so rapidly that people may refuse to accept it. Because money is practically useless, sellers may feel compelled to barter their products for other goods. Such barter transactions are very cumbersome and time-consuming.

Most inflations do not accelerate into hyperinflation. Hyperinflation is relatively rare, except for losers during wartime or early postwar periods. There are, however, a few exceptions, such as in present-day Bolivia, where a hyperinflation is raging even though the country has not been defeated in a war.

There are two important types of efficiency. *Technological efficiency* means getting the most output from a given set of inputs (labor, machinery, raw materials). *Allocative efficiency* occurs when the economy is producing the best combination of outputs, using the lowest-cost combination of inputs. Allocative efficiency means producing the goods and services which the consuming public wants most. It is possible for an economic system to produce "white elephants" in a technologically efficient manner. But this system would not be producing what people want; it would not be allocatively efficient. Similarly, if everyone were a lawyer, and nobody a doctor, there would be allocative inefficiency—even if everyone were a superb lawyer.

Equity means *fairness*, and that raises the question of what fairness means. There can be obvious disagreements. Those with low incomes are likely to argue that a more equal distribution of income would be fairer.

Those with higher incomes often argue that their high incomes are the result of hard work; it is fair for them to be paid more because they have worked harder.

Many people would, however, agree that the government should take some steps to help those who are poverty-stricken, for example, by taxing the rich to provide services for the needy. The question arises, however, as to how far this process should be taken. Clearly, if the government confiscated all income above the average, and gave the revenues to low income people, then it would severely interfere with the incentive to work hard. (This would also greatly increase the incentive to cheat on taxes!) Even less drastic steps to redistribute income can decrease incentives, and thus decrease the size of the national "pie." The size of the pie depends in part on how it is cut up.

Economic growth is often advocated for its own sake. In a growing company, we enjoy more goods and services. Furthermore, growth may make it easier to meet other goals, such as reducing poverty. However, we should not simply assume that the more growth, the better. Growth comes at a cost. Most obviously, if we produce more machinery and equipment to help us grow, then we will give up the current consumer goods that might have been produced instead of the machinery and equipment.

Some goals—such as a high level of employment and an elimination of poverty—are *complementary*. Progress on the one contributes to progress on the other. If jobs are provided for people, they are less likely to be poor.

Other goals are *in conflict*. If people buy more goods and services, they will help to increase the number of jobs. But they will also make it easier for sellers to raise their prices. Thus, if the government takes steps to encourage spending, it may help ease one problem (unemployment) while making another worse (inflation). In such circumstances, good policies may be particularly difficult to develop.

Important Terms: Match the Columns

Match the term in the first column with the corresponding phrase in the second column.

_____ 1. Laissez faire	a. Total number of people in a country
_____ 2. Great Depression	b. An increase in the average level of prices
_____ 3. Labor force	c. Change in relative prices
_____ 4. Population	d. Pursuing one helps in attainment of other
_____ 5. Recession	e. A decrease in the average level of prices
_____ 6. J. M. Keynes	f. When large-scale unemployment existed
_____ 7. Inflation	g. Producing the best combination of outputs, using the lowest-cost combination of inputs
_____ 8. Deflation	h. Pursuing one makes other more difficult to attain
_____ 9. Allocative efficiency	

_____ **10.** Complementary goals

_____ **11.** Conflicting goals

_____ **12.** This can help promote allocative efficiency

i. A broad decline in production, involving many sectors of the economy

j. Leave the economy alone

k. Idea that government should spend for public works when necessary to get economy out of depression, and restore full employment

l. Sum of those employed and those unemployed

True-False

T F **1.** The United States was the only advanced country whose rate of growth of output fell after the first great increase in oil prices in 1973–1974.

T F **2.** The length of the average manufacturing workweek in the United States declined about 25% between 1900 and 1950, but has changed very little since that time.

T F **3.** By the term "invisible hand," Adam Smith was expressing the idea that once people gain power in a government, they generally are interested in the public good.

T F **4.** Since 1970, recessions have been much less severe than those of the 1950s and 1960s.

T F **5.** A recession is a decline in total output, employment, and income, and is marked by a widespread contraction in *many* industries.

T F **6.** Changes in the average rate of inflation make an important contribution, since they are the key to improvements in allocative efficiency.

T F **7.** Most economists would agree that some degree of income inequality is desirable, as a way of providing people with an incentive to work hard.

T F **8.** Not all families have the same needs. For example, a large family spends more for food than does a small one. Yet this difference has been ignored by the government in picking the income figure which represents the poverty line.

T F **9.** The percentage of the population living in poverty declined during the 1960s, but has increased since 1979.

T F **10.** Over the past three decades, there has been a consistent trend in the United States: the rich have gotten richer, and the poor have gotten poorer.

T F **11.** Changes in the overall level of prices and changes in relative prices present roughly equal problems, and the government should give about equal importance to reducing changes in the average price level and changes in relative prices.

Multiple Choice

1. Between 1929 and 1933, during the early part of the Great Depression, total output in the United States:

　a. declined about 30%

　b. declined about 20%

　c. declined about 10%

　d. declined about 5%

　e. remained approximately stable; the depression represented an interruption of growth, not an actual decline in output

2. Since 1900, output per capita in the United States:

　a. has approximately doubled, while the length of the workweek has declined

　b. has approximately quadrupled, while the length of the workweek has declined

　c. has approximately doubled, while the length of the workweek has remained stable

　d. has approximately quadrupled, while the length of the workweek has remained stable

　e. has remained stable, while the length of the workweek has declined sharply; all the gains have come in the form of more leisure

3. By the term "invisible hand," Adam Smith was expressing the idea that:

　a. there are no economic conflicts among nations

　b. there would be no economic conflicts among nations, if countries would eliminate tariffs

　c. there are no conflicts between what is good for an individual, and what is good for the government

　d. by pursuing their own individual interests, people frequently promote the interests of society

　e. business executives have a natural interest in keeping prices down, and preventing inflation

4. The main criticism of a tariff on automobiles is that it:

　a. increases unemployment

　b. increases government spending

　c. increases government deficits

d. raises the costs of automobile companies

e. raises the price of cars bought by the public

5. In his *General Theory*, Keynes's principal concern was with the goal of:

    a. stable prices   **d.** technological efficiency

    b. low unemployment   **e.** an equitable distribution of

    c. allocative efficiency   income

6. In his *General Theory*, Keynes argued that the best way to restore full employment was by:

    a. increases in prices, which would give employers an incentive to produce more

    b. decreases in wages, which would give employers an incentive to hire more labor

    c. increases in spending for public works, which would provide people with jobs

    d. cuts in defense spending, which would provide incentives to produce nondefense goods

    e. cuts in nondefense spending of the government, which would provide incentives to produce goods for the private sectors of the economy

7. Which of the following is counted as being unemployed?

    a. someone who has just retired at age 65

    b. a full-time student not looking for a job

    c. someone who has recently graduated from college, and is looking for his or her first full-time job

    d. convicts in prisons

    e. all of the above

8. Hyperinflation is most likely to occur:

    a. during depressions

    b. during recessions

    c. when the growth of output is very rapid

    d. in losing countries, during or shortly after a war

    e. in winning countries, during or shortly after a war

9. During the past two decades, the prices of computers have fallen, while the price of oil has risen. As a result, manufacturers and other businesses have used more computers, and have conserved on energy. This switch toward more computers and less energy is an illustration of:

    a. allocative efficiency

    b. technological efficiency

    c. the effects of inflation

    d. a less equal distribution of income

    e. a more equal distribution of income

10. Allocative efficiency occurs when:

    a. growth is at a maximum

    b. the economy has reached its best size, and stopped growing

    c. income per capita has reached its best size, and has leveled out

    d. the best combination of outputs is produced, using the lowest-cost combination of inputs

    e. the best combination of outputs is produced, regardless of the cost

11. Which is the best example of *allocative* inefficiency?

    a. producing too many cars, and not enough housing

    b. slow growth

    c. inequality of incomes

    d. inflation

    e. hyperinflation

12. Which is the best example of *technological* inefficiency?

    a. producing too many cars, and not enough housing

    b. slow growth

    c. inflation

    d. inequality of incomes

    e. sloppy management

13. *Equity* in the distribution of income means:

    a. equality

    b. fairness

    c. more for everyone, as a result of growth

    d. more for those who can't work

    e. more for those who work hard

14. Which is a cost of economic growth?

    a. less current output

    b. less future output

    c. less current consumption

    d. less allocative efficiency

    e. more unemployment in the future

Exercise

In the following passage, choose the correct word or phrase in the brackets.

Economic history is a story of both progress and problems. Some evidence of progress shows up in Figure 1-1 in the textbook. Here we see that output per person has increased by approximately [100%, 200%, 300%] since 1900, and about [25%, 75%, 150%] since 1960. If we were to look at total output of the economy—rather than at output *per person*—we would find that total output has increased by [an even greater percentage than output per person, a somewhat smaller percentage].

The right-hand panel of Figure 1-1 shows another source of gain. Not only have we produced more, but we have done so with a shorter workweek. The decline in the workweek occurred mainly in the period from [1900 to 1950, 1950 to 1985]. Notice also the very sharp drop between 1925 and 1935. This decrease was [the result of a much more rapidly improving economy which allowed more leisure, one of the unfortunate effects of the depression which reduced the demand for output]. We conclude that a shorter workweek may be an indication of either an improvement—where people voluntarily work shorter hours because they can afford it—or an indication that work is hard to get.

Successes and problems also show up in Figure 1-3 in the textbook. The [upward trend in output, downward trend in unemployment, both] since 1950 show(s) how things have improved. One of the problems is shown by the vertical shaded bars, which mark periods of [recession, depression, inflation, poverty]. During such periods, [the unemployment rate increases, output declines, both]. The longest period without a recession was between [1940 and 1955, 1950 and 1960, 1961 and 1969, 1975 and 1985].

Figure 1-4 shows the average level of prices. A rise in this curve is an indication of inflation. The more rapid is inflation, the steeper is the curve. We see that infla-

tion was very rapid between [1950 and 1960, 1960 and 1970, 1970 and 1980].

Finally, Figure 1-5 shows the percentage of the population living in poverty; a decline in the percentage is a sign of success. Observe that, at the beginning of the period shown, the incidence of poverty declined, from about [15%, 22%, 30%] in 1960 to about [5%, 8%, 11%] when it reached its low point in the 1970s. By 1984, the percentage living in poverty had increased to about [15%, 22%, 30%].

Answers

Important Terms: 1 j 2 f 3 l 4 a 5 i 6 k 7 b 8 e 9 g 10 d 11 h 12 c
True-False: 1 F 2 T 3 F 4 F 5 T 6 F 7 T 8 F 9 T 10 F 11 F
Multiple Choice: 1 a 2 b 3 d 4 e 5 b 6 c 7 c 8 d 9 a 10 d 11 a 12 e 13 b 14 c
Exercise: 300%, 75%, an even greater percentage than output per person, 1900 to 1950, one of the unfortunate effects of the depression which reduced the demand for output, upward trend in output, recession, both, 1961 and 1969, 1970 and 1980, 22%, 11%, 15%.

APPENDIX

This appendix provides additional information and practice for those who have already studied the appendix to Chapter 1 in the textbook.

Graphs

During rainy spells, sales of lawn furniture decline. A simple version of the relationship between weather and lawn furniture sales is illustrated in Figure 1-1 below.

The two measures used in this graph—furniture sales and rainfall—are examples of **variables**. A variable

is something that can change, or vary, from time to time or from place to place. For example, the amount of rain can vary from April to July.

The statement that the sales of lawn furniture decline during rainy spells means that there is a relationship between the two variables in Figure 1-1. In particular, it means that when rainfall increases, then sales decrease. We want to see how this relationship is indicated by the graph.

Notice the two *axes* with the numbers marked on them, that meet at the point labeled 0. The *vertical axis* has sales of lawn furniture on it. Every time you go up a notch this means that sales of lawn furniture go up by $1,000. The amount of rainfall is marked on the horizontal axis. Every time you go one notch to the right this indicates 1 more inch of rainfall per month. The point where the axes meet is the *origin*. This is the zero point on both axes—the point where there would be no rainfall and no one would sell any lawn furniture.

The relationship between the two variables is depicted by the line marked with the letters A through F. You "read" this line by using the axes. For example, consider point A. You can measure the height of this point on the vertical axis, just as you can measure a child's height on a wall. The dashed line going to the left from A is like a book held level on top of the child's head, showing that the height of A is 6. The distance that A lies to the right can be measured on the horizontal axis. The dashed line drawn down from A shows us that this distance is 1.

Here is the way to "read" point A. When there is only 1 inch of rainfall per month (when you go 1 notch to the right), then there is $6,000 worth of lawn furniture sold (6 notches up). Likewise, point B tells you that

FIGURE 1-1

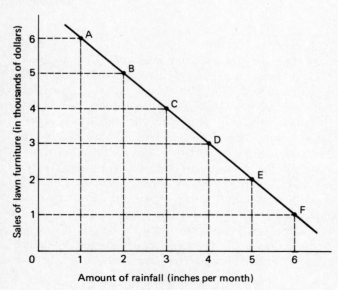

when there are 2 inches of rainfall then sales are $5,000. In this way, each time you read a point on the line you get one bit of information. These "bits" are shown in Table 1-1 below.

Table 1-1

Point	A	B	C	D	E	F
Rainfall	1	2	3	4	5	6
Sales	6	5	4	3	2	1

Thus, the rule for "reading" the graph goes as follows. Suppose you want to find out how much lawn furniture will be sold when there is some particular amount of rainfall (say, 2 inches per month). Start at the origin. Now mark off that amount of rainfall to the right, along the horizontal axis (go two notches to the right). Then the height of the line directly above that point (5) is the answer to your question. Question 1 at the end of this appendix gives an exercise in reading graphs.

Slope

The statement we began with doesn't just say that rainfall and sales are related. It also says something about the *direction* of that relationship. It says that when rainfall increases then sales don't increase, they decrease. In other words, sales are **negatively** related or **inversely** related to rainfall, because they change in the opposite direction.

You can tell the direction of this relationship by inspecting the line in Figure 1-1. Notice that it slopes downward to the right. This means that as you move to the right along the horizontal axis (as rainfall increases) the height of the line decreases (sales decrease). For example, compare points *A* and *B*. As rainfall increases from 1 to 2, sales decrease from 6 to 5.

A *positive* or *direct* relationship is shown in Figure 1-2. (See question 2 at the end of the appendix.) In this case, both variables change in the same direction. When snowfall increases, then sales of ski equipment increase as well. You can tell this from the way the line slopes upward to the right. As you move to the right (as snowfall increases) the line gets higher (sales increase).

You may wonder whether a graph is needed to show the direction of a relationship. After all, the same idea of direction can be expressed in simple English by our original statement that lawn furniture sales decline during rainy spells. Why use graphs? One reason is that a graph shows more than just the *direction* of a relationship. It also shows the *strength*. For example, when rainfall increases from 1 to 2 inches per month, Figure 1-1 doesn't just show that lawn furniture sales decrease. It also shows by *how much*—they decrease by $1,000, from $6,000 to $5,000. This goes beyond our original statement, which told us that sales would decrease, but not by how much.

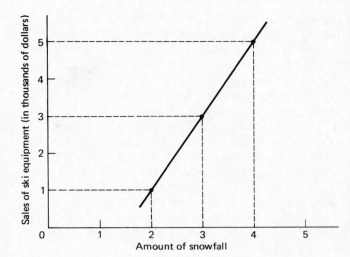

FIGURE 1-2

The *strength* of the relationship is indicated by *how steep* the line is. For example, the steep line in Figure 1-2 shows a strong relationship between snowfall and ski equipment sales. When snowfall increases by 1 (going, say, from 2 to 3), then sales increase by 2 (from 1 to 3). Compare this to the much weaker relationship shown by the flatter line in Figure 1-3. In this case, when snowfall increases from 2 to 3, sales increase only by ½ (from 1 to 1½).

Thus, both of these ideas—the direction and strength of a relationship—are shown by the way the line slopes. Direction is shown by whether the curve is slanted up or down. Strength is shown by how steep the line is.

There is a mathematical term that expresses both these ideas. This term is the **slope**. The slope of a line is defined as *the amount by which the height of the line changes when you go one more unit to the right on the horizontal axis*. For example, the slope of the line in Figure 1-2 is 2, because when snowfall increases by 1 unit (when you go 1 unit to the right), then sales of ski equipment (given by the height of the line) change by 2 units. The slope in Figure 1-1 is −1. This is negative

FIGURE 1-3

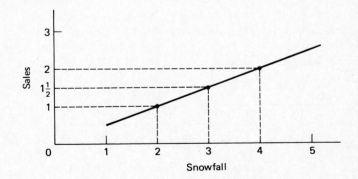

because when rainfall increases by 1 unit, then the change in sales (the change in the height of the line) is negative; sales decrease by 1 unit.

Thus, a positive slope indicates a line that slopes upward to the right, showing a positive relationship. A negative slope indicates a line that slopes downward to the right, showing a negative relationship.

Likewise, a larger slope indicates a steeper line, showing a stronger relationship. For example, the slope of the line in Figure 1-3 is only ½, showing that a 1-unit increase in snowfall increases sales by only $500 (½ of a unit). The slope of the steeper line in Figure 1-2 is 2, showing that the same increase in snowfall would increase sales by $2,000 (2 units). Questions 3 and 4 at the end of the appendix are designed to familiarize you with the idea of slope.

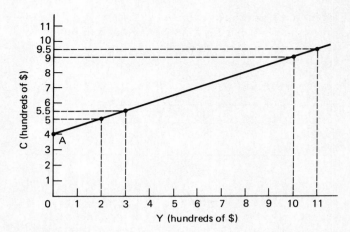

FIGURE 1-4

Linear Equations

Sometimes the relationship between two variables is shown not by a graph, but by an equation. Suppose you are told that my expenditures each month on consumer goods (C) depend upon my monthly income (Y) according to the equation:*

$$C = \$400 + 0.5Y$$

In simple English, this equation says I will spend $400 plus half my income. As my income varies from month to month the equation tells you how my expenditures will vary. It thus describes a relationship between these two variables, Y and C. Whatever my income (Y) is, the equation tells you how much I will spend (C).

For example, choose some convenient value for my income, like Y = 1,000. Then substitute this into the equation to get $C = 400 + 0.5 \times 1,000 = 400 + 500 = 900$. This tells us that when my income (Y) is 1,000, my expenditures (C) will be 900. Choose any other convenient value, like Y = 1,100. Substituting this into the equation tells you that when my income is 1,100, then my expenditures will be $C = 400 + 0.5 \times 1,100 = 950$. Each time you choose a value of Y and make this substitution you thus get one bit of information. These two bits are shown in Table 1-2. As an exercise, fill in the rest of the table.

Figure 1-4 shows this relationship in a graph. The slope of this line is 0.5. This is because every time my income increases by $100 (go to the right one unit along the horizontal axis), I spend another $50 (the rise in the line is 0.5 of a unit). If the equation had been C = 400 + 0.75Y, then it would have said I spend $400 plus three-

quarters of my income. In this case, the slope of the line would have been 0.75, because every time my income increased by $100 I would spend another $75.

In general, any equation of the sort $C = a + bY$ represents a line with a slope equal to b. Such an equation is called a *linear* equation. For example, the linear equation pictured in Figure 1-4 has a = 400 and b = 0.5.

The number b (that is, 0.5) is known as the *coefficient* of the variable Y. It indicates the slope of the line. The number a (400) shows how high the line is where it meets the vertical axis (point A). Thus, a is often called the *vertical intercept*. For example, the linear equation shown in Figure 1-4 has a = 400, and the line hits the vertical axis when C = 400.

At this point, you should try questions 5 and 6, which deal with linear equations.

Curves

So far we have drawn only straight lines. They are easy to use because they have a *constant* slope. For example, as you move down the line in Figure 1-1, from A to B, to C, and so on, every time you go 1 unit to the right the line falls by exactly 1 unit; not more or less. The slope stays constant at −1.

Not all relationships in economics can be described by straight lines. Some are described by curves, like the one in Figure 1-5. This curve shows how a student's final grade in economics depends on how many hours the student spends studying each day.

This curve does not have a constant slope. As you move to the right along the curve it gets flatter. For

Table 1-2

Y	100	200	300	400	500	600	700	800	900	1,000	1,100
C										900	950

* Note: To represent income, economists almost always use the letter Y, not I; they reserve I to denote investment.

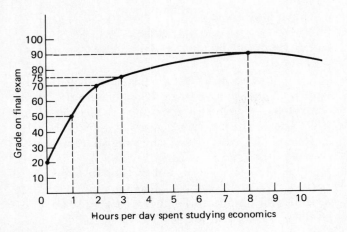

FIGURE 1-5

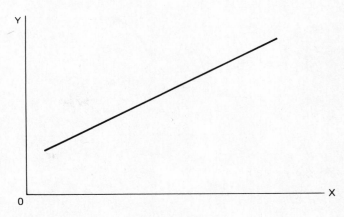

FIGURE 1-6

example, going from 0 hours to 1 hour makes the curve rise by 30—from 20 to 50. But then going from 1 hour to 2 hours makes it rise by only 20—from 50 to 70, and going from 2 to 3 hours makes it rise by only 5. Each time you go one more unit to the right on the horizontal axis, the curve rises by less than the last time.

When dealing with a curve, we can still define the *slope* the way we did before. The slope of a curve is the amount by which the height of the curve changes when you go one more unit to the right on the horizontal axis. But we must remember that this slope changes as you move along the curve. Starting at zero hours in Figure 1-5, the slope decreases, from 30, to 20, to 5, and so on.

The decreasing slope in Figure 1-5 indicates that as you spend more and more time studying, each extra hour may raise your grade, *but not by as much as the previous hour.* The first hour raises your grade by 30 marks, the next by only 20. After 2 hours per day, you are beginning to get saturated with economics, and the next hour raises your grade only 5 marks. Thus, the strength of the relationship between hours and grades is decreasing as you spend more hours. This is an example of diminishing returns; the payoff (in higher grades) diminishes as you study more and more.

Notice that, according to Figure 1-5, once you get beyond 8 hours per day, the relationship not only changes in strength, it also changes in direction, from positive to negative. After 8 hours the slope becomes negative. Studying beyond this point tires you so much it does more harm than good. Each extra hour causes your grade to decrease.

Thus, a curve with a changing slope shows a relationship whose strength or direction is changing instead of remaining constant.

Other Kinds of Graphs

Sometimes we don't bother to put numbers on the axes. For example, consider the linear relationship in Figure 1-6. The variables X and Y are shown on the axes,

but there are no numbers, except for the 0 at the origin. Without the numbers we can't tell exactly what the relationship is between X and Y. But the graph still tells us something. It tells us that the relationship is a positive one, because the line has a positive slope. It also tells us that the relationship is linear (with a constant direction and strength) because the line is straight (with a constant slope).

Sometimes instead of numbers we put letters, as in Figure 1-7. This still doesn't tell us the exact relationship. But the letters give us handy points of reference. For example, take point A on the horizontal axis. We don't know in numbers how far to the right this is. But whatever this distance is, from point O to point A, we call it the distance OA. Likewise, we describe the distance along the horizontal axis from point A to point B as the distance AB.

When describing movement from E to F along the line, it helps to look at the triangle EFG. The change in X is the difference between the distance OB and the distance OA; that is, the distance AB. It also equals the base of this triangle, EG. Likewise, the change in Y can be read from the vertical axis as CD, or from the triangle

FIGURE 1-7

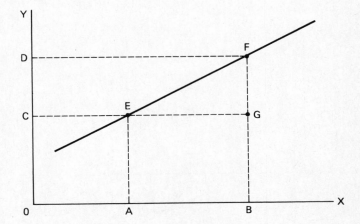

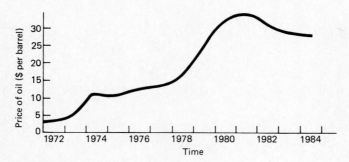

FIGURE 1-8

as *GF*. An exercise using this "letter code" is given in question 7.

Sometimes a graph will have numbers on it, but not starting at zero. For example, time is measured on the horizontal axis in Figure 1-8, starting at 1972. As long as each notch measures one more year, it doesn't matter that the "original" year is called 1972. A Moslem, whose time begins with Mohammed instead of Christ, would put 1392 on the origin of Figure 1-8. According to the Jewish calendar, the origin should be 5732. As long as we all know which convention is being used, the graph will mean the same.

The Ratio Scale

In Figure 1-8, every time you go one notch up the vertical axis, this represents the same change in the price of oil—$5. This is the way most graphs work—equal distances along an axis represent equal changes in the variable.

But there is an important exception to this rule. Look at Figure 1-9. In this graph, going up one notch on the vertical axis doesn't always mean the same change in the price level. The first notch takes you from 25 to 50—a change of 25. But when you move up to the second

FIGURE 1-9

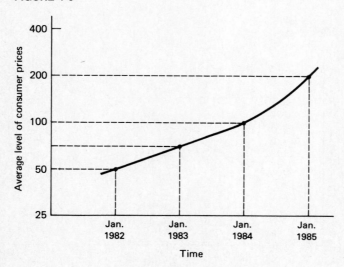

notch the price level goes from 50 to 100—a change this time of 50. The vertical axis measures the price level not on the usual scale, but on the **ratio scale**, or *logarithmic scale*.

As you move up a ratio scale, equal distances represent equal *percentage* changes. Going up from 25 to the first notch, the price level goes up by 100% to 50. Going to the second notch it again goes up by 100%—this time to 100. In this case, every notch higher represents a price level that is 100% higher.

We often use a ratio scale when we're primarily interested in the annual percentage rate of growth in a variable. For instance, when we're looking at the price level we usually want to know the rate of inflation. Ten percent inflation means that the price level has been growing at that rate per year.

The percentage rate of growth from one year to the next can be measured in such a diagram by the slope of the line. For example, as we go from January 1984 to January 1985 the change in the height of the curve is one notch, or 100%. (This is just an illustration. In fact, the rate of inflation in the United States that year was only 4%.) Thus, the slope of the curve is 100%. This tell us that over the calendar year 1984 there was 100% inflation.

In this kind of graph, a straight line represents something that grows at a constant percentage rate. Between January 1982 and January 1984 in Figure 1-9 the curve is a straight line, showing that the rate of inflation was constant over this 2-year interval. When the slope increases, as it does starting in January 1984, the rate of inflation is rising.

Geometric Series

There is one important technique that comes up frequently in economics that doesn't involve any graphs. Suppose someone gave you $1 today, then 50 cents tomorrow, then 25 cents the next day, and so on, each day giving you half as much as the day before. Let us suppose that the money is infinitely divisible so that you will continue to get 12½ cents, 6¼ cents, etc. If you stop to think how much you will be given in total, you will be faced with the problem of having to make the addition:

$$1 + \frac{1}{2} + \frac{1}{4} + \frac{1}{8} + \frac{1}{16} + \cdots$$

There is no end to the number of terms in this series. Nevertheless, there is an answer to the addition. For as each day passes the sum grows from $1 to $1.50 to $1.75 to $1.87½, to $1.93¾, and so forth. As you can see, the sum will approach an upper limit of $2. Every day, you are getting half of what it would take to get to $2. The shortfall keeps getting cut by half. You will never quite get there, because you will never get enough to bring you all the way up, just half that. But you will approach that sum asymptotically.

This is just an example of a problem that occurs often in economics. Suppose that a is some positive fraction, and you have to add the infinitely long series:

$$(1)\ S = 1 + a + a^2 + a^3 + a^4 + \cdots$$

This sum is called a geometric series. The previous example was obviously a special case of a geometric series, with $a = \frac{1}{2}$. There, I took a guess at the answer ($S = 2$), and showed how this would work. But it would be nice to be more systematic about it, especially when it gets to less obvious cases like $a = 0.8$. The following reasoning establishes a formula that can be used for any fraction a.

Multiply both sides of Equation (1) by a. Then, the two sides must continue to equal one another. Thus:

$$(2)\ aS = a(1 + a + a^2 + a^3 + a^4 + \cdots)$$

If we carry out the multiplication on the right-hand side of Equation (2) term by term we get:

$$(3)\ aS = a + a^2 + a^3 + a^4 + a^5 + \cdots$$

Now, suppose we subtract this equation from equation (1):

$$
\begin{aligned}
S &= 1 + a + a^2 + a^3 + \cdots \\
\text{Subtract}\quad aS &= \phantom{1 + {}} a + a^2 + a^3 + \cdots \\
\hline
S - aS &= 1 + 0 + 0 + 0 + \cdots
\end{aligned}
$$

Thus, we get the result $S(1 - a) = 1$. By dividing $(1 - a)$ into both sides of this last equation we get:

$$(4)\ S = \frac{1}{1 - a}$$

Equation (4) is the solution to our problem. This formula always gives the right answer. To check it out, note that when $a = \frac{1}{2}$, as in our example, then S indeed equals 2. (Now try $a = 0.8$).

Questions

1. Point A in Figure 1-10 has a height of _____, and lies a distance _____ to the right. Thus, it tells us that when there are _____ hundred police officers there will be _____ hundred crimes reported. If there are 600 officers there will be _____ hundred crimes, and with a thousand officers there will be _____ hundred crimes.

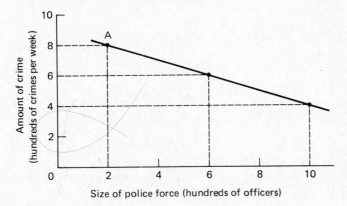

FIGURE 1-10

2. From Figure 1-2 fill in Table 1-3.

Table 1-3

Amount of snowfall	2	3	4
Sales of ski equipment			

3. Figure 1-11 has six different lines in it. Fill in Table 1-4 showing the slope of each line.

Table 1-4

Line	a	b	c	d	e	f
Slope						

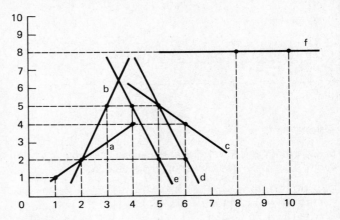

FIGURE 1-11

4. Which of the lines in Figure 1-12 show a positive relationship between the variables X and Y? _____. When X increases by 1 unit, which of these lines shows the greatest increase in Y? _____. When X increases by 1 unit, which one shows the greatest decrease in Y? _____.

FIGURE 1-12

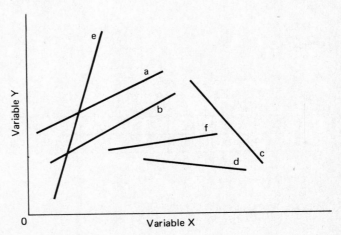

5. Consider any two variables, X and Y. Suppose they are related according to the linear equation $Y = 8 - 2X$. Fill in Table 1-5 according to this equation.

Table 1-5

X	0	1	2	3	4
Y					

This equation represents a straight line. Draw the straight line in Figure 1-13. The slope of this line is _____. The vertical intercept is _____. ˙

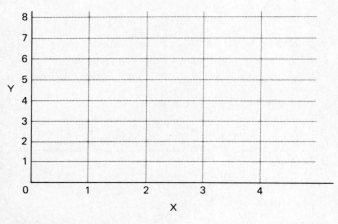

FIGURE 1-13

6. Consider the following linear equations, showing how one variable, Y, depends upon another variable, X.

    (a) $Y = 90 + 10X$
    (b) $Y = 50 + 15X$
    (c) $Y = 80 - 5X$
    (d) $Y = 3X$
    (e) $Y = -10 + 5X$
    (f) $Y = 50$

Each of these equations describes a different line.
    Line _____ has the largest vertical intercept and line _____ has the largest slope. When X increases by 1 unit, which line shows the largest increase in Y? _____. When $X = 0$, then the highest line is _____. Which show a posi-tive relationship? _____. Which a negative relationship? _____. What is the slope of line (f)? _____. What kind of relationship do you suppose is indicated by line (f)? _____

Which line has a vertical intercept of zero? _____. There-fore, which line passes through the origin in a graph? _____. Which line indicates that Y is always a constant multiple of X? _____. What does this suggest is always true of lines that pass through the origin? _____

What is the vertical intercept in line (e)? _____. How would this show up in a graph? _____

7. The amount of sunshine at point A in Figure 1-14 equals the distance _____, or _____. Sales of umbrellas at point A equal _____, or _____. At B the amount of sunshine equals _____, or _____, and sales of umbrellas equal _____, or _____. Going from A to B, the amount of sun-shine (increases, decreases) by _____, or _____, and sales of umbrellas (increase, decrease) by _____, or _____.

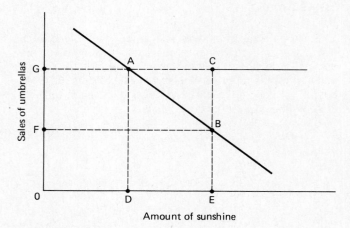

FIGURE 1-14

8. The sum $1 + 1/3 + 1/9 + 1/27 + \cdots$ equals _____.
9. Take any positive fraction a. Then the sum $a + a^2 + a^3 + a^4 + \cdots$ equals _____. [Hint: compare this with the sum (1), and use the formula (4).]

Answers

Linear Equations:

Table 1-2 completed:

Y	100	200	300	400	500	600	700	800	900	1000	1100
C	450	500	550	600	650	700	750	800	850	900	950

Geometric Series: When $a = 0.8$, then $S = 5$.
Questions:
1. 8, 2, 2, 8, 6, 4.

2. Table 1-3 completed:

2	3	4
1	3	5

3. Table 1-4 completed:

a	b	c	d	e	f
1	3	−1	−3	−3	0

4. (a, b, e, f), e, c.

5. Table 1-5 completed:

X	0	1	2	3	4
Y	8	6	4	2	0

    −2, 8

6. a, b, b, a, (a, b, d, e), c, 0; one in which Y does not vary as X changes; d, d, d, they always indicate that Y is a constant multiple of X; −10; if you extended the vertical axis down below the horizontal axis, the line would intersect the vertical axis on this lower segment.

7. OD or GA; OG or DA; OE or FB; OF or EB; increases; DE or AC; decrease; FG or BC.

8. 3/2.

9. $\dfrac{1}{1-a} - 1 = \dfrac{a}{1-a}$

Across

1. college degree
4. his *Wealth of Nations* was an early classic (2 names)
9. getting the most from efforts
11. shedder of light
12. preposition
16, 18. keeping government to a minimum
19. assist
20. the _____ countries, also known as the third world
24. major U.S. corporation
25. above
26. fairness
27. charged particle
29. during hyperinflation, this becomes practically worthless
31. advocated government spending to restore full employment
33. represents workers
34. losers in war often suffer this

Down

1. exist
2. labor organization
3. be ill
4. objective
5. the economic disease of the 1930s
6. indef. article
7. provider of long-distance telephone services
8. artificial (abbrev.)
10. a business degree
13. important source of information to buyers and sellers
14. an economic problem
15. international institution lending to developing nations (2 words)
17. rise in average level of prices
21. needed when looking for a job
22. large, powerful
23. early economist (see inside cover of text)
25. individuals
28. number
29. 1st person, possessive
30. holds corn or missiles
31. under lock and _____
32. its price skyrocketed in 1970s

Note to students: Answers to crossword puzzles are at the end of *Study Guide*.

CHAPTER 2

SCARCITY AND CHOICE

MAJOR PURPOSE

The major purpose of this chapter is to introduce the concept of *scarcity*. Because of limited resources, we cannot have all the goods and services that we want. We must therefore *make choices*, picking some items and foregoing others. This idea—that we face scarcity and therefore have to make choices—is at the center of economics. Indeed, economics is sometimes defined as "the study of the allocation of scarce resources to satisfy alternative, competing human wants."

The ideas of scarcity and choice are illustrated by the *production possibilities curve*. This illustrates the idea of *scarcity* because we are limited to a point on (or within) the curve; we cannot go outside the curve with our present resources and technological capabilities. The curve also illustrates the need to make *choices*. When we pick a specific point on the production possibilities curve, we pass over all the other points, and forego the goods which we might have had if we had picked some other point.

Finally, this chapter provides an introduction to *economic theory*. Economic theory *must* be a *simplification* of the real world. If we strove for a complete theory which took into account all the complexities of our world, we would get bogged down in a swamp of detail. When we simplify, we should keep in mind a central question: Does our theory include the most important relationships in the economy, or *have we left out something of critical importance*?

Learning Objectives

After you have studied this chapter in the textbook and study guide, you should be able to:

Understand why the combination of limited resources and unlimited wants require us to make choices

Define the three major factors of production

Explain the difference between real capital and financial capital, and explain why economists focus on real capital when estimating the productive capacity of the economy

Explain the concept of opportunity cost, and explain how it is related to the production possibilities curve (PPC)

Explain why the PPC slopes downward to the right

Explain why the PPC usually bows outward from the origin

Explain a circumstance in which the PPC might be a straight line, instead of bowing outward

Explain why production occurs within the PPC if there is large-scale unemployment

Explain the difference between a high-growth and a low-growth policy, using a PPC with capital goods on one axis and consumer goods on the other (Figure 2–5 in the textbook)

Explain why it is impossible to develop a theory without simplifying

HIGHLIGHTS OF CHAPTER

Scarcity is one of the most important concepts in economics. Scarcity requires us to *make choices*; we cannot have everything we want. Why? The answer is that our resources are limited, while our wants are not.

When we make choices, we pick some goods and services, and forego others. If we pick a college education, for example, we may have to put off buying a car for several years. The *opportunity cost* of our education is the car, and other things which we forego to pay tuition, room, and board. Similarly, for the society as a whole, opportunity cost is an important concept. When we decide to produce more weapons, we forego the consumer goods we might have produced instead. Individuals, corporations, and governments are continuously making choices among the options open to them.

The ideas of scarcity, the need to make choices, and opportunity cost are summarized by the production possibilities curve (PPC). The PPC shows the options from which a *choice* is made. The fact that we are limited by the PPC, and cannot pick a point outside it with our present resources and technology, illustrates the idea of *scarcity*. The *slope* of the PPC shows how much of one good we must forego when we choose more of another. In other words, the slope shows the *opportunity cost* of choosing more of a specific good.

The PPC has two important properties. First, it slopes downward to the right. This means that, if we decide to produce more of one good, we give up some of the other. The idea that there is an opportunity cost when we produce more of one good is illustrated by the downward slope of the PPC curve.

The second feature of the typical PPC curve is that it is "bowed out"—that is, it is *concave* to the origin. This is so because resources are *specialized*. If we decide to produce more and more wheat, we will use land which is less and less suited to the production of wheat, even though it was very good for producing cotton. For each additional unit of wheat, we will have to give up more cotton. Thus, the outward bend in the PPC illustrates the idea of *increasing opportunity cost*.

Under certain circumstances, however, the PPC need not bow outward. It is possible that two goods might require the same set of resources in their production. For example, radios and telephones might take the same combination of resources in their production—the same combination of copper, plastic, silicon, labor, etc.—in which case the PPC would be a *straight line*. In this particular case, the *opportunity cost of radios would*

be constant, in terms of the telephones foregone. (The opportunity cost of both radios and telephones might nevertheless still increase, in terms of the food or clothing foregone. In other words, the PPC would be a straight line if we put radios and telephones on the two axes, but would bow out if we put radios on one axis and food on the other.)

It is worth emphasizing that a downward slope and an outward bow are two *different* features. A PPC can slope downward without bowing outward—as in the example of radios and telephones. A downward slope means that the opportunity cost is *positive*. An outward bow means that the opportunity cost *increases* as more of a good is produced.

One of the important choices facing the society is the choice between consumer goods and capital goods. If we produce only a little capital, we will be able to enjoy a large quantity of consumer goods now. But, with little investment, we will have slow growth. In other words there is a *trade-off between a high current level of consumption and high growth*. This trade-off or choice is illustrated when we draw a PPC curve with consumer goods on one axis and capital goods on the other. For example, Figure 2-5 in the textbook illustrates the difference between a high-growth and a low-growth strategy. A high-growth strategy requires that a sizable fraction of our resources be committed to investment in plant and equipment (capital goods). But this makes possible a rapid growth, that is, a rapid outward movement of the PPC.

This chapter provides a brief introduction to economic theory. When we develop economic theories, we *must* simplify. The world is too complex to describe in all its detail. The objective of theory is to strip away the nonessential complications, in order to see the important relationships within the economy. Theory should not be dismissed because it fails to account for everything, just as a road map should not be discarded as useless just because it doesn't show everything. But, because of simplifications, theory must be used carefully. Just as last week's weather map is useless for planning a trip in a car, so the theory which helps to explain one aspect of the economy may be inappropriate or useless for explaining others.

Finally, this chapter explains the distinction between *positive* and *normative* economics. Positive or descriptive economics is aimed at explaining what has been happening and why. Normative economics deals with policies; it deals with the way things *ought* to be.

Important Terms: Match the Columns

Match the term in the first column with the corresponding phrase in the second column. But before you do so, write out your own definition of the term in the first column.

_____ 1. Economic resources
_____ 2. Financial capital
_____ 3. Real capital
_____ 4. Increase in real capital
_____ 5. Entrepreneur
_____ 6. PPC
_____ 7. Opportunity cost
_____ 8. Increasing opportunity cost
_____ 9. Constant opportunity cost
_____ 10. Cause of outward bow of PPC

a. Outward bow of PPC
b. Choices open to society
c. Specialized resources
d. Stocks and bonds
e. Straight-line PPC
f. Organizer of production
g. Basic inputs used in the production of goods and services
h. Investment
i. Alternative foregone
j. Machinery, equipment, and buildings

True-False

T F   1. Resources are said to be scarce because they are incapable of producing all the goods and services that people want; therefore, choices must be made.

T F   2. Wants were "unlimited" during the early days of the study of economics in the eighteenth and nineteenth centuries. But they are no longer unlimited in the affluent countries of North America and Western Europe.

T F   3. Suppose that a production possibilities curve meets the axes at 5 units of clothing, and at 20 units of food. This illustrates that the society can have a total of 5 units of clothing plus 20 units of food, but no more.

T F   4. The production possibilities curve bends outward because resources are not uniform in quality; some are better at producing one good than the other.

T F   5. Just as it is possible to select a combination of goods inside the PPC, so it is possible to choose a combination of goods that lies outside the PPC.

T F   6. An increase in the quantity of labor causes the production possibilities curve to move outward from the origin.

T F   7. Suppose that two countries, A and B, were identical in 1975. Suppose that, between 1975 and 1985, the economy of A grew at 4% per annum, while B grew at 3% per annum. Then, from that fact, we may conclude that economy A was allocatively more efficient than B during the period 1975–1985.

T F   8. In most less developed countries, an increase in population will make it more difficult to raise income per person. In such a country, an increase in population and in the quantity of labor will generally cause an inward movement of the production possibilities curve.

T F   9. Less developed countries have a special problem. If they want to grow, they have to forego some consumer goods. In the affluent countries of Europe and North America, no such choice is necessary.

T F   10. _Positive_ economics is the study of how policymakers can achieve desirable (that is, "positive") social goals.

Multiple Choice

1. Economists often speak of wants being "unlimited" because:
    a. the cost of living has increased; it costs more to meet our basic needs now than it did 20 years ago
    b. more people live in the cities now than in an earlier age, and it is more expensive to live in cities than on the farm
    c. even though our incomes have risen, we still want "more"; we do not believe all our wants are satisfied
    d. resources such as oil have become scarcer because we have been using them up
    e. as people's incomes have risen, they have decided to take more leisure, and work fewer hours

2. By real capital, economists mean:
    a. real estate, particularly land
    b. plant and equipment
    c. the real value of bonds, adjusted for inflation
    d. the real value of common stock, adjusted for inflation
    e. both (c) and (d)

3. The production possibilities curve has one major purpose—to illustrate the need to:

a. stop inflation
b. cut taxes
c. cut government spending
d. make choices
e. stop pollution

4. The textbook has a picture of a production possibilities curve (PPC), joining six points.
    a. All six points are equally desirable, since they all represent full employment.
    b. All six points are equally desirable, since they all are consistent with zero inflation.
    c. All six points are equally desirable, since they all provide for some growth.
    d. All six points are possible, but the PPC curve doesn't give enough information to tell which point is best.
    e. Only one of the six points is presently achievable; the others can be achieved only if the economy grows.

5. An _outward bow_ in the production possibilities curve illustrates what concept?
    a. scarcity
    b. unlimited wants
    c. increasing opportunity cost
    d. unemployment
    e. inflation

6. The opportunity cost of a good is measured by:

a. the slope of the PPC
b. how far the PPC is from the origin
c. the slope of a line from the origin out to the PPC
d. how far the economy is operating within the PPC
e. how fast the PPC is shifting outward

7. Suppose the production possibilities curve is a straight line if goods X and Y are put on the axis. Then we know that:
a. X and Y are really the same good
b. the problem of scarcity has been solved
c. we can have all the X and Y we want without incurring an opportunity cost, even though the general problem of scarcity has not been solved
d. the opportunity cost of X is zero, in terms of Y foregone
e. the opportunity cost of X is constant, in terms of Y foregone

8. We speak of a production possibilities curve as a "frontier" because:
a. we can produce within it or on it, but not beyond it with presently available resources and technology
b. it reflects the concept of scarcity, and goods were particularly scarce for U.S. settlers on the western frontier in the nineteenth century
c. it is no longer relevant, now that the U.S. frontier has been tamed and we have an affluent society
d. unemployment problems provide the frontier for economic research
e. differences among resources provide the frontier for economic research

9. Suppose that the society has only one objective, to maximize growth. Then, the best choice among the five points shown in Figure 2-1 is:
a. A   d. D
b. B   e. E
c. C

10. In Figure 2-1, a growth of the economy can be illustrated by:
a. a move from point A to B
b. a move from point B to A
c. a move from point A to E
d. a move from point D to E
e. an outward shift of the production possibilities curve

11. In Figure 2-1, suppose that the economy is originally at point E. Then there will be:

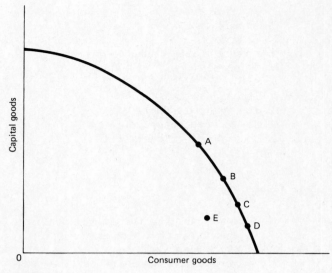

FIGURE 2-1

a. rapid growth
b. no capital formation
c. more capital formation than at points A, B, or C
d. a high rate of unemployment
e. rapid inflation

12. In the poorest of the less developed countries (LDCs), the growth process is more difficult than in the richer countries, because:
a. an increase in population causes the PPC curve to shift outward in the developed countries, but inward in the LDCs
b. an increase in capital causes the PPC curve to shift outward in the developed countries, but inward in the LDCs
c. it may be difficult to increase investment in the poorest LDCs without depressing consumption to the subsistence level
d. when LDCs invest, they pay a penalty in terms of consumer goods foregone, but the affluent countries pay no such penalty
e. all of the above

Exercises

1. Consider the following production possibilities table:

Table 2-1

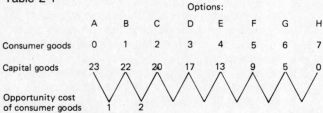

	A	B	C	D	E	F	G	H
Consumer goods	0	1	2	3	4	5	6	7
Capital goods	23	22	20	17	13	9	5	0
Opportunity cost of consumer goods		1	2					

a. Complete the third line, showing the opportunity cost of each additional unit of consumer goods.
b. Draw the PPC in Figure 2-2.
c. What is unusual about this curve?
d. In the range between points A and D, the PPC [bows outward, bows inward, is a straight line]. This shows that opportunity cost is [increasing, decreasing, constant] in this range. However, between points D and G, the curve [bows outward, bows inward, is a straight line]. This

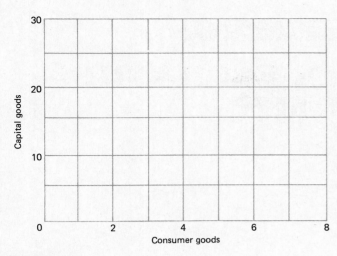

FIGURE 2-2

Table 2-2

Millions of labor hours	Thousands of houses
20	20
15	18
10	14
5	8
0	0

Table 2-3

Millions of labor hours	Hundreds of miles of road
20	10
15	9
10	7
5	4
0	0

shows that opportunity cost is [increasing, decreasing, constant] in this range.

2. Consider a hypothetical economy with a labor force of 10,000 workers, each of whom can be put to work building either houses or roads. Each worker is available for 2,000 hours per year. Thus, there are 20 million labor hours available during the year to produce houses and roads. Table 2-2 shows how many labor hours it takes to build various quantities of houses. For example, in order to build 18,000 houses, 15 million labor hours are needed. Likewise, Table 2-3 indicates how many labor hours are needed to build various amounts of roadway. In Figure 2-3, only one point, *A*, on the PPC has been plotted. It shows that if no houses are built, the 20 million labor hours can be used to produce 1,000 miles of road. Using the data in Tables 2-2 and 2-3, plot four other points, and draw a PPC to connect them.

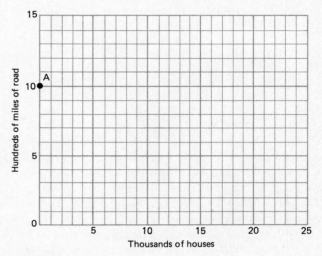

FIGURE 2-3

Answers

	B	C	D	E
Hundreds of miles	9	7	4	0
Thousands of houses	8	14	18	20

CHAPTER 3

SPECIALIZATION, EXCHANGE, AND MONEY

MAJOR PURPOSE

In this chapter, we study specialization, exchange, and money. People specialize and engage in exchange because there are *gains* from doing so: By specializing, they can achieve higher standards of living. There are *two major sources* of gain from specialization: (1) *comparative advantage*, and (2) *economies of scale*. These two phenomena are the forces that motivate specialization and exchange; that is, they are the twin *engines that drive commerce*.

Money, on the other hand, *is the oil* which makes the machinery of commerce run smoothly, with a minimum of friction. Without money, people would engage in cumbersome barter. But, if some money helps to make the system work smoothly, we should not conclude that more money would make it work even better. Just as too much oil can gum up an engine, so too much money can cause difficulty. Specifically, it causes inflation. The Federal Reserve (the central bank of the United States) acts as the chief mechanic. Its task is to create the right amount of "oil" (money)—neither too much, nor too little. The operations of the Federal Reserve will be considered in detail in Chapter 13.

Learning Objectives

After you have studied this chapter in the textbook and study guide, you should be able to:

Explain why specialization and exchange go hand in hand

Explain why barter is inferior to exchange with money

Explain why people may nevertheless revert to barter in some circumstances

Give an example of Gresham's law

Explain the two major reasons why there can be gains from specialization and exchange

Explain the difference between absolute advantage and comparative advantage

Explain why a country may have an absolute advantage in a product without having a comparative advantage in that product

Explain why a country cannot have a comparative advantage (nor a comparative disadvantage) in every product

HIGHLIGHTS OF CHAPTER

One reason for economic progress has been an increase in *specialization*. Individuals, cities, and countries are now more specialized than they were 100 years ago. When production is specialized, people engage in exchange, selling the products they produce to buy the wide variety of goods and services that they want to consume. We live in a highly interdependent economy, in which each of us depends on the specialized production of others.

Specialization and exchange would be very difficult without money. It is easy to imagine the difficulties that would arise if we tried to do without money, and engaged in barter exchange instead. Barter requires a *coincidence of wants*—people engaging in exchange must each be able to provide a good or service that the other wants. Furthermore, for barter to work, there must be some rough equivalence in the value of the two goods or services to be exchanged. To buy toothpaste, a farmer would scarcely offer a cow in exchange. However, with money, such problems of indivisibility do not arise. The farmer may sell the cow for $1,000 and spend just a bit of the money to buy toothpaste, using the rest for a wide variety of other purchases. Money provides people with *general purchasing power*; money can be used to buy any of the wide variety of goods and services on the market. Those wishing to make exchanges no longer have to search for unlikely coincidences (such as the ill-clad farmer looking for someone who not only has clothes to exchange, but who also wants to get beef in return).

Because it is so useful for those who wish to engage in exchange, money is used even in rudimentary societies with little or no government. The prisoner-of-war camp provides a modern example of such a simple society. However, governments have gotten deeply involved in the monetary system. Every country uses paper money printed by a central bank.

One reason for the government to be involved in the monetary system is that the government can provide a *uniform* currency. In the United States, for example, every $1 Federal Reserve Note (dollar bill) is worth the same as every other dollar bill. This uniformity of the money stock is very convenient. When selling something for $1, we only have to find out if the buyer has a $1 bill. Except for the rare cases where counterfeiting is suspected, we do not need to ask the much more complicated question of whether the dollar bill is inferior to some other dollar bill.

In passing, we might note that the United States has not always had a uniform currency. In the nineteenth century, privately owned banks issued currency. The value of this currency depended on the soundness of the bank that issued it. Thus, sellers did have to worry about the value of the dollar bills they accepted. Similar prob-lems have arisen throughout history. For example, gold coins have often been used, whose value depended primarily on the amount of gold they contained. Before the development of modern methods of producing coins with hard edges, such coins were sometimes "clipped." That is, people chipped off bits before spending them. As a result, not every coin was worth the same as every other coin of the same denomination. People had to examine the physical condition of the coins they were accepting.

In addition to providing a uniform currency, the Federal Reserve has the responsibility of providing an appropriate quantity of money. If too many dollar bills are created, there will be "too much money chasing too few goods." Inflation will result; the dollar will decline in value. On the other hand, if the quantity of money is allowed to decline sharply, spending will decline. Sellers will have a very difficult time finding buyers. Sales will fall, unemployment will rise, and prices will be under downward pressure. The authorities do not always perform their monetary duties well. In some countries, prices are galloping ahead by more than 100% per year. This reduces the convenience of money. If prices are rising rapidly, sellers feel under pressure to spend their money as soon as possible, before its value declines significantly.

With the proper quantity of money, the monetary system can work very smoothly, making transactions very convenient. But this is all that money does—it makes exchange convenient. It is not the reason why exchange is desirable in the first place.

There are two reasons why benefits come from specialization and exchange. The first is *comparative advantage*. The notion of comparative advantage is illustrated in the textbook by the example of the gardener and the lawyer. The lawyer has an absolute advantage in both the law and gardening; she can do both quicker than the gardener. It follows that the gardener has an absolute disadvantage in both the law and gardening—he is slower at both. However, the gardener has a comparative advantage in gardening, while the lawyer has a comparative advantage in the law. While the lawyer is superior in both activities, her superiority is greater in the law. In other words, her opportunity cost of drawing up wills or other legal documents is lower than the opportunity cost of the gardener. This provides the basis for mutually beneficial trade. Both the gardener and the lawyer can gain from specialization and exchange. (Details are provided in Box 3-3 in the textbook.)

Two points should be emphasized: (1) Absolute advantage is not necessary for gain; the gardener can gain by specializing in gardening, even though he is not the best gardener. (2) A person (or a nation) cannot have a comparative disadvantage in everything. In the simple case of two people and two activities (law and gardening), if one person has a comparative advantage in one activity, the other person *must* have the comparative advantage in the other activity.

Economies of scale provide the second major reason why there are gains from specialization and exchange. Economies of scale exist if an increase of $x\%$ in all inputs (labor, machinery, land, steel, etc.) leads to an increase of more than $x\%$ in output. Economies of scale are the major reason why big firms have an advantage in many industries, such as automobiles and mainframe computers. Economies of scale are the major reason why costs per unit of output often decline as more is produced. For example, a car company can produce 100,000 cars at a much lower cost per car than if it produces 20,000 cars. Clearly, if a person tried to put together a car in the back yard or in a small shop, it would be very expensive. There are gains when car production is left to the specialists.

Important Terms: Match the Columns

Match the term in the first column with the corresponding phrase in the second column. But before you do so, write out your own definition of the term in the first column.

_____ 1. Barter
_____ 2. Required by barter
_____ 3. General purchasing power
_____ 4. Function of money
_____ 5. Inflation
_____ 6. Gresham's law
_____ 7. Absolute advantage
_____ 8. Comparative advantage
_____ 9. Economies of scale
_____ 10. Example of economies of scale

a. Acts as medium of exchange
b. Bad money drives out good
c. Good can be produced at lower opportunity cost
d. Exchange of one good or service for another
e. Reason costs per unit fall as more is produced
f. Money
g. Adam Smith's pin factory
h. Good can be produced with fewest resources
i. Coincidence of wants
j. Fall in value of money

True-False

T F 1. One reason that barter is inconvenient is that many commodities cannot easily be divided into smaller parts.
T F 2. Monetary systems develop only when there is a strong national government, since strong national governments are required to provide money with value.
T F 3. Suppose that, in the prisoner-of-war camp with its "cigarette money," the value of cigarettes rises compared to the value of other items (such as beef, etc.) Such an increase is known as inflation.
T F 4. Comparative advantage is the reason why wheat is grown in Nebraska, and not in the city of Chicago.
T F 5. If everyone had the same abilities, then economies of scale would not exist.
T F 6. In the absence of a government, money is valuable only if it is useful. Therefore, cigarette money would be used exclusively in transactions between smokers in the prisoner-of-war camp.
T F 7. Consider a world with only two countries, A and B, and only two goods, X and Y. Then, if country A has a comparative advantage in good X, country B *must* have a comparative advantage in good Y.
T F 8. Even if everyone has the same abilities, specialization may be beneficial if there are economies of scale.

Multiple Choice

1. One of the problems with barter is that it requires a "coincidence of wants." This means that:
   a. everybody must want money
   b. everybody must want the same good
   c. at least two people must want the same good
   d. everybody must want my good, before I am able to exchange it
   e. for there to be an exchange between individuals A and B, individual A must want what B has, while B must want what A has

2. Money is said to represent "general purchasing power" because:

a. it can be used to buy any of the goods and services offered for sale
b. the government guarantees its value
c. the government is committed to accept money in payment of taxes
d. Gresham's law no longer is valid
e. Gresham's law applies to other goods, but not money

3. When we draw a diagram showing the circular flow of payments between households and businesses, the two major markets we show are:
   a. goods and services
   b. capital and labor

c. capital and land

d. consumer goods and economic resources

e. products made by private entrepreneurs, and those provided by the government

4. When the best-tasting cigarettes started to disappear from circulation in the prisoner-of-war camp, this was an example of:

a. economies of scale   d. inflation

b. absolute advantage   e. Gresham's law

c. comparative advantage

5. In the prisoner-of-war camp, in which cigarettes acted as money, suppose that the quantity of cigarettes coming into the camp remained constant, while the quantity of all other goods decreased. Then the most probable result would be:

a. a rise in the value of cigarettes, measured in terms of other items

b. a fall in the prices of other goods, measured in terms of cigarettes

c. inflation

d. deflation

e. bad money driving out good money

6. Suppose that a building supervisor can lay bricks more rapidly and better than a bricklayer. Then, considering only these two individuals, we may conclude that:

a. the bricklayer has an absolute advantage in bricklaying

b. the supervisor has an absolute advantage in bricklaying

c. the bricklayer has a comparative advantage in bricklaying

d. the supervisor has a comparative advantage in bricklaying

e. we can't tell which of the above is true without knowing how much bricks cost, compared to the wage for bricklayers

7. According to the theory of comparative advantage, a good should be produced in a country:

a. whose workers are most skillful at producing that good

b. which has the greatest number of workers capable of producing that good

c. which has the greatest quantity of capital capable of producing that good

d. which has the lowest opportunity cost of producing that good

e. where economies of scale are greatest in producing that good

8. Suppose that there are only two countries, A and B, and only two goods, food and clothing. If country A has a comparative advantage in the production of food, then we may conclude that:

a. country A must also have an absolute advantage in the production of food

b. country B probably has an absolute advantage in the production of food

c. country B probably has an absolute advantage in the production of clothing

d. country B probably has a comparative advantage in the production of clothing

e. country B must have a comparative advantage in the production of clothing

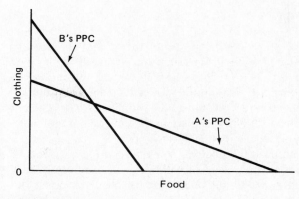

FIGURE 3-1

9. Figure 3-1 illustrates the PPCs of countries A and B.

a. Country A has a comparative advantage in the production of clothing, while country B has a comparative advantage in the production of food.

b. Country A has a comparative advantage in the production of food, while country B has a comparative advantage in the production of clothing.

c. Country A has a comparative advantage in the production of both goods.

d. Country A has an absolute advantage in the production of both goods.

e. Country B has an absolute advantage in the production of both goods.

10. Suppose that there are only two countries, A and B, and only two goods, food and clothing. We can conclude that A has a comparative advantage in the production of food if:

a. A's opportunity cost of producing food is less than B's opportunity cost of producing food

b. A's opportunity cost of producing food is less than A's opportunity cost of producing clothing

c. A's opportunity cost of producing food is less than B's opportunity cost of producing clothing

d. A has more capital than B

e. A has a larger population than B

11. Suppose that 10 workers with 1 machine can produce 100 TV sets in a month, while 20 workers with 2 machines can produce 250 TV sets in a month. This is an example of:

a. technological efficiency

b. allocative efficiency

c. economies of scale

d. comparative advantage

e. absolute advantage

12. Suppose that (1) there are economies of scale in the production of each good, and (2) land and labor have specialized capabilities—for example, land and the climate give Brazil a comparative advantage in coffee. Then the gains from specialization will probably be:

a. larger than if either (1) or (2) had existed alone

b. small, since (1) and (2) tend to offset each other

c. negative, since the combination of (1) and (2) creates confusion

d. about the same as with (1) alone, since (2) doesn't make much difference

e. about the same as with (2) alone, since (1) doesn't make much difference

Exercises

1. This exercise illustrates the idea of comparative advantage. Assume the following. A doctor working on home repairs can fix a leaky faucet in 10 minutes. A plumber takes 15 minutes. Then the [doctor, plumber] has an absolute advantage in plumbing. The doctor's time is worth $80 per hour in the practice of medicine. The plumber is paid $20 per hour.

Suppose the doctor's house has six leaky faucets. If he fixes them himself, it will take ＿＿ minutes. Thus, to fix the faucets, the doctor will use $＿＿ worth of his time. If the plumber is hired to fix the faucets, he will take ＿＿ minutes, which is [longer, shorter] than the doctor would take. The cost in this case is $＿＿, which is [more, less] by $＿＿ than if the doctor fixed the faucets himself. The [doctor, plumber] has a comparative advantage in plumbing.

2. Table 3-1 shows how many cars can be produced in a country with various amounts of inputs. Each unit of input represents a specific quantity of labor and capital. Table 3-2 provides similar information for TV sets. Table 3-1 illustrates the idea of [comparative advantage, absolute advantage, economies of scale, none of these]. Table 3-2 illustrates the idea of [comparative advantage, absolute advantage, economies of scale, none of these].

Suppose that the economy has 5 units of inputs to be devoted to cars and TV sets. Plot the PPC for these 5

Table 3-1
PRODUCTION OF CARS

Number of cars (millions)	Units of input
1	1
3	2
6	3
12	4
20	5

Table 3-2
PRODUCTION OF TV SETS

Number of TV sets (millions)	Units of input
20	1
40	2
60	3
80	4
100	5

units of input in Figure 3-2. How is the shape of the PPC different from the PPCs in Chapter 2? ＿＿. The opportunity cost of producing cars [increases, decreases, remains constant] as more are produced.

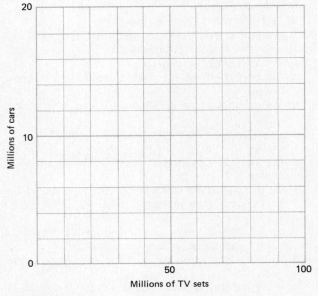

FIGURE 3-2

Essay Questions

1. The textbook explains why comparative advantage can mean that there are benefits from specialization and exchange. But it does not explain why specific people or nations might have a comparative advantage. How would you explain Iowa's comparative advantage over New England in producing corn? Why does Pennsylvania have a comparative advantage over most of the other states in the production of steel? Why does Taiwan have a comparative advantage in the production of transistor radios and TV sets?

2. Why do you think that most economists are usually in favor of reducing tariffs and other barriers to international trade? Why might anyone oppose the reduction of tariffs?

3. There are disadvantages associated with specialization, as well as advantages. What are they?

Answers

Important Terms: **1** d **2** i **3** f **4** a **5** j **6** b **7** h **8** c **9** e **10** g
True-False: **1** T **2** F **3** F **4** T **5** F **6** F **7** T **8** T

Multiple Choice: 1 e   2 a   3 d   4 e   5 c   6 b   7 d   8 e   9 b   10 a   11 c   12 a

Exercises: 1. doctor, 60, $80, 90, longer, $30, less, $50, plumber.   2. economies of scale, none of these, it bows inward, decreases.

Across

1, 4, 5. reason why there are gains from specialization
8. it's mightier than the sword
9. covering of spun silk
11. Princeton; also, capital of Bahamas
12. top of the cake
14. in a light spirit; jauntily
16. *really* bad
17. his 300-year-old law worked in the POW camp
19. factor of production, which has itself been produced
22. attribute of money (2 words)
24. for beneficial trade, this type of advantage is good enough
25. required for barter (3 words)

Down

1. if people specialize, this becomes necessary
2. oil for the wheels of commerce
3. a way of increasing living standards
4. above
5. because of this, not all our wants can be met
6. this advantage is desirable, but not necessary for specialization
7. if all incomes are _____, top 10% of population get 10% of total income
10. production possibilities _____
13. the type of economics that deals with policy
15. doctors' organization (abbrev.)
18. sharp (Lat.)
20. what someone does in an economy with no money
21. item produced for exchange
23. all

CHAPTER 4

DEMAND AND SUPPLY:

THE MARKET MECHANISM

MAJOR PURPOSE

This chapter is one of the most important in the book. It introduces the concepts of *demand* and *supply*, which help us to understand what is happening in the markets for specific products. The demand curve illustrates how buyers respond to various possible prices: At lower prices, they buy more. On the other hand, sellers react negatively to low prices: They offer less for sale. This response of sellers is illustrated by the supply curve.

When drawing a demand or supply curve, we isolate the effect of *price alone* on the behavior of buyers and sellers. Of course, many other things besides price can affect their behavior. When we draw a demand or supply curve and look at the effect of price alone, we make the *ceteris paribus* assumption—that all these other things do not change. In cases where they do in fact change, we are no longer on a single demand or supply curve; the demand or supply curve *shifts*.

Other important concepts introduced in this chapter are the concept of *equilibrium*, *surplus* and *shortage*, and *substitutes* and *complementary goods*.

Learning Objectives

After you have studied this chapter in the textbook and study guide, you should be able to:

Explain why the demand curve slopes downward to the right

Explain why the supply curve slopes upward to the right

Explain why a price which begins away from equilibrium will move to equilibrium

List and explain three things that can shift the demand curve, and four that can shift the supply curve

Give one example each of a pair of goods that are (1) substitutes in use, (2) complements in use, (3) substitutes in production, and (4) complements in production. In each case, you should be able to explain why the pair fits into the category.

Explain the distinction between product makets and markets for factors of production

Explain how the factor markets can help answer the question, For whom?

Explain how changes in factor markets can affect what happens in a product market, and vice versa

Explain the main strengths and main shortcomings of the market mechanism as a way of answering the questions, What? How? and For whom?

HIGHLIGHTS OF CHAPTER

In every economy, some mechanism is needed to decide three major questions: *What* will be produced? *How* will it be produced? And *for whom* will it be produced? There are two major ways of answering these questions: (1) through the market—that is, through voluntary exchanges between buyers and sellers, and (2) through governmental decision making. (Other ways are sometimes used—for example, in a family or in a monastery. But we are not primarily interested in these alternatives.)

All nations have some reliance on markets, and some reliance on governmental decision making. However, there are substantial differences among nations. In the United States, the market is the most important mechanism, although the government does play a significant role in modifying the outcome of the market. In the U.S.S.R., government plays a much more central role, although there is some reliance on markets.

The central feature of a market is *price*. Different prices for different goods provide *incentives* for producers to make some goods rather than others, and incentives for consumers to purchase cheap goods rather than expensive ones. *Prices* also provide *signals* and *information* to buyers and sellers. For example, the willingness of buyers to pay a high price acts as a signal to producers, showing that people are eager to obtain the product.

To study how buyers respond to different prices, we use a *demand curve* or *demand schedule*. This curve or schedule shows the quantity of a specific good that buyers would be willing and able to purchase at various different prices. The demand curve slopes downward to the right, illustrating that people are more eager to buy at lower prices. A major reason is that, at a lower price, people have an incentive to *switch* away from other products, and buy the product whose price is lower instead.

On the other side of the market, the supply curve shows how much sellers would be willing to offer at various prices. It slopes upward to the right, because sellers will be increasingly eager to sell as the price rises. Again, the willingness to *switch* is an important reason for the slope. If the price of a good is higher, firms have an incentive to drop other products, and make more of this good instead.

What happens in the market depends on both demand and supply. To find the *equilibrium* price and quantity, we put the demand and supply curves together, to find where they intersect. At this price, the quantity offered by sellers is equal to the quantity which buyers want to purchase. There is no unfulfilled demand to pull prices up, nor any excess offers to pull prices down.

If the price were not at its equilibrium, there would be pressures on the price to change. If the price were below its equilibrium, for example, there would be eager buyers who would not be able to find the good for sale. In other words, there would be a *shortage*. Producers would notice this, and conclude that they could sell at a higher price. The price would rise to its equilibrium level. On the other hand, if the price were initially above its equilibrium, there would be a *surplus*. Eager sellers would be unable to find buyers. They would become willing to sell at a lower price. The price would fall to its equilibrium level.

When we draw a demand or supply curve, we are looking at the way in which buyers and sellers respond to price, and to price *alone*. In practice, of course, buyers and sellers are influenced by many other things than the price of the good—for example, buyers generally purchase more when their incomes rise, and sellers are less willing to sell when the costs of their inputs rise. But these other things are held stable when a single demand or supply curve is drawn. This is the important assumption of *ceteris paribus*, that other things do not change. If they do change, the demand or supply curve *shifts*. For example, an increase in income generally causes a rightward shift in the whole demand curve. However, in the case of inferior goods, the demand curve shifts left; when people can afford better alternatives, they do so.

If the demand curve shifts to the right while the supply curve remains stable, then both price and quantity will increase. On the other hand, if the supply curve shifts right while the demand curve remains stable, then quantity will increase but price will fall. In brief, *a change in demand makes price and quantity change in the same direction, whereas a change in supply makes price and quantity move in opposite directions*. In practice, of course, many things can happen at once; often the demand and supply curves both shift. In this case, it becomes more difficult to predict what will happen.

Supply and demand theory is often used to study the market for a single good. However, there are strong connections among markets. When a price changes in one market, it can change conditions in other markets. For example, an increase in the price of gasoline in the 1970s caused a decline in the demand for large cars. This is an example of *complementary goods*—large cars and gasoline are used *together*. When the price of gasoline increases, the demand for large cars shifts left.

Whereas gasoline and cars are complements, some other products—such as bus tickets and train tickets—are *substitutes*. A person wanting to travel to the next city can go either by train or by bus. The higher is the train fare, the more people will use busses instead. Thus, a higher price of train tickets causes the demand for bus tickets to shift to the right.

Goods may also be substitutes or complements in production. Substitutes in production are goods which use the same inputs; the inputs can be used to produce either the one good or the other. For example, land can be used to produce either wheat or corn. If there is a crop failure abroad, and the United States exports much more wheat, the price of wheat will be bid up. Farmers will be encouraged to switch out of the production of corn, and produce additional wheat instead. The supply curve for corn will shift to the left.

On the other hand, complements are produced together. For example, wheat and straw are produced together. If the price of wheat is bid up, more wheat will be produced. In the process, more straw will be produced as a by-product. The supply curve of straw will shift to the right.

The question of *what* will be produced is decided primarily in the product market. To throw light on the other two questions—*how?* and *for whom?*—we should look first at the markets for inputs. For example, the market for labor helps to answer these two questions. If the demand for labor is high compared to its supply, then wage rates will be high. For example, wage rates are much higher in the United States than in India, because there are fewer workers for each unit of land and capital in the United States. As a result of the high wage, producers in the United States have an incentive to use only a little labor, and substitute capital instead. In an Indian factory, in contrast, many more things will be done by hand because of the low wage rate. The wage rate not only helps to determine how things are produced, but it also helps to determine who gets the product. Because wage rates are high in the United States, the American worker can buy and consume many more products than the Indian worker.

Observe that high wage rates affect what the worker can buy; with high wages, workers are more likely to buy TV sets and homes. This means that wages—determined in the factor markets in the lower box in Figure 4-9 in

the textbook—have an impact on the demand for TV sets, homes, and other products in the upper box. Thus, there are important connections among markets.

Finally, this chapter summarizes the strengths and weaknesses of the market as a mechanism for answering the three central questions. The strong points of the market are that (1) it encourages producers to make what consumers want, (2) it provides people with an incentive to acquire useful skills, (3) it encourages consumers to conserve scarce goods, (4) it encourages producers to conserve scarce resources, (5) it provides a high degree of economic freedom, and (6) it provides buyers and sellers with information on market conditions, including local conditions.

The market mechanism is also subject to major criticisms: (1) some people may be left in desperate poverty, (2) a market economy may be unstable, (3) monopolies and oligopolies may have the power to keep production down and keep prices up, (4) the market does not provide a strong incentive for producers to limit pollution and other negative side effects, (5) markets don't work in the case of public goods, where people benefit regardless of who pays for the good, and (6) producers may simply be satisfying a want that they have created in the first place through advertising.

To evaluate the market, it is important to compare it with the alternatives which exist in fact, not with some ideal, unattainable system. The textbook outlines a few of the problems which can arise when the government sets prices—in particular, the problem of black markets and shortages. A form of price regulation, rent control, is discussed in Box 4-1. One problem with rent control is that it may offer tenants short-run gains, and thus may be popular among the voting public, even though the results are bad in the long run.

Important Terms: Match the Columns

Match the term in the first column with the corresponding phrase in the second column. But before you do so, write out your own definition of the term in the first column.

_____ 1. Capitalism
_____ 2. Monopoly
_____ 3. Oligopoly
_____ 4. Perfect competition
_____ 5. Industry
_____ 6. Firm
_____ 7. Excess supply
_____ 8. Excess demand
_____ 9. Inferior good
_____ 10. Complementary goods
_____ 11. Substitutes
_____ 12. *Ceteris paribus*

a. All the producers of a single good
b. If price of A rises, demand for B increases
c. Surplus
d. Free enterprise
e. Demand for this declines as income rises
f. Nothing else changes
g. Goods used together
h. Market with only one seller
i. Where every buyer and seller is a price taker
j. Shortage
k. A single business organization, such as General Motors
l. Market dominated by a few sellers

True-False

T F **1.** Perfect competition exists only when the government fixes the price, so that no single buyer or seller is able to influence the price of the good.

T F **2.** Perfect competition will not exist in a market if there is only one seller, or if there is only one buyer.

T F **3.** In a perfectly competitive industry, every buyer and seller takes the quantity as given, and is left with only a pricing decision.

T F **4.** Even if there are many buyers, imperfect competition can exist in a market.

T F **5.** Even if there are many sellers, imperfect competition can exist in a market.

T F **6.** In a capitalist economy, most of the capital equipment is owned by the government.

T F **7.** A surplus drives the price down; a shortage drives the price up.

T F **8.** If the price of wheat increases, the supply curve of straw will probably shift to the right.

T F **9.** The demand curve for Pepsi Cola will probably shift to the right if the price of Coke rises.

T F **10.** If the price of paper increases, the supply curve of books will probably shift to the right.

T F **11.** If demand increases while supply decreases, the price will increase.

T F **12.** If the demand curve shifts to the right, the result will be an increase in the quantity sold and an increase in the market price.

T F **13.** If both the demand and supply curves for a product shift to the right, we can expect the quantity sold to increase, but we cannot be sure whether the price will rise or fall.

T F **14.** One essential characteristic of a free-enterprise economy is that the government make it easier to enter businesses freely by subsidizing new businesses.

T F **15.** Factor markets are different from the markets for most goods, in that goods markets are generally perfectly competitive, while the markets for factors are usually monopolized.

Multiple Choice

1. The U.S. government uses four major ways to influence what will be produced, how, and for whom. It uses every one of the following except one. Which one does not belong on this list?

  a. spending
  b. taxes
  c. regulation
  d. comprehensive central planning
  e. public enterprises

2. What is the most important characteristic of perfect competition?

  a. each seller has at least one powerful competitor to worry about

  b. there is at least one powerful, efficient producer who acts to keep prices down

  c. every buyer can go to at least three or four sellers to see who has the lowest price

  d. every buyer and seller is a price taker; none has any power to set price

  e. there must be many buyers, and at least three or four sellers

3. A market with one seller and a few buyers is an example of:

  a. monopoly
  b. oligopoly
  c. perfect competition
  d. technological inefficiency
  e. a black market

4. A surplus of wheat exists when:

  a. wheat production is lower than last year

  b. wheat production is higher than last year

  c. wheat production exceeds the production of all other grains combined

  d. the quantity of wheat demanded exceeds the quantity supplied

  e. the quantity of wheat supplied exceeds the quantity demanded

5. Suppose that a surplus exists in a market. Then we may conclude that:

  a. the price is below the equilibrium
  b. the price is above the equilibrium
  c. the government has imposed a price ceiling
  d. the quantity demanded has decreased
  e. the quantity supplied has increased

6. When incomes increase, the demand curve for an individual good:

  a. usually shifts down
  b. always shifts down
  c. usually shifts to the right
  d. always shifts to the right
  e. doesn't move, since only price affects demand

7. Peanuts and tobacco can be grown on similar land. Therefore, they are:

  a. substitutes in production
  b. joint products
  c. inferior goods
  d. normal goods
  e. an oligopoly

8. Tennis rackets and tennis balls are:

  a. substitutes
  b. complementary goods
  c. inferior goods
  d. unrelated goods
  e. monopolistic goods

9. Apples and textbooks are:

  a. substitutes
  b. complementary goods
  c. inferior goods
  d. independent goods
  e. monopolistic goods

10. Suppose that the demand for beef increases. This is most likely to cause:

a. a rightward shift in the supply curve for beef
b. a leftward shift in the supply curve for beef
c. a fall in the price of beef
d. a fall in the price of leather
e. an upward shift in the demand for leather

11. Suppose that, between year 1 and year 2, the demand curve and the supply curve for wheat both shift to the right. From this information, we may conclude that, in year 2:

a. the quantity of wheat sold will be larger, while the price will be higher
b. the quantity of wheat sold will be larger, while the price will be lower
c. the quantity of wheat sold will be larger, while we do not have enough information to tell if the price will be higher or lower
d. the quantity of wheat sold will be smaller, while we do not have enough information to tell if the price will be higher or lower

12. A black market is most likely to exist when:

a. the government controls the price of a good
b. the supply of a good is controlled by a monopolist
c. the supply of a good is controlled by two or three producers

d. the government imposes an excise tax on a good
e. the government urges producers to produce more to promote the general welfare of the public

13. The advantages of the market mechanism (as contrasted to government controls) as a way of deciding what, how, and for whom include:

a. prices provide incentives for producers to make what the public wants
b. prices provide incentives for producers to conserve scarce resources
c. prices provide incentives for consumers to conserve scarce goods
d. high wages in skilled occupations act as an incentive for workers to undertake training
e. all of the above

14. When we draw the demand curve for a product, we assume that:

a. there are many sellers
b. there are only a few sellers
c. all "supply shifters" are held constant
d. all "demand shifters" are held constant
e. both (c) and (d)

Exercises

1. Using the demand and supply schedules in the table below, plot the demand and supply curves in Figure 4-1. Label the axes, and mark in appropriate numbers on each axis. Then fill in the last column of the table.

a. The equilibrium quantity is _____ .
b. The equilibrium price is _____ .
c. At the equilibrium price, what is the surplus or shortage shown in the last column? _____ . Does this confirm that this price is an equilibrium?
d. Now suppose that the government sets a price of 60 cents. At this price, there will be a [surplus, shortage] of _____ .

2. Box 4-1 in the textbook describes what happens when the government sets a price below the equilibrium. In other cases, the government prevents the price from falling to its equilibrium. For example, the government has taken steps to keep the prices of agricultural commodities up.

Figure 4-2 illustrates some of the issues that arise when the government undertakes price supports. *D*

FIGURE 4-1

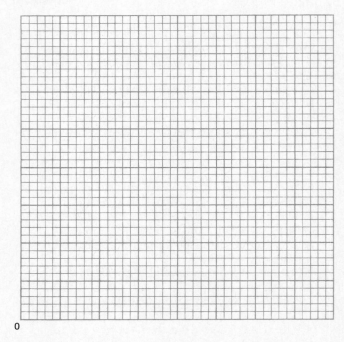

0

Price of hamburgers	Quantity demanded (thousands per week)	Quantity supplied (thousands per week)	Surplus (+) or shortage (−)
$1.40	200	700	
$1.20	240	600	
$1.00	300	500	
$0.80	400	400	
$0.60	600	300	
$0.50	800	250	

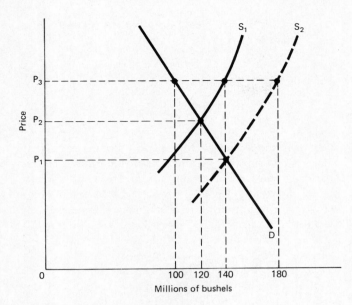

FIGURE 4-2

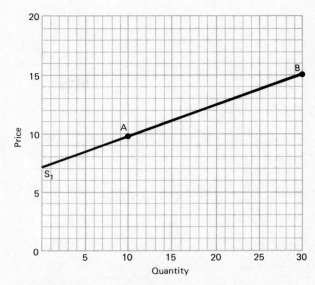

FIGURE 4-3

shows the demand curve, and S_1 the supply curve. Initially, the equilibrium quantity is _____ million bushels, and the price is _____. Now suppose that the government passes a rule that says that wheat cannot be sold at a price less than P_3. The result of this law will be a [surplus, shortage] amounting to _____ million bushels.

If all the government does is set a high price, not all wheat farmers will be better off. Those who are better off will be those who [cut back production, sell their wheat at the high price]. On the other hand, some will be worse off, specifically those who [are unable to sell their wheat at the high price, sell their wheat at a low price]. To ensure that wheat farmers are better off, the government can [buy the surplus wheat, reduce the price to P_1].

Now, suppose that the government undertakes irrigation projects to help agriculture in dry areas. This will cause an increase in supply from S_1 to S_2, and the [surplus, shortage] of wheat will [increase, decrease] to _____ million bushels. The government will find the costs of its price support program [increasing, decreasing]. If it now eliminates the price support, the free-market price will settle at _____.

3. Suppose that supply is given by the equation

$$Q = -30 + 4P$$

This supply is plotted in Figure 4-3 in the following way. First, choose some convenient value for P, such as 10. Put this value into the equation to get $Q = -30 + 40 = 10$. This means that when $P = 10$, $Q = 10$, so that point A is on the supply "curve." Then, choose another value of P, say $P = 15$. Substituting this into the equation, we find that the corresponding $Q = $ _____. This is plotted as point B. The supply relationship is a straight line; there are no squared terms or other reasons for

supply to bend. Thus, with the two points A and B, we can draw the straight–line supply S_1.

a. Suppose that demand is also a straight line:

$$Q = 20 - P$$

Then, if $P = 15$, $Q = $ _____, and if $P = 5$, $Q = $ _____. Plot demand in Figure 4-3 and label it D_1. On this figure, we see that the equilibrium price is _____ and the equilibrium quantity _____. Confirm these figures by solving the two equations algebraically, to find P and Q.

b. Suppose now that income increases and demand consequently increases, with 15 more units being demanded at each price. Thus, the new demand is

$$Q = 35 - P$$

To plot this new demand, we find two points. For example, if $P = 15$, $Q = $ _____, and if $P = 5$, $Q = $ _____. Plot the new equilibrium demand, labeling it D_2. At the new equilibrium, $P = $ _____ and $Q = $ _____. Again, confirm these numbers by solving the demand and supply equations. The price has [increased, decreased], and the quantity has [increased, decreased] as a result of this increase in demand.

c. Now, suppose we are back with the original demand, D_1, but that supply is now

$$Q = -10 + 2P$$

If $P = 10$, $Q = $ _____, and if $P = 15$, $Q = $ _____. Plot this new supply and label it S_2. With supply S_2 and demand D_1, the equilibrium price is _____, while quantity is _____. Again, confirm these numbers by solving the demand and supply equations.

d. Finally, suppose that demand shifts from D_1 to D_2, while supply remains at S_2. At the new equilibrium $P =$ _____ and $Q =$ _____. When the demand curve shifted this time, why is it that the price rose more, and the quantity less, than in part (b)?

Answer: _____.

Essay Questions

1. A demand or supply curve applies to a specific time and a specific location. For example, the market for milk in Washington, D.C., is not the same thing as the market for milk in Baltimore. Would you expect the price of milk in these two cities to be similar? Precisely the same? Explain.

2. Suppose that, as a result of an increase in the population of Washington, there were an increase in the demand for milk in that city. If you were an all-powerful social planner, you would probably want to persuade people in Baltimore to give up some of their milk in order to provide for the higher number of people in Washington. What sort of rationing scheme might you devise to accomplish this goal? How would you know how much to allocate to each family? How large a staff do you think you would need?

Suppose, alternatively, that you allowed market forces to work freely. What would happen to the price of milk in Washington? What would happen to the quantity? How would the changing conditions in Washington affect the supply curve for milk in Baltimore? What would happen to the price of milk in Baltimore? To the quantity? Draw demand and supply curves for Washington and Baltimore to illustrate what is happening. Would your intentions as a social planner be carried out by the market instead? Which policy—rationing or the market—works more efficiently? Are there any disadvantages to the more efficient system?

3. The prices printed on a restaurant menu apply whether the restaurant is crowded or half empty on any particular evening. If you ran a restauraut:

a. Would you charge higher prices on Friday and Saturday evenings, when the restaurant is crowded, than on other evenings?

b. Would you charge higher prices during the evening than for an identical meal at lunch? Why or why not? (Or, under what circumstances might you?)

c. Does McDonalds behave in the way you have suggested? How do you explain that?

Answers

Important Terms: 1 d 2 h 3 l 4 i 5 a 6 k 7 c 8 j 9 e 10 g 11 b 12 f

True-False: 1 F 2 T 3 F 4 T 5 T 6 F 7 T 8 T 9 T 10 F 11 T 12 T 13 T 14 F 15 F

Multiple Choice: 1 d 2 d 3 a 4 e 5 b 6 c 7 a 8 b 9 d 10 d 11 c 12 a 13 e 14 d

Exercises: **1a.** 400 **1b.** $0.80 **1c.** zero, yes **1d.** shortage, 300 **2.** 120, P_2, surplus, 40, sell their wheat at the high price, are unable to sell their wheat at the high price, buy the surplus wheat, surplus, increase, 80, increasing, P_1 **3.** 30 **a.** 5, 15, 10, 10 **b.** 20, 30, 13, 22, increased, increased **c.** 10, 20, 10, 10 **d.** 15, 20, because S_2 is steeper than S_1

CHAPTER 5

THE ECONOMIC ROLE OF GOVERNMENT

MAJOR PURPOSE

The major objective of this chapter is to explain how the government affects the economy. It does so in four ways: spending, taxation, regulation, and the operation of public enterprises. In the United States, public enterprises are much less important than in other countries, and the other three are the principal ways in which the government affects the economy.

There are a number of reasons for government intervention in the economy. (1) The government provides *public goods*—that is, goods that everyone can enjoy, whether they actually pay for them or not. An example is police protection; we all gain the benefits from an orderly society, whether we pay taxes or not. (2) The government can control or discourage externalities, such as pollution. Free markets don't work very well in polluting industries, since they provide no incentive to keep pollution down. (3) The government provides merit goods—such as education—that it considers particularly important for the society. (4) The government provides programs to help the poor.

Learning Objectives

After you have studied this chapter in the textbook and study guide, you should be able to:

Describe the four ways in which the government affects the economy

Describe the major programs of the three levels of government

Explain the difference between government spending for goods and services, and transfer payments

Explain the difference between a progressive and a regressive tax, and give an example of each

Describe the five major reasons for government intervention in the economy

Explain the objectives that should be kept in mind when designing a tax system

Explain the difference between the *benefit principle* and the *ability to pay principle*

Explain why the U.S. tax system is less progressive than we might guess by looking at the income tax schedule

HIGHLIGHTS OF CHAPTER

The government affects the economy in four major ways: (1) spending, (2) taxation, (3) regulation, and (4) public enterprises. There are some public enterprises in the United States—for example, the Tennessee Valley Authority and the Post Office. However, public enterprise is much less important in the United States than in many other countries, as we saw in Chapter 4. This chapter therefore concentrates on the first three points.

Spending

In dollar terms, government spending has risen very rapidly in the United States, from $100 billion per year in 1955 to $1,250 billion by 1984. However, if we look at the size of the government relative to the economy, we get a much less spectacular picture. Indeed, government *purchases of goods and services* have remained approximately stable as a percentage of GNP in the past three decades; increases at the state and local levels have been offset by decreases at the federal level. Nevertheless, if transfer payments are included, government spending has been going up as a percentage of GNP. In other words, the increase in the size of the government reflects mainly the increase in transfer payments, of which social security is the most important program.

Taxes

The primary purpose of taxes is to raise the revenues to finance government spending programs. Personal income taxes and social security taxes are the largest revenue raisers—by a wide margin. Social security tax revenues have grown very rapidly, by more than 50% in the 4 years from 1980 to 1984, and further increases are scheduled for the coming years. These large increases have been necessary to finance the large increases in pensions and other benefits under the social security system.

On most income—up to a maximum of $39,600 in 1985—the social security tax is *proportional*; it is a flat percentage of each $1 in income. However, no tax is collected on incomes over the maximum, which means that the social security tax is somewhat *regressive*. That is, it is a smaller percentage of an income of $50,000 than of an income of $25,000. Nevertheless, the overall social security system is *progressive*, because the benefits to lower-income people are greater, compared to the taxes they have paid, than the benefits of higher-income people.

The income tax rates are *progressive*—the tax rate on high incomes is larger than the tax rate on low incomes. However, the overall tax system is less progressive that the tax rates suggest, both because of the existence of regressive taxes such as social security, and because of "loopholes"—various tax deductions or tax credits. The term "loophole" implies that the deduction or credit is undesirable, and there is considerable debate over what is desirable and what is not. One item sometimes put on the list of loopholes—the provision that homeowners can deduct the interest on their mortgages from their taxable incomes—has such overwhelming political support that it is rarely questioned in the ongoing discussion of tax reform. (President Carter once hinted that the interest deduction might be eliminated, but there was such a storm of protest that he quickly dropped the idea.)

Other than raising revenues, there are a number of other objectives that should be considered in designing a tax code:

1. One objective is *equity*, or fairness. As we suggested in Chapter 1, there is some controversy over just what is fair. Nevertheless, discussions of fairness usually begin with one of two approaches to taxation:

    a. *Ability to pay.* According to this idea, taxes should be imposed according to income or wealth; people with high incomes should pay more because they are better able to do so. The progressive income tax is one application of this principle. (The inheritance tax is another.)

    b. *Benefit principle.* According to this idea, taxes should depend on who benefits most from government programs. Those who benefit most should pay the most.

2. *Simplicity* is an important objective in the tax system. Discussions of tax reform in recent years have often centered around the criticism that the income tax has become hopelessly complicated. Even some ex-commissioners of the Internal Revenue Service find the income tax too complicated for them to make out their own forms; they get professional help.

3. *Neutrality.* As a starting point, most economists believe that the tax system should be designed to disturb market forces as little as possible. It should not capriciously introduce incentives for people to change their behavior in order to avoid taxes.

4. *Meeting social objectives.* Nevertheless, in some cases it may be desirable to encourage people to change their behavior. For example, in order to encourage people to give to charities, the government allows people to deduct their contributions to charities from their taxable income. Taxes may also be used to discourage businesses from polluting the air or water.

Regulation

More direct means are available for encouraging some behavior, and discouraging other activities. For example, there are regulations limiting the amount of pollutants that factories are allowed to discharge into the air and water. In the early days of regulation about 100 years ago, the government took steps to discourage monopolistic behavior by the so-called "robber barons" of the time. Other regulations are aimed at protecting the safety of workers and discouraging discrimination.

Government regulations are generally aimed at reducing major problems. Nevertheless, regulation has been a source of controversy. There are two major problems with regulation: (1) regulatory agencies may require major reporting efforts from business, and sometimes generate expensive red tape of little value; and (2) regulatory agencies sometimes come under the control of the industry they are supposedly regulating. The government may be the means for an industry gaining oligopolistic or monopolistic power.

Reasons for Government Activity

The government becomes involved in the economy for many reasons. Here are the five most important:

1. Governments often provide goods and services which the private sector would otherwise fail to provide or would provide only with difficulty and at a high cost. Roads are one example. If the roads within a city were run by private entrepreneurs, motorists would have to stop frequently to pay tolls. National defense is unlikely to be organized and paid for privately. There is a problem of *free riders*—people who let others pay because they will reap the benefits even if they don't contribute. If people benefit whether they pay or not, we have an example of a *public good*.

2. The government may intervene when *side effects* prevent people from making socially desirable decisions. For example, vaccinations protect not only the individuals who are vaccinated; they also protect the public from communicable diseases. Smallpox has been eradicated by the combined action of governments and international organizations.

Benefits that go to people other than those who are vaccinated (or their doctors) are known as *external benefits*. There also can be *external costs*, such as the cost to people downwind from a polluting factory. Just as the government encourages activities with external benefits—such as vaccinations—so it may discourage those with external costs.

3. The government may provide *merit* goods or services, such as education, that it considers very desirable from a social viewpoint.

4. The government has programs to *help the poor*; for example, food stamps and welfare programs.

5. The government may increase or decrease its expenditures in order to *promote economic stability*. For example, during a period of high unemployment, it may undertake public projects in order to provide jobs.

Important Terms:

Match the term in the first column with the corresponding phrase in the second column. But before you do so, write out your own definition of the term in the first column.

_____ **1.** Transfer payment
_____ **2.** Progressive tax
_____ **3.** Proportional tax
_____ **4.** Average tax rate
_____ **5.** Marginal tax rate
_____ **6.** Deficit
_____ **7.** Revenue sharing
_____ **8.** Externality
_____ **9.** Public good
_____ **10.** Neutral tax
_____ **11.** Incidence of tax
_____ **12.** Tax credit
_____ **13.** Deduction

a. Tax paid divided by income
b. One which takes the same percentage of high and low incomes
c. Grants by the federal government to states and localities
d. Subtraction from tax payable
e. People get the benefit of this, regardless of who pays
f. Expenditure by government, for which government receives no good or service in return
g. Tax which leaves market forces undisturbed
h. Who ultimately pays tax
i. Excess of expenditures over revenues
j. Subtraction from taxable income
k. One which takes a higher percentage of high incomes
l. Side effect of production or consumption
m. Percentage of increase in income paid in tax

True-False

T F **1.** A tax is progressive if high-income people pay a larger percentage of their income than low income-people.
T F **2.** Defense expenditures have risen consistently as a percentage of national product since the beginning of the conflict in Vietnam.
T F **3.** Since 1960, transfer expenditures by the federal government have risen, both as a fraction of total federal government expenditures, and as a fraction of national product.

T F   4. Suppose that a state imposes a tax of 5% of all income. Because it "hits the poor as hard as the rich," such a tax is regressive.

T F   5. According to the benefit principle of taxation, government expenditures should be undertaken if they benefit the public.

T F   6. According to the ability-to-pay principle of taxation, only those who have enough income that they are able to save should be required to pay taxes.

T F   7. The term "merit good" is used in describing a feature of the British economy. Specifically, a merit good is one which the upper class consumes more heavily than the lower classes.

T F   8. Suppose that one wanted to make the tax system more progressive. A replacement of deductions with tax credits would be a step in this direction.

Multiple Choice

1. Which of the following is the best example of government expenditure for goods or services?
- **a.** salaries of judges
- **b.** social security pensions paid to the elderly
- **c.** welfare payments
- **d.** unemployment compensation
- **e.** the progressive income tax

2. Since 1980, the fastest-growing item of federal government spending has been:
- **a.** defense spending
- **b.** social security expenditures
- **c.** education
- **d.** interest
- **e.** veterans' benefits

3. Over the past three decades, transfer payments by the federal government have been rising as a percentage of GNP. From this, we may conclude that:
- **a.** transfer payments have become too large
- **b.** transfer payments may or may not be too large now, but they were too small in 1955
- **c.** transfer payments are still too small, since they are still rising
- **d.** transfer payments will sooner or later bankrupt the government
- **e.** we don't have enough information to come to any of the above conclusions

4. If a tax takes $1,000 from someone with an income of $10,000, and $2,000 from someone with an income of $50,000, that tax is:
- **a.** neutral
- **b.** progressive
- **c.** regressive
- **d.** proportional
- **e.** marginal

5. An excise tax is a tax:
- **a.** that has been cut out of the tax code
- **b.** on goods such as gasoline or cigarettes
- **c.** on corporate profits
- **d.** on excess corporate profits
- **e.** on incomes above $100,000

6. An important component of President Reagan's economic plan when he came into office in 1981 was:
- **a.** tighter regulation of polluters
- **b.** more generous social security pensions
- **c.** cuts in defense expenditures, to help balance the budget
- **d.** increases in tax rates, to help balance the budget
- **e.** cuts in tax rates

7. More than two-thirds of federal government expenditures are made up of three large categories. Those three categories are:
- **a.** defense, education, and social security
- **b.** defense, education, and agriculture
- **c.** defense, social security, and agriculture
- **d.** social security, agriculture, and interest on the national debt
- **e.** social security, defense, and interest on the national debt

8. A public good:
- **a.** creates no positive externalities
- **b.** creates no negative externalities
- **c.** cannot be produced by a private corporation
- **d.** can be enjoyed by all, even those who do not pay for it
- **e.** must be provided by the federal government, if it is to be provided at all

9. Which of the following is the best example of a negative economic externality?
- **a.** air pollution created by a steel mill
- **b.** the rise in the price of steel when the government requires steel mills to reduce pollution
- **c.** vaccinations
- **d.** an increase in the international price of oil
- **e.** an increase in the international price of grain

10. According to the "neutrality" principle of taxation:
- **a.** taxes should be imposed only on goods about which people are neutral (that is, neither very enthusiastic nor very negative)
- **b.** taxes should be imposed on tobacco and alcoholic beverages
- **c.** taxes should be designed to disturb market forces as little as possible
- **d.** income taxes should be progressive
- **e.** the government should rely on the corporate profits tax, not the personal income tax

11. Which of the following is designed specifically to be *non*neutral?
- **a.** a tax on polluters
- **b.** a proportional income tax
- **c.** a general sales tax of 5%
- **d.** all of the above
- **e.** none of the above

12. The presence of externalities means that:
- **a.** a tax system that seems to be progressive will in fact be regressive

b. a tax system that seems to be regressive will in fact be progressive

c. the market system will generally not work as well as it would in the absence of externalities

d. the rich will generally get richer, and the poor poorer

e. the federal government will find it much more difficult to balance its budget

13. Which of the following is the best example of a "flat" tax?

a. a tax that collects the same number of dollars from everyone

b. a proportional income tax

c. a progressive income tax

d. a regressive income tax

e. an excise tax on beer and wine

Exercises

1. The table below shows two different taxes—tax A and tax B. For each of these taxes, fill in the column showing the average tax rate at various incomes, and the marginal tax rate. Also note on the last line whether the tax is proportional, regressive, or progressive.

2. Suppose that a family with an income of $35,000 pays $5,000 in interest on its mortgage, and is allowed to deduct that $5,000 from its taxable income. As a result, taxable income falls from $35,000 to $30,000. This would mean a reduction of $_____ in tax payable under tax A, and a reduction of $_____ under tax B. Thus, the higher is the marginal tax rate, the [greater, less] is the tax saving from a deduction.

Income	Tax A Average rate	Marginal rate	Tax B Average rate	Marginal rate
$10,000	$1,500 ____%		$1,500 ____%	
		____%		____%
$20,000	3,000 ____%		3,500 ____%	
		____%		____%
$30,000	4,500 ____%		6,000 ____%	
		____%		____%
$40,000	6,000 ____%		9,000 ____%	
Type of tax:	_____		_____	

Essay Questions

1. During the past 15 years, there has been a controversy over the appropriate scope of government regulation. Take the government agencies on pages 85 and 86 in the textbook, and divide them into three lists— agencies that you consider clearly desirable, those that are clearly undesirable, and ones you are not sure about. (You are not required to put any particular number on any of the lists. One or two of the lists may be blank, if there are no such agencies.) In each case, explain briefly why you put the agency on the list you did.

2. In most communities, the following services are provided by the local government: (a) police, (b) elementary education, (c) street cleaning, and (d) garbage collection. Could these be provided by private enterprise? Is there any advantage in having them provided by the government? Would there be any advantage in having them provided by the private sector?

3. What externalities are created when individuals (a) drive on a highway, (b) mow their lawns, and (c) smoke in a theater. In each case, do you think that the government should do anything to encourage or discourage the activity? If so, what, and why? If not, why not?

Answers

Important Terms: 1 f 2 k 3 b 4 a 5 m 6 i 7 c 8 l 9 e 10 g 11 h 12 d 13 j
True-False: 1 T 2 F 3 T 4 F 5 F 6 F 7 F 8 T
Multiple-Choice: 1 a 2 d 3 e 4 c 5 b 6 e 7 e 8 d 9 a 10 c 11 a 12 c 13 b
Exercises: **1.** Tax A. Average rates: 15%, 15%, 15%, 15%. Marginal rates: 15%, 15%, 15%. The tax is proportional. Tax B. Average rates: 15%, 17.5%, 20%, 22.5%. Marginal rates: 20%, 25%, 30%. The tax is progressive. **2.** $750, $1,500, greater.

Across

1. it is important to distinguish these two tax rates (2 words)
7. two
8. era
9. preposition
10. desirable characteristic for tax base
13. what a completely flat tax would do to tax rate
15. file your tax _____
18. a tax-deferred way of saving (abbrev.)
20. part of Roosevelt's economic program (abbrev.)
22. Economic Recovery Tax Act of 1981
23. 2nd person
24. above
26. generally considered an undesirable type of tax
27. spiritual guide (Hind.)
29. for an expense account, this is a no-no
30. Batman's home
33. a government commission
35. what people do with pen
36. the (Fr.)
37. distant
41. major government program (2 words)
45. that is
46, 47. U.S. hasn't had this for many years

Down

1. one guide in designing taxes (3 words)
2. famous international trade theorist (see inside cover of text)
3. what marginal tax rate does as your income increases
4. his theories shook the world
5. before this time
6. raise
11. in your car, to be avoided
12. determines who pays tax
14. worth
16. social security is an example
17. an airline (abbrev.)
19. what a defeated army does
21. what people do at bank
25. generally, a desirable characteristic of tax
28. a status at a university (abbrev.)
31. informal greeting
32. 1st person
34. in Britain, it's sometimes said you get this by going to school (2 words)
38. government agency
39. not so
40. claim against property
42. U.S. spying agency (abbrev.)
43. glum
44. defunct government agency (abbrev.)

CHAPTER 6

BUSINESS ORGANIZATION AND FINANCE

MAJOR PURPOSES

The major purposes of this chapter are to (1) explain the three forms of business organization, (2) describe how businesses finance expansion, (3) explain the differences between a balance sheet and an income statement, and (4) describe some of the problems that arise in the financial markets.

For big business, the major legal form is the corporation. This provides owners with the protection of *limited liability*. Stockholders are not responsible for the debts of their business, and can lose only the funds they have already spent to acquire a share of ownership.

Limited liability is one of the reasons why there is such a broad market in common stock, and why it is relatively easy for corporations to raise funds by selling additional stock.

One of the major functions of the markets for financial capital—such as the stock market and the bond market—is to provide funds to new and expanding companies. People have an incentive to buy the securities of rapidly growing, profitable, and financially sound corporations. The capital markets do a fairly good job of providing resources to the most profitable and promising corporations.

Learning Objectives

After you have studied this chapter in the textbook and study guide, you should be able to:

Describe the three major types of business organization, and explain the major advantages and disadvantages of each

Describe the ways in which a corporation can raise funds for expansion

Explain what a balance sheet is, and how it differs from an income statement

Explain the advantages and disadvantages to the corporation of issuing common stock rather than bonds

Explain the advantages and disadvantages of buying common stocks rather than bonds

Explain leverage and its relation to the risks faced by corporations and bondholders

Describe the major motives of the people who buy securities, and the major motives of those who issue securities

Describe two major problems in the financial markets

HIGHLIGHTS OF CHAPTER

There are three major types of business organization:

1. The *single proprietorship*, owned and operated by an individual. Many small businesses are single proprietorships.

2. The *partnership*, which is quite similar to the single proprietorship, except that there are several owners and operators. With a few exceptions, partnerships are quite small businesses.

3. The *corporation*, which is the standard organization for large businesses. The corporation provides *limited liability* to the stockholder-owners. This is a great advantage, because the stockholder-owners don't have to worry about being stuck with the obligations undertaken by any of the other owners. As a result, a large, well-known corporation may be able to sell shares of common stock (that is, shares of ownership) to a wide variety of people. Thus, the corporate form of organization has the advantage of making it *easier to finance growth*. A third advantage of the corporation is that it has *automatic continuity*. When one of the stockholder-owners dies, the stock goes to the heirs. The corporation continues uninterrupted. Because of the protection offered by limited liability, an heir need not be concerned about accepting the stock.

Many small corporations are not well known, and the desire to raise funds is not the reason for incorporation. For many small businesses, tax considerations are important in the decision whether to incorporate or not. The income of a proprietorship or partnership is taxed as the personal income of the owner or owners. Corporate profits are taxed differently; they are subject to a corporation income tax. For small corporations, the tax on the corporate profits may be less that the tax on an individual proprietor's income. Thus, there can be an advantage in incorporating. But there can also be a disadvantage. The corporation pays tax on its profits. Then, when the profits are paid out as dividends to stockholders, the stockholder-owners have to pay taxes on these dividends. Thus, profits distributed to stockholders are taxed twice: once by the corporate income tax, and once by the personal income tax on the stockholders.

The corporation can raise funds by (1) issuing additional shares of *common stock*, each representing a fraction of the ownership of the corporation; (2) *selling bonds*, which is a way of borrowing money for a long period of time from the person who buys the bond; (3) issuing shorter-term debt, such as *notes* or *commercial paper*; (4) *borrowing from a bank* or other financial institution; and (5) issuing securities that are between common stock and standard bonds—specifically, shares of *preferred stock* and *convertible bonds*. Dividends on preferred shares are somewhat more certain than dividends on common stock; the preferred dividends must be paid if any dividends at all are paid on common stock. Convertible bonds can be exchanged for common stock, and thus are a way of participating in the bright future of a corporation.

All of these securities can normally be bought and sold in markets. For example, a person who owns stock or bonds of a corporation may sell them to anyone who is willing to buy. Transactions in such securities are usually facilitated by *brokers* or *dealers*. (Brokers bring buyers and sellers together. A bond dealer may be the actual buyer or seller of a bond.) Similarly, government bonds and shorter-term securities may be sold by the present holder to someone else. Thus, if the government or corporation issues long-term bonds, it has a guaranteed use of the funds for a long period of time. But the buyer is not necessarily tying up funds for a similar long period: the bond may be sold at any time. Thus, the financial markets provide *liquidity* to bondholders.

The prices of securities in the financial markets are determined by supply and demand; the prices of common stocks, bonds, and other financial assets can fluctuate as conditions change. The major determinant of the price of common stock is the *expected profitability* of the corporation. The person who buys the share will participate in the good fortune (if any) of the corporation. Even though bonds provide a fixed contract—for, say $12,000 in interest payments each year over 20 years—they may nevertheless fluctuate in value. In the marketplace, people have the choice of buying new bonds or old bonds. If a new bond will pay more interest—say $14,000—then the amount people will be willing to pay for the old bond (with $12,000 interest per year) will go down.

Although interest payments on bonds are set by the bond contract, the payment of interest is not guaranteed. If the issuing corporation runs into trouble, it may not have the funds to pay interest. In this case, the bondholder has the legal right to sue, and may push the corporation into the bankruptcy courts. Even then, there is no assurance that the bondholder will be paid, because the corporation may simply not have enough assets to cover its liabilities. If a corporation is in difficulty, there may be an agreement among bondholders and other creditors to give it more time to pay, and perhaps take smaller interest payments.

Because bondholders are not guaranteed payment, they must be concerned with the prospects that the issuer will in fact be able to make interest payments on schedule, and repay the principal when the bond reaches maturity. If a corporation is shaky, people will avoid its bonds unless they offer an extra amount of interest to compensate for the risk—the so-called risk premium. Because of differences in risk, some bonds offer substantially higher interest rates than others. Interest rates can also differ because of the tax law. For example, interest on state and local government bonds is exempt from federal income tax. This makes them attractive, and states and localities can therefore offer lower interest rates on their bonds than do corporations or the federal government.

In deciding which securities to buy, potential bond buyers weigh a number of factors—*risk, return, liquidity,* and *taxes.* Issuers of securities also have a number of factors to consider. One of their most important decisions is whether they will issue additional common stock or additional bonds. If they issue stock, they will be taking on additional part-owners. Thus, they will have to share their future profits among more people. If they issue additional bonds, they will be increasing the *leverage* of the corporation. If the business does well, the owners will only have to pay the interest; they will not have to share their profits with the bondholders. But they will be legally committted to pay the interest, whether the firm does well or not. Thus, leverage can add to the risks that the company may fail in the future.

The major function of financial markets is to allocate the saving of society to the various investment projects that can be undertaken. On the whole, the financial markets do a fairly good job in allocating funds among various projects. People who buy bonds or stocks have an incentive to put their funds into the corporation with the best prospects. Nevertheless, major mistakes are made. Some mistakes are inevitable in an risky and uncertain world—the best buggy whip manufacturer in America became obsolete with the invention of the motor car. But some mistakes can be avoided if people have more information. This is where the Securities and Exchange Commission plays an important role. It requires corporations to disclose their financial condition. By enforcing a reasonable rule—that information be disclosed—the government can help the private capital markets work better.

Important Terms: Match the Columns

Match the term in the first column with the corresponding phrase in the second column. But before you do so, write out your own definition of the term in the first column.

_____ 1. Proprietorship	a. Long-term debt
_____ 2. Limited liability	b. Example of financial intermediary
_____ 3. Bond	c. Debt divided by net worth
_____ 4. Commercial paper	d. Way of allocating cost of capital to various years
_____ 5. Net worth	e. Unincorporated enterprise
_____ 6. Leverage	f. Assets minus liabilities
_____ 7. Book value	g. A short-term debt
_____ 8. Depreciation	h. Chief advantage of forming a corporation
_____ 9. Savings and loan association	i. Net worth divided by number of shares

True-False

T F   1. Partnerships have "unlimited liability." This means that there is no limit to the amount of bonds and other liabilities they can issue.

T F   2. Corporation profits paid out to stockholders as dividends are subject to double taxation.

T F   3. A partnership with two partners (A and B) has its income taxed twice—once as the income of A, and once as the income of B.

T F   4. A corporation's balance sheet shows its assets and liabilities at a *point* in time.

T F   5. A corporation's income statement shows its sales and costs over a *period* of time.

T F   6. A firm's net worth is the amount that stockholders originally paid into the corporation when they bought their shares.

T F   7. A government bond is generally more liquid than a house.

T F   8. Issuing additional common stock increases the leverage of a corporation.

T F   9. Businesses that increase their leverage usually do so to reduce the risk of bankruptcy.

T F 10. If a corporation buys machinery with the proceeds from newly issued bonds, the issuing of the bonds does not increase the corporation's leverage.

Multiple Choice

1. In a standard partnership, each partner:
   a. must pay personal income tax on all the income of the partnership
   b. has unlimited liability, but only for the debts which he or she undertook personally
   c. has unlimited liability, but only for his or her share of the debts of the corporation
   d. has unlimited liability for all the debts of the partnership, including those undertaken by the other partners
   e. can lose the amount of his or her initial investment, but no more

2. Corporations provide "limited liability." This means that:
   a. the stockholder-owners are not personally liable for debts of the corporation
   b. the corporation is not legally liable for debts of more than one-half its net worth in any one year
   c. officers of the corporation cannot be held legally liable for any fraudulent activities of the corporation
   d. the corporation is legally required to make contributions to the pension fund only in the years when it is profitable
   e. corporations do not have to pay dividends if they are unprofitable

3. People sometimes talk of the "double taxation" applying to corporations. Which of the following is subject to double taxation?
   a. interest paid by the corporation
   b. interest received by the corporation
   c. retained profits
   d. dividends paid by the corporation
   e. wages paid by the corporation

4. In the balance sheet of a corporation:
   a. net worth = assets + liabilties
   b. assets = net worth − liabilties
   c. assets = liabilities − net worth
   d. assets = liabilities + net worth
   e. profits = sales − depreciation

5. The book value of a share of common stock is equal to:
   a. the value of the share when it was initially issued by the corporation
   b. today's price of a share on the books of brokerage houses
   c. the market price of a share when the books were closed at the end of the most recent fiscal year
   d. retained earnings of the company divided by the number of shares outstanding
   e. net worth of the company divided by the number of shares outstanding

6. What appears on the income statement of a corporation?
   a. depreciation
   b. income before taxes
   c. income after taxes
   d. all of the above
   e. none of the above

7. If depreciation is "accelerated," this means that:
   a. machines are wearing out more quickly
   b. technological change is occurring more quickly
   c. firms speed up the rate at which they depreciate capital

d. taxes must be paid more quickly on the depreciated value of plant
   e. taxes must be paid more quickly on the depreciated value of equipment

8. Financial intermediaries:
   a. offer liquidity to creditors
   b. issue only long-term securities, such as bonds
   c. hold only long-term securities, such as bonds
   d. hold mainly the warrants of other corporations
   e. require unlimited liability of their creditors

9. Those who underwrite the shares of a corporation are called:
   a. investment banks
   b. central banks
   c. savings and loan associations
   d. brokers
   e. buccaneers

10. Financial leverage is measured by:
   a. the trend in net worth, measured in dollars
   b. the trend in debt, measured in dollars
   c. the trend in debt, after adjustment for inflation
   d. the ratio of debt to net worth
   e. the price-earnings ratio

11. Whenever a corporation issues bonds, rather than raising funds by issuing new common stock, it:
   a. increases its leverage
   b. decreases its leverage
   c. decreases the risks faced by stockholders
   d. decreases the risks faced by bondholders
   e. increases the tax it has to pay

12. In the spring of 1985, the yield on high-grade corporate bonds was about 12.5%, while the yield on lower-grade corporate bonds was about 13.7%. The 1.2% difference was:
   a. a tax premium
   b. a risk premium
   c. an inflation premium
   d. an incentive for risky businesses to borrow
   e. a sign of malfunctioning capital markets

13. A commitment by a bank to lend up to a predetermined limit to a specific customer is known as a:
   a. warrant
   b. stock option
   c. commercial paper
   d. line of credit
   e. illegal overdraft

14. Interest rates on state bonds are generally lower than interest rates on bonds of the federal government. The major reason is that:
   a. the federal government has been running large deficits
   b. the federal government has been running large surpluses
   c. state governments have been running large deficits
   d. Cleveland and New York almost went bankrupt during the 1970s
   e. interest from state bonds is exempt from federal income tax

15. Interest rates on government bonds are most likely to rise during:
   a. recessions
   b. depressions
   c. deflationary periods

d. periods of rising inflation
e. the period just prior to income tax time in April of each year

16. A major purpose of the Securities and Exchange Commission (SEC) is to require corporations to:
a. issue stock periodically so as to decrease leverage
b. issue stock periodically so as to increase leverage
c. issue bonds periodically so as to decrease leverage
d. issue bonds periodically so as to provide bondholders a stable source of income
e. make information available to the public

Exercises

1. The numbers below apply to XYZ Corporation.
   a. Prepare a balance sheet for the XYZ Corporation in Table 6-1. There are no assets and liabilities other than those listed below. However, *not* all items should be included in the balance sheet. *Use only the ones that belong.*
   b. Some of the numbers are not used in part (*a*) belong in the income statement. Use them to complete the income statement in Table 6-2. This corporation pays 30% of its income in taxes.
   c. The book value of each share of stock of the XYZ Corporation is [$15, $19.50, $20, $34.50].

2. The owners of a corporation are called _____. Compared with the owners of a partnership, they have a major advantage: _____. The corporation can raise funds by issuing two types of stock, namely: _____. If it issues _____ instead, its leverage will increase. Leverage is disadvantageous, in that it increases _____.

   The profits of a corporation are equal to _____ less _____. To find net profit, we also have to subtract _____.

Accounts payable	$ 800,000
Sales during year	$1,900,000
Accounts receivable	$ 900,000
Wages paid during year	$ 850,000
Long-term bonds of XYZ Corp. outstanding	$1,000,000
Plant and equipment (current value, after depreciation)	$2,000,000
Inventory on hand	$ 300,000
Revenue from service contracts	$ 250,000
Bank deposits and other cash items	$ 200,000
Depreciation during year	$ 300,000
Net interest paid	$ 150,000
Other costs	$ 250,000
Accrued liabilities	$ 150,000
Number of shares of common stock outstanding	$ 100,000
Holdings of notes issued by ABC Corp.	$ 50,000

Table 6-1
BALANCE SHEET (THOUSANDS OF DOLLARS)

Assets	Liabilities
	Net worth
Total assets =	Total liabilities and net worth =

Table 6-2
INCOME STATEMENT (THOUSANDS OF DOLLARS)
1. Revenues:

   Total:
2. Costs:

   Total:
3. Profit before taxes:
4. Tax:
5. Net profit:
6. Addendum: profit per share:

Essay Questions

1. To find net worth, what do we subtract from assets? Is it possible for the net worth of a corporation to be negative? If so, what could we say about the book value of each share of common stock of a corporation with a negative net worth? Would it ever pay to buy shares in a firm with a negative net worth? If it is not possible, explain why not. Specifically, explain what will happen as the net worth of the corporation shrinks toward zero.

2. Suppose that you are in charge of finance for a large corporation. How would you go about raising funds to (*a*) finance the construction of a large plant with an expected useful life of 25 years, (*b*) acquire larger inventories of raw materials, and (*c*) meet a temporary shortage of cash resulting from a decision by your customers to wait an extra month before paying their bills? Under what circumstances might you issue new common stock rather than borrow? Might it ever be a good idea to cut the dividend by, say, 50% to pay for any of the above? Explain why or why not. Might it ever be a good idea to cut the dividend for other reasons? Explain.

Answers

Important Terms: 1 e 2 h 3 a 4 g 5 f 6 c 7 i 8 d 9 b
True-False: 1 F 2 T 3 F 4 T 5 T 6 F 7 T 8 F 9 F 10 F
Multiple Choice: 1 d 2 a 3 d 4 d 5 e 6 d 7 c 8 a 9 a 10 d 11 a 12 b 13 d 14 e 15 d 16 e
Exercises:

1a. Table 6-1
BALANCE SHEET (THOUSANDS OF DOLLARS)

Assets		Liabilities	
Cash	$ 200	Accounts payable	$ 800
ABC Corp. notes	50	Accrued liabilities	150
Accounts receivable	900	XYZ Corp. bonds	1,000
Inventory	300	Total liabilities	1,950
Plant and equip.	2,000	Net worth	1,500
Total assets =	3,450	Total liabilities and net worth =	3,450

1b. Table 6-2
INCOME STATEMENT (THOUSANDS OF DOLLARS)

1. Revenues:		
Sales	$1,900	
Service contracts	250	
Total:	$2,150	
2. Costs:		
Wages	$ 850	
Depreciation	300	
Net interest	150	
Other	250	
Total:	$1,550	
3. Profit before taxes:	$ 600	
4. Tax:	$ 180	
5. Net profit:	$ 420	
6. Addendum:		
Profit per share:	$ 4.20	

1c. $15. **2.** stockholders, limited liability, common stock and preferred stock, bonds (or debt), risk, revenues, costs, taxes.

PART TWO

HIGH EMPLOYMENT AND A STABLE PRICE LEVEL

**Special note for students using the paperback,
AN INTRODUCTION TO MICROECONOMICS**

If you are using the microeconomics paperback, note that the study guide has corresponded with your book for the first six chapters. But now you should skip Chapters 7 through 19 in this study guide (the chapters on macroeconomics), and proceed to Chapter 20. This corresponds to Chapter 7 in the microeconomics paperback. For each chapter beginning with Chapter 7 in the microeconomics paperback, add 13 to get the number of the corresponding chapter in this manual.

MEASURING NATIONAL PRODUCT AND NATIONAL INCOME

MAJOR PURPOSE

Macroeconomics is about the overall magnitudes in the economy—total output and the average level of prices. The main purpose of this chapter is to provide an introduction to macroeconomics by explaining how total output and the average level of prices are measured. In calculating total output—or GNP—we want to count everything that is produced once, but only once. This means that there is an important problem to be avoided—the problem of double counting. This problem can be avoided by counting only final products such as TV sets, and excluding intermediate products such as the wire and chips that went into the TV set.

Another important objective of the chapter is to draw a distinction between *nominal* (or current dollar) magnitudes and *real* (or constant dollar) magnitudes. Through time, GNP measured in dollar terms goes up rapidly. This rapid increase is the combined result of two things: (1) there is an increase in the quantity of goods and services that we are producing, and (2) the prices at which these goods and services are sold are going up. The first of these is desirable; the second is not. To see what is happening in real terms, national product accountants eliminate the effects of inflation. They do this by measuring the GNP of each year in the prices of a single base year, 1972.

Learning Objectives

After you have studied this chapter in the textbook and study guide, you should be able to:

Explain what GNP measures, and why the distinction between final products and intermediate products is important

State the relationship between gross investment, net investment, depreciation, and the change in the stock of capital

State the major differences between GNP and NNP, between NNP and national income, between national income and personal income, and between personal income and disposable personal income. (See Figure 7-3 in the textbook.)

State the relationship between nominal GNP, real GNP, and the GNP deflator. That is, you should understand equation 7-6 in the textbook.

Explain why the GNP deflator is not exactly the same as the consumer price index

Explain why real GNP is a better measure of how we are doing than is nominal GNP

Explain why real GNP is nevertheless not a very good way to measure how well we are doing

Explain why it is so hard to calculate a more comprehensive measure of economic welfare

Explain why the "underground economy" exists, why its size may have increased in recent years, and why this is of concern to economists

HIGHLIGHTS OF CHAPTER

This chapter explains how national product is measured, in both real and nominal terms. It also explains some of the limitations of GNP as a measure of economic welfare.

To calculate the total output of the nation, we must somehow add apples and oranges, steel and airplanes, haircuts and medical services. The only reasonable way to add up different goods and services is to add together the total amount of money spent on each of them. Thus, when we put together a measure of national product, we use *market prices* as a way of judging the comparative importance of each product. A car selling for $10,000 contributes as much to national product as do 20,000 bottles of Coca-Cola selling for 50 cents each.

When we measure national product, we want to measure everything produced in the economy (except for antisocial, illegal products). However, we have to be careful. If we took the value of all the cars produced in the economy, plus all the steel and all the tires, then we would be exaggerating our output. Why is that? The answer is, because much of the steel and many of the tires were used by car manufacturers to produce their cars. We didn't produce a car plus four tires, but the car into which the four tires went.

To avoid double counting of tires, steel, and other intermediate products, national product accountants concentrate on *final products*. These are placed in four main categories: (1) consumer expenditures for goods and services, (2) investment, (3) government purchases of goods and services, and (4) net exports (that is, exports minus imports).

Investment is perhaps the trickiest of these four to understand precisely. The first important point is that we are dealing with the production of capital goods—buildings, machines, etc.—and not what Wall Streeters mean by "investment." That is, we do not include financial investments—such as the purchase of common stock—in the investment category of GNP. The reason is straightforward. When individual A buys 100 shares of common stock from individual B, there is simply a transfer of ownership, not a direct increase in production. (Of course, the ability of firms to issue stock or bonds may help them to finance new factories, and these new factories are included in GNP.) Recall that this distinction between financial capital (such as stocks and bonds) and capital goods (such as factories) was made back in Chapter 2.

A second complication with investment is that it includes some intermediate products, such as steel, tires, or wheat. Specifically, it includes the *increases* in our inventories of such products. These inventory increases are something we have produced during the year. They are not included elsewhere—for example, they have not yet been used in the production of consumer goods. Thus, they have not yet been included

when we count consumer goods. Therefore, they are counted here, in the investment category.

The final complication is that, when we count all the factories and machines produced during the year, we are in an important sense exaggerating what we have produced. The reason is that existing factories and machines have been wearing out and becoming obsolete during the year. What we should be measuring is not the total production of capital goods during the year, but only the *increase* in our capital stock. In other words, it would make sense to include only the *increase* in the stock of equipment, plant, and residential buildings, just as we include only the increase in the stocks of inventories.

This leads to the distinction between net investment and gross investment. *Gross investment* (I_g) is total output of plant, equipment, residential buildings, and increases in inventories. *Net investment* (I_n) is just the increase in our stock of plant, equipment, residential buildings, and inventories. The difference between the two is depreciation (Figure 7-2). GNP includes gross investment; NNP includes net investment. Accordingly, the difference between GNP and NNP is also depreciation (Figure 7-3 in the textbook).

Other important magnitudes—national income, personal income, and disposable personal income—are also shown in Figure 7-3. While you should not try to memorize the numbers on that figure, you should know the differences between the five major measures. You should also have a general idea of the magnitudes. For example, you should know that personal saving is less than 10% of disposable income; it is not 20% or 30%.

We have seen that market prices provide a feasible way to add various products. But, when we use market prices, we run into difficulty. Today, a person can use $100 to buy food, or clothing, or other things. The relative prices of food, clothing, or other things represent the relative amounts that people pay for the various goods; it is a way of measuring their relative value. But a person can't shop now out of the Sears catalog of 1970. We should not conclude that a $10,000 car bought now is worth four times as much as the car that sold for $2,500 in 1965. Money has lost some of its value as a result of inflation.

This raises an important problem. We want to use GNP figures as one measure of how well the economy is performing, of how healthy the economy is now as compared to the way it was 5 or 10 years ago. If we simply used GNP measured at current prices, we would not know what to do with the comparison. Does a higher GNP today reflect success; are we producing more? Or does it simply reflect our failure to prevent inflation? In practice, it is likely to reflect both.

In order to separate the undesirable increase in prices from the desirable increase in output, national product accountants calculate *constant-dollar GNP*. That is, they calculate what GNP would have been if prices had remained what they were in a single base year. Such constant dollar or real GNP figures represent what has been happening to output over time.

Although real GNP is an important measure of the performance of the economy, it has major defects which mean that we should not concentrate single-mindedly on increasing real GNP. A lot of important things don't appear in GNP—the quality of the physical environment, the stability of the political system, or the degree of social harmony, to name but a few. Because of limits of GNP as a measure of welfare, some economists have considered the possibility of a broader measure, to include important features of our economic performance that are left out of GNP. This attempt has not been very successful. The problems are apparently insoluble. In particular, it is not clear how leisure should be counted. In the period studied by Nordhaus and Tobin, per capital real NNP rose 90%, while leisure per capita rose 22%. It is not clear what this means, in terms of an overall measure. Were we more than 90% better off, since we had 90% more goods and more leisure too? Or was the improvement only some average of the 90% and the 22%? The answer is not clear. The most promising approach is therefore not to search for some comprehensive single measure of welfare, but to look at a number of measures simultaneously—for example, not only real NNP, but also literacy, life expectancy, infant mortality, etc.

Important Terms: Match the Columns

Match the term in the first column with the corresponding phrase in the second column. But before you do so, write out your own definition of the term in the first column.

_____ 1. GNP	**a.** Personal income − income taxes and other personal taxes
_____ 2. NNP	**b.** Remove the effects of inflation from a time series
_____ 3. National income	**c.** Good intended for resale or further processing
_____ 4. Disposable income	**d.** NNP + depreciation
_____ 5. Depreciation	**e.** Sales − cost of intermediate products bought from outside suppliers
_____ 6. Intermediate product	**f.** NNP − sales taxes
_____ 7. Value added	**g.** Unreported income
_____ 8. Deflate	**h.** GNP − NNP
_____ 9. Underground economy	**i.** $C + G + I_n + X - M$

True-False

T F **1.** GNP can be determined by adding sales taxes to NNP.

T F **2.** The easiest way to calculate GNP is to add the sales of all corporations.

T F **3.** It is possible for net exports to be negative during a year.

T F **4.** Gross private domestic investment includes all the money spent on U.S. stock exchanges during the year, but it excludes money spent by Americans on foreign stock exchanges.

T F **5.** During the typical business cycle, investment fluctuates by a larger percentage than does GNP.

T F **6.** Suppose that there are no sales taxes in an economy. Then personal income will be the same as national income.

T F **7.** Gross investment is most likely to be small, as a fraction of GNP, during a depression.

T F **8.** If real GNP has gone up and the price index has gone up, then we can be sure that nominal GNP has gone up.

Multiple Choice

1. In the GNP accounts, increases in inventories are:
   a. excluded, since they are made up mostly of intermediate goods
   b. included as part of the consumption category, since they are made up mostly of consumer goods
   c. included as part of the government category, together with other miscellaneous items
   d. included as part of the investment category
   e. included as an item separate from C, I, and G

2. Suppose we know $C + I_g + G$. Then, to get GNP, we should:
   a. add depreciation
   b. subtract depreciation
   c. add the increase in inventories
   d. add sales taxes
   e. add exports and subtract imports

3. In the GNP accounts, which of the following is included as a final product?

a. a plane bought by the government
b. government expenditures to resurface roads
c. purchases of washing machines by households
d. purchases of washing machines by laundromats
e. all of the above

4. Last year, the XYZ Corporation issued $10 million in new common stock, and used $8 million of the proceeds to build a new factory. The other $2 billion was used to repay bank loans, and replenish XYZ's deposits at its banks. As a result, GNP went up by:

a. the $8 million spent for the factory
b. the $10 million in new common stock
c. $12 million
d. $18 million
e. $20 million

5. Consider the following incorrect definition: National income equals the sum of wages and salaries, rent and interest, proprietors' income, net exports, and corporation profits. To make this statement correct, one item should be deleted. This item is:

a. wages and salaries
b. rent and interest
c. proprietors' income
d. net exports
e. corporation profits

6. Some years ago, the Department of Commerce published a statistical report that, in 1932, gross private domestic investment in the United States was $1.0 billion, while depreciation was $7.6 billion. We may conclude that:

a. net investment was larger than gross investment
b. net investment was negative; the capital stock was smaller at the end of the year than at the beginning
c. most investment was in the form of inventory accumulation
d. imports were larger than exports
e. there is something wrong with the statistics; maybe the Department of Commerce got gross investment and depreciation mixed up

7. Suppose that gross investment has been 10% of GNP, but then it falls to zero during the current year. In the current year:

a. depreciation is the same size as net investment
b. depreciation is the same size as gross investment
c. depreciation is also zero
d. net investment is also zero
e. net investment is negative

8. Suppose that a firm sells its output for $40,000. It pays $22,000 in wages and salaries, $10,000 for materials bought from other firms, $3,000 for interest on its bonds, and it has profits of $5,000. Then its value added is:

a. $18,000
b. $22,000
c. $30,000
d. $35,000
e. $37,000

The next six questions are based on the following table, which shows national product in a simple economy with only guns and consumer goods.

9. In this simple economy, current-dollar GNP in 1972 was:

a. $700,000
b. $1,250,000
c. $1,900,000
d. $3,500,000
e. $4,200,000

10. In this simple economy, current-dollar GNP in 1986 is:

a. $700,000
b. $1,250,000
c. $1,900,000
d. $3,500,000
e. $4,200,000

11. Suppose that 1972 is the base year in this simple economy. Real GNP in 1986 is:

a. 700,000
b. $1,250,000
c. $1,900,000
d. $3,500,000
e. $4,200,000

12. Suppose that 1972 is the base year in this simple economy. In this economy, the GNP deflator in 1986 is:

a. 162.5
b. 250
c. 271
d. 280
e. 300

13. In this economy, how much did the average level of prices rise between 1972 and 1986?

a. 150%
b. 171%
c. 180%
d. 200%
e. 280%

14. In this economy, how much did real GNP rise between 1972 and 1986?

a. 52%
b. 79%
c. 152%
d. 179%
e. 204%

15. Suppose we divide current-dollar GNP for 1986 by constant-dollar GNP for 1986. Then the resulting figure is a measure of:

a. inflation during 1986
b. real output during 1986
c. nominal output during 1986
d. the GNP price deflator for 1986
e. depreciation

16. If the price index has gone up and current-dollar GNP also has gone up, then we know that:

a. real GNP has gone up
b. real GNP has gone down
c. real GNP has stayed constant
d. we cannot tell from the facts cited whether (a), (b), or (c) has happened

17. Last year, Sam Brown spent each Saturday from May to November building a new wing on his family home. In last year's GNP:

a. the full market value of the wing is included
b. the lumber, windows, paint, and other materials he bought at the store were included, but the value of his labor was not
c. the full market value of the wing was included, plus an additional 10% if the Commerce Department's survey found that he actually enjoyed building the wing

	Production of guns	Price of guns	Production of consumer goods	Price of consumer goods
1972	200	$1,000	1,000	$500
1986	250	$2,000	2,000	$1,500

d. the wing was not included at all, since it was not a market transaction

e. the wing was not included at all, since it probably is not as good as one built by a professional builder

18. In the official GNP statistics, pollution:

a. has no effect on GNP

b. results in an addition to GNP, insofar as businesses buy pollution control equipment

c. results in a subtraction from GNP, insofar as resources are diverted into the production of pollution control equipment

d. results in a subtraction from GNP, equal to the estimated discomfort to those downstream and downwind

e. results in subtractions from GNP, equal to the estimated discomfort to those downstream and downwind, and the estimated extra cost of medical care

Exercises

1. Suppose you have the following incomplete data:

C	$900
I_g	400
Wages and salaries	800
Interest and rent	100
Corporate profits (after taxes)	250
Personal taxes	350
Depreciation	50
G	450
Corporate income taxes	150
Contributions to social security	0
Sales taxes	200
Transfer payments	200
Undistributed corporate profits	150
Proprietors income	400

Compute the following:
NI _____
NNP _____

GNP	_____
X − M	_____
Personal income	_____
Personal disposable income	_____
I_n	_____

2. Suppose that a country produces two goods, a consumption good and an investment good. The first two rows of Table 7-1 give the current-dollar value of the total production of the two goods. Fill in the next row indicating nominal GNP each year. The next two rows indicate the market prices of the two goods each year. Fill in the next two rows giving the number of units of each good produced each year. Then fill in the final four rows, using 1972 as the base year.

Table 7-1

	1972	1980	1985
Current-dollar value of C production	200	450	600
Current-dollar value of I production	100	150	200
Nominal GNP			
Price of C	5	9	10
Price of I	20	25	40
Quantity of C production			
Quantity of I production			
Constant-dollar value of C production			
Constant-dollar value of I production			
Real GNP			
GNP deflator			

Essay Questions

1. In what ways does GNP overstate economic well-being? In what ways does it understate economic well-being?

2. Do the per capita NNP figures of two countries give a measure of their relative economic welfare? Explain the major deficiencies of NNP as a way of comparing welfare in different countries.

3. "Transfer payments to the poor and the elderly are not included in the G segment of national product. But the assistance to the poor and elderly make very important contributions to economic welfare. Therefore, transfer payments should be added, to get a better measure of GNP." Do you agree or not? Explain why.

4. Suppose you buy a house in January, and its value goes up by $10,000 by the end of the year. Would you consider this part of your income for the year? As part of your disposable income? Should the national income accountant include it as part of national income? Why or why not?

Answers

Important Terms: 1 d 2 i 3 f 4 a 5 h 6 c 7 e 8 b 9 g
True-False: 1 F 2 F 3 T 4 F 5 T 6 F 7 T 8 T
Multiple Choice: 1 d 2 e 3 e 4 a 5 d 6 b 7 e 8 c 9 a 10 d 11 b 12 d 13 c 14 b 15 d 16 d 17 b 18 b

Exercises:

1.
NI	1,700
NNP	1,900
GNP	1,950
X − M	200
Personal income	1,600
Personal disposable income	1,250
I_n	350

2. **Table 7–1**

	1972	1980	1985
Nominal GNP	300	600	800
Quantity of C production	40	50	60
Quantity of I production	5	6	5
Constant-dollar value of C production	200	250	300
Constant-dollar value of I production	100	120	100
Real GNP	300	370	400
GNP deflator	100	162	200

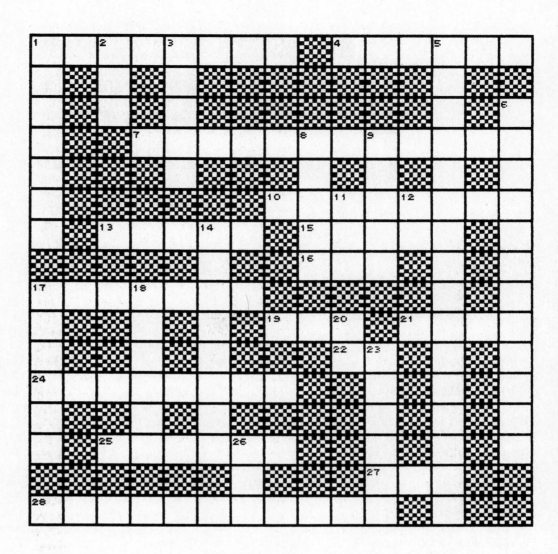

Across

1, 4. after inflation is removed, this is the measure of GNP that remains

7. to calculate NNP, subtract this from GNP

10. what some capital becomes when new inventions are made

13, 15. value of sales, less intermediate products bought from outside producers

16. a British college, famous for its teaching of economics (abbrev.)

17. to remove effects of price changes, do this to a time series

19. a measure of the nation's output

21. a factor of production

22. the (Ital.)

24. ratio of debt to net worth

25. these appear in a balance sheet

27. major U.S. conglomerate

28. this type of product is missed by GNP accountants

Down

17. _____ _____ GNP; that is, GNP before the effects of inflation are removed

2. a better measure of welfare than GNP

3. your condition after much studying

5. an advantage of incorporating (2 words)

6. these goods are not counted separately by GNP accountants

8. group of plotters

9. home

11. a student organization of the late 1960s (abbrev.)

12. the (Fr.)

14. consumption is the _____ goal of economic activity

18. more than friends

20. 3.14

23. assets with this characteristic can easily be sold

26. used for repairing roads

CHAPTER 8

FLUCTUATIONS IN ECONOMIC ACTIVITY:

UNEMPLOYMENT AND INFLATION

MAJOR PURPOSE

This chapter describes the two major macroeconomic problems—*unemployment* and *inflation*. These two problems are closely related to *economic fluctuations*. During recessions, when output is declining, fewer workers are needed by business, and the unemployment rate increases. During a rapid expansion, when spending by businesses and consumers is rising rapidly, inflation generally becomes more severe. Economic conditions were most unstable in the United States during the period between the two world wars. Between 1929 and 1933, output collapsed and the unemployment rate shot upward.

This chapter describes how the unemployment rate is calculated, and the various major types of unemployment. *Cyclical* unemployment is the result of fluctuations in overall economic activity. Reducing this type of unemployment is one of the major objectives of economic policy. *Frictional* unemployment results from the normal turnover of the labor force; some amount of frictional unemployment is inevitable. *Structural* unemployment arises when the labor force does not have the type of skills needed for available jobs, or if workers live a long distance from available jobs. This type of unemployment is more severe than frictional unemployment. To escape structural unemployment, people must move or switch to different types of work.

Finally, this chapter describes some of the problems created by inflation. Specifically, inflation can cause an *arbitrary redistribution of wealth and income*. This effect is particularly strong when inflation is *unexpected*. When it is expected, people can take steps to protect themselves.

Learning Objectives

After you have studied this chapter in the textbook and study guide, you should be able to:

Describe the four phases of the business cycle

Explain why people may disagree whether a downturn should be called a "recession" or not

Describe the major features of the Great Depression of the 1930s

Explain the major features of recent business cycles—for example, what happens to profits, investment, and the purchase of consumer durables during recessions

Explain how the labor force and the unemployment rate are calculated

Explain why the unemployment rate may understate the problem of unemployment during a recession

Explain why the productivity of labor is adversely affected by recessions

State Okun's law

List the three major types of unemployment, and explain how they are different

Explain potential GNP and the GNP gap

Explain who loses from inflation, and who gains, and why

Explain why unanticipated inflation creates greater problems than anticipated inflation

HIGHLIGHTS OF CHAPTER

The business cycle has four phases. During a *recession*, economic activity declines, and the unemployment rate increases. Economic activity reaches its low point at the *trough*. This is followed by the *expansion* phase, which ends at the upper turning point, or *peak*. The key to identifying a business cycle is to tell when a recession has occurred. Not every downward jiggle is called a recession; the downward movement must be significant. The National Bureau of Economic Research decides whether downturns are significant enough to be called recessions. Its starting point is historical: Is the downward slide as severe as the declines of the past which have been called recessions? A simpler rule of thumb has often been used as a quick and ready method of identifying a recession: Has real GNP declined for two or more quarters? However, this rule of thumb is not foolproof. Output did not decline for two quarters during the recession of 1980.

The most severe downturn in U.S. history occurred between 1929 and 1933, as the economy collapsed into the Great Depression. In this chapter, the main events of the Great Depression are summarized. Although the depression may seem like ancient history, it remains a lesson in how badly things can go wrong. It thus provides a reason for studying macroeconomics. If things can go this badly when macroeconomic policy is mismanaged, it is important for us to have some idea of what macroeconomic policy is all about.

Between 1929 and 1933, the unemployment rate rose to almost 25%, real GNP fell 30%, and the average level of prices declined more than 20%. The production of capital equipment, buildings, and consumer durables fell particularly sharply. On the farm, the depression caused a collapse of prices.

Recent recessions have been *much* milder than the downturn of 1929–1933. Some have been very short and mild indeed—for example, the recession of early 1980. However, there has been no noticeable tendency for recessions to become progressively more mild over the past four decades. Two recent recessions were severe—those of 1973–1975 and 1981–1982.

The unemployment rate is calculated by the Bureau of Labor Statistics, as a percentage of the labor force. The unemployed are people who are out of work who (1) are temporarily laid off, (2) are waiting to report to a new job, or (3) have been looking for work in the previous four weeks. If people without jobs do not meet one of these conditions, they are considered to be out of the labor force. The labor force is made up of those with jobs, plus those who are unemployed according to the above criteria.

During recessions, it becomes harder and harder to find a job. As a result, those out of work may become discouraged and stop looking for work. In this case, they drop out of the officially measured labor force and out of the ranks of those who are counted as unemployed. Consequently, the unemployment rate may understate the unemployment problem during recessions. Nevertheless, the unemployment rate is one important indicator of what is happening during recessions.

During recessions, as sales of products fall, businesses lay off some employees. However, they are often reluctant to lay off highly skilled workers, since these workers may take jobs elsewhere and be unavailable when sales recover. Hence, employment does not fall as much as output. There is a decline in output per worker—that is, in the productivity of labor.

As the unemployment rate increases during recessions, so does the number of those who have been unemployed for a long period of time. Not only are more people unemployed, but the hardship faced by the average unemployed person also becomes more severe. Not all groups are affected equally by unemployment. The unemployment rate for teenagers—particularly minority teenagers—is much higher than for adults.

No matter how prosperous the economy becomes, it is not possible to eliminate unemployment altogether. *Frictional* unemployment represents those who are temporarily unemployed because they are looking for a better job, or because of adjustments associated with a dynamic, changing economy. In a changing economy, there is always some frictional unemployment.

Thus, if "full employment" is to be a meaningful goal, it cannot mean an unemployment rate of zero. There is some debate over the unemployment rate that should be considered full employment. During the 1960s, an unemployment rate of 4% was frequently looked on as representing full employment. Most economists now put the figure higher—at 6% or even 7%. Several explanations have been offered for the upward trend in unemployment: (1) changes in the labor force; for example, there has been an increase in the number of teenagers, who tend to have high unemployment rates (2) increases in the minimum wage and in the number of people covered by the minimum wage; some low-skilled workers have been priced out of the market (3) reduced pressures on unemployed workers to take jobs quickly.

Potential GNP is estimated as the GNP path along which the economy would move if there were no business cycles and a high level of employment were maintained continuously. The shortfall of actual GNP below the estimated potential is called the *GNP gap*. It gives a measure of the output lost because of recessions.

The costs of inflation are much less easy to identify than the costs of unemployment. One reason is that high unemployment represents a clear net loss to society—the output foregone when people are idle. On the other hand, there are both winners and losers from inflation. Winners include those who have borrowed and who are able to repay with less valuable money. Losers include bondholders, who are repaid with money whose value has declined, and people whose money incomes are stable in the face of inflation. Between 1973 and 1979, the average hourly earning of workers did not keep up with inflation, and their real earnings therefore declined.

There are ways in which people can be protected from inflation. The incomes of some people are *indexed*—that is, the money incomes are automatically increased in line with the rising index of prices. For example, social security payments to retirees are indexed. During the 1970s, labor unions responded to the rising rate of inflation by negotiating more cost-of-living adjustments in their contracts. This represented another form of indexation.

Owners of assets can try to protect themselves in another way. They can avoid bonds and acquire different assets instead—for example, common stock or real estate. When they do this, they will reduce the amount of funds flowing to the bond market. With fewer funds, interest rates will be bid up. If interest rates rise enough to compensate for inflation, people will be able to buy bonds without being penalized by inflation.

In protecting oneself, the *predictability* of inflation is of central importance. For example, if asset holders accurately anticipate inflation, they can refuse to buy bonds unless interest rates rise enough to compensate for the inflation. But suppose that they have already bought bonds on the expectation that inflation will be 3%, and it turns out to be 10%. They will not have protected themselves, and will lose from the unexpected inflation.

This is a very important point, to which we will return in later chapters. The effects on various groups in the economy are much greater if inflation is *unexpected* than if people expect it and take steps to protect themselves.

Important Terms: Match the Columns

Match the term in the first column with the corresponding phrase in the second column. But before you do so, write out your own definition of the term in the first column.

_____ 1. Recession
_____ 2. Trough
_____ 3. Peak
_____ 4. Underemployed
_____ 5. Discouraged workers
_____ 6. Okun's law
_____ 7. Frictional unemployment
_____ 8. Structural unemployment
_____ 9. Cyclical unemployment
_____ 10. Potential GNP
_____ 11. GNP gap

a. Discouraged workers, plus those who are not kept busy because demand is low
b. To reduce this unemployment, people must move or acquire new skills
c. What output would be if the economy were at full employment
d. Observation that unemployment rate moves less strongly than output during the business cycle
e. Turning point at the end of a recession
f. Unemployment caused by recessions
g. Turning point as a recession is about to begin
h. Potential output less actual output
i. Unemployment associated with adjustments in a changing, dynamic economy
j. Downward movement of the economy, usually lasting two quarters or more
k. Those who have dropped out of the labor force because they were unable to find work

True-False

T F   1. Recessions in the U.S. economy have become consistently less and less severe over the past three decades.
T F   2. In most U.S. recessions, seasonally adjusted real national product has declined for two or more consecutive quarters.
T F   3. In percentage terms, investment fluctuates less than consumption, but more than total GNP, during the typical business cycle.
T F   4. Calculated as a percentage of the total labor force, the unemployment rate is smaller than when calculated as a percentage of the civilian labor force.
T F   5. As the economy declines into recession, the number of people employed generally declines. Furthermore, the productivity of those still at work also generally declines.

T F 6. During the Great Depression, the prices of agricultural products fell much more than the prices of manufactured products.

T F 7. The Great Depression was confined to the United States. Other countries experienced only mild recessions during the 1930s.

T F 8. During the business cycle, consumer spending for nondurable goods fluctuates more than consumer spending for durable goods.

T F 9. People temporarily laid off, but waiting to be recalled, are included among the unemployed.

T F 10. During a recession, as workers are laid off, the remaining workers can use the best equipment. Therefore, productivity of those remaining at work generally increases rapidly during a recession.

T F 11. Inflation is more likely to lead to an arbitrary and unfair reshuffling of income and wealth when it is anticipated than when it is unanticipated.

Multiple Choice

1. After the expansion phase of the business cycle, which comes next?
  - **a.** recession
  - **b.** depression
  - **c.** peak
  - **d.** trough
  - **e.** upswing

2. Between the peak of 1929 and the trough of the Great Depression in 1933, real GNP fell by approximately:
  - **a.** 30%
  - **b.** 15%
  - **c.** 10%
  - **d.** 5%
  - **e.** 2%

3. Between the peak of 1929 and the trough of the Great Depression in 1933, the prices of farm commodities:
  - **a.** rose about 15%, in spite of the decline in the prices of most other goods
  - **b.** remained stable, in spite of the decline in the prices of most other goods
  - **c.** remained stable, in spite of the increase in the prices of most other goods
  - **d.** fell about 10%, or slightly less than the average of other prices
  - **e.** fell about 60%, or much more than the average of other prices

4. During the typical recession, profits:
  - **a.** fall by about as much as the decline in output
  - **b.** fall by a much greater percentage than output falls
  - **c.** fall, but by less than the fall in output
  - **d.** remain approximately stable, as companies raise prices by whatever amount is needed to maintain their profits
  - **e.** rise substantially, as companies raise prices

5. During the typical recession:
  - **a.** government spending falls more than consumption
  - **b.** government spending falls more than investment
  - **c.** consumption falls more than investment
  - **d.** investment falls more than consumption
  - **e.** consumption and investment generally increase, but at a slow rate

6. During recent decades, one sector of GNP has accounted for much of the downward movement during recessions. Recent recessions are therefore often referred to as:
  - **a.** export recessions
  - **b.** tax recessions
  - **c.** inventory recessions
  - **d.** government recessions
  - **e.** consumption recessions

7. Assume that the population is 200 million, the labor force is 100 million, and 90 million people are employed. Then, the unemployment rate is:
  - **a.** 4.5%
  - **b.** 5%
  - **c.** 9%
  - **d.** 10%
  - **e.** 55%

8. Suppose a person quit a job in construction last month, and has already lined up a job in a factory, to begin next week. This person is:
  - **a.** counted as still being employed in construction
  - **b.** counted as being employed in the factory job
  - **c.** frictionally unemployed
  - **d.** structurally unemployed
  - **e.** cyclically unemployed

9. A major objective of macroeconomic policy is to reduce:
  - **a.** cyclical unemployment
  - **b.** frictional unemployment
  - **c.** labor mobility
  - **d.** product innovations
  - **e.** all of the above

10. During the past three decades, the unemployment rate generally considered to represent "full employment":
  - **a.** has been stable at 0%; at no other rate is there "full employment"
  - **b.** has been stable, at about 4%
  - **c.** has risen, from about 4% to 6% or 7%
  - **d.** has fallen, from about 10% to about 4%, as the economy recovered from the Great Depression
  - **e.** has fallen, from about 7% to about 4%

11. Suppose that the unemployment rate this month is 10%. Then we can conclude that:
  - **a.** the economy is still declining into a recession
  - **b.** the economy is at the trough
  - **c.** the economy has passed the trough, and is now in a recovery
  - **d.** actual GNP is less than potential GNP
  - **e.** potential GNP is less than actual GNP

12. During an unexpected inflation, who are the clearest gainers?
  - **a.** employers
  - **b.** workers
  - **c.** foreigners
  - **d.** bondholders
  - **e.** those who have borrowed

13. Inflation is most likely to lead to an arbitrary reshuffling of wealth and income if it is:
  - **a.** erratic and unexpected
  - **b.** erratic and expected
  - **c.** predictable

d. increasing slowly

e. decreasing slowly

14. Who is most likely to gain from unexpected inflation?

   a. someone who bought a house before the inflation began, paying cash

   b. someone who bought a house before the inflation began, taking out a mortgage for most of the purchase price

   c. someone who sold a house before the inflation began, receiving cash

   d. someone who sold a house before the inflation began, taking most of the purchase price in the form of a mortgage

   e. someone who sold one house for cash, and used the proceeds to buy another

Exercises

1. During recessions, output declines. So does employment, [by even more than output, although less than output]. The relationship between changes in output and changes in unemployment is known as [Keynes's law, Okun's law]. This relationship is reflected in a [rapid rise in productivity, fall in productivity] during the typical recession.

When a recession becomes very severe, it is called a [depression, stagnation]. One occurred during the 1930s. At such times, prices fall, particularly those of [manufactured goods, agricultural commodities]. Output declines very sharply, especially the output of [manufactured goods, agricultural commodities]. There is a particularly sharp decline in the output of [consumer goods, capital goods]. At such times, [cyclical, frictional, structural] unemployment becomes very high.

2. Figure 8-1 shows fluctuations in real output. Recessions occurred during the time periods _____ and _____, and expansions during the periods _____ and _____. Peaks occurred at _____ and _____, while troughs occurred at _____ and _____.

3. When the economy is at full employment, the unemployment rate is not zero. Rather, the full-employ-

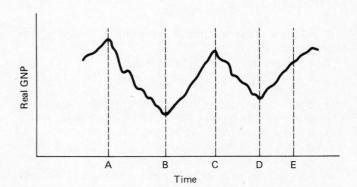

FIGURE 8-1

ment rate is now generally believed to be around _____%. The rate considered to represent full employment has [increased, decreased] in the past quarter century. In the early 1960s, _____% was usually identified as the full-employment rate of unemployment. Several explanations have been offered for this [increase, decrease] over the past quarter century, specifically: (*a*) _____, (*b*) _____, and (*c*) _____.

Essay Questions

1. Explain why, during a recession, (*a*) production of consumer durable goods decreases more than production of consumer nondurables, (*b*) production of capital goods decreases more than production of consumer nondurable goods, (*c*) output generally declines more than employment, and (*d*) labor productivity generally declines.

2. Explain the conceptual difference between structural and frictional unemployment. Explain also why it may be difficult in practice to distinguish whether specific unemployed individuals are part of "structural" or "frictional" unemployment. Might it also be difficult

to tell if specific individuals are part of "frictional" or "cyclical" unemployment? Why or why not?

3. Suppose that you expect inflation to rise from a present level of, say, 4% to 10%, but nobody else does. What might you do to gain? How would you be benefited by these actions if inflation did in fact occur? How might you lose if, contrary to your expectations, inflation declined?

4. Now suppose that you are not alone in expecting an increase in inflation, but that everybody shares your expectation. How might this affect your ability to gain from the inflation when it does occur?

Answers

Important Terms: 1 j 2 e 3 g 4 a 5 k 6 d 7 i 8 b 9 f 10 c 11 h
True-False: 1 F 2 T 3 F 4 T 5 T 6 T 7 F 8 F 9 T 10 F 11 F
Multiple Choice: 1 c 2 a 3 e 4 b 5 d 6 c 7 d 8 c 9 a 10 c 11 d 12 e 13 a 14 b
Exercises: **1.** although less than output, Okun's law, fall in productivity, depression, agricultural commodities, manufactured goods, capital goods, cyclical. **2.** *AB, CD, BC, DE, A, C, B, D.* **3.** 6% or 7%, increased, 4%, increase, change in composition of labor force, increases in minimum wage and its coverage, reduced pressure on the unemployed to find jobs.

CHAPTER 9

EXPLAINING UNEMPLOYMENT AND INFLATION:

AGGREGATE SUPPLY AND AGGREGATE DEMAND

MAJOR PURPOSE

Chapter 8 provided an overview of macroeconomic problems—fluctuations in the overall level of production, periods of high unemployment, and the problem of inflation. The purpose of this chapter is to begin a study of *why* these macroeconomic problems arise. In explaining macroeconomic events, *aggregate supply* and *aggregate demand* are useful tools, just as supply and demand

are useful in figuring out what is happening in the market for individual products such as hamburgers, shoes, or wheat.

The Great Depression of the 1930s was caused by a collapse in aggregate demand, while the milder business cycles of recent decades have been caused by more moderate fluctuations in aggregate demand. Thus, a more stable aggregate demand is the key to reducing fluctuations in output and employment.

Learning Objectives

After you have studied this chapter in the textbook and study guide, you should be able to:

Explain why we should not assume that aggregate demand and supply curves look like demand and supply curves for an individual product

Draw the aggregate demand curve of classical economists, and explain why it slopes downward to the right

Explain why classical economists drew the aggregate supply function as a vertical line

Explain why the simple version of the Keynesian aggregate supply curve is a reversed L, and what the explanation is for the horizontal section

List the four major components of aggregate demand that Keynesians consider in detail to determine what is happening to aggregate demand as a whole

Explain why classical economists believed that equilibrium would occur at full employment, while Keynesian economists believed that equilibrium might occur either at full employment or with large-scale unemployment

Summarize how classical economists explained the Great Depression of the 1930s

Summarize the three major propositions in Keynes's *General Theory*, including his major policy conclusion

Summarize the major points of agreement between Keynesians and those in the classical tradition, and the remaining points of disagreement

HIGHLIGHTS OF CHAPTER

When studying the market for a specific good (such as apples or hamburgers), we use demand and supply curves. To study the overall behavior of the economy as a whole—changes in total output and the average level of prices—we likewise use aggregate demand and aggregate supply curves.

There are major differences between demand and supply in an individual market, and aggregate demand and aggregate supply for the economy as a whole. The major difference is that when drawing a demand or supply curve for, say, hamburgers, we are looking at what happens when *only* the price of this one good changes. (Recall the *ceteris paribus* assumption—that everything else remains unchanged.) Thus, an increase in the price of hamburgers represents a change in *relative* prices; the price of hamburgers rises *relative* to the prices of other goods. Consumers and producers respond to the change in relative prices. Consumers *switch* away from hamburgers, and buy hot dogs or other products instead. Such switching is the major reason that the quantity of hamburgers is smaller when the price is higher. Similarly, producers have an incentive to *switch*. When the price of hamburgers rises, producers have an incentive to make hamburgers instead of other products. Their willingness to switch from other products, and to produce hamburgers instead, is the principal reason why the supply curve slopes upward to the right.

On the other hand, when we look at *aggregate* demand and aggregate supply, we are looking at the responses of buyers and sellers when the *overall* level of prices rises. In simple terms, we are looking at what happens when *all* prices rise by, say, 10%. Since all prices are rising, there is no change in *relative* prices. Thus, there is no reason for either buyers or sellers to switch as a result. Switching does *not* provide a reason for the slope of the aggregate demand or aggregate supply curve.

Nevertheless, classical economists believed that the aggregate demand curve sloped downward to the right. The reason was that a fall in the average level of prices would increase the purchasing power of money. With the money in their pockets and their bank accounts, people would be able to buy more goods and services. Therefore, they would buy more.

However, classical economists did not draw the aggregate supply curve sloping upward to the right. Instead, they believed that it was vertical, at the full-employment or potential quantity of output. If, starting at full employment, all prices—including the price of raw materials and labor—were to increase by, say, 10%, then producers would have no incentive to produce more. They would get 10% more for their products, it is true, but they would have to pay 10% more for their inputs. Because they had the same incentive to produce, the total amount offered for sale would remain constant, regardless of the level of prices.

Equilibrium occurred at the intersection of aggregate demand and aggregate supply. Because they drew the aggregate supply curve as a vertical line at the full-employment output, classical economists believed that the equilibrium had to be at a position of full employment. This raised a question: How was the depression to be explained? Classical economists believed that it was a result of disturbances that resulted in a temporary *disequilibrium*. The economy had moved away from its full employment equilibrium as a result of the reduction in the money stock and a fall in aggregate demand. Classical economists believed that full employment could be restored by an increase in the money stock, which would bring aggregate demand back up, or by a decrease in wages and prices, which would lead to a new equilibrium at a lower overall price level.

Keynes saw the world differently. He believed that there could be a *long-lasting equilibrium* with high unemployment. The simplest way to illustrate this is with the reversed-L aggregate supply function. In the horizontal range, prices and wages are downwardly rigid. If aggregate demand leaves the economy in this horizontal range, then an unemployment equilibrium can persist. The solution to the depression, said Keynes, was to increase aggregate demand. The best way to get an increase would be through direct government action. The government had the responsibility, said Keynes, to increase its spending and thereby increase overall demand, leading the economy back toward full employment. (This major policy conclusion of Keynesian economics will be explained in detail in Chapter 11.)

The theoretical frameworks of both classical and Keynesian economics are still important, since they are both still used—in modified form—by present-day economists. In spite of the different approaches, there is a widespread agreement among economists on a number of central points:

1. A sharp decline in aggregate demand can cause large-scale unemployment, as it did during the depression.

2. More moderate fluctuations in aggregate demand can cause milder business cycles and temporary periods of high unemployment.

3. If aggregate demand can be stabilized, the amplitude of business cycles can be reduced.

4. When the economy is already at full employment, any large increase in aggregate demand will cause inflation.

Nevertheless, some differences in theoretical approach and in policy conclusions remain between economists in the Keynesian tradition and those in the classical tradition. Most important are the following differences:

1. Although most economists believe that both monetary and fiscal policies are important, those in the classical tradition (monetarists) emphasize monetary policy, while those in the Keynesian tradition generally emphasize fiscal policies.

2. Keynesians believe that the government has the responsibility to *manage aggregate demand* by changing fiscal and monetary polices from time to time, in order to stabilize demand and minimize business fluctuations. Monetarists believe that active management is more likely to destabilize than to stabilize aggregate demand. They advocate a *policy rule*—the authorities should aim for a slow, steady increase in the stock of money. They believe that this will result in a slow, steady increase in aggregate demand and keep the economy at or close to full employment, without causing inflation.

Important Terms: Match the Columns

Match the term in the first column with the corresponding phrase in the second column. But before you do so, write out your own definition of the term in the first column.

_____ **1.** Purchasing power of money
_____ **2.** Stickiness of prices
_____ **3.** Long run
_____ **4.** Classical aggregate supply
_____ **5.** Keynesian aggregate supply
_____ **6.** The classical equilibrium
_____ **7.** Cause of unemployment
_____ **8.** Monetarist
_____ **9.** Cause of inflation
_____ **10.** Keynesian policy
_____ **11.** Monetarist policy

a. Decline in aggregate demand
b. Reversed L
c. Active demand management
d. What a dollar will buy
e. Too much aggregate demand
f. Money rule
g. This accounts for the horizontal section of Keynesian aggregate supply function
h. Vertical line
i. Present-day classicist
j. Full employment
k. In classical economics, the period when prices and wages adjust to their equilibrium levels

True-False

T F **1.** Even if relative prices remain stable, the aggregate demand curve can nevertheless slope downward to the right.

T F **2.** The aggregate demand curve slopes downward to the right because people switch away from services, and buy goods instead, when the average price of goods declines.

T F **3.** According to classical economists, brief recessions represented periods of disequilibrium, but the economy could be in an unemployment equilibrium during a major depression.

T F **4.** Classical economists explained the Great Depression as the result of a fall in the money stock, plus downward stickiness of wages and prices.

T F **5.** According to classical economists, full employment could have been reestablished during the 1930s if *either* of two conditions had been met: a large increase in the money stock or flexibility of wages and prices.

T F **6.** Sticky wages and prices are the reason for the horizontal section of the Keynesian aggregate supply curve.

T F **7.** Classical macroeconomists defined the long run as any period over 1 year.

T F **8.** One major shortcoming of Keynesian economics is that it assumes prices are permanently fixed. Inflation therefore cannot be explained within this theory.

T F **9.** There is general agreement among economists that very large increases in aggregate demand will lead to inflation.

T F **10.** Monetarists advocate a slow, steady increase in the money stock because they believe that the economy will work best with a slow, steady inflation.

Multiple Choice

1. According to the classical approach, people buy .more goods and services when the price level falls (*ceteris paribus*) because:

a. they switch among products when prices fall
b. the purchasing power of their money has increased
c. the purchasing power of their money has decreased

d. the economy is coming out of a recession

e. potential GNP has increased because of past investment

2. According to classical economists, the aggregate supply curve was:

    a. upward sloping, like the supply curve for wheat

    b. downward sloping, like the supply curve for wheat

    c. vertical, at potential GNP

    d. an L

    e. a reversed L

3. In its simplest form, the Keynesian aggregate supply function was:

    a. upward sloping, like the supply curve for wheat

    b. downward sloping, like the supply curve for wheat

    c. vertical, at potential GNP

    d. an L

    e. a reversed L

4. According to classical economists, when the economy was at equilibrium, then real GNP would be:

    a. about 10% above the level in the most recent recession

    b. above potential GNP

    c. at potential GNP

    d. below potential GNP

    e. either (c) or (d), but we can't tell which without information on aggregate demand

5. According to Keynes, when the economy was at equilibrium, then real GNP would be:

    a. about 10% above the level in the most recent recession

    b. above potential GNP

    c. at potential GNP

    d. below potential GNP

    e. either (c) or (d), but we can't tell which without information on aggregate demand

6. There is an important reason why we cannot conclude that the aggregate demand curve must slope downward to the right, just because the demand for an individual product slopes downward to the right. The reason is:

    a. there are no "other goods" for consumers to switch from

    b. relative prices rather than absolute prices are on the axis

    c. absolute prices rather than relative prices are on the axis

    d. nominal prices rather than real prices are on the axis

    e. real prices rather than nominal prices are on the axis

7. According to classical economists, the Great Depression represented a disequilibrium caused by:

    a. an increase in government spending, which made the economy less efficient

    b. a collapse in government spending

    c. a collapse in government spending, combined with inflation

    d. a fall in the quantity of money, combined with downward stickiness of prices and wages

    e. a collapse in government spending, combined with downward stickiness of prices and wages

8. According to classical economists, the best thing the government could do to prevent recessions and depressions is to:

    a. cut government spending

    b. increase government spending

    c. provide a steady increase in the money stock

    d. promote investment

    e. promote imports

9. According to Keynes, the primary cause of large-scale unemployment is:

    a. high prices   **d.** low exports

    b. low prices   **e.** inadequate aggregate

    c. high exports   demand

10. Consider the reversed L aggregate supply function of Keynesian economics. The effects of an increase in aggregate demand will differ, depending on where the economy begins. Specifically, an increase in aggregate demand will lead to:

    a. an increase in prices if the economy starts in the horizontal section, but an increase in output if it starts in the vertical section

    b. an increase in prices if the economy starts in the vertical section, but an increase in output if it starts in the horizontal section

    c. an increase in prices if the economy starts in the horizontal section, but a decrease in prices if it starts in the vertical section

    d. an increase in prices if the economy starts in the vertical section, but a decrease in prices if it starts in the horizontal section

    e. an increase in prices if the economy starts in the horizontal section, but a decrease in employment if it starts in the vertical section

11. According to Keynes:

    a. a collapse in investment demand was the primary cause of the depression, and an increase in investment demand provided the best hope of recovery

    b. a collapse in government spending was the primary cause of the depression, and an increase in government spending provided the best hope of recovery

    c. a collapse in investment demand was the primary cause of the depression, but an increase in government spending provided the best hope of recovery

    d. a collapse in government spending was the primary cause of the depression, but an increase in investment demand provided the best hope of recovery

    e. a collapse in government spending was the primary cause of the depression, but an increase in saving provided the best hope of recovery

12. Shifts in aggregate demand, rather than shifts in aggregate supply, seem to be the primary reason for fluctuations in output. We come to that conclusion because declines in output are usually associated with:

    a. rising inflation   **d.** less unemployment

    b. declining inflation   **e.** increase in government

    c. more unemployment   spending

13. Those in the classical and Keynesian traditions agree that:

    a. a decline in aggregate demand was the principal cause of the Great Depression

    b. a decline in the money stock was the principal cause of the Great Depression

    c. a decline in investment demand was the principal cause of the Great Depression

d. fluctuations in aggregate supply have been the major cause of fluctuations in output and employment in recent decades

e. the government now has the responsibility to manage aggregate demand actively

14. To stabilize aggregate demand and reduce the amplitude of business cycles, monetarists propose:

a. active management of monetary policy

b. active management of both monetary and fiscal policies

c. active management of the government's financial accounts

d. a monetary rule, requiring the authorities to aim for a slow, steady increase in the quantity of money

e. a monetary rule, requiring the authorities to aim for a slow, steady increase in the price level

Exercises

1. In Figure 9-1 below, AS_1 represents the part of the aggregate supply function above point A. A classical economist completing this function would draw the dashed section shown as [AS_a, AS_b]. However, a Keynesian economist would be more likely to complete it with [AS_a, AS_b].

Suppose that AD_1 is the initial aggregate demand curve. Then the initial equilibrium will be at point _____, where the equilibrium quantity of output will be $OQ\_\_$. According to [classical, Keynesian, both] economists, there will be full employment at this initial equilibrium.

Now suppose that aggregate demand collapses to AD_2. According to classical economists, the economy will move in the short run to a point such as _____.

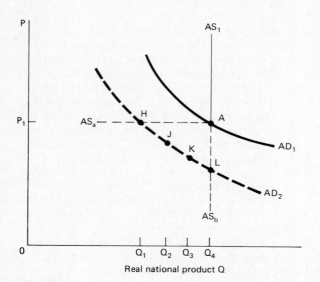

FIGURE 9-1

However, this point does not represent a new equilibrium, since [the economy is not at full employment, prices are below P_1]. If aggregate demand remains at AD_2, prices will [rise, fall], and the economy will move to a new equilibrium at point _____. At this new equilibrium, there will be [full employment, large-scale unemployment].

In the face of a fall in aggregate demand from its initial AD_1 to AD_2, Keynesians see a different outcome. In the short run, the economy will move to point _____. If aggregate demand remains stable at AD_2, the long-run equilibrium will be at point _____, with output $OQ\_\_$. With this output, there will be [full employment, large-scale unemployment].

2. On many matters, Keynesian economists and those in the classical tradition agree. However, there are still some disagreements. Mark each of the views below with a C if it is more likely to be held with those in the classical tradition, or with K if it is more likely to be held by Keynesians:

_____ **a.** Money is by far the most important determinant of aggregate demand.

_____ **b.** The government should manage aggregate demand to reduce cyclical swings in the economy.

_____ **c.** Even when the unemployment rate is high, wages and prices will move down only slightly, if at all.

_____ **d.** Following a rule, rather than periodically adjusting policies, is more likely to lead to a stable economy.

_____ **e.** The best policy to follow is to increase the quantity of money at a slow, steady rate.

_____ **f.** Large-scale unemployment represents a temporary disequilibrium.

ESSAY QUESTIONS

1. Using diagrams, explain briefly how classical economists drew the aggregate demand and aggregate supply curve. What might cause a depression? How might the economy move out of a depression and to full employment?

2. Summarize the three main points in Keynes's *General Theory*. Which points, if any, might a classical economist agree with?

Answers

Important Terms: 1 d   2 g   3 k   4 h   5 b   6 j   7 a   8 i   9 e   10 c   11 f

True-False: 1 T   2 F   3 F   4 T   5 T   6 T   7 F   8 F   9 T   10 F

Multiple Choice: 1 b   2 c   3 e   4 c   5 e   6 a   7 d   8 c   9 e   10 b   11 c   12 b   13 a   14 d

Exercises: **1.** AS_b, AS_a, A, OQ_4, both, J, the economy is not at full employment, fall, L, full employment, H, H, OQ_1, large-scale unemployment. **2. a** C **b** K **c** K **d** C **e** C **f** C.

Across

1. to reduce fluctuations, some recommend this (2 words)
5. an early economist who was interested in money (see inside cover of text)
9. not (Fr.)
10. builder
11. important economic objective (2 words)
15. metal
16. a fruit, or a computer
17. before
18. road (abbrev.)
19. one of the three basic factors of production
20. in cards, it's either high or low
21. to banks and pension funds, this is important
23. where lawyers are called
24. he revolutionized economists' views on macroeconomics
25. two directions (abbrev.)
26. peace (Russian)
28. according to Marx, capitalism would do this to the working class
32, 36. according to classical economists, these were one reason why the depression lasted so long
37. Greek letter, now means something very small
38. 3rd "person"
39. they decide who's president
41. unhappy
43. the (Sp.)
44. according to Keynesians, this is the best type of policy
46. money has this type of power

Down

2. major economic problem
3. this describes the Great Depression
4. type of income
6. someone who gets the good of a product
7. too much causes inflation
8. a football player
9. Lenin's economic program (abbrev.)
10. 1st person, possessive
11. one of the two major policies for managing aggregate demand
12. the (Fr.)
13. some advocate this for managing economy
14. providers of finance
20. rough and hard
21. exist
22. the intellectual ancestors of monetarists belonged to this school
24. what the guy in 8 down does
27. major European organization (abbrev.)
29. British political organization (abbrev.)
30. _____, ye prisoners of starvation!
31. when you look for a job, you need this
33. type of equipment
34. major U.S. corporation (abbrev.)
35. French city
40. part of window
42. Roosevelt's New _____
45. from (Ger.)

CHAPTER 10

EQUILIBRIUM WITH UNEMPLOYMENT:

THE KEYNESIAN APPROACH

MAJOR PURPOSE

In Chapter 9, the main outlines of Keynesian and classical economics were presented. The purpose of this chapter is to explain the central proposition of Keynesian economics—*that the economy may reach an equilibrium with large-scale unemployment*. This happens when aggregate demand is too low to buy all the goods and services that could be produced by the economy at full employment. When aggregate demand is too low, businesses can't sell many of their products. Lacking sales, they cut back on production and lay off workers.

Aggregate demand is made up of four major components: demand by consumers, investment demand, government purchases of goods and services, and net exports. In order to present the simplest explanation, this chapter deals with an economy with only consumption and investment—that is, the government and the foreign sectors are ignored for the time being. Furthermore, investment demand is not explained here; we simply assume that investment demand exists, and see what happens when it changes. (In Chapters 14 and 15, we will look at the reasons for a change in investment demand.) Thus, consumption is the only type of demand studied in detail. The main determinant of consumption is disposable income—when people have more income, they generally spend more. This has important implications for what happens when *investment* demand increases. People are put to work producing factories and machines. Their incomes rise. Therefore, they consume more. Therefore, an increase in investment demand causes—or *induces*—an increase in consumption demand, too. As a result, an increase in investment demand has a *multiplier effect*—national product goes up by a multiple of the increase in investment.

Learning Objectives

After you have studied this chapter in the textbook and study guide, you should be able to:

Explain the relationship between disposable income and consumer expenditures

Explain what the MPC is, and why it is the same as the slope of the consumption function

Explain why, when we put disposable income (or national product) on the horizontal axis, we can also measure disposable income (or national product) as the distance up to the 45° line

Derive the saving function from the consumption function

Explain the relationship between the MPC and the MPS

Explain why equilibrium national product is found where the aggregate demand function cuts the 45° line

Explain what will happen if national product is greater or less than this equilibrium quantity

Explain why there may be large-scale unemployment at equilibrium

Explain the difference between a leakage and an injection, and give an illustration of each

Explain why an increase in investment has a multiplied effect on aggregate demand and national product

Write the two equations for the multiplier in the simple economy with no taxes or international transactions

Express the equilibrium condition for national product in three different ways, and explain why these three different statements amount to the same thing

HIGHLIGHTS OF CHAPTER

This chapter introduces the basic framework of Keynesian theory. Keynes's major innovation was the proposition that the economy could reach an equilibrium with large-scale unemployment. National product would not automatically move to the full-employment level; it could stay much below that level if aggregate demand were low.

As we saw in the previous chapter, there are four components of aggregate demand: consumption demand, investment demand, government expenditures for goods and services, and net exports. However, to make things simple, this chapter deals with an economy with only consumption and investment.

Consumption expenditures (C) depend on disposable income (DI). The relationship between C and DI is known as the *consumption function*. This function has three main characteristics:

1. As DI increases, so does consumption. This means that the consumption function *slopes upward*.

2. The change in C (ΔC) is less than the change in DI (ΔDI). The change in C, as a *fraction* of the change in DI, is known as the *marginal propensity to consume* (MPC). This fraction, $\Delta C/\Delta$DI, is also the *slope* of the consumption function. Because the MPC is less than one, the slope of the consumption function is likewise less than one.

3. Below some level of DI—known as the *break-even point*—C is larger than DI. That is, people spend more than their incomes; they *dissave*. They do this by running down their assets or by borrowing.

These characteristics are illustrated by Figure 10-2 in the textbook.

In order to simplify the discussion, the consumption function is also given a fourth characteristic: it is drawn as a *straight line* in textbooks. This means that the MPC is constant. The evidence on consumer behavior shown in Figure 10-1 suggests that the MPC need not in fact be constant. Thus, we should file away in the back of our minds that we have made an assumption that is not necessarily correct.

The break-even point may be identified by drawing a 45° line on the consumption function diagram. The 45° line is equidistant from the two axes; measuring up to the 45° line gives the same number as measuring horizontally to the line. Because we measure disposable income on the horizontal axis, we may also measure disposable income in an upward direction; it is the height of the 45° line. The break-even point is the point where C = DI—that is, the point where the consumption function and the 45° line intersect.

Saving equals DI − C. (It is standard procedure to use this simple relationship, and ignore the interest paid to consumers shown in Figure 7-3 in the textbook.) Thus, a saving function can be derived directly from the consumption function. Specifically, the height of the saving function (Figure 10-3) is the vertical distance between the consumption function and the 45° line (Figure 10-2). The saving function has three main characteristics:

1. As DI increases, so does saving. This means that the saving function *slopes upward*.

2. The change in S (ΔS) is less than the change in DI (ΔDI). The change in S, as a *fraction* of the change in DI, is the *marginal propensity to save* (MPS). This fraction, $\Delta S/\Delta$DI, is also the *slope* of the saving function. Because the MPS is less than 1, the slope of the consumption function is likewise less than 1.

3. Below the *break-even point*, S is negative. That is, people *dissave*.

Because each $1 of additional disposable income is either consumed or saved, MPC + MPS = 1.

To see a simple illustration of equilibrium, we look at a simple economy in which there is no depreciation and no government. In such an economy GNP = NNP, and we can talk simply of national product, NP. Furthermore, in the absence of taxes and transfers, NP = NI = DI, and we can therefore redraw the consumption function with NP measured along the horizontal axis or up to the 45° line. To find aggregate demand (AD), we add investment demand (I^*) vertically to the consumption function. Equilibrium occurs where AD = NP—that is, where the AD function cuts the 45° line. At this point, producers are able to sell what they produce. If national product were larger—say at L in Figure 10-5 in the textbook, then production would be greater than aggregate demand. Unsold goods would pile up in *undesired inventory accumulation*. In order to reduce their undesired inventories, businesses would cut back on orders from suppliers and reduce their production. Output would fall back to its equilibrium at K. At equilibrium, aggregate demand may fall below the level needed for full employment. That is, equilibrium national product K may be to the left of full-employment point F, as shown in Figure 10-5. Figure 10-5 is one of the half dozen most important diagrams in the book.

The circumstances under which there is equilibrium may be stated in three different ways, all of which amount to the same thing. Equilibrium occurs when:

1. AD = NP, as shown by the intersection of AD and the 45° NP line in Figure 10-5. At this point of intersection, there is a demand for all the goods and services produced. That is:

2. Undesired inventory accumulation equals zero, and $I = I^*$.

3. $S = I^*$, as shown in Figure 10-6.

If investment demand increases, the additional investment demand is added vertically to the AD function; the AD function shifts upward. As a result, national product increases. As it does so, incomes increase. People spend more. Thus, a $1 increase in investment demand leads not only to $1 more in the output of capital goods; it leads to more output of consumer goods and services, too. Overall output increases by a multiple of the $1 increase in investment. This is the important *multiplier* concept. Specifically, the multiplier is equal to $\Delta NP/\Delta I^*$. In the simple economy, this equals 1/MPS. Details on the multiplier are given in Figure 10-11 and Table 10-3 in the textbook.

Important Terms: Match the Columns

Match the term in the first column with the corresponding phrase in the second column. But before you do so, write out your own definition of the term in the first column.

_____ **1.** Break-even point
_____ **2.** Marginal propensity to consume
_____ **3.** Marginal propensity to save
_____ **4.** Saving
_____ **5.** Equilibrium national product
_____ **6.** Undesired inventory accumulation
_____ **7.** A leakage
_____ **8.** An injection
_____ **9.** Multiplier

a. Saving
b. NP = AD
c. 1/MPS
d. *I* minus *I**
e. $\Delta C/\Delta DI$
f. *I**
g. DI − C
h. C = DI
i. 1 minus MPC

True-False

T F **1.** The slope of the saving function = 1 − MPC.
T F **2.** At the break-even point of consumers, saving equals zero.
T F **3.** If national product is above its equilibrium, then actual investment is greater than desired investment.
T F **4.** If undesired inventory accumulation is positive, then actual national product exceeds equilibrium national product.
T F **5.** If the MPC is constant, then the MPS is equal to the MPC.
T F **6.** If the consumption function is a straight line, then the MPC is greater than 1.
T F **7.** Because all goods must be demanded if they are to be produced, the slope of the aggregate demand schedule equals 45°.
T F **8.** Businesses respond to undesired inventory accumulation by increasing their orders for goods.
T F **9.** The higher is the MPC, the larger is the multiplier.
T F **10.** The slope of the aggregate demand function is equal to the MPS.

Multiple Choice

1. In Keynesian theory, aggregate demand is studied as the sum of four components, including each of the items below *except one*. Which one?
   a. personal consumption expenditures
   b. personal saving
   c. investment demand
   d. government purchases of goods and services
   e. net exports

2. The *break-even point* in the consumption function is the point where:

   a. C + I* = national product
   b. C + I* = aggregate demand
   c. personal income = disposable income
   d. MPC = 1
   e. saving = 0

3. The slope of the consumption function is equal to:
   a. the MPC
   b. the MPS
   c. the MPS + 1
   d. the multiplier
   e. 1/(the multiplier)

4. Suppose that the consumption function is a straight line. Then:

a. consumption is a constant fraction of income
b. saving is a constant fraction of income
c. the MPC is constant
d. the MPC becomes smaller as income becomes smaller
e. the MPS becomes smaller as income becomes smaller

5. If the slope of the consumption function rises, then we may conclude that:
a. the slope of the saving function has fallen
b. the marginal propensity to save has risen
c. the marginal propensity to consume has fallen
d. the multiplier has become smaller
e. undesired inventory accumulation has become larger

6. National product is at its equilibrium when:
a. aggregate demand = $C + I^* + G$
b. aggregate demand = national product
c. saving = undesired inventory accumulation
d. saving = desired inventory accumulation
e. government spending = tax revenues

7. When undesired inventory accumulation equals zero:
a. $S = 0$
b. $I = 0$
c. $I^* = 0$
d. government spending = tax revenues
e. national product is at its equilibrium level

8. Actual investment minus investment demand equals:
a. one
b. zero
c. inventory investment
d. undesired inventory investment
e. desired inventory investment

9. Suppose that, in a simple Keynesian system, national product exceeds its equilibrium quantity. Then:
a. aggregate demand exceeds national product
b. investment demand exceeds saving
c. actual investment exceeds investment demand

d. the multiplier equals 1
e. MPC = MPS − 1

10. The condition for equilibrium may be stated in three different ways—in each of the following ways *except one*. Which is the exception?
a. aggregate demand = national product
b. $I = I^*$
c. $S = I^*$
d. $S = I$

11. In the circular flow of spending:
a. investment is an injection, and saving a leakage
b. saving is an injection, and investment a leakage
c. saving and investment are both leakages, and consumption is an injection
d. saving and investment are both injections, and consumption is a leakage
e. consumption and saving are both leakages, and investment is an injection

12. Consider a simple economy, with no government or international trade, and with an MPC of 0.9. According to the multiplier theory, if investment demand increases by $100 billion, equilibrium national product will rise by a multiple of the $100 billion. Specifically, equilibrium national product will rise by:
a. $1,000 billion, made up of the original $100 billion in investment plus an additional $900 billion of investment stimulated by the initial investment
b. $1,000 billion, made up of the $100 billion in investment plus $900 billion in consumption as consumers move along the consumption function
c. $500 billion, made up of $100 billion in investment plus $400 billion in consumption
d. $500 billion, made up of the original $100 billion in investment plus an additional $400 billion of investment stimulated by the initial investment
e. $500 billion, made up of $100 billion in investment, $200 billion of consumption, and $200 billion of government spending for goods and services

Exercises

1. Figure 10-1 shows a simple economy with only two components of demand—consumption demand and investment demand. In this economy, equilibrium occurs at point _____, with national product of _____. At this national product, consumption is distance _____, desired investment is distance _____, actual investment is distance _____, saving is distance _____, and undesired inventory accumulation is distance. _____. Now, suppose that national product is equal to *OC*. At this national product, consumption is distance _____, desired investment is distance _____, actual investment is distance _____, saving is distance _____, and undesired inventory accumulation is distance _____.

In this diagram, we can also tell the size of the multiplier. If, from an initial point of equilibrium, investment were to fall to zero, the equilibrium point would move to _____. That is, when investment demand fell by distance _____, national product would

FIGURE 10-1

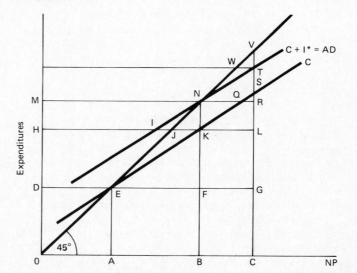

fall by distance _____. Thus, the size of the multiplier is distance *AB* divided by distance _____.

We can also tell the MPC in this diagram. Specifically, it is distance _____ divided by distance *EF*.

2. Table 10-1 below represents the same sort of simple economy as the one studied in this chapter. Suppose that the MPC = 0.8. Fill in the second column, giving the level of consumption demand at each level of DI. Suppose that the demand for investment is 40. Then fill in the third column, giving the level of aggregate demand at each level of NP. Now fill in the fourth and fifth columns, giving (respectively) the amount of saving and the amount of undesired inventory investment that would occur at each level of NP. Then fill in the sixth column, giving *S* minus investment demand.

3. Suppose that the equation of the consumption function is *C* = 25 + (0.75) DI. In other words, if DI equals, say, 100, then *C* = 25 + (0.75 × 100) = 100. Plot out the consumption function in Figure 10-2. Plot

the saving function in Figure 10-3. Suppose that the demand for investment equals 25. Plot the demand for investment in Figure 10-3. Plot the aggregate demand schedule and the 45-degree line in Figure 10-2. The MPC equals _____, the MPS equals _____, the multiplier equals _____, and the equilibrium level of NP equals _____. Now, suppose that the demand for investment increases by 25; it now equals 50. Plot the new aggregate demand schedule in Figure 10-2 and the new investment demand schedule in Figure 10-3. The new equilibrium NP equals _____. At the value of NP that used to be the equilibrium, aggregate demand is now [more, less] than NP by the amount _____, saving is now [more, less] than the demand for investment by the amount _____, and the level of undesired inventory investment equals _____.

4. Suppose that the MPC equals 0.5 and that investment demand rises by 400. In the first column of Table 10-2 fill in the increase in demand at each round of

Table 10-1

(1) DI (= NP)	(2) C	(3) Aggregate demand	(4) Saving	(5) Undesired inventory investment	(6) S minus investment demand
0	20	_____	_____	_____	_____
100	_____	_____	_____	_____	_____
200	_____	_____	_____	_____	_____
300	_____	_____	_____	_____	_____
400	_____	_____	_____	_____	_____
500	_____	_____	_____	_____	_____

FIGURE 10-2

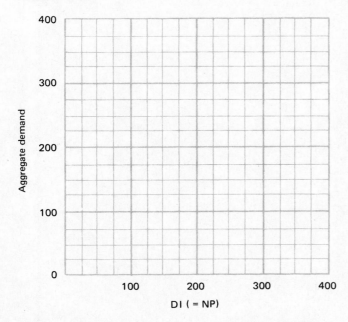

FIGURE 10-3

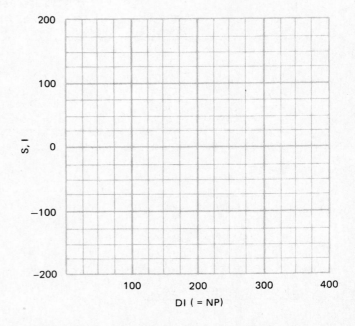

Table 10-2

		(1) Change in aggregate demand	(2) Cumulative total
First round	Investment of		
Second round	Consumption of		
Third round	Consumption of		
Fourth round	Consumption of		
Fifth round	Consumption of		
Sixth round	Consumption of		
Seventh round	Consumption of		

spending, as in Table 10-3 in the textbook. In the second column fill in the total increase in demand (investment plus consumption) that has occurred up to and including that round. The total increase in demand in *all* the rounds (if the series is continued indefinitely) will be _____ .

Essay Questions

1. In the textbook, disposable income is the main determinant of consumption expenditures. But consumption can depend on other things, too. What other variables do you think are important, and why? (Hints: What beside disposable income determines the expenditures of a retiree in Florida? Does it make sense for a student to consume more than his or her disposable income? Why?)

2. In the textbook, the level of investment is initially assumed to be constant, and then it is assumed to change without explanation. What do you think would be the important determinants of investment? Would investment demand depend on national product? *If so,* how would this change the way in which Figures 10-5 and 10-6 were drawn in the textbook? Would it make the economy more or less stable through time? *If not,* why do you think other determinants are more important than national product?

Answers

Important Terms: 1 h 2 e 3 i 4 g 5 b 6 d 7 a 8 f 9 c
True-False: 1 T 2 T 3 T 4 T 5 F 6 F 7 F 8 F 9 T 10 F
Multiple Choice: 1 b 2 e 3 a 4 c 5 a 6 b 7 e 8 d 9 c 10 d 11 a 12 b
Exercises: 1 N, OB, BK, KN, KN, KN, zero, CS, ST, SV, SV, TV, E, KN, AB, KN, FK.

2. Table 10-1

DI(NP)	C	Aggregate demand	Saving	Undesired inventory investment	S minus investment demand
0	20	60	−20	−60	−60
100	100	140	0	−40	−40
200	180	220	20	−20	−20
300	260	300	40	0	0
400	340	380	60	20	20
500	420	460	80	40	40

3. 0.75, 0.25, 4, 200, 300, more, 25, less, 25, −25.   4. 800.

Table 10-2

	1	2
First	400	400
Second	200	600
Third	100	700
Fourth	50	750
Fifth	25	775
Sixth	12½	787½
Seventh	6¼	793¾

PART THREE

AGGREGATE DEMAND POLICIES

CHAPTER 11

FISCAL POLICY

MAJOR PURPOSE

The principal cause of recessions and depressions is the instability of aggregate demand. The authorities have two tools with which to stabilize aggregate demand—fiscal policy and monetary policy. Fiscal policy, in turn, can be subdivided under two headings—changes in government spending and changes in tax rates. The major purpose of this chapter is to explain how these two fiscal policy tools can be used to influence aggregate demand.

Government spending for goods and services constitutes one of the components of aggregate demand, and an increase in such spending therefore increases aggregate demand directly. If, during a depression, the government builds new roads, people will be put to work building the roads and providing materials to construc-

tion companies. The initial increase in output and employment will be followed by a multiplier effect, as those engaged in roadbuilding activities find that their incomes are higher and therefore buy more consumer goods.

A change in tax rates does not affect aggregate demand in the same way; taxes are not a component of demand. However, a cut in tax rates leaves the public with more disposable income, and therefore encourages consumption.

Ideally, the government should cut taxes to fight recessions and raise taxes to fight inflation, thereby stabilizing the path of demand. In practice, however, the U.S. government has had only partial success in using its fiscal policy tools.

Learning Objectives

After you have studied this chapter in the textbook and study guide, you should be able to:

Explain why an increase in government spending causes an increase in aggregate demand

Explain why a cut in tax rates causes an increase in aggregate demand

Explain why a $100 change in government spending can have a more powerful effect on aggregate demand than a $100 change in taxes

Explain why taxes have nevertheless become the primary tool of fiscal policy

Explain why an increase in tax rates causes the aggregate demand function to become flatter, thereby decreasing the size of the multiplier

Give an illustration of an automatic stabilizer, and explain how it acts to stabilize the economy

Describe how the full-employment budget is measured

Explain what the full-employment budget is used for

Explain why the government may destabilize the economy if it attempts to balance the budget every year

Explain why a large and growing national debt can be a problem

HIGHLIGHTS OF CHAPTER

This chapter explains how the government can change its expenditures or tax policies in order to influence aggregate demand.

During a depression or severe recession, aggregate demand is below full employment. If we look at the height of the aggregate demand function at the full-employment national product, we will find that it lies below the 45° line. The vertical distance between the two lines, measured at the full-employment NP, is the *recessionary gap*. This is the amount by which the aggregate demand curve should be shifted upward to get the economy to full employment. The government can eliminate a recessionary gap of, say, $10 billion by increasing its spending by that amount. If, on the other hand, aggregate demand is too high and causing inflation, an *inflationary gap* exists. Again, it can be eliminated by a change in government spending. In this case, it is appropriate for the government to cut its spending by the amount of the gap.

Government spending, like investment spending, contributes directly to aggregate demand. Furthermore, a change in government spending has the same multiplied effect on aggregate demand as do changes in investment. Once government is included in the economy, the aggregate demand function represents the vertical addition of $C + I^* + G$.

Changes in tax rates also affect national product, but not in the same direct way, because taxes are not a component of aggregate demand. However, changes in taxes affect disposable income and therefore affect consumption. For example, an increase in tax rates reduces the disposable income of the public, thereby discouraging consumption. As a result, the consumption function is lowered, and the aggregate demand function is likewise lowered.

An increase in tax rates also has a second important effect on the consumption function and aggregate demand. Not only are these functions *lower*; they are also *flatter*. The reason is that an increase of, say, 10% in taxes will take more income from the public if national product is large than if it is small. Therefore, the larger is national product—that is, the further we go to the right in the 45° diagram—the greater will be the depressing effect of taxes on consumption.

In an economy with a high tax rate, the consumption function is quite flat, and this means that consumers respond weakly to a change in national product. Only a small amount of consumption is induced by a change in investment or government spending. The multiplier is small. Fluctuations in investment demand have only a weak effect on aggregate demand. Because the existence of taxes means that the multiplier is smaller, the economy is stabilized *automatically*. Tax rates do not have to be adjusted for taxes to have a stabilizing effect. Automatic stabilizers mean that the government deficit *automatically* tends to increase during recessions.

While these automatic deficits help to stabilize the economy, they introduce two important complications into fiscal policy. First, they present a *trap* for the policymaker. If the government follows a superficially plausible strategy of trying to balance the budget every year, it will end up destabilizing the economy. As the economy swings into recession, deficits will automatically appear. If the authorities raise taxes or cut spending in an attempt to balance the budget, they will be following precisely the wrong fiscal policy; they will be depressing aggregate demand further, and adding to the depth of the recession. President Hoover and the Congress fell into this trap in 1932 when they imposed a substantial tax increase. This added to the downward momentum of the economy. One of Keynes's major objectives was to warn against such blunders. He argued that it was important for fiscal policy to be aimed at *balancing the economy, not the budget*.

The second complication is the problem of *measuring* fiscal policy. Deficits *automatically* increase during a recession. Just because deficits rise during recessions, we should not conclude that the authorities are following countercyclical fiscal policies; they may be doing nothing. In order to determine what is happening to fiscal *policy*, some measure other than the actual budgetary surplus or deficit is needed. The *full-employment budget* provides such a measure. This budget gives a measure of the deficit or surplus that would occur with current tax rates and spending programs *if* the economy were at full employment. Because the full-employment budget is always measured at full employment, it does not automatically swing into deficit when the economy moves into a recession. However, the size of the deficit or surplus does change when tax rates or spending programs are changed. In brief, the full-employment budget changes when policies change; it does not change when the economy falls into recession. It therefore may be taken as a measure of fiscal policy.

Keynesian economists showed how the old objective of balancing the actual budget could lead to the wrong policies. But if the president and Congress are not held responsible for balancing the budget, what will restrain their spending? One possibility would be to have a guideline that would require restraint, while avoiding the trap of balancing the budget every year. Suggested guidelines include: (1) balancing the full-employment budget every year, (2) balancing the actual budget over the business cycle, with surpluses during prosperity to offset the deficits during recessions, or (3) limiting government spending to, say, 21% of GNP. While all of these options have been discussed, none has become a firm basis for policy. The question of restraint has become increasingly important in recent years. Government deficits have grown rapidly, to about $200 billion per year, and large deficits will continue unless there are policy changes.

When the government runs deficits, it borrows the difference between its expenditures and receipts. That is, it issues bonds or shorter-term securities. A $200 billion deficit therefore leads to a $200 billion increase in the national debt. The high deficits of recent years have made the national debt soar. A national debt is different from a personal or corporate debt, because we "owe most of it to ourselves." That is, even though we as taxpayers have to pay interest on the debt, we also receive most of the interest payments. We may not always be aware of this, because some of the interest payments are not obvious to us. For example, government bonds may be held by our pension funds, and the interest is paid into our pension funds without our necessarily being aware of the fact.

However, the national debt does raise a number of problems, particularly if it is increasing rapidly. (1) Some of the debt may *not* represent what we owe to ourselves; some government bonds may be held by foreigners. In this case, the nation is less well off. In the future, we will be taxed to make interest payments to foreign countries. This aspect of the national debt has attracted much attention in recent years. Large U.S. government deficits have been accompanied by a large increase in foreign claims on the United States. Only a few years ago, we were major international creditors. That is, U.S.

assets abroad were much larger than foreign claims on the United States. However, by 1985, we had dissipated our creditor position; we became net international debtors for the first time since 1914. (2) Even when we own our government's bonds, and pay interest to ourselves, the debt is not problem-free. To pay the interest, taxes are levied. The public has an incentive to alter its behavior to avoid the taxes. When this happens, the economy generally becomes less efficient. This decrease in efficiency is known as the *excess burden* of taxes. (3) If the national debt rises high enough, the government may find it very difficult to collect enough taxes to pay the interest. It may simply borrow more and more, to service the ever-growing debt. In other words, the debt may *grow on itself*. Again, this is an issue which has attracted much greater attention in the past few years because of the combination of rising debt and high interest rates. Interest on the national debt rose from 1.4% of GNP in 1975 to an estimated 3.7% by 1986. (See Table 11-1 in the textbook.) (4) Finally, as interest payments balloon, the government may be tempted to print money to meet these payments. If it does so to any great extent, this will add to inflationary pressures in the economy. (The government prints money via a complicated procedure. The U.S. Treasury issues bonds, and the Federal Reserve prints money to buy these bonds. This is a subject that will be studied in the next few chapters.)

Important Terms: Match the Columns

Match the term in the first column with the corresponding phrase in the second column. But before you do so, write out your own definition of the term in the first column.

_____ 1. Recessionary gap
_____ 2. Inflationary gap
_____ 3. Output gap
_____ 4. An injection
_____ 5. A leakage
_____ 6. Deficit
_____ 7. Full-employment surplus
_____ 8. Automatic stabilizer
_____ 9. Policy trap
_____ 10. Excess burden of tax

a. The opposite of a surplus
b. The decrease in economic efficiency when people change their behavior to reduce their taxes
c. Any tax or spending program that makes the budgetary deficit rise during recession, even if no policy change is made
d. Vertical distance from the aggregate demand function up to the 45° line, measured at full-employment NP
e. $R_{FE} - G_{FE}$
f. The annually balanced budget
g. Government purchases of goods and services
h. Full-employment NP − actual NP
i. Taxes
j. Vertical distance from the aggregate demand function down to the 45° line, measured at full-employment NP

True-False

T   F   1. An increase in tax rates reduces equilibrium national product.
T   F   2. An increase in government purchases of goods and services will increase aggregate demand, but an increase in transfer payments by the government will not.

T F 3. An across-the-board increase in income taxes by, say, 5% has an effect similar to an increase in a lump-sum tax: It causes the consumption function to move down, but it does not change its slope.

T F 4. An automatic stabilizer acts to stabilize the size of the government's surplus or deficit.

T F 5. When the economy moves into a recession, the actual budget automatically moves toward deficit, but the full-employment budget does not.

T F 6. If the government tries to balance the full-employment budget every year, it will fall into a policy trap; it will increase the severity of recessions by raising tax rates or cutting spending during recessions.

T F 7. An increase in government spending to build roads will move both the actual budget and the full-employment budget toward deficit.

T F 8. A decline into recession causes an increase in the deficit in the actual budget.

T F 9. A cyclically balanced budget requires the full-employment budget to be balanced every year.

T F 10. Foreign-held debt imposes no burden, because we pay foreigners with exports of goods and services, and exports make the economy stronger.

Multiple Choice

1. To restrain aggregate demand during an inflationary boom, the appropriate fiscal policy is:
   a. an increase in taxes and/or an increase in government spending
   b. an increase in taxes and/or a decrease in government spending
   c. a decrease in taxes and/or an increase in government spending
   d. a decrease in taxes and/or a decrease in government spending
   e. an increase in government purchases and/or an increase in transfer payments

2. The recessionary gap is:
   a. the amount by which actual GNP falls short of equilibrium GNP
   b. the amount by which actual GNP falls short of full-employment GNP
   c. the vertical distance from the aggregate demand line to the 45° line, measured at equilibrium national product
   d. the vertical distance from the aggregate demand line to the 45° line, measured at the full-employment national product
   e. the vertical distance from equilibrium national product to the aggregate demand function

3. When the economy is in equilibrium, the vertical distance between the aggregate demand function and the 45° line is equal to:
   a. the output gap   **d.** saving
   b. the recessionary gap   **e.** zero
   c. investment demand

4. There is a relationship between the recessionary gap and the output gap. Specifically, the output gap is the recessionary gap:
   a. times the multiplier
   b. divided by the multiplier
   c. times the average tax rate
   d. divided by the average tax rate
   e. minus the average tax rate

5. In a diagram with aggregate demand on the vertical axis and national product on the horizontal axis, an across-the-board cut of one-half in all income tax rates will cause the consumption function to become:

   a. lower, with no change in slope
   b. lower and flatter
   c. lower and steeper
   d. higher and flatter
   e. higher and steeper

6. Suppose that MPC equals 0.75 and that all taxes are lump-sum taxes. If equilibrium national product is $3,000 billion and full-employment national product is $3,400 billion, then the recessionary gap is:
   a. $100 billion   **d.** $700 billion
   b. $400 billion   **e.** $1,600 billion
   c. $600 billion

7. An increase in income tax rates:
   a. makes the aggregate demand function steeper, and therefore lowers the size of the multiplier
   b. makes the aggregate demand function steeper, and therefore raises the size of the multiplier
   c. makes the aggregate demand function flatter, and therefore lowers the size of the multiplier
   d. makes the aggregate demand function flatter, and therefore raises the size of the multiplier
   e. lowers aggregate demand, but has no effect on the size of the multiplier

8. An illustration of the term "automatic stabilizer" is provided by:
   a. the tendency of tax collections to rise as the economy moves into a recession
   b. the tendency of tax collections to fall as the economy moves into a recession
   c. increases in tax rates as the economy moves into a recession
   d. decreases in tax rates as the economy moves into a recession
   e. public works designed to get the economy out of a depression

9. The principal purpose of the full-employment budget is to measure:
   a. changes in fiscal policy
   b. the size of the deflationary gap
   c. the size of the inflationary gap
   d. the cut in taxes needed to get the economy to full employment
   e. the increase in taxes needed to get the economy to full employment

10. The full-employment budget:
   a. differs from the actual budget because it does not include transfer payments
   b. differs from the actual budget because it includes transfer payments, whereas the actual budget does not
   c. is in surplus whenever the economy falls short of full employment
   d. is more likely to show a surplus than is the actual budget
   e. is less likely to show a surplus than is the actual budget

11. A number of guidelines have been proposed as a way of exerting restraint on the government. Which of the following possible guidelines provides the greatest opportunity for an active fiscal policy aimed at reducing the amplitude of business fluctuations?
   a. balance the actual budget every year
   b. balance the full-employment budget every year
   c. balance the actual budget over the business cycle
   d. allow the government to increase spending whenever an increase in tax receipts pushes the budget into surplus
   e. none of the above allows an active countercyclical fiscal policy

12. In which of the following cases does the government fall into a "policy trap"?
   a. it cuts taxes as the economy falls into a recession, since its deficits will increase as a result

b. it increases spending as the economy falls into a recession, since its deficits will increase as a result
   c. it increases tax rates as the economy falls into a recession, since it will depress aggregate demand
   d. it attempts to balance the full-employment budget every year, since this will destabilize aggregate demand
   e. it moves toward a full-employment deficit during recessions, since this will destabilize aggregate demand

13. The opportunity cost of government spending is:
   a. borne entirely by future generations
   b. larger if the economy is at full employment than if there is large-scale unemployment
   c. larger if there is large-scale unemployment than if the economy is at full employment
   d. zero, provided that the spending is financed entirely from taxes
   e. always the same, regardless of the rate of unemployment and tax rates

14. The inflationary effects of deficit spending by the federal government will be greatest if the government finances the deficit by:
   a. borrowing abroad
   b. borrowing from individuals
   c. borrowing from corporations
   d. borrowing from state governments
   e. printing money

Exercises

1. Figure 11-1 below shows a consumption function in an economy with no taxes. Its equation is $C = 200 + 0.5DI$, where units are billions of dollars and DI stands

FIGURE 11-1

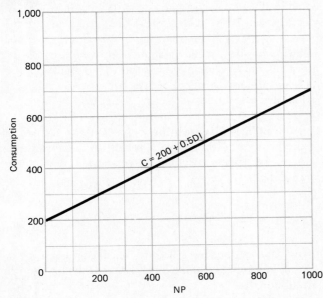

for disposable income. In the no-tax economy, DI = NP. The MPC equals _____. Now suppose that the government imposes a *lump-sum* tax of $200 billion. When NP = $400 billion, DI = $_____ billion, and C = $_____ billion. When NP = $600 billion, DI = $_____ billion, and C = $_____ billion. Plot this consumption function in the same diagram. The new consumption function is [flatter than, steeper than, has the same slope as] the initial consumption function.

Now suppose that the lump-sum tax is eliminated, and replaced with a proportional tax: $T = (1/3)DI$. The marginal tax rate is _____. When NP = $300 billion, T = $_____ billion, DI = $_____ billion, and C = $_____ billion. When NP = $600 billion, T = $_____ billion, DI = $_____ billion, and C = $_____ billion. Plot this new consumption function on the same diagram. This new consumption function is [flatter than, steeper than, has the same slope as] the initial consumption function. How do you account for the different behavior of the slope here, compared to what happened when a tax was imposed in the previous paragraph?

2. Figure 11-2 shows aggregate demand and its components. In this economy, equilibrium is at point _____, with national product = _____. At this equi-

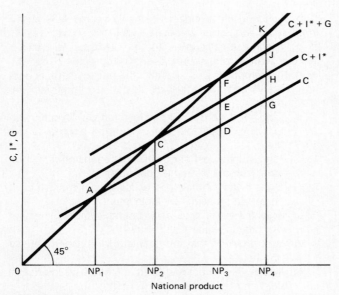

FIGURE 11-2

librium, government purchases of goods and services (G) amounts to distance _____, I* = _____, and I = _____. *Personal saving* (S) equals [DE, DF, we don't have enough information to say].

Now, suppose that national product is at the disequilibrium amount NP_4. I* = _____, while I = _____, and undesired inventory [accumulation, decumulation] = _____.

Now, suppose that this disequilibrium quantity NP_4 represents the full-employment output. There is an [inflationary, recessionary] gap equal to distance _____. The appropriate fiscal policy is an [increase, decrease] in government purchases of goods and services amounting to distance _____.

3. The government's tax revenues increase as national product increases, and fall during recessions. This means that the budget automatically tends to move into [surplus, deficit] during recession.

The automatic [surpluses, deficits] during recessions introduce two major complications into fiscal policy. First, they present a trap for the policymaker. If the government follows a superficially plausible strategy of trying to balance the budget [every year, over the business cycle], it will end up [stabilizing, destabilizing] the economy. As the economy swings into recession, [surpluses, deficits] will automatically appear. If the authorities [raise, lower] taxes or [raise, lower] spending in

an attempt to balance the budget, they will be following the [correct, wrong] fiscal policy; they will be [slowing the decline of demand, depressing aggregate demand further], and [adding to, reducing] the depth of the recession. This was illustrated most clearly in [1932, 1942, 1961, 1981] when tax rates were [increased, cut] substantially. This [reduced, added to] the downward momentum of the economy. One of Keynes's major objectives was to [show how fiscal policy could be used in this manner to restore full employment, warn against such blunders]. He argued that it was important for fiscal policy to be aimed at balancing the [budget, economy, both, neither].

The second complication is the problem of measuring fiscal policy. [Surpluses, Deficits] *automatically* increase during a recession. Just because [surpluses, deficits] rise during recessions, we should not conclude that the authorities are following countercyclical fiscal policies; they may be doing nothing. In order to determine what is happening to fiscal *policy*, some measure other than the actual budgetary surplus or deficit is needed. The [actual, full-employment, long-term] budget provides such a measure. This budget gives a measure of the deficit or surplus that would occur with current tax rates and spending programs *if* the economy were at [equilibrium, full employment]. Because it is always measured at [equilibrium, full employment], this budget does not automatically swing into [surplus, deficit] when the economy moves into a recession. However, the size of the deficit or surplus does change when tax rates or spending programs are changed. In brief, this budget changes when policies change; it does not change when the economy falls into recession. It therefore may be taken as a measure of fiscal policy.

Keynesian economists showed how the old objective of balancing the [actual, full-employment] budget could lead to the wrong policies. But if the president and Congress are not held responsible for balancing this budget, what will restrain their spending? One possibility would be to have a guideline which would require restraint, while avoiding the trap of balancing the [actual, full-employment] budget every year. Suggested guidelines include (a) _____, (b) _____, and (c) _____. Current policy is based firmly on option [(a), (b), (c), all of them, none of them]. As a result, the government's budget has [been successfully restrained, has shown large deficits] in recent years.

Essay Questions

1. For each of the following, state whether you agree or disagree, and explain why: (a) A tax acts as an automatic stabilizer only if it makes the aggregate demand function flatter; (b) whenever the aggregate de-

mand function becomes flatter, the multiplier is lower; and (c) automatic stabilizers reduce the size of the multiplier.

2. If the government increases transfer payments,

how does this affect aggregate demand? Will a $100 increase in transfer payments have the same effect as a $100 million increase in government purchases of goods and services? Why or why not?

3. Critically evaluate the following statement: "Any system of unemployment insurance will be completely useless as a way of reducing business cycles. Even though the payment of benefits to the unemployed will help to raise aggregate demand during recessions, the taxes to support the system will lower aggregate demand."

Answers

Important Terms: 1 d 2 j 3 h 4 g 5 i 6 a 7 e 8 c 9 f 10 b

True-False: 1 T 2 F 3 F 4 F 5 T 6 F 7 T 8 T 9 F 10 F

Multiple Choice: 1 b 2 d 3 e 4 a 5 e 6 a 7 c 8 b 9 a 10 d 11 c 12 c 13 b 14 e

Exercises: **1.** 0.5, $200, $300, $400, $400, has the same slope as, 1/3, $100, $200, $300, $200, $400, $400, flatter than, here the tax increases with NP while it did not do so with the lump-sum tax in the previous paragraph. **2.** F, NP_3, EF, DE, DE, we don't have enough information to say because in equilibrium, $I^* + G = S + T$; the diagram tells us what G and I^* are, but we can't tell what S is unless we also know T, GH, $GH + JK$, accumulation, JK, recessionary, JK, increase, JK. **3.** (Note: This exercise is based directly on the chapter highlights section.) deficit, deficits, every year, destabilizing, deficits, raise, lower, wrong, depressing aggregate demand further, adding to, 1932, increased, added to, warn against such blunders, economy, Deficits, deficits, full-employment, full employment, full employment, deficit, actual, actual, (*a*) balancing the full-employment budget every year, (*b*) balancing the actual budget over the business cycle, with surpluses during prosperity to offset the deficits during recessions, and (*c*) limiting government spending to a fixed percentage of GNP, none of them, has shown large deficits.

Across

4. a way to combat a depression (2 words)
7, 10. this can be a trap for fiscal policymakers
14. a type of investment
15. when government runs a deficit, the national _____ increases
18. no (slang)
19. what you do with disposable income that you do not spend on consumption
20. change in saving, divided by change in disposable income
23. change in equilibrium national product, divided by change in government spending for goods and services
26. the party of Eisenhower and Reagan (abbrev.)
28. one of the factors of production
29. investment or government spending
32. he said an increase in real holdings of money leads to an increase in consumption
33. $C + I^* + G + X - M$ (2 words)
35. largest component of national product

Down

1. saving and taxes
2. huge bodies of water
3. national income + sales taxes
5. he was a billionaire
6. an insecticide
8. one (Germ.)
9. this carries the code of life (abbrev.)
10. to _____, or not to _____
11. to reduce this, deficit spending may be desirable
12. move
13. make a mistake
16. college degree
17. a popular type of entertainment (abbrev.)
21. should precede action
22. transgression
24. small picture case worn as pendant
25. remove errors from a manuscript
26. NNP + depreciation
27. a medium-sized mammal
30. number (abbrev.)
31. famous student of psychology
34. government spending can be used to fill recessionary _____

CHAPTER 12

MONEY AND THE BANKING SYSTEM

MAJOR PURPOSE

The major purpose of this chapter is to explain how the banking system creates money. The details of money creation, as set out in the various tables in this chapter, are important. A number of specific conclusions are also important: (1) Even though the banking system can create money equal to a multiple of its reserves, an individual bank cannot do so. (2) Instead, an individual bank receiving a deposit of $100 can lend only a fraction of this $100 (specifically, $100 × 0.8, if the required reserve ratio is 0.2). (3) The bank sees nothing particularly magical or peculiar about such loans, even though they result in an increase in the money stock. (4) Fractional-reserve banking developed as a natural result of the desire to make profits. (5) Fractional-reserve banks can be subject to runs. Because each bank holds reserves equal to only a fraction of its deposit liabilities, no bank can withstand an all-out run without outside help, no matter how sound the bank was originally. (6) Bank runs are not only unfortunate for the banks and individual depositors who are too late to get their funds; they also can have strong adverse effects on the economy. Because reserves are being withdrawn from the base of the monetary pyramid, bank runs cause strong downward pressures on the money stock. One of the major tasks of the monetary authorities is to prevent bank runs and instability of the monetary supply, as we shall see in the next chapter.

Learning Objectives

After you have studied this chapter in the textbook and study guide, you should be able to:

Describe the three basic functions of money

Explain the differences between M1, M2, and M3

Explain why a bank might want to hold only fractional reserves, rather than reserves equal to 100% of its deposit liabilities

Explain why fractional-reserve banking leads to the risk of a bank run, and why no bank can withstand a severe run without outside help

Describe some of the major changes in financial institutions in recent years

Explain in detail (using balance sheets) how an individual bank responds to an increase in its reserves and how the overall banking system can increase money by a multiple of the increase in reserves

State the formula for the deposit multiplier

Give two reasons why the actual expansion of deposits is likely to be less than indicated by this formula

HIGHLIGHTS OF CHAPTER

This chapter introduces the basic concepts of money and banking, as a background for studying monetary policy in the next chapter.

Money performs three interrelated functions:

1. It is a *medium of exchange*; that is, it is used to buy goods and services.

2. It is a *standard of value*; that is, we keep accounts, quote prices, and sign contracts in dollar terms.

3. It is a *store of value*; that is, you can hold money for future purchases rather than spending it right away.

The basic definition of the money stock, M1, includes items which are used as money in everyday transactions—coins, paper currency, and checking accounts in banks and similar financial institutions. Each of these items represents wealth to the holder; if you have $100 in your pocket, you are better off than you would be without it. In this way, money is different from a credit card, which represents a convenient way to run up debt, rather than an asset. Thus, even though credit cards (and the corresponding lines of credit) are often used to make purchases, lines of credit are not included in the money stock.

M2 includes M1 plus noncheckable savings deposits and small time deposits. Although such deposits are not used directly in making purchases, they can be quickly switched into money. Thus, they can have a powerful effect on people's spending behavior. When we are concerned about the relationship between "money" and aggregate demand, we often use the broader definition of money, M2. Even broader concepts are M3 (which includes large time deposits), and liquid assets, *L*.

Commercial banks and similar financial institutions—such as savings and loan associations—accept deposits, using most of the proceeds to make loans. They hold reserves equal to only a fraction of their deposit liabilities. *Fractional-reserve banking* developed centuries ago, when financial institutions realized that they could cover their costs and make profits from the interest on loans. Through history, fractional-reserve banks have been plagued by the problem of runs, which have not only been dangerous for them, but have also had very disruptive effects on the economy. One conspicuous example occurred in 1932–1933, when the U.S. banking system collapsed, adding to the downslide into the depression. On a much smaller—but still serious—scale, there were runs on state-chartered S&Ls in Ohio and Maryland in 1985. Some of the reasons for these runs will be explained in the next chapter.

Even in olden times, when there were no required reserve ratios, banks kept reserves to use as working balances and to meet unexpected withdrawals; they pro-vided some modest protection against a run. Now, the function of reserves is not to provide protection against a run. Rather, it is to give the authorities control over the money stock. The Federal Reserve, which is the central bank of the United States, is empowered to set reserve requirements within limits specified by Congress. If the required reserve ratio is, say, 0.10, then a $100 withdrawal from a bank deposit will reduce the required reserves by only $10. The other $90 will have to be obtained elsewhere by the bank, most likely by reducing its portfolio of loans or bonds. In other words, reserves in this case would only provide one-tenth of the funds needed to meet the withdrawal.

If there is a required reserve ratio specified by law, then the banking system as a whole can increase its deposit liabilities by as much as $1/R$ times any increase in its reserves. Tables 12-4 to 12-9 in the text explain in detail how banks do this. These tables are not repeated here, but they are of central importance in any study of the monetary system. They often appear on examinations. Students should go over them particularly carefully, together with the balance sheets in the exercises below. This idea—of the multiple expansion of bank deposits—is one of the most important and difficult in introductory economics.

The deposit multiplier, $D = 1/R$, shows the *maximum* increase in deposits that can occur when the banking system acquires additional reserves. In practice, the actual increase is likely to be much less, for two reasons. Most important is that, as people acquire more checking deposit money, they are likely to want to hold some of the additional money in the form of currency. When they make withdrawals from their banks, the reserves of banks are reduced. The second reason is that banks may hold excess reserves rather than lending all they are permitted. In recent years, excess reserves have been very small, and this second point represents only a minor complication. However, it was quite important back in the 1930s, when excess reserves at times amounted to almost half of total reserves. There were two reasons for this. Interest rates were very low, which meant that bankers didn't forego much interest when they kept excess reserves. Second, bankers were frightened to lend to businesses, since so many businesses were going bankrupt. This failure to lend was unfortunate, since more lending and more money would have promoted economic recovery. This was but one illustration of the difference between what is good for an individual or an institution, and what is good for the economy as a whole. Risky bank lending would have increased the money stock and contributed to economic recovery. But it could have meant financial suicide for any bank making risky loans. Bankers cannot be expected to commit suicide for the public good. It is up to the Federal Reserve, not up to individual banks, to see that the money stock is at the right level to keep aggregate demand close to its desired path. How the Fed does this will be studied in the next chapter.

(A second example of the conflict between what is good for the individual and what is good for the overall economy occurs during a bank run. Each individual has an incentive to be first in line. But severe bank runs can disrupt the economy.)

Important Terms: Match the Columns

Match the term in the first column with the corresponding phrase in the second column. But before you do so, write out your own definition of the term in the first column.

_____ 1. Currency	**a.** Assets − net worth
_____ 2. M1	**b.** Deposit liabilities × *R*
_____ 3. Liquid assets	**c.** Major reason for risk of runs
_____ 4. Liabilities	**d.** Actual reserves − required reserves
_____ 5. What a single bank can prudently lend	**e.** Coins, paper currency, and checking deposits
_____ 6. Required reserves	**f.** Increase in reserves × 1/*R*
_____ 7. Maximum increase in deposits	**g.** Short-term government securities and savings bonds
_____ 8. Fractional-reserve banking	**h.** Coins and paper currency

True-False

T F   1. Checking deposits held by manufacturing corporations—such as General Motors—are included in the money stock (M1).

T F   2. Bank deposits owned by the U.S. Treasury are included in the money supply, provided they are checking deposits.

T F   3. Reserve deposits held by the Chase Manhattan bank are included in the money stock (M1).

T F   4. When General Motors deposits $100,000 in the Chase Manhattan bank, the resulting deposit appears as an asset on the GM balance sheet, and the same deposit appears as a liability on the Chase Manhattan balance sheet.

T F   5. Fractional-reserve banking was invented by the Federal Reserve.

T F   6. In the modern U.S. banking system, most commercial banks reserves are held in the form of gold.

T F   7. If a commercial bank receives a deposit of currency, then its actual reserves and excess reserves both increase by the same amount (specifically, by the amount of the deposit).

T F   8. If a commercial bank receives the deposit of a check drawn against an account in another bank, then its actual reserves and its excess reserves both increase as a consequence.

T F   9. A bank can safely lend the amount of its excess reserves × 1/*R*.

T F   10. Banks are more likely to hold excess reserves during a depression than during prosperity.

Multiple Choice

  1. Between 1929 and 1933, during the early part of the Great Depression:
  a. the quantity of money rose, but aggregate demand nonetheless collapsed
  b. the quantity of money fell, but prices nevertheless rose moderately
  c. there was hyperinflation, even though the money stock fell
  d. the quantity of money fell, and this contributed to the downturn
  e. the quantity of money increased at a slow, steady rate, as advocated by monetarists, but the depression nevertheless occurred

  2. Even though credit cards are used by many people in making purchases, they are not included in M1. A major reason is that:
  a. credit cards are a way of going into debt, whereas the components of M1 represent assets
  b. credit cards had not yet been invented when money was defined

c. some credit cards are issued by stores (such as Sears), whereas all money is issued by banks

d. credit cards are much less liquid than M1

e. credit cards don't affect consumer expenditures, whereas M1 does

3. Checking deposits are included in the money stock M1:

a. only if they are owned by individuals

b. if they are owned by individuals or nonbank corporations (such as IBM or a local car dealer)

c. if they are owned by individuals, other banks, or the Federal Reserve

d. if they are owned by individuals, other banks, or the U.S. Treasury

e. if they are owned by individuals, the Federal Reserve, or the U.S. Treasury

4. Suppose we know M1, and want to calculate M2. To do so, which of the following do we add to M1?

a. coins

b. paper currency

c. checking deposits

d. noncheckable savings deposits

e. Treasury bills

5. Which of the following is the best example of a liquid asset?

a. real estate whose price has been rising

b. real estate whose price has been falling

c. short-term securities issued by the U.S. Treasury

d. long-term corporate bonds

e. common stock of the Fortune 500

6. The primary reason why the activities of early goldsmiths developed into "fractional-reserve banking" was the desire to:

a. keep the money stock down to a fraction of its earlier level, in order to restrain inflation

b. increase the quantity of money, in order to finance the growth of trade

c. provide a more stable money system, in order to reduce the size of business fluctuations

d. provide a broader range of financial services to their customers

e. increase profits, by lending out some of the gold deposited with them

7. A bank run is most likely to occur at a time when:

a. government surpluses are high

b. tax rates are high

c. many nonbank businesses are going bankrupt

d. investment by nonbank businesses is large

e. banks have reserves equal to 100% of their deposit liabilities

8. The Federal Reserve performs all the following functions *except one*. Which is the exception? The Fed:

a. issues paper currency

b. conducts fiscal policy

c. controls the quantity of money in the United States

d. acts as the federal government's bank

e. acts as a bankers' bank

9. Commercial banks are required by law to hold reserves. These reserves are specified as percentages of a bank's:

a. total assets

b. total liabilities

c. deposit liabilities

d. holdings of government securities

e. net worth

10. Suppose that the required reserve ratio is 20% and that a

person deposits $100 in his or her bank. Then that single bank can create:

a. $80 in additional money by lending $80

b. $100 in additional money by lending $100

c. $400 in additional money by lending $400

d. $500 in additional money by lending $500

e. no additional money; it takes the actions of the whole banking system to create more money, not just one bank

11. Suppose that the required reserve ratio of a commercial bank is represented by the fraction R. Suppose that this commercial bank receives a deposit of currency of $100. Then, as a result, *this single commercial bank* can make a loan of as much as:

a. $100/R$

b. $100 \times R$

c. $100/(1 - R)$

d. $100 \times (1 - R)$

12. Suppose that someone in New York, who banks at the Citibank, sends a check for $1,000 to someone in California, who deposits it in the Bank of America. The required reserve ratio is R. In the process of check clearing, the reserves of Citibank will:

a. increase by $1,000, while those of the Bank of America will decrease by $1,000

b. decrease by $1,000, while those of the Bank of America will increase by $1,000

c. increase by $1,000 $\times$ R, while those of the Bank of America will decrease by $1,000 \times R$

d. decrease by $1,000 $\times$ R, while those of the Bank of America will increase by $1,000 \times R$

e. increase by $1,000 divided by R, while those of the Bank of America will decrease by $1,000/R$

13. An increase in the required reserve ratio on checking deposits would most likely cause:

a. an increase in M1

b. a decrease in M1

c. an increase in checking deposits

d. an increase in bank profits

e. an increase in the checking deposit multiplier

14. Banks are most likely to hold significant quantities of excess reserves:

a. when their profits are high, and they can afford to hold excess reserves

b. when economic activity is buoyant, and interest rates are high

c. when economic activity is buoyant, and interest rates are low

d. when economic activity is slack, and interest rates are high

e. when economic activity is slack, and interest rates are low

15. The monetary system is sometimes said to form an inverted pyramid. By this, we mean that:

a. a large quantity of checking deposit money can be built on a small quantity of reserves

b. a large quantity of reserves can be built on a small quantity of checking deposit money

c. a large quantity of currency can be built on a small quantity of checking deposit money

d. checking deposits are the largest component of M1

e. currency is the largest component of M1

Exercises

1a. If I deposit $100,000 in currency into a checking deposit with bank A and the required reserve ratio is 20%, then the immediate increase in bank A's total reserves is $_____, and the immediate increase in bank A's required reserves is _____. Thus, the immediate increase in bank A's excess reserves is _____. As a result of this transaction, the total amount of currency in the hands of the public has gone [up, down] by the amount _____, the total amount of checking deposits has gone [up, down] by the amount _____, the total amount of M1 has [increased, decreased, not changed], and the total amount of M2 has [increased, decreased, not changed].

1b. If bank A now lends its new excess reserves and the proceeds of the loan are deposited into a checking deposit in bank B, then the immediate effect is to make bank A's total reserves go [up, down] by _____, to make bank A's required reserves [increase, decrease, stay unchanged], to make bank A's excess reserves go [up, down] by _____, to make bank B's total reserves go [up, down] by _____, to make bank B's required reserves go [up, down] by _____, and to make bank B's excess reserves go [up, down] by _____. As a result of this loan and subsequent deposit, the total amount of currency in the hands of the public has [increased, decreased, stayed the same], the total amount of checking deposits has [increased by _____, decreased by _____, stayed the same], the total amount of M1 has gone [up, down] by _____, and the total amount of M2 has [increased by _____, decreased by _____, stayed the same].

1c. If the process continues like this until all excess reserves have been eliminated, then the result of the whole process, starting from my initial deposit, will have been to make the total supply of currency in the hands of the public go [up, down] by _____, to make the total amount of checking deposits go [up, down] by _____, to make M1 go [up, down] by _____, and to make M2 [go up by _____, go down by _____, stay the same].

2. Show what happens as a direct result of each of the following transactions by filling in the appropriate number for that transaction in the balance sheet. Each balance sheet should represent the *change* in total assets and total liabilities of all banks. In each case, suppose that the required reserve ratio on checking deposits is 20%, and on all other deposits is 10%. Each transaction should be considered separately from all the others.

a. Someone puts $25,000 of currency into a checking deposit.

b. Someone makes a cash withdrawal of $100,000 from a noncheckable savings account, in order to hold the money in the form of currency.

c. Someone switches $200,000 from a checking deposit to a noncheckable savings deposit.

d. A bank lends $40,000 to someone who takes the proceeds of that loan in the form of currency.

e. A bank lends $100,000 to someone who uses that $100,000 to pay off a loan to someone who puts the $100,000 into a noncheckable savings deposit.

BALANCE SHEET A

Change in assets		Change in liabilities	
Loans	_____		
Total reserves	_____		
		Checking deposits	_____
Required reserves	_____	Other deposits	_____
Excess reserves	_____		

BALANCE SHEET B

Change in assets		Change in liabilities	
Loans	_____		
Total reserves	_____		
		Checking deposits	_____
Required reserves	_____	Other deposits	_____
Excess reserves	_____		

BALANCE SHEET C

Change in assets		Change in liabilities	
Loans	_____		
Total reserves	_____		
		Checking deposits	_____
Required reserves	_____		
		Other deposits	_____
Excess reserves	_____		

BALANCE SHEET D

Change in assets		Change in liabilities	
Loans	_____		
Total reserves	_____		
		Checking deposits	_____
Required reserves	_____		
		Other deposits	_____
Excess reserves	_____		

BALANCE SHEET E

Change in assets		Change in liabilities	
Loans	_____		
Total reserves	_____		
		Checking deposits	_____
Required reserves	_____		
		Other deposits	_____
Excess reserves	_____		

Essay Questions

1. Why are bank runs most likely to occur during a depression or severe recession? Are bank runs most damaging to the economy at such times? Why or why not?

2. Deposits in most banks and S&Ls are now covered by federal insurance. If your bank doesn't have the money, the federal government will make good, up to a maximum of $100,000 per deposit. As a result, runs on banks and other financial institutions have been *much* less common than they were during the 1930s, prior to federal deposit insurance. Nevertheless, runs still occasionally occur. Why do you suppose they still do?

3. By his term "invisible hand," Adam Smith sug- gested that self-interested actions tend to benefit society. This chapter has explained two cases where pursuit of self-interest leads to undesirable results for the society as a whole. What are these two cases, and why does self-interest lead to socially undesirable outcomes? Can you think of any way to deal with these problems?

4. Individual bankers often argue, "We don't create money; we just lend money that has already been deposited with us." Is this correct? If so, explain why. If not, explain why not.

5. What would happen if Congress abolished all reserve requirements?

Answers

Important Terms: 1 h 2 e 3 g 4 a 5 d 6 b 7 f 8 c
True-False: 1 T 2 F 3 F 4 T 5 F 6 F 7 F 8 T 9 F 10 T
Multiple Choice: 1 d 2 a 3 b 4 d 5 c 6 e 7 c 8 b 9 c 10 a 11 d 12 b 13 b 14 e 15 a

2. BALANCE SHEET A

Change in assets		Change in liabilities	
Loans	0		
Total reserves	25,000		
		Checking deposits	25,000
Required reserves	5,000		
		Other deposits	0
Excess reserves	20,000		

BALANCE SHEET B

Change in assets		Change in liabilities	
Loans	0		
Total reserves	− 100,000		
		Checking deposits	0
Required reserves	− 10,000		
		Other deposits	− 100,000
Excess reserves	− 90,000		

BALANCE SHEET C

Change in assets		Change in liabilities	
Loans	0		
Total reserves	0		
		Checking deposits	− 200,000
Required reserves	− 20,000		
		Other deposits	+ 200,000
Excess reserves	+ 20,000		

BALANCE SHEET D

Change in assets		Change in liabilities	
Loans	+ 40,000		
Total reserves	− 40,000		
		Checking deposits	0
Required reserves	0		
		Other deposits	0
Excess reserves	− 40,000		

BALANCE SHEET E

Change in assets		Change in liabilities	
Loans	100,000		
Total reserves	0		
		Checking deposits	0
Required reserves	+ 10,000		
		Other deposits	100,000
Excess reserves	− 10,000		

CHAPTER 13

THE FEDERAL RESERVE AND MONETARY POLICY

MAJOR PURPOSE

There are two major tools for controlling aggregate demand—fiscal policy and monetary policy. Fiscal policy, which involves changes in tax rates and in government spending, is in the hands of the Congress and the president. Monetary policy, which involves changes in the rate of growth of the money stock, is in the hands of the Federal Reserve. The major purpose of this chapter is to explain how the Federal Reserve (the "Fed") can influence the money stock.

As we saw in Chapter 12, most of the money stock consists of checking deposits in banks and other similar institutions. The amount of money that banks can create depends on the quantity of reserves which they own, and on the required reserve ratio. The Federal Reserve has three principal tools with which it can influence the quantity of money:

1. It can *purchase securities on the open market.* When it does so, it increases the reserves of the banks.

2. It can *change the discount rate,* changing the banks' desire to borrow from the Fed. Since the reserves of banks increase when they borrow from the Fed, changes in the discount rate influence the total quantity of reserves that the banks hold.

3. It can *change the required reserve ratio,* thereby changing the quantity of deposits that can be created on any given reserve base.

Learning Objectives

After you have studied this chapter in the textbook and study guide, you should be able to:

Describe the organization of the Federal Reserve

Describe how the Fed can use each of its three major tools to affect the size of the money stock

Explain how open market operations affect not only the size of the money stock, but also interest rates

Give an example which shows why the yield (interest rate) on a Treasury bill falls when its price rises

Explain why a restrictive monetary policy usually does not involve an open market sale, but rather just a reduction in the rate of purchases on the open market

Explain what a "penalty rate" would be, and why some economists recommend that the Fed use such a rate

Explain why large changes in the required reserve ratio would be very disruptive, and give an historical example

Explain why a margin requirement may add to the stability of the stock market, even if the margin requirement is never changed

Explain why the concentration of gold in the Federal Reserve did not guarantee against a run on banks

Explain why federal deposit insurance reduces the risk of a run on banks

Explain why there have been some runs on financial institutions in recent years (for example, in Ohio and Maryland)

Explain why stabilization of the interest rate may be a "trap" for the Federal Reserve, just as aiming for an annually balanced budget may be a trap for fiscal policymakers

HIGHLIGHTS OF CHAPTER

The Federal Reserve is the central bank of the United States. It is the "bankers' bank," and it is responsible for controlling the quantity of money. When the Federal Reserve was established, there were deep concerns over the power of centralized financial institutions, and therefore the Fed is decentralized. There are 12 Federal Reserve districts, with a Federal Reserve bank in each district. In Washington, there is a Board of Governors with seven members. The most important policy body of the Fed—the Federal Open Market Committee (FOMC)—is made up of seven members of the board, plus five of the presidents of the regional Federal Reserve banks. At the FOMC meetings, these five presidents explain to the other members of the FOMC the economic and financial conditions in their districts. (So do the other presidents, who are nonvoting members of the FOMC.) Thus, conditions in the various regions are taken into account when developing monetary policy.

The Fed has three major tools with which it can affect the quantity of money: (1) *open market operations* (2) *changes in the discount rate*, and (3) *changes in reserve requirements*. Open market operations are the most important tool; they are used for the everyday, "bread and butter" activities of the Fed.

When it buys securities worth, say, $10 million on the open market, the Fed increases bank reserves by the same $10 million. Because they have additional reserves, the banks are able to make loans; the money stock can increase by a multiple of the $10 million. As we saw in Chapter 12, the *maximum* increase in the money stock is the $10 million times $1/R$, where R is the required reserve ratio. However, in practice, the actual increase is not likely to be this great. As banks make loans and the quantity of money increases, the public is likely to want not only more checking deposits, but more currency too. People therefore withdraw some currency from their bank accounts. When they do so, the reserves of banks decline, and the amount of money they can create likewise declines.

The maximum increase in the money stock depends on the size of the open market operation ($10 million in the above example) and on the required reserve ratio. It does not depend on whether a commercial bank, a nonbank corporation, or an individual sells the securities to the Fed. However, the details of the way in which the money supply increases will vary, depending on who the seller is. If a nonbank corporation—such as IBM—or an individual is the seller, then the money stock will go up immediately as a result of the open market purchase. For example, if IBM sells the $10 million in securities which the Fed buys, IBM will deposit the proceeds from the sale in its checking deposit, and its holdings of money will therefore increase by $10 million. IBM's bank will now have larger deposit liabilities, and its

required reserves will rise—by $10 million times the required reserve ratio. If this ratio is, say, 15%, the bank will have $8.5 million of excess reserves (the $10 addition to reserves less the increase of $1.5 million in required reserves). It will safely be able to lend the $8.5 million. There will be a series of expansions: $10 million + ($10 × 0.85) million + ($10 × 0.85²) million, and so on.

On the other hand, if a commercial bank sells the $10 million in securities, there is no initial increase in the quantity of money, since the checking deposits held by the public have not been affected. Required reserves likewise remain unchanged, but the banks have $10 million in excess reserves. They can therefore lend the full $10 million, again initiating an expansion of $10 million + ($10 × 0.85) million + ($10 × 0.85²) million, and so on. Although the initial, first round effects of the two types of transaction are different, their ultimate effects on the money stock will be the same.

Thus, when the Fed buys securities on the open market, the money stock increases. If the Fed sold securities on the open market, it would likewise cause a multiple decrease in the money stock. However, this would cause *very* tight monetary conditions. In our growing economy, the money stock can grow at a moderate rate without causing inflation. Therefore, when the Fed wants to tighten monetary conditions, it normally does not sell securities. Instead, it simply *reduces the rate of purchases* on the open market.

When it buys securities on the open market, the Fed bids their prices *up*. But this is just another way of saying that it bids interest rates *down*. As a result of the Fed's purchase, the banks have excess reserves. As they make loans or buy bonds with these reserves, the banks bid interest rates down even further.

Changes in the discount rate are the second major tool of the Fed. By cutting the discount rate, the Fed encourages banks to borrow more. When they borrow more, their reserves increase. Thus, a cut in the discount rate is an expansionary policy; increases in the rate are a contractionary policy. The Fed is sometimes spoken of as the "lender of last resort"; the banks can go to the Fed to borrow reserves if they are temporarily short and cannot get funds elsewhere.

The third major tool of the Fed is a change in the required reserve ratio. As we have seen in Chapter 12, checking deposits can be as much as $1/R$ times reserves, where R is the required reserve ratio. By changing R, the Fed can thus change the size of the deposit multiplier. Relatively small changes in R can have a powerful effect on the size of the money stock. In order to avoid disruption of monetary conditions, the Fed is now careful to make only small changes when it does adjust R.

The Fed also has a number of other ways of influencing monetary and financial conditions. It imposes *margin requirements*, limiting the amount that can be borrowed by those who are buying stocks or bonds. The Fed has the power to adjust these requirements, but it has in fact kept the rate on stocks stable at 50% in recent years. For requirements to have a stabilizing effect, it is not necessary that they be adjusted. A steady 50% rate means that stockholders will not be wiped out by moderate reverses in the stock market, and will not be forced to dump their stocks. If they had been able to borrow, say, 90% of the value of the stock, their rush to get out of the stock market could change a small retreat into a stock market collapse.

Finally, the Fed can influence bank behavior by *moral suasion*—suggestions to bankers regarding appropriate policy.

When the Fed purchases securities on the open market, it creates money "out of thin air." Our money is not backed by gold. Money retains its value because the Fed limits its supply; money is scarce. Checking deposits are backed not only by the assets of the banks, but also by the Federal Deposit Insurance Corporation. Insurance is important for individual depositors; it offers them protection. It is also important for the stability of the system as a whole: Federal insurance greatly reduces the risk of a run on banks.

At times in our history, money has also been backed by gold (and silver). This system had one great advantage, in that it limited the amount of money that could be created, and thus acted as a restraint on reckless, inflationary expansions in the money stock. However, it had two great defects: (1) Increases in the quantity of gold played a function similar to open market purchases in the present system; they increased bank reserves, and permitted a multiple increase in the money stock. However, there was no assurance that the amount of gold mined or imported from abroad would provide the amount of money needed for a full-employment, noninflationary economy. (2) The gold standard pyramid was vulnerable to runs. Whenever gold was withdrawn from the base of the pyramid, there was a powerful contractionary effect on the quantity of money. In other words, the gold standard could make financial crises and recessions worse—as it did in the early 1930s. This was the major reason for the abandonment of the gold standard.

Finally, this chapter explains how the Fed faces a policy trap, somewhat similar to the fiscal trap of attempting to balance the budget every year. If the Fed follows a policy of stabilizing interest rates, its policy is passive. It increases the money stock in response to rising demands from the public for funds. Responding in such a passive way can be a great mistake. The money supply will go up particularly rapidly during prosperity, when people are clamoring for loans. This can make the prosperity turn into an inflationary boom.

Important Terms: Match the Columns

Match the term in the first column with the corresponding phrase in the second column. But before you do so, write out your own definition of the term in the first column.

_____ 1. The Federal Reserve
_____ 2. Open market operation
_____ 3. Example of restrictive policy
_____ 4. Example of the expansive policy
_____ 5. U.S. Treasury
_____ 6. Discount rate
_____ 7. Prime rate
_____ 8. Price of a Treasury bill
_____ 9. Margin requirement
_____ 10. Legal tender
_____ 11. Fiat money
_____ 12. Meet the "needs of trade"

a. Money unbacked by gold or silver; it is money because the government says so
b. Acts to stabilize stock market
c. Interest rate on Fed's loans to commercial banks
d. Creditors must accept this money in repayment of debts
e. This rises when interest rates fall
f. Central bank of the United States
g. Possibly, a monetary policy trap
h. Reduction of discount rate
i. Purchase or sale of government securities by the Fed
j. A bank's publicly announced interest rate for short-term loans
k. This institution initially issues securities bought or sold in open market operations
l. Increase in the required reserve ratio

True-False

T F   **1.** Open market policy is determined by the Federal Open Market Committee, which meets in Washington. However, actual open market operations are carried out by the New York Fed.

T F   **2.** Changes in required reserve ratios are the most commonly used tool of monetary policy.

T F   **3.** If the required reserve ratio of the commercial banks is 10%, then an open market purchase of $1 million by the Federal Reserve permits the banks to increase their checking deposits by a maximum of $10 million.

T F   4. The appropriate strategy for the Federal Reserve during a depression is to sell government bonds, to make low-risk, sound assets available for the commercial banks to buy.

T F   5. When the Fed sells securities to the commercial banks, it increases their earning assets, and thus makes possible an increase in the money stock.

T F   6. When the Fed increases its purchases of government securities, it is engaging in an expansionary act; when it sells government securities, it is engaging in a restrictive act.

T F   7. If the interest rate doubles, then the price of a Treasury bill falls by 50%.

T F   8. Federal Reserve notes (the paper currency of the United States) are backed dollar for dollar with gold held by the Fed.

T F   9. The existence of federal insurance for bank depositors reduces the danger of bank runs. Indeed, one of the major purposes of such insurance is to reduce this danger.

T F   10. Federal Deposit Insurance protects the public, which has deposited money in the banks. But it does not help banks, since they must pay premiums for the insurance, and they get only what they pay for.

Multiple Choice

1. When the Fed purchases securities on the open market, the securities it buys are generally:
   a. common stock of the U.S. corporations whose stocks are included in the Dow-Jones industrial average
   b. corporate bonds
   c. securities issued by state governments
   d. securities issued by the federal government
   e. any of the above; as it is a transaction on "the open market," the Fed buys whatever is offered for sale at the best price

2. During a depression, the best strategy of the Federal Reserve is to:
   a. buy government securities
   b. sell government bonds, in order to make low-risk, sound assets available for commercial banks to buy
   c. sell government bonds, in order to reduce the size of the government's deficits
   d. sell government bonds, in order to increase aggregate demand
   e. exhort banks not to lend to businesses, in order to reduce their risks of loss

3. Suppose that (a) the Fed purchases a $100,000 government security on the open market, (b) the required reserve ratio is 20%, (c) IBM sells the security, and (d) IBM deposits the proceeds from the sale in a checking deposit in its commercial bank. The effect of this single transaction will be to increase the money stock by:
   a. $20,000   d. $500,000
   b. $100,000   e. zero
   c. $200,000

4. If checking deposits are $10 billion, bank reserves are $2 billion, and excess reserves are $500 million, then the required reserve ratio is:
   a. 5%   d. 20%
   b. 10%   e. 25%
   c. 15%

5. If the price of a Treasury bill falls, then:
   a. all interest rates certainly fall
   b. all interest rates probably fall
   c. the interest rate on this bill certainly falls

   d. the interest rate on this bill probably rises
   e. the interest rate on this bill certainly rises

6. When the Fed purchases Treasury bills on the open market, then:
   a. the quantity of bank reserves falls
   b. the interest rate on Treasury bills rises
   c. the price of Treasury bills rises
   d. the risk premium on business loans usually rises
   e. required reserves of banks fall

7. If the required reserve ratio is 20%, and if commercial banks borrow $100 million from the Federal Reserve, then the effect on commercial bank reserves is:
   a. an increase of $100 million
   b. an increase of $500 million
   c. a decrease of $100 million
   d. a decrease of $500 million
   e. no change

8. The Fed *tightens* monetary conditions by *lowering*:
   a. required reserve ratios
   b. the margin requirements on stocks
   c. the discount rate
   d. the interest rate on Treasury bills
   e. the rate at which it is buying securities on the open market

9. The discount rate refers to:
   a. the penalty paid by risky bank borrowers; that is, the amount of interest they pay in excess of the prime rate
   b. the rate at which banks write off bad loans
   c. the rate at which assets lose their real value as a result of inflation
   d. the rate at which money loses its value as a result of inflation
   e. the rate of interest that the Fed charges on loans to commercial banks

10. Commercial banks receive a hidden subsidy when the discount rate is:
   a. above the interest rate on Treasury bills
   b. below the interest rate on Treasury bills
   c. above the required reserve ratio

d. below the required reserve ratio

e. above the penalty rate

11. The discounting procedure of the Fed is sometimes said to create "slippage" in the effects of monetary policy because:

   a. the discount rate is slipped up and down too often

   b. the discounting procedure increases the leakage of reserves out of the banking system and into the hands of the public

   c. the discounting procedure prevents the Fed from engaging in open market operations as vigorously as it should; it acts as a "brake" on open market operations

   d. the commercial banks may borrow to replenish their reserves when the Fed is undertaking restrictive open market operations

   e. discounting causes an automatic erosion of required reserve ratios

12. A margin requirement tends to make the stock market less unstable:

   a. only if it is backed up by open market operations

   b. only if the margin requirement is increased during an upswing in stock prices, and decreased during a downswing in stock prices

   c. only if the margin requirement is decreased during an upswing in stock prices, and increased during a downswing in stock prices

   d. only if the margin requirement is decreased whenever the rate of business bankruptcy increases

   e. even if it is kept perfectly stable, at (say) 50%

13. The Federal Reserve issues paper currency which acts as money in the United States. It is most accurate to say that this money is "backed" by Federal Reserve assets in the form of:

   a. loans to member banks

   b. U.S. government securities

   c. gold (or gold certificates)

   d. required reserves of the commercial banks

   e. the value of Federal Reserve buildings

14. Suppose that you were a central banker facing the problems of the Great Depression in the early 1930s. You fear a run on the banks. To reduce this risk, the best of the following options would be to:

   a. increase required reserves, so that banks will have greater reserves and be more able to meet withdrawals of depositors

   b. hold firm to the gold standard, in order to restore confidence

   c. centralize the banking system's gold reserves in the central bank, in order to restore confidence

   d. centralize the banking system's gold reserves in the central bank, in order to have more reserves available to meet any run

   e. purchase securities on the open market in order to increase bank reserves

15. Economists sometimes speak of the "monetary pyramid" under the old gold standard, such as that in the United States in the 1920s. By this they mean that:

   a. the money stock was just a small fraction of the quantity of gold

   b. reserve ratios automatically fell whenever the quantity of gold increased

   c. required reserve ratios automatically rose whenever the quantity of gold increased

   d. the quantity of money could be a multiple of the quantity of gold

   e. bank reserves increased whenever the public decided to hold more money in the form of gold

16. There are two traps facing macroeconomic policymakers. Specifically, they are quite likely to destabilize aggregate demand if they attempt to:

   a. balance the full-employment budget every year, and stabilize interest rates

   b. balance the actual employment budget every year, and stabilize interest rates

   c. balance the full-employment budget every year, and stabilize the money stock

   d. balance the actual employment budget every year, and stabilize the money stock

   e. stabilize the growth in reserves and in the money stock

Exercises

1. Suppose the required reserve ratio on all deposits is 20 percent.

   a. In balance sheets A, show the initial effects of an open market purchase of $10 million of securities by the Fed where the seller is a corporation that deposits the proceeds of the sale immediately with its bank, which keeps the funds in the form of a deposit with the Fed.

   b. In balance sheets B, show the ultimate effects of the above transaction, assuming that the deposit expansion process continues up to its maximum limit given by the deposit multiplier. Assume that each bank in the process holds all its extra reserves in the form of deposits with the Fed.

   c. In balance sheets C, show the initial effects of an open market purchase of $10 million of securities by the Fed where the seller is a commercial bank. Is the initial change in the money stock the same as in part a? Why or why not?

   d. In balance sheets D, show the ultimate effects of the open market purchase in part c, assuming that the deposit expansion process continues up to its maximum limit given by the deposit multiplier. Assume that each bank holds all its extra reserves in the form of deposits in the Fed. Compare the results with those in part b.

BALANCE SHEETS A

Federal Reserve System		All commercial banks	
Federal government securities _____	Federal Reserve notes _____	Loans _____ Total reserves _____	Deposits _____
	Deposits of member banks _____ Net worth _____	Required reserves _____ Excess reserves _____	

BALANCE SHEETS B

Federal Reserve System		All commercial banks	
Federal government securities _____	Federal Reserve notes _____	Loans _____ Total reserves _____	Deposits _____
	Deposits of member banks _____ Net worth _____	Required reserves _____ Excess reserves _____	

BALANCE SHEETS C

Federal Reserve System		All commercial banks	
Federal government securities _____	Federal Reserve notes _____	Loans _____ Government securities _____ Total reserves _____	Deposits _____
	Deposits of member banks _____ Net worth _____	Required reserves _____ Excess reserves _____	

BALANCE SHEETS D

Federal Reserve System		All commercial banks	
Federal government securities _____	Federal Reserve notes _____	Loans _____ Government securities _____ Total reserves _____	Deposits _____
	Deposits of member banks _____ Net worth _____	Required reserves _____ Excess reserves _____	

2. The Great Depression of the 1930s provided many lessons for macroeconomists; it was a painful demonstration in how badly things may go wrong if poor policies are pursued.

Specifically, the Great Depression was a time of [large-scale unemployment, inflation, both]. Major mistakes were made in both monetary and fiscal policies. Specifically, the government [cut, raised] tax rates in an attempt to eliminate deficits and move the budget toward balance. This change in taxes [increased, decreased] disposable income, and thus caused an [increase, decrease] in aggregate demand. This made the problem of [unemployment, inflation, both] worse.

The Federal Reserve allowed the money stock to [increase, decrease] by more than 25% between 1929 and 1933, thereby adding to the problem of [inflation, unemployment, both]. This rapid change in the quantity of money may be attributed partly to the [gold standard, the idea that banks should "meet the needs of trade," both]. During this period, the Federal Reserve Board took the position that vigorous open market operations would be unsound. However, the collapse into the depression would have been less severe if the Fed had made vigorous [purchases, sales] of government securities on the open market.

3. (This exercise is only for those who have studied Box 13-1 in the textbook.) Consider a $100 bond with an annual coupon of $10. In the table below, fill in the approximate price of the bond under the different assumptions concerning the term to maturity and the rate of interest. What general proposition is suggested by this example concerning the relationship between (a) the term to maturity of the bond and (b) the size of the effect upon the price of the bond of a change in the rate of interest?

TERM TO MATURITY

Rate of interest	1 year	2 years	Perpetuity
8%	_____	_____	_____
10%	_____	_____	_____
12%	_____	_____	_____

Essay Questions

1. Open market operations constitute the most important tool with which the Fed affects the money stock. But the Fed can also change the quantity of money by changing required reserve ratios. Why should the Fed rely primarily on open market operations rather than changes in required reserve ratios?

2. Savings and loan associations have traditionally held most of their assets in the form of mortgages on homes, with initial terms of 20, 25, or 30 years. Suppose that many of these mortgages are made at interest rates of 8% or 9%. Then suppose that long-term interest rates increase to 12%. What happens to the value of a S&L's mortgages? Can the S&L continue to offer low interest rates in order to keep interest payments less than interest receipts? If it does so, what is likely to happen? Do you see why many S&Ls ran into difficulty when interest rates soared in the late 1970s?

3. Show by means of an example how, if you buy shares on a 50% margin, your gains if stock prices rise will be 100% higher than if you bought for cash, and your losses if stock prices fall will be 100% greater. (Ignore brokerage fees, interest payments on the loan, and dividends on the stock.)

Answers

Important Terms: 1 f 2 i 3 l 4 h 5 k 6 c 7 j 8 e 9 b 10 d 11 a 12 g

True-False: 1 T 2 F 3 T 4 F 5 F 6 T 7 F 8 F 9 T 10 F

Multiple Choice: 1 d 2 a 3 b 4 c 5 e 6 c 7 a 8 e 9 e 10 b 11 d 12 e 13 b 14 e 15 d 16 b

Exercises:

1. BALANCE SHEETS A

Federal Reserve System		All commercial banks		
Federal government securities $10 million	Federal Reserve notes 0	Loans 0		Deposits $10 million
		Total reserves $10 million		
	Deposits of member banks $10 million	Required reserves $ 2 million		
	Net worth 0	Excess reserves $ 8 million		

BALANCE SHEETS B

Federal Reserve System		All commercial banks		
Federal government securities $10 million	Federal Reserve notes 0	Loans $40 million		Deposits $50 million
		Total reserves $10 million		
	Deposits of member banks $10 million	Required reserves $10 million		
	Net worth 0	Excess reserves 0		

BALANCE SHEETS C

Federal Reserve System		All commercial banks		
Federal government securities $10 million	Federal Reserve notes 0	Loans 0		
		Government securities −$10 million	Deposits 0	
		Total reserves $10 million		
	Deposits of member banks $10 million	Required reserves 0		
	Net worth 0	Excess reserves $10 million		

BALANCE SHEETS D

Federal Reserve System		All commercial banks		
Federal government securities $10 million	Federal Reserve notes 0	Loans $50 million		
		Government securities −$10 million	Deposits $50 million	
		Total reserves $10 million		
	Deposits of member banks $10 million	Required reserves $10 million		
	Net worth 0	Excess reserves 0		

2. large-scale unemployment, raised, decreased, decrease, unemployment, decrease, unemployment, both, purchases.

3.

Rate of interest	1 year	2 years	Perpetuity
8%	$101.85	$103.57	$125.00
10%	$100.00	$100.00	$100.00
12%	$ 98.21	$ 96.62	$ 83.33

The longer the term to maturity the greater the change in the price of the bond for any change in the interest rate.

Across

2. major policy-making body (abbrev.)
4. reserves are a _____ of deposit liabilities
6. claim on property, as security for a debt
9. continent in the western hemisphere (abbrev.)
11. when bankers say this, watch out! (3 words)
15. cause of monetary instability, particularly with gold standard
18. what sometimes is done to coins
22, 23. central bank of United States
24. a set of Federal Reserve notes held by a typical bank
25. unbacked paper currency is _____ money
26. Dad
27. _____ Rand, author of *Atlas Shrugged*
28. what one does to each side of a balance sheet
30. yes (Russian)
31. O say, can you _____
32. former middle eastern organization (abbrev.)
33. computer measure
34. make a mistake
35. Federal Reserve influence

Down

1. historically, has been at base of monetary pyramid
2. this can lead to a bank run
3. above
5. bankers fear this
7. return on a loan
8. bankers and others try to avoid this
10. this institution has made bank runs less likely (abbrev.)
12. Dr. Jekyll's alter ego
13. material for fixing roads
14. the price of this commodity is of great interest to Mexico's bankers
15. some say, the discount rate should be a _____ rate
16. banks are required to hold these
17. open _____ operation
18. average
19. the (Fr.)
20. main financial department of U.S. government
21. a Federal Reserve note is legal _____ in the U.S.
22. a dandy
23. currency of Saudi Arabia
25. passing fashion
29. what money is said to be, when interest rates are high

PART FOUR

GREAT MACROECONOMIC ISSUES OF OUR TIME

CHAPTER 14

MONETARY POLICY AND FISCAL POLICY:

WHICH IS THE KEY TO AGGREGATE DEMAND?

MAJOR PURPOSE

One of the important controversies of recent decades has been over the relative importance of monetary and fiscal policies. If the economy is heading into an inflationary boom or into a recession, should we turn to fiscal policy to stabilize the economy? Or to monetary policy? Most economists would now say that a *combination* of monetary and fiscal policies is best. However, there has been a sharp debate between Keynesians—who have often emphasized fiscal policy—and monetarists, who have emphasized that money is the key to aggregate demand. The purpose of this chapter is to review the highlights of this debate, and explain why it is unwise to rely exclusively on either monetary or fiscal policy.

Keynes suggested that the effects of monetary policy be looked on as a three-step process: (1) the effect of a change in the quantity of money on the interest rate, (2) the effect of a change in interest rates on investment demand, and (3) the multiplier process, whereby the change in investment demand has a magnified effect on aggregate demand. Keynes believed that expansive monetary policies might be of little value during the Great Depression, because interest rates were already low, and therefore not much would happen at step 1. Until about 1960, his followers also had major doubts about the second stage. Now, however, almost all Keynesians see an important role for monetary policy. On the other side, some monetarists are quite skeptical that fiscal policy has much effect on aggregate demand. The effects of an increase in government spending can be offset if interest rates increase and cause a reduction in investment or in net exports.

Learning Objectives

After you have studied this chapter in the textbook and study guide, you should be able to:

Describe the three steps in the Keynesian explanation of how a change in the quantity of money can cause a change in aggregate demand

Explain how problems at two of these three steps might mean that aggregate demand will not change much as a result of a change in the quantity of money

Explain how, at the first step, the quantity of money and people's willingness to hold money determine the rate of interest

Explain what the MEI curve means, and what is measured on the vertical axis

Explain why monetary policy might be quite effective, even if the MEI curve is very steep

Explain why monetary policy might be less effective in expanding aggregate demand than in restraining it

Explain the key propositions of monetarists, and the major points of disagreement between monetarists and Keynesians

Explain how deficit spending may lead to a decrease in investment and/or in net exports

Explain the case for using both monetary and fiscal policies in cooperation

Explain why, in spite of strength of the case for using both policies, the United States has nevertheless relied almost exclusively on monetary.policy as a demand-management tool in recent years

HIGHLIGHTS OF CHAPTER

This chapter deals with the controversy over the relative importance of monetary and fiscal policies. Although most economists take an intermediate position, two extreme views may be identified. One position—the position of strong Keynesians, particularly during the 1950s and 1960s—is that fiscal policy is very important, while monetary policy has little or no effect. The other extreme position—the strong monetarist view—is just the opposite. An earlier chapter explained the Keynesian view of how fiscal policy affects aggregate demand. This chapter rounds out the discussion by explaining (1) the reasons why strong Keynesians have dismissed monetary policy, (2) the monetarist view as to why monetary policy is important, and (3) the monetarist view as to why fiscal policy may not have much effect on aggregate demand. This chapter also explains why the historical evidence does not give unqualified support to either extreme view; we are left with a case for using both monetary and fiscal policies.

The Keynesian View of Monetary Policy

In the Keynesian view, there are three links in the chain of events whereby an open market purchase can increase aggregate demand. At the *first link*, an open market purchase can cause a *fall in interest rates*. We have already seen in Chapter 13 why. Specifically, the initial increase in the Fed's demand for bonds, and the secondary increase in bond purchases by commercial banks, will both work to bid up the prices of bonds; that is, interest rates will fall. This chapter explains this first link in more detail.

To see how monetary policy affects interest rates, Keynesian economists look at the demand and supply of money. By the supply of money, they mean the quantity which exists in the economy. By the demand, they mean the *willingness* of people to hold money. This willingness depends in part on interest rates—the lower are interest rates, the more money people are willing to hold. This is reflected in the downward slope of the demand curve in Figure 14-2 in the textbook.

Now, suppose that the economy is initially in equilibrium, and that the Fed then increases the quantity of money. At the existing interest rate, people now have more money than they are willing to hold. They try to reduce their money balances. How do they do so? The answer is: by buying bonds. As people buy bonds, bond prices rise. That is, interest rates fall. Once the interest rate has fallen to its equilibrium, people no longer have more money than they are willing to hold; the demand for bonds levels off.

The *second link* represents the *effect that a change in interest rates has on investment*. Businesses will undertake investment projects as long as their *rate of return* is at least as great as the interest rate. The rate of return can be calculated if we know (1) the initial cost of the investment project, (2) the lifetime of the project, (3) the additional sales from the project, and (4) the costs associated with running the project. For the economy as a whole, the potential investment projects can be ranked according to their rates of return. When this is done, we have a schedule or curve which shows how much investment will yield at least 15%, how much 14%, how much 13%, and so on.

This is the marginal efficiency of investment (MEI) curve, also known as the investment demand curve. It shows the amount that will be invested at various rates of interest. For example, if the interest rate is 12%, businesses have an incentive to undertake any project whose return is more than 12%—that is, any project whose return is high enough to meet interest payments and leave something over to be added to profits. If, then, the interest rate falls to 11% as a result of an expansionary monetary policy, more investment will be undertaken. In other words, the policy leads to an increase in investment at this second step.

At *the third step*, an increase in investment has a *multiplied effect on aggregate demand*. The theory of the multiplier was explained in detail in Chapter 10.

Keynesian economists foresee two situations in which monetary policy may not have much effect. First, Keynes himself saw a problem at the first step. He was skeptical that monetary policy could be used as a way out of the depression of the 1930s. Interest rates were already very low, and there was not much prospect that they could be lowered significantly with monetary policy. After all, there is a downward limit on interest rates—they cannot be pushed below zero. In other words, in the special case of the depression when interest rates were already low, Keynes believed that the authorities could not rely on monetary policy. They would have to use fiscal policy to get the economy out of the depression.

Some of his followers had a more general skepticism regarding monetary policy; they doubted its effectiveness even during more normal times. Specifically, they foresaw a problem at the second step. They believed that the MEI curve might be almost vertical. As a result, they were skeptical that changes in interest rates would lead to a significant change in investment. Even if monetary policy did change interest rates at step 1, there might be very little change in investment at step 2.

One rebuttal was that monetary policy might have an effect *even if* the MEI curve were almost vertical. When the Fed tightens monetary policy, it restricts bank reserves. Because they must meet required reserve ratios, banks *must* limit their loans—regardless of the demand by businesses. As a consequence, investment may be limited by a *unavailability of funds*, rather than by a lack of desire by businesses to invest. Banks may *ration* their available funds among eager buyers.

For three reasons, a restrictive monetary policy may be more effective than an expansive policy:

1. The rate of interest cannot be driven below zero, but there is no limit to how high it can be driven.

2. Banks cannot increase their loans and other earning assets when they lack excess reserves; the Fed can firmly restrain their lending by limiting their reserves. But when the Fed increases bank reserves, it cannot force banks to lend. They may hold large excess reserves—as many of them in fact did during the late 1930s.

3. Through credit rationing, banks can keep loans below the amounts demanded by businesses. But banks cannot force businesses to borrow more than they want.

The Monetarist View of Monetary Policy

The monetarist view can be expressed in terms of the equation of exchange: $MV = PQ$, where M is the stock of money, V is the velocity of money, P is the average level of prices, and Q is the quantity of output (that is, real national product). This equation is not a "theory," because it is simply true *by definition*. Specifically, V is defined as PQ/M. However, on this equation a theory has been built. This theory—the *quantity theory*—is the proposition that V is stable. If this is so, then a change in M will cause an approximately proportional change in PQ. In other words, monetary policy has a strong and predictable effect on nominal GNP.

Five key propositions of monetarism are:

1. The money supply M is the most important determinant of aggregate demand and nominal national product PQ.

2. In the *long run*, real GNP tends toward its full employment level. Consequently, the only long run effect of M is on P, not on Q.

3. However, in the short run, an increase (decrease) in M can cause *both* P and Q to increase (decrease).

4. If M is increased at a slow, stable rate, then aggregate demand will also increase at a slow, stable rate.

5. Such a slow, stable increase in aggregate demand is the best way to reduce the magnitude of business cycles and keep inflation down. Therefore, the central bank should follow a monetary *rule*, aiming for a slow, steady increase in M.

The Monetarist View of Fiscal Policy

Monetarists doubt that fiscal policy has a strong and predictable effect on aggregate demand. The major reason for this is because of "crowding out." Suppose that the government spends more, and finances the resulting deficit by borrowing from the public. Interest rates will rise. As a result, businesses will move upward to the left along the MEI curve; investment demand will decline.

Thus, the government spending will *crowd out* investment; the net effect on aggregate demand will be smaller than foreseen in the simple discussion of Chapter 11. The strength of this crowding out effect will depend on the slope of the MEI curve. The flatter it is, the more investment will fall for any increase in the interest rate. Monetarists generally believe that the MEI curve is quite flat (in contrast to the almost vertical curve of early Keynesians). As a result, they foresee a strong crowding-out effect, with little or no net effect of fiscal policy on aggregate demand.

This crowding-out argument is based on the assumption that the government sells bonds *to the public*. In this case, there will be no effect on the money stock; this will be a *pure* fiscal policy. If, on the other hand, the Fed buys the additional government bonds, interest rates may be kept down and investment demand and aggregate demand will increase. But the money stock will rise, and a monetarist will consider money, not government spending, to be the cause of the increase in aggregate demand. Thus, if we want to distinguish between the Keynesian and monetarist viewpoints, we should look at a *pure* fiscal policy—a change in G or in tax rates with no change in M—and compare it with what we might call a *pure* monetary policy: an open market operation and a change in M with no change in fiscal policy. If an expansive fiscal policy is accompanied by an increase in M, there is no disagreement: aggregate demand will increase. Keynesians will generally attribute the increase to fiscal policy, and monetarists to a change in M.

A second reason that deficit spending may have a weak effect on aggregate demand has attracted considerable attention in recent years. An increase in deficit spending by the governrment can cause an increase in interest rates, encouraging foreigners to buy U.S. bonds and bidding up the price of the U.S. dollar in terms of foreign currencies. U.S. exports are discouraged, and imports stimulated. In other words, a budgetary deficit can cause a deficit in international trade, with the trade deficit offsetting the stimulative effects of the government's deficit spending.

Statistical evidence does not give unqualified support to either the strong monetarist nor to the strong Keynesian view. There is still some uncertainty over the relative effectiveness of monetary and fiscal policies. Because we do not know exactly how the economy operates, it makes sense to diversify—to use some of each policy, rather than putting all our eggs in one basket. But, while the importance of diversification is widely recognized, we have in fact placed almost exclusive reliance on monetary policy as a demand-management tool in recent years. The reason is that fiscal policy is caught in a political impasse. Many people believe that smaller deficits would be desirable, but there is little agreement on how to achieve that goal.

Important Terms: Match the Columns

Match the term in the first column with the corresponding phrase in the second column. But before you do so, write out your own definition of the term in the first column.

_____ 1. MEI curve
_____ 2. Credit rationing
_____ 3. Credit crunch
_____ 4. Quantity theory
_____ 5. Equation of exchange
_____ 6. Velocity
_____ 7. Crowding out
_____ 8. Pure fiscal policy

a. Severe credit rationing
b. $MV = PQ$
c. Change in G with no change in rate of growth of M
d. Relationship between interest rate and $I*$
e. G leads to higher i, which leads to less $I*$
f. Funds are unavailable, even for credit-worthy borrowers
g. Proposition that V is stable
h. PQ/M

True-False

T F 1. According to Keynes, interest rates might be low during a depression. He argued that in this case, expansive monetary policy would not be an effective tool for promoting recovery.

T F 2. The flatter is the marginal efficiency of investment curve, the more effective is monetary policy as a way of controlling aggregate demand.

T F 3. The flatter is the marginal efficiency of investment curve, the more effective is fiscal policy as a way of controlling aggregate demand.

T F 4. Most Keynesians argue that the equation of exchange is incorrect; specifically, they argue that V does not equal PQ/M.

T F 5. According to the quantity theory of money, V tends to be stable through time, and PQ therefore tends to change by about the same percentage as M.

T F 6. According to quantity theorists, a change in M will have little or no effect on P in the long run.

T F 7. According to quantity theorists, a change in M will have a greater effect on P in the long run than in the short run.

T F 8. According to monetarists, fiscal policy can have a powerful effect on aggregate demand, provided that changes in government spending are financed by borrowing from the central bank.

T F 9. The stronger is the crowding out effect, the more powerful will be the effect of fiscal policy on aggregate demand.

T F 10. The steeper is the aggregate supply curve, the more powerful is fiscal policy as a way of changing output and employment.

Multiple Choice

1. Which of the following is most likely to *decrease* when the quantity of money *increases*?
   a. P
   b. Q
   c. $P \times Q$
   d. the interest rate
   e. the quantity of money demanded

2. In the Keynesian approach to monetary policy, if the quantity of money exceeds the quantity demanded, the most likely result is a:
   a. fall in the interest rate
   b. rise in the interest rate
   c. fall in investment
   d. fall in national product
   e. fall in the size of the multiplier

3. Suppose that the amount of money people have exceeds the quantity that they want to hold. Then, Keynesian theory emphasizes that they will try to get rid of excess money balances by:
   a. saving more
   b. buying bonds
   c. buying goods
   d. switching from currency to checking deposits
   e. switching from checking deposits to currency

4. Suppose that the amount of money people have exceeds the quantity that they want to hold. Then, monetarists emphasize that they will try to get rid of excess money balances by:
   a. saving more
   b. buying bonds
   c. buying goods
   d. switching from currency to checking deposits
   e. switching from checking deposits to currency

5. Suppose that a company is going to buy a machine costing $100,000 which is expected to last one year, after which it will have no scrap value. With this machine, the company can produce $250,000 worth of additional goods, while spending $100,000 for additional raw materials, supplies, and labor. Then the expected rate of return on that machine is:

a. -100%　　　　**d.** 50%
b. 0　　　　　　**e.** 150%
c. 10%

6. If the marginal efficiency of investment curve is quite flat, then we would expect the effects on aggregate demand of:
  a. monetary policy to be strong while fiscal policy is weak
  b. fiscal policy to be strong while monetary policy is weak
  c. both monetary and fiscal policies to be strong
  d. both monetary and fiscal policies to be weak

7. If credit rationing occurs, then:
  a. the interest rate will be above its equilibrium level
  b. bond prices will rise
  c. funds will flow from the corporate sector into housing
  d. investment will be at a point to the left of the MEI curve
  e. saving will be greater than investment

8. The quantity theory of money is best described as the proposition that:
  a. Q is stable　　　**d.** $MV = PQ$
  b. P is stable　　　**e.** $MQ = PV$
  c. V is stable

9. Keynesians and monetarists are most likely to agree that:
  a. monetary policy is more effective than fiscal policy
  b. fiscal policy is more effective than monetary policy
  c. neither fiscal nor monetary policy can affect Q; the only effect will be on P
  d. the MEI curve is generally steep
  e. $V = PQ/M$

10. Which of the following views is most likely to be held by a monetarist?
  a. a decrease in the rate of growth of the money stock will cause the level of national product to stay below the full employment level permanently
  b. the money stock should be increased at a steady, constant rate
  c. investment demand is quite unresponsive to changes in the rate of interest
  d. the quantity of money demanded responds strongly to changes in the rate of interest
  e. monetary policy is like trying to control aggregate demand with a string

11. According to monetarists, an increase in M will have a strong effect in the long run on:
  a. V　　　　　　**d.** current-dollar national
  b. Q　　　　　　　　product
  c. real national product　**e.** none of the above

12. The "crowding-out" effect of fiscal policy applies to which of the following ideas?

a. an increase in G leads to an increase in interest rates, which leads to an increase in I^*
b. an increase in G leads to a decrease in interest rates, which leads to an increase in I^*
c. an increase in G leads to an increase in interest rates, which leads to a decline in I^*
d. an increase in G leads to an increase in I^*, which leads to an increase in interest rates
e. an increase in G leads to an increase in I^*, which leads to a decrease in interest rates

13. By "pure" fiscal policies, economists mean:
  a. fiscal policies uninfluenced by special interests
  b. fiscal policies where all changes take place in the nondefense sectors of the government's budget
  c. fiscal policies concentrated in the defense sectors of the government's budget, because these have little effect on the productive capacity of the economy
  d. changes in government spending or tax rates unaccompanied by changes in the rate of growth of the money stock
  e. changes in government spending or tax rates while interest rates are held constant

14. Some economists believe that expansions will be *lopsided* if large U.S. government deficits persist. By this, they mean that during expansions, production of:
  a. exports will be too high, and production of capital goods too low
  b. capital goods will be too low, and exports will also be too low
  c. capital goods will be too high, and exports will also be too high
  d. capital goods will be too high, and exports too low
  e. consumption goods will be too low, and capital goods too high

15. If the aggregate supply curve is quite steep, then:
  a. an expansive monetary policy will have a powerful effect on aggregate demand, but an expansive fiscal policy will not
  b. an expansive fiscal policy will have a powerful effect on aggregate demand, but an expansive monetary policy will not
  c. an expansive monetary policy will have a powerful effect on real output, but an expansive fiscal policy will not
  d. an expansive fiscal policy will have a powerful effect on real output, but an expansive monetary policy will not
  e. neither an expansive fiscal nor an expansive monetary policy will have a powerful effect on real output

Exercises

1. According to Keynesians, money can affect aggregate demand as a result of a three-step process. Specifically, an increase in the quantity of money will lead to (a) _____, which in turn will cause (b) _____, which in turn will lead to (c) _____.

Keynesians foresee no problem at the third step.

However, problems might occur at each of the first two steps. Specifically, there might be a problem at the first step, particularly if [interest rates were already very low, interest rates were already high, the rate of inflation were high]. There also could be a major problem at the second step, if [the demand for money, the MEI curve, the consumption function] were steep.

In Keynesian theory, if the amount of money people have exceeds the quantity that they want to hold, they will [buy bonds, buy goods, save more]. As a result, [prices will rise, interest rates will fall]. Monetarists foresee a somewhat different response. If the amount of money people have exceeds the quantity that they want to hold, they will [buy bonds, buy goods, save more]. As a result, [aggregate demand will increase, interest rates will fall]. In the short run, monetarists believe that this will lead to [higher P, higher Q, both]; in the long run, it will cause [higher P, higher Q, both]. Monetarism is based on the quantity theory of money. That is, it is based on the view that [M, V, P, Q, all of them] is/are stable.

2. Suppose that the MEI curve is very steep. This suggests that monetary policy will be [effective, weak]. Specifically, suppose the Federal Reserve engages in a very restrictive policy, selling Treasury bills on the open market. As a result, the prices of bills will [fall, rise], and their interest rates or yields will [fall, rise]. This will lead to an [increase, decrease] in I^*, with the size of this effect being very [large, small] because of the steepness of the MEI curve.

Some economists suggest that monetary policy can be quite [effective, ineffective] even if the MEI curve is steep, because of what happens to the availability of funds. Specifically, the open market sale will lead to an [increase, decrease] in bank reserves. As a result, banks will be *forced* to [increase, decrease] their portfolio of loans and other earning assets. Businesses will find that bank loans are [easier to get, rationed]. This will mean that I^* is [greater, less] than we would have expected by looking simply at the MEI curve and interest rates.

3. In Figure 14-1 below, the curves labeled A and B are two alternative ways the MEI curve may be drawn. Of the two, curve [A, B] is the one in which I^* is the more responsive to changes in the rate of interest. According to curve A, when the rate of interest is 10%, I^* will be _____; when the rate of interest is 5%, I^* will be _____. According to curve B, when the rate of interest is 10%, I^* will be _____; when the rate of interest is 5%, I^* will be _____. If the two economies are identical except for the MEI, then monetary policy will be more powerful in economy [A, B], and fiscal policy will be more powerful in economy [A, B].

Figure 14-2 shows the 45° line and the line indicating consumption demand plus government demand for goods and services in either economy A or B. The slope of this line is equal to _____. This means that the

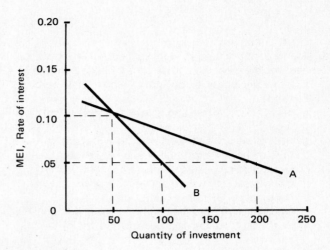

FIGURE 14-1

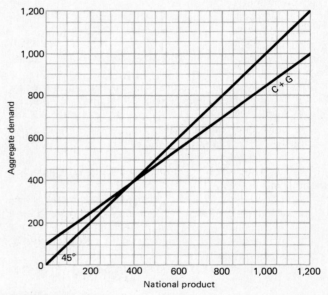

FIGURE 14-2

multiplier is equal to _____. (If you have trouble with this point, refer back to Chapter 10.) Suppose that the interest rate in economy A is 10%. Draw the aggregate demand line ($C + I^* + G$) for economy A. The equilibrium is at a national product of _____. Now suppose that the interest rate decreases to 5%. I^* will [increase, decrease] from _____ to _____ in economy A. Draw in a new aggregate demand line. The new equilibrium national product is _____. From your last two answers, confirm the size of the multiplier shown earlier in the paragraph.

Now go through the same exercise for economy B. That is, draw in the aggregate demand line when the interest rate is equal to 10%, and then when it is equal to 5%. As a result of the fall in the interest rate, investment [increases, decreases] from _____ to _____, and equilibrium national product [increases, decreases] from

_____ to _____. By comparing answers, we see that the multiplier is [higher than in A, lower than in A, the same as in A]. (Do you see why this is so?) A fall in interest rates from 10% to 5% has [a more powerful, a less powerful, the same] effect on national product in economy B, compared with economy A.

Essay Questions

1. One reason for using both monetary and fiscal policies together is that diversification spreads the benefit or pain. For each of the following policies, explain who the major gainers and losers are, and why: (*a*) expansive monetary policy, (*b*) expansive fiscal policy, (*c*) restrictive monetary policy, and (*d*) restrictive fiscal policy.

2. Suppose one economist told you that the MEI curve was quite steep, and another told you it was quite flat. Which is more likely to be a monetarist, and which a Keynesian? Explain.

3. "The equation of exchange, $MV = PQ$, is a tautology. Therefore it is useless in helping us understand how the economy works." Evaluate this statement. Also evaluate the following: "The basic Keynesian equation, aggregate demand $= C + I^* + G + X_n$, is also a tautology. Therefore it is also useless in helping us understand how the economy works."

Answers

Important Terms: 1 d 2 f 3 a 4 g 5 b 6 h 7 e 8 c
True-False: 1 T 2 T 3 F 4 F 5 T 6 F 7 T 8 T 9 F 10 F
Multiple Choice: 1 d 2 a 3 b 4 c 5 d 6 a 7 d 8 c 9 e 10 b 11 d 12 c 13 d 14 b 15 e
Exercises: **1a.** a fall in the interest rate **1b.** a rise in investment demand **1c.** a multiplied increase in aggregate demand, interest rates were already very low, the MEI curve, buy bonds, interest rates will fall, buy goods, aggregate demand will increase, both, higher *P*, *V*. **2.** weak, fall, rise, decrease, small, effective, decrease, decrease, rationed, less. **3.** A, 50, 200, 50, 100, A, B, 0.75, 4, 600, increase, 50, 200, 1,200, increases, 50, 100, increases, 600, 800, the same as in A (because the multiplier depends on the slope of the aggregate demand function, which is the same in the two countries), less powerful.

Figure 14-2 completed:

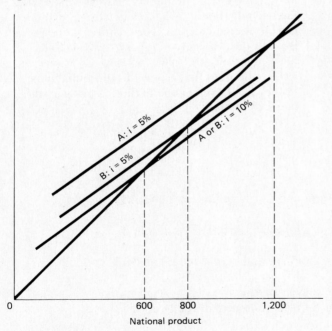

FIGURE 14-2

CHAPTER 15

FINE TUNING OR STABLE POLICY SETTINGS?

MAJOR PURPOSE

This chapter deals with one of the major, continuing controversies in macroeconomics: Should aggregate demand policies be adjusted as conditions change, or should the Fed follow a monetary policy rule? On the one side are those in the Keynesian tradition, who argue that aggregate demand should be *actively managed* in pursuit of the goals of high employment and stable prices. On the other side are the monetarists, who favor a rule: The Fed should aim for a *slow, steady increase in the money stock*. No matter how well intentioned the authorities, they do not know enough to stabilize the economy. Discretionary policies do not work in practice. So say the monetarists.

This debate has been dominated by strong advocates of rules, on the one hand, and strong opponents, on the other. One of the major conclusions of this chapter is that the question before us is not really whether we should chose a rigid, permanent rule that would be followed without regard to "how the chips" fall. There is no way that future policymakers could be bound firmly to such a rule. (Even if it were feasible to enshrine a policy rule in the Constitution, the Constitution could be amended again.) There is, however, a *very* important policy issue which remains—even if rigid, permanent rules are discarded as a logical impossibility. The issue is: Should policies be adjusted frequently in the light of unfolding conditions? Or would we be better off to aim for a stable growth of the money stock, and make adjustments only rarely, when very strong evidence for a change accumulates? Unfortunately, the experience of the past quarter century does not provide a clear answer. Sometimes discretionary policies have worked quite well; sometimes they have not. The ambiguous lesson of history is, of course, one of the reasons why the controversy continues.

Learning Objectives

After you have studied this chapter in the textbook and study guide, you should be able to:

Describe the various steps in the active Keynesian approach to aggregate demand management

Explain why lags make it difficult to stabilize aggregate demand through active management

Explain the important role of potential GNP in the active approach

Explain how problems in estimating potential were a major source of difficulty during the 1970s

Explain the case for and the case against a discretionary policy

If you study the appendix, you should also be able to:

Explain why investment is much more volatile than consumption during the business cycle

Explain why a moderate expansion may be more likely to last than a very rapid expansion

HIGHLIGHTS OF CHAPTER

Keynes and his followers argued that the government has the responsibility to maintain full employment and reasonably stable prices. Particularly in the early years between 1935 and 1965, Keynesians believed that an untended market economy would suffer from two major problems: Aggregate demand would be (1) often inadequate, and (2) unstable. Authorities should actively intervene to bring aggregate demand up to the full employment level, and then manage it on a continuing basis to offset forces of instability.

This idea was particularly influential during the 1960s, a decade that has sometimes been called the "age of Keynes." Figure 15-1 in the textbook illustrates the general Keynesian demand-management strategy; Figure 15-2 presents the same idea applied to the situation in the early 1960s. There were several major steps in bringing aggregate demand up to the full-employment level: (1) First, the path of potential GNP was estimated. (2) Next, forecasts were made of where actual GNP would go in the absence of policy changes; in other words, the size of the prospective GNP gap was estimated. (3) Finally, fiscal and monetary policies were adjusted with the objective of closing the gap in a reasonably brief period. Until 1965–1966, this strategy was very successful. The estimated GNP gap closed, and prices remained reasonably stable. However, by the late 1960s, inflation was accelerating. This was only partly the result of failures in economic analysis. Even more fundamentally, it was a result of political problems in changing policies. By the mid 1960s, the Council of Economic Advisers was becoming concerned with the growing inflationary pressures. They recommended to President Johnson that taxes be increased in order to restrain aggregate demand and thus reduce inflationary pressures. President Johnson waited several years before passing this recommendation along to Congress; he was reluctant to ask the public to pay higher taxes to finance an unpopular war. This was just one extreme example of the problem of lags.

Critics of active management make five major arguments:

1. *Lags* in the operation of policies mean that the government, like the panicky helmsman, may overreact to current events.

2. Because of lags, policies developed today must be designed to deal with problems several months in the future. But economists are *only moderately successful in their ability to forecast* either the probable course of the economy in the absence of policy changes, or the effects of policy changes themselves.

3. *Prices respond even more slowly* than real output when monetary and fiscal policies are changed. As a consequence, there may be an *inflationary bias* to discretionary policies. Decision-makers may choose expansionary policies for the short-run benefits of higher output, and worry later about the inflationary consequences.

4. Activists may *overestimate potential GNP*. As a result, they may strive to achieve an unattainable goal, creating strong inflationary pressures in the process. Figure 15-4 in the textbook illustrates this argument in general terms; Figure 15-5 applies it to the 1970s.

5. The active management of aggregate demand involves additional government meddling in the economy; rules are more consistent with *economic freedom* than are discretionary policies.

Advocates of rules recognize, of course, that it is important to pick the correct rule—one that is consistent with economic stability. It won't do to pick any old rule. Some seemingly plausible rules would be a mistake. For example, the gold standard rule made the banking system vulnerable to runs; it added to the banking chaos of 1931–1933. However, proponents of rules believe that if the money stock were increased at a slow, steady rate, the economy would be more stable than it has been in the past, when proponents of active demand management were in charge. The proposal for a slow, steady increase in the money stock is based directly on the quantity theory of money—that is, on the view that velocity V is stable. If V is in fact stable, then a stable increase in M will mean a stable increase in nominal income PQ.

Opponents of a monetary rule emphasize four points:

1. The government would be foolish to adopt rigid rules that may become outdated as circumstances change in unforeseen ways. Indeed, a truly rigid rule is a *logical impossibility*. Future decision-makers cannot be bound inflexibly by the present. The *real issue is one of degree*: Will policies be adjusted in the light of a moderate amount of new information, or will policy changes be postponed until the evidence becomes overwhelming? While advocates of policy rules are correct in pointing out that lags create difficulties for discretionary policies, their proposals would increase lags in a major way. The government would be so committed to a course of action that it would not change policy until conditions became very bad indeed.

2. When strong evidence does accumulate that something is wrong, the government may then make abrupt changes in policy. In other words, the desire to follow a stable policy rule may paradoxically lead to *abrupt changes in practice*.

3. There is no guarantee that stable monetary growth will lead to a stable increase in aggregate demand. In the period since 1975, there have been two major, unpredictable changes in velocity—an abnormal rise in velocity in 1975 and 1978, and a sharp decline in 1982. The 1982 slowdown in velocity added to the recession, and led the Fed to increase its target for monetary growth. Earlier, in 1979, the Fed had moved toward the monetarist position in order to fight inflation more vigorously. In 1982, the Fed backed away from this position, in order to combat the recession. It was persuaded to change its monetary target by a moderate amount of evidence—quite rightly so, said the critics of rules.

4. The rule advocated by monetarists—a slow, steady growth in the money stock—may lead to aggregate demand that is too low to buy the increasing volume of goods and services that the economy is capable of producing. In other words, the adoption of a rule aimed at slow growth of demand and stable prices may result in high unemployment and slow growth of real output.

Note the contrast between this last point and the fourth point in the earlier list of the criticisms of fine tuning. There is a significant difference in the approach of the two groups to the problems of inflation and unemployment. Advocates of discretionary policies consider monetarists heartless in their willingness to accept unemployment; monetarists consider some Keynesians to be crude inflationists.

As noted earlier, forecasting is required for the implementation of discretionary policies. Some forecasting, either formal or informal, is also needed by businesses that are planning their investment programs. Economic forecasters often use *econometric models*, modified by the results from surveys and the judgment of the forecaster. The record of forecasters is fair. It is much better than would come from a very simple approach, such as projecting the trends of the previous year or so. However, forecasters have not done a very good job in anticipating what will happen during recessions. In particular, they substantially underestimated the depth of the severe recessions of 1974 and 1982. This is worrisome to the advocates of active demand management. It is particularly important to anticipate recessions, in order to be able to shift to more expansive policies in a timely manner.

Important Terms: Match the Columns

Match the term in the first column with the corresponding phrase in the second column. But before you do so, write out your own definition of the term in the first column.

_____ **1.** Potential GNP
_____ **2.** GNP gap
_____ **3.** V
_____ **4.** Policy rule
_____ **5.** Recognition lag
_____ **6.** Action lag
_____ **7.** Impact lag

a. From time weakness is recognized until policies are changed
b. Keep money growth low and stable
c. From time policy is changed until aggregate demand responds
d. Aggregate demand policies are aimed at eliminating this
e. If this isn't stable, money rule won't work
f. Target path for those who manage aggregate demand
g. From time weakness begins until time it is recognized

True-False

T F **1.** Monetarists advocate that the money stock be adjusted to keep interest rates stable.

T F **2.** "Fine tuner" is a term applied to someone who wants to adjust policy frequently to stabilize demand.

T F **3.** The "recognition lag" is the interval between the time when a problem is recognized and the time when corrective action is taken.

T F **4.** The "action lag" is the interval between the time when action is taken, and when the action has its effect on aggregate demand.

T F **5.** The case for active, discretionary monetary and fiscal policies would be stronger if economists could forecast better.

T F **6.** If the potential GNP path is overestimated, active demand managers are likely as a consequence to follow overly stimulative demand management policies.

T F **7.** If the rate of increase in productivity unexpectedly falls, potential GNP is likely as a result to be overestimated.

T F **8.** Because of the errors in estimating potential GNP during the 1970s, almost all economists now believe in a monetary policy rule.

T F **9.** Those who advocate a monetary "rule" argue that a rule is more conducive to freedom than is discretion by policymakers.

T F **10.** The inflation rate is a leading indicator.

Multiple Choice

1. An economist is most likely to favor discretionary aggregate demand policies, rather than a policy rule, if he or she is in which economic tradition?
- **a.** Keynesian
- **b.** classical
- **c.** monetarist
- **d.** marginalist
- **e.** libertarian

2. Economists who argue for a policy rule aimed at stabilizing aggregate demand are most likely to favor which rule?
- **a.** the gold standard
- **b.** a balanced actual budget
- **c.** a balanced full-employment budget
- **d.** a steady growth in the money stock
- **e.** all the above rules are equally good; the thing that matters is to have *some* rule

3. A monetarist is most likely to advocate which of the following policy rules?
- **a.** increase the money stock, measured in dollars, by 4% every year
- **b.** increase the money stock by 4% in real terms; that is, increase the money stock by 4% plus the amount of inflation
- **c.** increase the money stock, measured in dollars, by 4% plus a fraction of the output gap
- **d.** increase the real money stock by 4% plus a fraction of the output gap
- **e.** increase the real money stock by 4% plus a fraction of the inflationary gap

4. The discretionary policies of the 1960s involved each of the following steps *except one*. Which is the exception?
- **a.** estimate potential GNP
- **b.** forecast the probable course of GNP in the absence of policy changes
- **c.** forecast the effects of various changes in aggregate demand policies
- **d.** select the policies aimed at closing the GNP gap in a reasonably brief time
- **e.** revise the potential GNP path upward, since an even better performance now becomes possible

5. Suppose that the Council of Economic Advisers forecasts a GNP gap of $100 billion for the coming year if no change is made in policies. Then an advocate of:
- **a.** rules would prescribe a faster growth in the quantity of money
- **b.** rules would prescribe a faster growth in government spending
- **c.** active management would prescribe an increase in tax rates, to balance the budget
- **d.** active management would prescribe an increase in government spending
- **e.** active management would prescribe an increase in government spending to increase real output, plus a decrease in the money stock to reduce inflation

6. The recognition lag is the lag between the time when:
- **a.** a problem is recognized and the time when corrective action is taken
- **b.** a problem is recognized and the time when it is corrected
- **c.** a recession begins and the time when the authorities recognize it has begun

d. aggregate demand increases and the time when producers realize that they can raise their prices
e. aggregate demand increases and producers recognize that they should produce more

7. The "helmsman's dilemma" illustrates the difficulty of making policy in the presence of:
- **a.** inflation
- **b.** deflation
- **c.** unemployment
- **d.** low growth
- **e.** lags

8. Those who advocate policy rules rather than active management argue that active managers tend to:
- **a.** overestimate potential, and therefore follow inflationary policies
- **b.** underestimate potential, and therefore follow deflationary policies
- **c.** underestimate growth, and therefore follow inflationary policies
- **d.** underestimate the effects of government spending, and therefore rely too much on monetary policy
- **e.** underestimate the effects of tax changes, and therefore rely too much on monetary policy

9. At times during the business cycle, "everything seems to be going right"—that is, output is rising, unemployment falling, and the rate of inflation falling. This is most likely to occur:
- **a.** at the peak of the expansion
- **b.** early in the expansion
- **c.** late in the expansion, about 3 or 4 months before the peak
- **d.** late in the recession, when people are beginning to become more optimistic
- **e.** at the trough, when people are beginning to become more optimistic

10. The monetarist case is based on each of the following propositions *except one*. Which is the exception?
- **a.** The desirable path of aggregate demand is one of steady, moderate growth.
- **b.** The desirable trend of prices is a gradual upward movement, by about 4% per year.
- **c.** The best way to get a steady, moderate increase in aggregate demand is by a steady, moderate increase in the money stock.
- **d.** Following a monetary rule increases economic freedom, and probably political freedom, too.

11. Suppose that you were looking for a set of policy rules to keep aggregate demand reasonably stable. Which set of rules would hold the most promise?
- **a.** Keep interest rates fixed, and balance the actual budget each year.
- **b.** Keep interest rates fixed, and balance the full-employment budget each year.
- **c.** Increase the quantity of money at a steady rate, and balance the actual budget each year.
- **d.** Increase the quantity of money at a steady rate, and balance the full-employment budget every year.
- **e.** Reestablish the gold standard.

12. Those who advocate active demand management oppose policy rules on a number of grounds, including the argument that:

a. proposed rules are likely to result in excessive unemployment

b. proposed rules are likely to result in ever-increasing inflation

c. rules won't work unless "you can fool some of the people all the time, or all the people some of the time"

d. rules require an estimate of potential GNP, and we are able to estimate potential GNP only imperfectly

e. rules will result in too much saving and investment

13. Opponents of a monetary rule argue that there cannot in fact be a rigid rule because:

a. it would be unconstitutional

b. the Fed in fact has almost no control over the money stock

c. money does not affect aggregate demand

d. money does not affect interest rates

e. future governments cannot be committed to a rule regardless of the consequences

14. Suppose that $C = 0.5$ GNP; $I^*_g = 500$; $G = 700$; $X = 300$; and imports are 10% of GNP. Then equilibrium GNP equals:

a. 2,500   **d.** 3,950

b. 3,000   **e.** 5,200

c. 3,750

Exercises

1. There are three lags before monetary and fiscal policies affect aggregate demand. First is the _____ lag, next the _____ lag, and then the _____ lag. In addition, there is another lag that occurs after aggregate demand changes. Specifically, the effects of demand on [output, prices] generally lags behind its effect on [output, prices]. Critics of active demand management argue that the first three lag means that policies may destabilize the economy. The fourth lag means that discretionary policies can have an [inflationary, deflationary] bias.

Lags are, however, not the only problem facing the managers of aggregate demand. They also have the difficult task of estimating [the path of potential GNP, the effects of monetary policy on demand, the effects of fiscal policy on demand, all of these]. Suppose they overestimate the potential path. This means that, starting from a recession, they are likely to [keep expansive policies too long, abandon expansive policies too soon]. The reason is that [the economy will remain below the potential path, they will soon give up trying]. As a result, the problem of [inflation, low growth] may become worse.

2. In this exercise you must choose a fiscal policy. See if you can learn from this what kind of problems beset policymakers.

a. Suppose your advisers tell you that potential GNP is now $990 billion and that it will grow by $60 billion per year for each of the next four years. (All figures are in constant dollars.) Last year (year zero) and the year before, actual GNP was $810 billion and G (the level of government spending on goods and services) was $250 billion. Next, suppose that your advisers tell you that the government spending multiplier is 3, that they do not forsee any lags in the economic system, and that aggregate demand will not change unless G changes. In Table 15-1, chart the behavior of potential GNP, and of actual GNP and the GNP gap under different assumptions about G. In this example, policy [A, B, C]

Table 15-1

	Year 1	Year 2	Year 3	Year 4
Potential GNP	990			
G	250	250	250	250
A. Actual GNP	810	810	810	810
GNP gap	180			
G	310	330	350	370
B. Actual GNP				
GNP gap				
G	280	310	340	370
C. Actual GNP				
GNP gap				

is the neutral policy of keeping the same level of government spending, policy [A, B, C] is the activist policy of trying to eliminate the GNP gap immediately, and policy [A, B, C] is the "gradualist" policy of eliminating the GNP gap in stages over 4 years.

b. Now suppose that your advisers were mistaken. Instead of no lag, the multiplier operates with a 1-year lag, so that any change by one unit in G this year would cause a 3-unit change in GNP *next* year, but no change in GNP *this* year. Then, show the results of the three policies in Table 15-2.

Table 15-2

G	Year 1	Year 2	Year 3	Year 4
A. Actual GNP	810	810	810	810
GNP gap	180			
B. Actual GNP	810			
GNP gap				
C. Actual GNP				
GNP gap				

c. Next, suppose that as well as the lag there are shifts in aggregate demand that were unforeseen by your advisers. Suppose that the changes in investment from one year to the next were as indicated in Table 15-3, and that these changes, just like changes in G, affected GNP with a multiplier of 3 and with a 1-year delay. Show in Table 15-4 the outcomes of the three policies. Table 15-4 shows a potential hazard of activist policies. The activist policy, B, instead of just closing the GNP gap in years 2, 3, and 4, would

Table 15-3

	Year 0	Year 1	Year 2	Year 3
Change in investment over previous year	0	+50	+40	+20

Table 15-4

	Year 1	Year 2	Year 3	Year 4
A. Actual GNP				
GNP gap				
B. Actual GNP				
GNP gap				
C. Actual GNP				
GNP gap				

result in a sizable [recessionary, inflationary] gap. The less active, "gradualist" policy, C, would result in a [smaller, larger] gap. And the best policy in terms of producing the smallest average gap over the years 2 through 4, would be the [neutral, activist, gradualist] policy.

Essay Questions

1. Why can't the government always eliminate the GNP gap by continuing to increase its spending as long as the gap exists?

2. Suppose that a 4% monetary rule were adopted. Then suppose that the introduction of an electronic transfer system for making payments caused a large increase in the velocity of money. What would happen to the price level? Could this have been avoided if the rule hadn't been adopted? Can you think of a rule that would allow for such contingencies?

3. Presidents have objectives in addition to their economic goals—for example, national defense and get-ting reelected. How do these other goals strengthen or weaken the case for discretionary policies, rather than a monetary rule?

4. A passage in the chapter highlights section reads as follows: "Advocates of discretionary policies consider monetarists heartless in their willingness to accept unemployment; monetarists consider some Keynesians to be crude inflationists." Explain why these criticisms are made. In the first case, what defense might a monetarist have? (Hint: Does it depend on the aggregate supply function?) In the second case, what defense might a Keynesian have?

Answers

Important Terms: 1 f 2 d 3 e 4 b 5 g 6 a 7 c
True-False: 1 F 2 T 3 F 4 F 5 T 6 T 7 T 8 F 9 T 10 F
Multiple Choice: 1 a 2 d 3 a 4 e 5 d 6 c 7 e 8 a 9 b 10 b 11 d 12 a 13 e 14 a
Exercises: **1.** recognition, action, impact, prices, output, inflationary, all of these, keep expansive policies too long, the economy will remain below the potential path, inflation.

2a. Table 15-1

Year 1	Year 2	Year 3	Year 4
990	1050	1110	1170
180	240	300	360
990	1050	1110	1170
0	0	0	0
900	990	1080	1170
90	60	30	0

A, B, C

2b. Table 15-2

Year 1	Year 2	Year 3	Year 4
810	810	810	810
180	240	300	360
810	990	1050	1110
180	60	60	60
810	900	990	1080
180	150	120	90

2c. Table 15-4

inflationary, smaller, neutral

Year 1	Year 2	Year 3	Year 4
810	960	1080	1140
180	90	30	30
810	1140	1320	1440
180	−90	−210	−270
810	1050	1260	1410
180	0	−150	−240

Across

1. someone to whom money is owed
6. holiday season
8. type of lag
12. a chemical element (abbrev.)
13. type of radio (abbrev.)
14. this is watched by forecasters (2 words)
18. this group has made projections of potential GNP (abbrev.)
19. _____ of money is the key, say prononents of rules
20. a healthy economy does this
22. policymakers want to keep this high
25. sound of disapproval
27. should we use this, or follow rules?
30. old
33. this level of GNP is sometimes used as a target
34. classical macroeconomics is built on the _____ of exchange

Down

1. the business _____ is major macroeconomic problem
2. alternative to active management
3. Keynesian aggregate supply reverses this
4. our condition in the long run, said Keynes
5, 24. peak or trough
7, 28. what monetarists want
9. famous mouse
10. type of lag
11. they advise Congress on the budget (abbrev.)
15. here (Fr.)
16. fraction of a week
17. type of lag
20. eliminating this may be a policy objective (2 "words")
21. spider's home
23. stylish (slang)
26. group
29. researchers get paid for this
31. U.S. political party (abbrev.)
32. animal's home

CHAPTER 16

AGGREGATE SUPPLY:

HOW CAN INFLATION AND UNEMPLOYMENT COEXIST?

MAJOR PURPOSE

For several decades following the Great Depression, macroeconomists concentrated on the management of aggregate demand. When the economy was declining into a recession, they advocated expansive demand policies to keep output and employment at high levels. When inflationary pressures were strong, they advocated tighter policies to restrain demand and keep inflation down.

However, during the past two decades, the economy has from time to time given conflicting signals. There have been bouts of *stagflation*—that is, periods when high unemployment was combined with rapid inflation. The high unemployment suggested that demand should be expanded; the rapid inflation indicated the opposite. To understand this complex economy, we must look not only at aggregate demand, but also at aggregate supply. Our purpose in Chapter 16 is to study aggregate supply, and, in doing so, to explore stagflation.

The simplest way to approach aggregate supply is the one presented earlier, in a diagram with real national product on the horizonal axis and the average level of prices on the vertical. However, this is not the approach most commonly used. Instead, economists generally begin with a diagram with the two macroeconomic problems—unemployment and inflation—on the axes. The smooth curve traced out by historical data during some periods, such as the 1960s, is known as a *Phillips curve*. However, the Phillips curve has not been stable in recent decades. One of the major purposes of this chapter is to try to explain why the Phillips curve shifts.

Learning Objectives

After you have studied this chapter in the textbook and study guide, you should be able to:

Summarize the experience of the United States with inflation and unemployment since 1960

Explain why demand-management authorities sometimes feel that they face a policy dilemma

Explain the two major reasons why the (short-run) Phillips curve can shift upward

Explain the difference between cost-push inflation and demand-pull inflation, and explain why cost-push inflation can lead to higher prices *and* higher unemployment

Explain why demand-management authorities face a very difficult problem when there is a large upward shift in the Phillips curve (such as in 1973–1974 and 1979–1980)

Explain why inflation can accelerate to higher and higher rates if the authorities try to keep unemployment below the natural rate

Explain why many economists believe that the long-run Phillips curve is vertical

Explain why Milton Friedman argues that "there is *always* a *temporary* trade-off between inflation and unemployment; there is *no permanent trade-off*"

Explain why some economists argue that there is no trade-off—even in the short run (if you have studied Box 16-2)

Explain why the process of reducing inflation can be painful, in terms of high unemployment

Explain why a stable path of aggregate demand results in a lower average rate of unemployment than a fluctuating path

Describe the major incomes policies used since 1960, and explain the pros and cons of using such policies

HIGHLIGHTS OF CHAPTER

When the demand for a specific commodity—such as wheat—changes, there is a movement *along* the supply curve (as illustrated in Figure 4-8 on page 62 of the textbook). Similarly, when aggregate demand changes, the economy moves along the aggregate supply curve. Thus, when we study aggregate supply in this chapter, we are studying how the economy responds to a change in aggregate demand. This is an important and puzzling topic. From time to time, the economy has suffered from *stagflation*—a combination of high unemployment and high inflation. In such circumstances. it is not clear what the authorities should do. If they take steps to increase aggregate demand in an attempt to increase output and employment, they may get more inflation instead. If they restrain demand in an attempt to reduce inflation, they may get more unemployment. Making sense of the aggregate supply puzzle is an important topic; it is the main purpose of this chapter.

To study aggregate supply, it is possible to use the aggregate supply curve introduced in Chapter 9, with real national product (Q) on the horizontal axis and the average level of prices (P) on the horizontal axis. However, this is not the approach most commonly used. Instead, economists generally begin with a diagram with the two macroeconomic problems—unemployment and inflation—on the axes.

When historical data are plotted on such a diagram in Figure 16-3, two main conclusions stand out:

1. Between 1961 and 1969, the points trace out a smooth curve, sloping upward to the left. This is known as a *Phillips curve*.

2. Since 1970, the observations have been above and to the right of that Phillips curve. We have gotten more unemployment *and* more inflation. Strong movements in a "northeast" direction (upward and to the right) occurred between 1969 and 1970, between 1973 and 1975, and between 1978 and 1980.

During the 1960s, when most economists believed that the Phillips curve being traced out by the data represented a stable relationship, authorities felt trapped on the horns of a *dilemma*. If they expanded aggregate demand briskly, they would get more output and employment. But inflation would rise. On the other hand, if they restrained demand in order to keep inflation down, the unemployment rate would remain high. They hoped to escape from this dilemma by using expansive aggregate demand policies to reduce unemployment, and incomes policies to directly restrain inflation. They were not entirely successful. Inflation in fact did increase as output expanded and unemployment declined. The economy in fact did move upward as it moved to the left in Figure 16-3 in the text.

Shifts in the Phillips Curve

Even worse problems were to come in the 1970s, however, as both inflation and unemployment increased. Two of the three strong movements to the "northeast" in Figure 16-3 coincided with the spiraling price of oil on the international markets. This suggests one explanation for the stagflation since 1970: Rising oil prices shifted the Phillips curve upward, and meant more inflation combined with more unemployment. Inflation was caused by the *upward push of costs*.

Oil prices certainly do not provide the whole explanation, however. The first major movement to the northeast, between 1969 and 1970, occurred while international oil prices were stable at a very low level. In fact, there was something of a glut on the international oil market.

To explain this early episode of stagflation, we must look elsewhere. The *accelerationist theory* provides the most generally accepted explanation.

The Accelerationist Theory

The accelerationist theory, put forward in the late 1960s by Ned Phelps and Milton Friedman, has one core idea. The Phillips curve—such as that observed in the 1960s—is fundamentally *unstable*. If the authorities attempt to reduce the unemployment rate to a very low level, they will succeed, but *only temporarily*. In particular, they will succeed only during the interval between the time when demand is expanded and the time when contracts are renegotiated to take the resulting inflation into account. When people renegotiate contracts, they will demand compensation for inflation; wages and other contractual prices will be adjusted upward. Inflation will accelerate; a *wage-price spiral* will gain momentum. This is illustrated by points H, J, and K in Figure 16-7 of the text. At each of these points, actual inflation is higher than people expected when they negotiated contracts. For example, at H, people expected zero inflation (as illustrated by the Phillips curve), but get 2% instead. They then renegotiate contracts on the expectation of 2% inflation. But, with higher costs, businesses raise prices; the economy moves to J. People expected 2% inflation; they get 4% instead.

How, then, can we return to macroeconomic equilibrium, once the wage-price spiral has begun? Equilibrium occurs only when *people get the amount of inflation they expected*. It is easiest for this to happen when the rate of inflation levels out. For inflation to level out, the authorities must depart from their single-minded attempt to keep unemployment low; they must introduce a degree of restraint in aggregate demand policies. As restraint occurs, businesses will find it hard to raise prices more and more rapidly; inflation will indeed level off. However, as it becomes hard to sell goods, output wil increase more slowly and the unemployment rate will rise.

Once people get the amount of inflation they expect, the unemployment rate will move back to its *natural* or *equilibrium* rate, illustrated by point N in Figure 16-8 of the text. A central proposition of the accelerationist theory is that this equilibrium rate of unemployment *doesn't depend on the rate of inflation*; once people adjust completely to inflation, the inflation rate doesn't affect their behavior. They are neither more nor less willing to work, and businesses are neither more nor less willing to hire them. Because the equilibrium rate of unemployment isn't affected by inflation—once people have gotten used to it—*the long-run Phillips curve is vertical*. In the short run, the central bank can lower the rate of unemployment by an inflationary policy. But in the long run, their willingness to accept an inflation rate of, say, 6% will not result in any gain in output and employment. There is a *short-run trade-off* between the goals of low inflation and low unemployment, but there is *no long-run trade-off*.

Just as low unemployment is associated with an acceleration of inflation, so high unemployment is associated with a deceleration of inflation. If aggregate demand is too low to buy the goods and services being offered at the current rate of inflation, output will fall and businesses will settle for smaller increases in price. This is illustrated by point V in Figure 16-11 of the text. V is not a good place to be; the unemployed are being used as cannon fodder in the war against inflation. In order to avoid painful periods at points like V, it is important to stop the inflationary spiral from gathering momentum in the first place. To those who asked in the 1970s how we might get out of stagflation, there was only one easy—although unsatisfactory—answer: Go back to 1965 and do it right this time. Stop inflation from accelerating in the first place. But, of course, we could not go back to 1965 again. The economy was in fact dragged through the severe recession of 1982 before the inflation rate was brought down to 4%—a rate that was still much higher than that of the period from 1955 to 1965.

Incomes Policies

Incomes policies are sometimes used in an effort to ease the transition to a lower rate of inflation. For example, the wage-price freeze of the Nixon administration was intended to break inflationary expectations without an extended period of high unemployment (at points like V in Figure 16-11). At other times, incomes policies are used to stop inflation from gathering momentum in the first place—for example, the wage-price guideposts of the Kennedy and Johnson administrations.

Incomes policies are controversial. Proponents say that they are the only compassionate way to deal with the inflationary problem—the only alternative is to use the unemployed as draftees in the war against inflation. Opponents say that incomes policies may do more harm than good. For example, by suppressing inflationary pressures temporarily, they may provide the illusion of success, with the authorities unwittingly continuing expansive policies as underlying inflationary pressures build up. The result can be an explosion of inflation, and a worse situation than would be faced if the inflation had not been temporarily suppressed.

Important Terms: Match the Columns

Match the term in the first column with the corresponding phrase in the second column. But before you do so, write out your own definition of the term in the first column.

_____ 1. Phillips curve
_____ 2. Trade-off
_____ 3. Stagflation
_____ 4. Cost-push inflation
_____ 5. Natural rate of unemployment
_____ 6. Accelerationist theory
_____ 7. Incomes policy
_____ 8. Wage-price guideposts
_____ 9. Wage-price freeze
_____ 10. TIP

a. The incomes policy of President Nixon
b. This is aimed at easing the inflation-unemployment dilemma
c. Equilibrium rate of unemployment
d. The incomes policy of Presidents Kennedy and Johnson
e. Relationship between inflation and unemployment
f. High unemployment combined with high inflation
g. An incomes policy backed up with tax incentives
h. View that there is trade-off in the short run, but not in the long run
i. Choice between conflicting goals
j. The rise in the international price of oil is an example

True-False

T F   1. According to the aggregate supply function of simple Keynesian theory, large-scale unemployment *or* rapid inflation can exist, but not both simultaneously.

T F   2. Suppose that money wages were constant through time. Then it would be possible to have a continuous downward trend in prices, if productivity rises.

T F   3. Those who emphasize cost-push inflation are more likely to believe that market power is important than are advocates of the accelerationist theory.

T F   4. According to the accelerationist theory, the economy can be in equilibrium only when the inflation rate is zero; any positive rate of inflation will tend to accelerate.

T F   5. Even when the unemployment rate is at its natural level, there is still frictional unemployment.

T F   6. Even when the unemployment rate is at its natural level, there is still structural unemployment.

T F   7. The short-run Phillips curve has shifted down since 1960; it is now lower than it was in 1960.

T F   8. If the long-run Phillips curve is vertical, then the average rate of unemployment over the long run is independent of both the trend and stability of aggregate demand; aggregate demand is irrelevant in determining the average unemployment rate.

T F   9. Although the actual rate of unemployment has been on an upward trend during the past two decades, the evidence indicates that the natural rate has declined.

T F   10. The TIP proposal is supposed to work by stimulating aggregate demand.

Multiple Choice

1. If we compare the U.S. experience since 1970 with that of the 1960s, we find that, on average:
  a. the rate of unemployment and the rate of inflation have both been lower since 1970 than during the 1960s
  b. the rate of unemployment has been lower since 1970 than during the 1960s, but the rate of inflation has been higher
  c. the rate of inflation has been lower since 1970 than during the 1960s, but the rate of unemployment has been higher
  d. the rate of unemployment and the rate of inflation have both been higher since 1970 than during the 1960s

2. The Phillips curve traced out by the U.S. data of the 1960s suggested that there was a policy "trade-off." Specifically, there seemed to be a conflict between achieving the goal of high employment and the goal of:
  a. an equitable distribution of income   **d.** high growth
  b. allocative efficiency   **e.** low inflation
  c. technological efficiency

3. Economists are most likely to conclude that "cost push" inflation is occurring when a rise in the rate of inflation is accompanied by an increase in:
  a. output
  b. the rate of growth of output
  c. the unemployment rate
  d. government deficits
  e. the money stock

4. Which of the following is an assumption of the accelerationist theory of inflation?
  a. there is downward rigidity in nominal wages
  b. inflation is caused mainly by unions
  c. inflation is caused mainly by OPEC
  d. inflation is caused mainly by an acceleration in investment
  e. people's expectations of inflation have an important effect on the contracts they negotiate

5. Suppose we draw a diagram with both a short-run Phillips curve and a long-run Phillips curve. At the point where they intersect:
  a. the inflation rate is zero
  b. the unemployment rate is zero

  c. actual inflation is the same as expected inflation
  d. inflation is accelerating
  e. the rate of unemployment is rising

6. According to the accelerationist theory, the unemployment rate will be greater than the natural rate when inflation is:
  a. greater than people expected   **d.** high and steady
  b. less than people expected   **e.** zero
  c. low and steady

The next three questions are based on Figure 16-1.

FIGURE 16-1

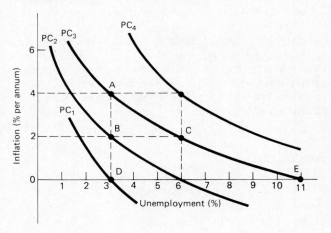

7. In Figure 16-1, the natural rate of unemployment is 6%. Which of the points represents an equilibrium?
  a. A   **d.** D
  b. B   **e.** E
  c. C

8. In Figure 16-1, the natural rate of unemployment is 6%. When the economy is at point A on Phillips curve PC_3, the expected rate of inflation is:
  a. zero   **d.** 4%
  b. 2%   **e.** 6%
  c. 3%

9. In Figure 16-1, the natural rate of unemployment is 6%. Last year, the economy was at point A on short-run Phillips curve PC_3. If contracts are now renegotiated, which of the short-run Phillips curves is most likely to result?

   a. PC_1
   b. PC_2
   c. PC_3
   d. PC_4
   e. either PC_1 or PC_2, but we can't be sure which

10. According to the accelerationist theory, equilibrium can exist only when:

   a. the unemployment rate is at its natural rate
   b. the inflation rate is zero, since any nonzero rate of inflation will tend to accelerate
   c. the expected inflation rate is zero, since inflation will accelerate otherwise
   d. the growth of the money stock is zero, since inflation will accelerate otherwise
   e. all of the above conditions are met

11. Which of the following is likely to cause the highest average rate of unemployment in the long run?

   a. a highly variable rate of growth of aggregate demand
   b. a steady rate of growth of aggregate demand at about 5% per annum
   c. a steady rate of growth of aggregate demand at about 10% per annum
   d. a reduction in the minimum wage
   e. a reduction in the fraction of teenagers in the labor force.

12. Which of the following is likely to reduce the natural rate of unemployment?

   a. a rise in the minimum wage
   b. a fall in the proportion of teenagers in the labor force
   c. more emphasis on fiscal policy, and less on monetary policy
   d. more generous unemployment insurance benefits
   e. all of the above

13. According to the Kennedy-Johnson wage guideposts, the increase in nominal wages was to be held to 3.2% per year. The figure of 3.2% was chosen because that was the estimated rate of:

   a. inflation, and workers therefore needed 3.2% to keep their real wage from falling
   b. inflation, and workers therefore needed 3.2% to keep consumption up and prevent a recession
   c. increase in productivity, and therefore workers could be paid this amount without causing inflation
   d. increase in real GNP, and therefore workers had to get this amount in order to prevent their share of GNP from falling
   e. increase in nominal GNP, and therefore workers had to get this amount in order to prevent their share of GNP from falling

14. The major case for wage-price guideposts or controls is that:

   a. they are the only way to stop inflation
   b. they are the only way to keep profits from falling when labor unions bargain aggressively for higher wages
   c. they are essential if income is to be distributed in a more equitable way
   d. if we rely solely on the restraint of aggregate demand, the fight against inflation will have a high cost in terms of unemployment
   e. they help to shift the long-run Phillips curve to the right

15. Price controls sometime create shortages. Shortages are most likely in the markets for:

   a. luxuries, since their prices are likely to be controlled most tightly
   b. necessities, since their prices are likely to be controlled most tightly
   c. luxuries, since producers will realize that they're not very important socially, and cut back on their production
   d. necessities, since there is a tendency for the demand for necessities to increase at the most rapid rate
   e. services, since their prices are harder to control than goods

Exercises

1. Figure 16-2 represents the Phillips curve for year 1, when the expected rate of inflation is zero. The natural rate of unemployment is _____%. If unemployment is at the natural rate, the rate of inflation will be _____ in year 1. If, alternatively, the unemployment rate is 3%, the actual rate of inflation will be [more, less] than the expected rate by _____%.

Suppose now that the expected rate of inflation is 2% in year 2. Draw the Phillips curve for year 2 in Figure 16-2. If the rate of unemployment is still 3% in year 2, the rate of inflation will be _____%.

If, on the other hand, inflation is 3% in year 2, the rate of unemployment will be slightly more than _____%. Now suppose that the rate of inflation is kept at 3% indefinitely, into years 3, 4, 5. . . . The expected rate of inflation will move to _____%. Alternatively, if

FIGURE 16-2

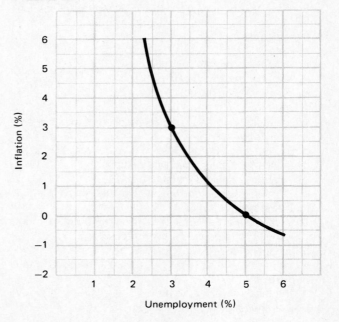

aggregate demand policies are aimed at keeping the unemployment rate at 3%, the rate of inflation will _____.

2a. Suppose the economy is initially at point A on Phillips curve 1 in Figure 16-3. Now the curve shifts to Phillips curve 2. If policymakers pursue restrictive monetary and fiscal policies that keep inflation from increasing, then unemployment will [increase, decrease] by the amount _____. If, on the other hand, they keep the rate of unemployment constant by following more expansionary policies, then inflation will [increase, decrease] by the amount _____.

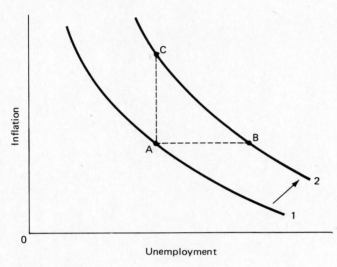

FIGURE 16-3

2b. Suppose this shift in the Phillips curve was caused by workers observing a rate of inflation higher than they had expected. Then, according to the accelerationist theory, the rate of unemployment at A must have been [higher than, lower than, equal to] the natural rate. Therefore, the attempt by policymakers to go to point C

Essay Questions

1. According to the accelerationist theory, the rate of unemployment cannot be kept permanently below the natural rate by an expansive aggregate demand policy. Explain why. Can the rate be kept permanently above the natural rate by a restrictive aggregate demand policy? Explain why or why not.

2. The short-run Phillips curve indicates that when unemployment rises, inflation should fall. But in some years, both inflation *and* unemployment rise. How

this year will cause the Phillips curve to _____ next year.

3. In Figure 16-4, the curve labeled PC_1 is a short-run Phillips curve of the usual shape, based on an expected rate of inflation of 5%. According to this curve, if inflation equals 5% every year, then the rate of unemployment will equal _____% every year. The natural rate of unemployment is _____%. Suppose that the rate of expected inflation remains constant at 5%. Then, if the actual rate of inflation is increased temporarily to 6%, the rate of unemployment will [increase, decrease] to _____%, and if the actual rate of inflation is decreased to 4%, the rate of unemployment will [increase, decrease] to _____%. Therefore, if actual inflation is 6% half the time and 4% the other half of the time, the average rate of inflation will be [higher, lower, no different] than if the rate of inflation was 5% all the time, but the average rate of unemployment will be [more, less] by an amount equal to _____%.

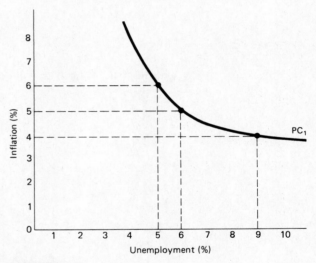

FIGURE 16-4

would an accelerationist explain this? Is there any other explanation?

3. Critics argue that the use of wage-price controls is like trying to cure a sick person by using a thermometer that won't register higher than 98.6°. Why? How can wage-price controls lead to a "sicker" economic patient? How would the defenders of wage-price controls respond?

Answers

Important Terms 1 e 2 i 3 f 4 j 5 c 6 h 7 b 8 d 9 a 10 g
True-False: 1 T 2 T 3 T 4 F 5 T 6 T 7 F 8 F 9 F 10 F

Multiple Choice: 1 d 2 e 3 c 4 e 5 c 6 b 7 c 8 b 9 d 10 a 11 a 12 b 13 c 14 d 15 b
Exercises: 1. 5, 0, more, 3, 5, 4, 3, become more and more rapid.
Figure 16-2 completed:

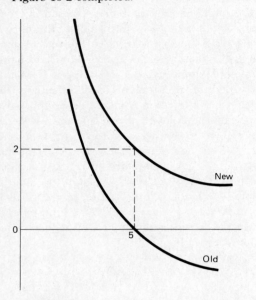

FIGURE 16-2

2a. increase, *AB*, increase, *AC*. **2b.** lower than, shift further up. **3.** 6, 6, decrease, 5, increase, 9, no different, more, 1.

CHAPTER 17

HOW DO WE ADJUST TO INFLATION?

MAJOR PURPOSE

In the previous chapter, we have seen how wage contracts can be adjusted to take account of inflation. The theory of the vertical Phillips curve is based on the view that inflation won't have any affect on the unemployment rate, once people get used to the inflation and adjust to it. This chapter deals with the way in which individuals, businesses, and the government adjust to an inflationary environment. By adjusting, they reduce the effects of inflation on real magnitudes, such as real output and real wages. However, even after two decades of rather rapid inflation, the economy has not adjusted fully to inflation; inflation has significant real consequences. The purpose of this chapter is to study the ways in which the economy does and does not adjust to inflation.

One important set of adjustments is in the market for bonds and other debt instruments. Unanticipated inflation hurts bondholders; they are repaid in less valuable dollars. If they anticipate inflation, however, they can adjust for it. They can withdraw from the bond market until interest rates rise to compensate for inflation. However, even if this happens, with real interest rates remaining constant, inflation can still have important consequences for borrowers and lenders. In particular, the combination of high inflation and high nominal rates of interest means that debt is front-loaded—payments in the early years are high, in real terms. As a result, young people have difficulty buying their first homes.

Another important issue is the effect of inflation on the tax system. Some of the effects of inflation can be offset by *indexation* of tax brackets, deductions, etc. Such indexation was introduced in 1985. However, there are other important effects, such as those arising from the taxation of nominal interest, that are not so easily dealt with. Inflation continues to cause quirks and distortions in the tax system.

Learning Objectives

After you have studied this chapter in the textbook and study guide, you should be able to:

Explain why unanticipated inflation has much stronger effects on the economy than anticipated inflation

Give examples of those who lose from unanticipated inflation, and those who gain

Explain how the real rate of interest is related to the nominal rate of interest and the expected rate of inflation (equation 17-1)

Explain how the behavior of borrowers and lenders tends to stabilize real interest rates

Explain how borrowers—and particularly purchasers of first homes—can be adversely affected by inflation, even if the real rate of interest remains constant

Explain how a graduated payment mortgage can deal with the problem of front-loaded debt

Give an example of how the after-tax real rate of interest may be negative, even though the pretax real rate has remained constant in the face of higher inflation

Explain why a high, uncertain rate of inflation can cause problems in the bond market

Explain the advantages and disadvantages of indexed wages

Explain the problems that can arise if the government uses the real government deficit as a measure of fiscal policy, or if the Fed uses the real quantity of money as a measure of monetary policy

HIGHLIGHTS OF CHAPTER

In Chapter 16, we began to see how the economy can adjust to inflation. As inflation continues, people come to expect it and change their behavior accordingly. For example, labor unions bargain for higher nominal wages to compensate for the increase they have come to expect in the cost of living. If people's expectations are accurate, then the inflation need not affect real wages; it will be taken into account by both workers (who will demand higher money wages) and employers (who will be willing to pay higher money wages). In addition, the rate of unemployment may be unaffected; this was the idea behind the vertical long-run Phillips curve of Chapter 16.

The Real Rate of Interest

Adjustments like this can occur not only in the labor market, but also in other markets. Among the most important are the markets for corporate bonds, government bonds, mortgages, and other debt instruments. If owners of bonds fail to adjust to inflation, they can be severely hurt; they will be repaid in dollars with smaller value. If they anticipate inflation, they will take steps to protect themselves. They can switch out of bonds and into other assets, such as common stock or real estate. When they do so, bond prices fall; that is, interest rates rise. The rise in interest rates is reinforced by the eagerness of borrowers. Because they will be able to repay in less valuable dollars, they have an incentive to borrow more as inflation increases.

The *real rate of interest* is the rate of interest after account is taken of inflation. It is (approximately) the nominal rate of interest less the expected rate of inflation. For example, if the nominal interest rate is 10%, someone lending $100 today will be repaid $110 in one year's time. If the rate of inflation is 10% during that year, the $110 will buy no more than $100 would have bought originally. In real terms, the lender has no gain. The nominal interest rate of 10% is no more than enough to compensate for the 10% inflation; the real interest rate is zero (10% − 10%). This is not very good from the lender's viewpoint. Lenders are therefore likely to be reluctant to make loans, causing a further rise in interest rate. When this happens, the real interest rate becomes positive. Many observers of financial markets believe that the behavior of lenders and borrowers will act to stabilize the real interest rate. This is a difficult hypothesis to test, because the *expected* rate of inflation provides the motive for borrowers and lenders, and expected inflation is not directly observable. Until the early 1970s, evidence suggested that the real interest rate was quite stable. In the early 1980s, however, there was evidence that the real interest rate was high by historical standards.

Even if the real interest rate is constant and infla-

tion is perfectly anticipated, a combination of high inflation and a high nominal interest rate can have an important effect on borrowers and lenders. There are two main reasons for this. The first has to do with front loading; the second has to do with the tax system.

The Duration of Debt: Front Loading

Bonds, mortgages, and other types of debt usually specify a constant *nominal* rate of interest. In a world of zero inflation, a nominal interest rate of 3% represents a real rate of 3%. Someone who has issued a bond with a face value of $100,000 will pay $3,000 in interest each year.

Suppose now that inflation accelerates to 10%, with the nominal rate of interest keeping step at 13%. Someone issuing a $100,000 bond will now have to pay $13,000 in interest per year. This $13,000 includes $10,000 to compensate for the loss of value by the $100,000 principal over the year. The remaining $3,000 represents a real interest payment. In a sense, $10,000 of the $13,000 may be looked on as a partial repayment of principal. In real terms, the borrower is not only paying interest, but is also repaying part of the principal each year. Payments in early years are very high in real terms—the $13,000 represents a lot in the first year. The debt is *front-loaded*.

During periods of rapid inflation and high nominal interest rates, mortgages are similarly front-loaded. As a result, it is very difficult for first-time buyers to afford homes. If they take out a mortgage now, they may face a crushing burden in the early years. This problem would be solved if mortgage payments were fully graduated—that is, if nominal payments rose through the years to keep real payments stable. Such fully graduated mortgages are not available, nor are they likely to become available. The major reason is that they would lead to a rise in the burden of mortgage payments through time if inflation unexpectedly slowed down.

Taxation and Inflation

Taxation is another reason that inflation can have lasting real consequences, even if it is perfectly anticipated. Some taxes, like sales taxes, are a constant percentage of expenditures. If all incomes and prices rise by 10%, so will the number of dollars spent on sales taxes. In real terms, there will be no change in the taxes paid.

Income taxes are different, however. The income tax schedule is progressive; tax rates rise as incomes rise. Thus, there has been a problem of tax-bracket "creep." When prices doubled and incomes doubled in money terms, people were pushed into higher tax brackets. The percentage of their incomes paid in taxes rose. In order to correct the unlegislated increase in taxes that resulted from inflation, the income tax was *indexed*, beginning in 1985. Tax brackets, exemptions, etc., now rise in proportion to prices. If all prices and incomes increase at the same rate, so do tax payments.

However, inflation still has peculiar effects on taxes. Most notably, people pay taxes on their *nominal* interest, and can generally deduct their nominal interest payments from their taxable income. In the earlier example, with $13,000 interest on a $100,000 bond, the taxpayer in the 50% bracket would pay half of the $13,000 in taxes, leaving only $6,500, or 6.5% after taxes. But this would not be enough to compensate for the 10% inflation. The after-tax real rate of interest would be negative.

Inflation and Uncertainty

Another complication that prevents perfect adjustment to inflation is uncertainty. Periods of *rapid* inflation also tend to be periods of *erratic* inflation. This means that bond buyers are taking a risk. High nominal interest rates may compensate for the inflation they expected when they bought the bond. But suppose that inflation speeds up unexpectedly. The bondholder will lose. Similarly, there are risks for the borrower: If inflation unexpectedly slows down, the real burden of interest payments increases. Because erratic inflation poses risks for both borrowers and lenders, a high, erratic inflation may cause the long-term bond market to dry up.

One way to deal with the problem of uncertainty is to have periodic adjustments in interest during the period of the loan. For example, most new mortgages in the United States now have adjustable rates. With the introduction of adjustable rate mortgages, the mortgage market has dealt quite effectively with the problem of *erratic* inflation. But it has not been able to deal with the front-loading problem associated with *high* rates of inflation and interest. Fully graduated mortgages are unavailable.

Indexed Wages

Indexed wages—with adjustments for changes in the cost of living during the contract period—are another way of responding to erratic inflation. Wage indexation became much more common during the 1970s, when inflation was becoming both higher and more erratic.

Indexation is a natural response of labor negotiators to the uncertainties they face. The question arises as to whether indexation makes the economic system work better or not. The answer is that it may. In particular, it may make it easier to unwind inflation without long periods of unemployment. But, on the other hand, indexed wages can speed up a wage-price spiral. Indexation—which represents a way in which labor tries to protect itself from erratic inflation—tends to make inflation even more erratic.

Real Magnitudes and Fiscal and Monetary Policies

Finally, this chapter considers how the government itself might respond to an inflationary situation. One question is how we should measure fiscal policy. Some argue that we should look at the changes in the real deficit of the government. When inflation is rapid—say, at 10%—then the first 10% in interest doesn't really represent interest; it represents a partial repayment of the real value of the debt. Thus, a government with a $1 trillion debt and a $100 billion deficit is not running a deficit at all. In real terms, its budget is balanced; the real value of its debt is constant.

This is a rather interesting idea, but it presents a problem. Indeed, it represents a trap that can be added to the earlier list of traps—such as an annually balanced budget or a monetary policy aimed at a stable nominal rate of interest. Specifically, if inflation increases, the real value of the debt declines. This causes a swing toward surplus in the real budget. If we take the real budget as our guide, we may respond by increasing government spending or cutting taxes. But these steps will increase aggregate demand and make inflation worse.

Similarly, it would be a trap for the Fed to focus on the real quantity of money. During periods of inflation, the real value of the outstanding money stock declines. If the Fed responds by increasing the amount of money in order to restore the real quantity, it will make inflation worse.

Nevertheless, the real debt and the real quantity of money are important. For example, the real quantity of money is an important determinant of how much people will buy. The problem is that real measures must be used *very* cautiously by policymakers. One of the problems with inflation is that it introduces an element of confusion and chaos into the debate over aggregate demand policies.

Important Terms: Match the Columns

Match the term in the first column with the corresponding phrase in the second column. But before you do so, write out your own definition of the term in the first column.

_____ 1. Anticipated inflation
_____ 2. Unanticipated inflation
_____ 3. The real rate of interest
_____ 4. Front loading

a. A limit on indexation
b. A way of dealing with the problem of front loading
c. The effect of inflation in making people pay higher tax rates in an unindexed tax system

_____ 5. Graduated-payment mortgage
_____ 6. Adjustable-rate mortgage
_____ 7. Tax-bracket "creep"
_____ 8. Indexation
_____ 9. Cap

d. This type of inflation has relatively small real effects
e. Automatic adjustment for inflation, as in wages or a tax system
f. This type of inflation has large real effects
g. An effect of inflation, even if real interest rates are constant
h. A way of dealing with the problem of erratic inflation
i. The nominal rate, less the expected rate of inflation

True-False

T F **1.** People who have borrowed large sums usually gain from unanticipated inflation.
T F **2.** Inflation makes lenders more eager to lend, and borrowers less eager to borrow.
T F **3.** When nominal interest rates rise, a new mortgage is "front-loaded" as a result, even if monthly payments on that mortgage are constant in dollar terms throughout the life of the mortgage.
T F **4.** A variable-rate mortgage eliminates the "front loading" of mortgages.
T F **5.** Once tax brackets, the standard deduction, and exemptions are indexed, inflation has no further effect on the real taxes paid by individuals or corporations.
T F **6.** Inflation provides one incentive for borrowers to borrow. The tax system provides another.
T F **7.** If replacement-cost depreciation were introduced in the United States, businesses would face heavier tax burdens.
T F **8.** Wage indexation reduces uncertainty about real wage rates, but increases uncertainty about nominal wage rates.
T F **9.** A COLA clause in an indexed wage contract provides a fixed amount to cover an increase in the cost of living, no matter what the rate of inflation.
T F **10.** Wage indexation generally leads to a more stable, predictable rate of inflation.

Multiple Choice

1. Unanticipated inflation:
a. inflicts losses on bond owners
b. inflicts losses on people who have borrowed
c. provides gains to bond owners, while leaving borrowers unaffected
d. inflicts losses on borrowers, while leaving bond owners unaffected
e. has no effect on real magnitudes because people adjust to it

2. Someone who has taken out a mortgage to buy a house will probably:
a. lose from inflation, especially if it was unexpected when the house was bought
b. lose from inflation, especially if it was expected when the house was bought
c. gain from inflation, especially if it was unexpected when the house was bought
d. gain from inflation, especially if it was expected when the house was bought
e. lose from inflation, but only if there is no mortgage on the house

3. If the nominal rate of interest is 12% and the real rate of interest is 3%, then the expected rate of inflation is:
a. 18%   **d.** 9%
b. 15%   **e.** 3%
c. 12%

4. Market forces can work to keep real interest rates stable. Specifically, in the event of an accelerating inflation:

a. lenders become more eager, and borrowers less eager, causing a rise in the nominal rate of interest
b. borrowers become more eager, and lenders less eager, causing a rise in the nominal rate of interest
c. lenders become more eager, and borrowers less eager, causing a fall in the nominal rate of interest
d. borrowers become more eager, and lenders less eager, causing a fall in the nominal rate of interest

5. A mortgage is most likely to be front-loaded if:
a. nominal interest rates are high, reflecting a high rate of inflation
b. real interest rates are high
c. real interest rates are low
d. inflation decelerates after the house is bought
e. taxes rise after the house is bought

6. If you have a "fully graduated" mortgage:
a. real payments would rise when prices rose
b. real payments would rise when your real income rose
c. real payments would rise when the value of the home rose
d. nominal payments would rise when prices rose, keeping real payments constant
e. nominal payments would rise when your nominal income rose, keeping payments at a constant fraction of your income

7. If the tax code were fully indexed and your money income exactly kept up with inflation, then your:
a. nominal income tax would stay the same

b. real income tax would fall
c. nominal income tax would rise by the same percent as prices, keeping your real tax constant
d. real income tax would rise by the same percent as prices, keeping your nominal tax constant
e. real income tax would rise, but by less than the rate of inflation

8. Consider someone in the 25% tax bracket, holding a bank account paying 8% interest. The rate of inflation is 6%. Then the after-tax real return to that individual is:

a. −2% d. 4%
b. 0 e. 6%
c. 2%

9. Since 1980, real interest rates have been very high, as normally calculated (the nominal interest rate less the current rate of inflation). The most plausible explanation for the high real rates has been:
a. the acceleration of inflation since 1980
b. high unemployment
c. a collapsing stock market
d. rising tax rates
e. large government deficits

10. Adjustable-rate mortgages are aimed primarily at dealing with the problem created by:
a. the tendency of homes to depreciate
b. high inflation
c. erratic inflation
d. the combined effects of inflation and taxation
e. the tendency for real rates of interest to vary with the business cycle

11. During periods of rapid inflation, the real value of trading on the long-term bond market generally:
a. is high, because after-tax real interest rates are high
b. is high, because nominal interest rates are high
c. is low, because the real return on bonds is unpredictable
d. is low, because the real return on bonds is low relative to the real return on short-term securities
e. increases while inflation is accelerating, but then decreases when inflation levels out

12. Which of the following is the strongest argument against the indexation of wages? Wage indexation:
a. makes the rate of inflation more volatile
b. is not compatible with the indexation of the tax code, and tax indexation is more important
c. is not possible without the indexation of the tax code, and tax indexation is undesirable
d. increases the costs, in terms of unemployment, of an anti-inflationary policy
e. keeps the unemployment rate permanently above the natural rate

13. The rule of thumb most likely to stabilize real economic activity and prices is:
a. a slow, steady increase in the real quantity of money
b. a slow, steady increase in the nominal quantity of money
c. a slow, steady increase in the real value of the government's debt
d. a balanced budget every year
e. a stable nominal rate of interest

Exercises

Suppose that you put $200 into a savings account and keep it there for 1 year, at which time it has grown to $220. Then the nominal rate of interest is _____%. If you expected inflation to be 4% during the year, you anticipated a real rate of interest of _____%. Suppose that inflation turned out to be 6% instead. Then, after the year, you would find that your real return was only _____%.

1b. If you are in a 40% tax bracket, you will pay $_____ in taxes. Your after-tax nominal rate of interest will be _____%, and your after-tax real return will be _____%.

2. Figure 17-1 shows the demand and supply for loanable funds in a noninflationary situation. The equilibrium interest rate is _____%. In the same diagram, draw the supply and demand curves that would exist if everyone expected 2% inflation and the economy had adjusted completely to this rate of inflation. The equilibrium nominal rate of interest is now _____%, and the equilibrium real rate _____%. The equilibrium quantity of funds, in real terms, is now [more than, less than, the same as] in the initial situation.

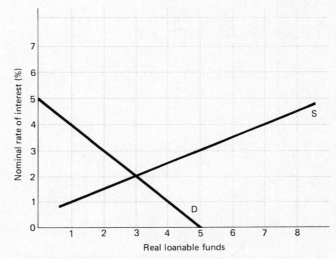

FIGURE 17-1

3. Table 17-1 illustrates a simple progressive income tax.
a. Suppose you have an income of $20,000 initially. Your income tax is $_____, or _____% of your

Table 17-1

Income before tax	Tax
Less than $10,000	0
$10,000 to $20,000	10% of income over $10,000
Over $20,000	$1,000 + 20% of income over $20,000

income. You are left with an after-tax income of $_____ .

b. Now, suppose that one year later, prices are 25% higher than in the initial year. Your pretax income has also increased by 25%, to $25,000. Thus, your real pretax income has [increased, decreased, remained unchanged]. Your tax is now $_____ , or _____ % of your income. In real terms—that is, measured in dollars of the first year—your tax is $_____ . Thus, your real tax burden has [increased, decreased, remained unchanged]. Measured in current dollars, your after tax income is $_____ . Measured in dollars of the first year, this is equal to $_____ . Thus, in real terms, your after-tax income has [increased, decreased, remained unchanged].

c. In Table 17-2, show what the income tax schedule would be in the second year if the tax system were fully indexed.

d. If taxes were in fact fully indexed as shown in Table 17-2, you would pay $_____ in taxes in the second year, leaving $_____ in after-tax income. Measured at prices of the first year, you would pay $_____ in taxes in the second year, leaving $_____ in after-tax income. Thus, between the 2 years, when your real before-tax income was [increasing, decreasing, remaining constant], your real tax burden would [increase, decrease, remain constant].

Table 17-2

Income before tax	Tax
Less than $_____	0
$_____ to $_____	10% of income over $_____
Over $_____	$_____ + 20% of income over $_____

Answers

Important Terms: 1 d 2 f 3 i 4 g 5 b 6 h 7 c 8 e 9 a
True-False: 1 T 2 F 3 T 4 F 5 F 6 T 7 F 8 T 9 F 10 F
Multiple Choice: 1 a 2 c 3 d 4 b 5 a 6 d 7 c 8 b 9 e 10 c 11 c 12 a 13 b
Exercises: **1a.** 10, 6, 4. **1b.** 8, 6, 0. **2.** 2, 4, 2, the same as.
Figure 17-1 completed:

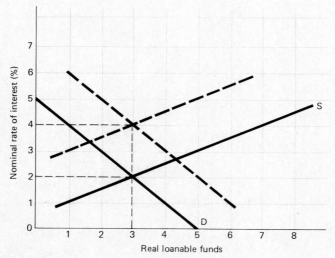

FIGURE 17-1

3a. 1,000, 5, 19,000.   **3b.** remained unchanged, $2,000 (that is, $1,000 + 20% of $5,000), 2/25 = 8%, $2,000 × 100/125 = $1,600, increased, $25,000 − $2,000 = $23,000, $23,000 × 100/125 = $18,400 (also equal to $20,000 in real income less $1,600 in real taxes), decreased.

3c. Table 17-2 completed:

Income before tax	Tax
Less than $12,500	0
$12,500 to $25,000	10% of income over $12,500
Over $25,000	$1,250 + 20% of income over $25,000

3d. $1,250, $23,750, $1,250 × 100/125 = $1,000, $23,750 × 100/125 = $19,000, remaining constant, remain constant.

Across

1, 5. unions may use this as a protection against unexpected inflation
7. common preposition
8. the Federal Reserve influences this (2 words)
11, 12. a characteristic of mortgages when inflation and nominal interest rates are high
13. way of enforcing wage-price guideposts
19, 20. a type of infl___ 'on
21, 22. policymakers often face this
23. on the interior of
24. used by Presidents Kennedy and Johnson to restrain inflation
27. title given to senior government leaders (abbrev.)
28. a way of preventing tax-bracket "creep"
30. a source of minerals
31, 32. a way the bond market may respond to erratic inflation

Down

2. combination of inflation and high unemployment
3. small but important part of a machine
4. person who acts on behalf of someone else
5. in a form that is unreadable by unauthorized persons
6. someone in the final year of college
9. an investigative office established by Congress (abbrev.)
10. à la _____
12. punctured
14. not very exciting
15. ___ West, young man!
16. a common problem at exam time
17. wall painting
18. this type of bank account is included in money supply, M1
21. what Adam Smith's factory made
25. what people do with goods
26. this is very important in a market economy
27. early monetary theorist (see inside cover of text)
28. man's name (abbrev.)
29. a teachers' organization (abbrev.)

CHAPTER 18

PRODUCTIVITY AND GROWTH:

WHY HAVE THEY BEEN DISAPPOINTING?

MAJOR PURPOSE

The major purpose of this chapter is to look at the sources of growth—why output increases. The major reasons are the increase in population, and, even more important, the increase in *productivity*. Economists have been able to identify some of the reasons for changes in productivity—the increase in the *capital stock*, the improved *education* of the labor force, and greater *economies of scale*. But economists do not have a good explanation why productivity slowed down so much during the 1970s. In the 1980s, productivity performance has shown signs of improvement. However, it is difficult to tell if the productivity problems of the 1970s are behind us. One reason is that productivity is *strongly affected by business cycles*. We cannot be sure how much of the recent improvement in productivity in 1983–1985 was due to the recovery from the deep recession, and how much was due to a stronger underlying growth trend.

Learning Objectives

After you have studied this chapter in the textbook and study guide, you should be able to:

Explain the relationship between total output, total number of hours worked, and productivity

Identify the period of most rapid growth in the twentieth century, and the period of slowest growth

Summarize Denison's main conclusions regarding (1) the reasons for increases in output per person in the period 1948–1973 and (2) the reasons for the slowdown of the period 1973–1981

State what the "unexplained residual" may include

Explain why we cannot be sure whether the strong productivity performance of 1983–1984 is the beginning of a strong new growth trend

Describe the relative productivity performances of the major industrial countries, and explain some of the reasons for the differences

Explain how the objective of growth may conflict with other important objectives

Explain why the concept of an "optimal" population is elusive

Explain the "supply-side" strategy, and how supply-side economists hope we might achieve lower inflation and lower unemployment at the same time

Draw a Laffer curve, and explain why it has the shape you have drawn

Using the Laffer curve, explain why an increase in taxes may sometimes lead to an increase in tax revenues, and sometimes lead to a decrease

Explain why a cut in taxes may stimulate investment in some ways, but discourage it in others

Explain the general idea of an "industrial policy," and why some economists are skeptical of such a policy

HIGHLIGHTS OF CHAPTER

The average productivity of labor is equal to total output (Q) divided by the number of labor hours worked (L). To understand the growth of output, we must look at the increases in labor hours and productivity.

Figure 18-1 in the textbook shows these changes since 1800. Over the past century, output has grown at an average rate between 3% and 4% per year. Population has grown somewhat more than 1% per year, while labor hours have grown somewhat less. Productivity has increased at an average annual rate between 2% and 3%.

This increase has not, however, been steady. The improvement in labor productivity was particularly rapid in the quarter century after the Second World War. It was very low—only 0.7% per year—between 1973 and 1981. Since 1981, there are signs that the productivity performance of the U.S. economy may be reviving.

Observe in Figure 18-1 in the text that productivity has generally improved very rapidly when labor hours were growing slowly, and vice versa. With more workers on the job, each works with less capital than would be the case with a lower growth in the labor force. As a result, there is a drag on output per labor hour. When the labor force increases, there are two important effects: (1) *total* output increases, since there is an increase in the labor input; and (2) output *per labor hour* decreases, since the amount of capital per worker is kept down.

Those who have studied productivity and growth in detail include Edward F. Denison. Denison has estimated the reasons for the increase in output per person employed. The first column of Table 18-1 in the text lists his estimates for the period from 1948 to 1973. The most important conclusion is that *no single* item accounted for most of the increase. There were a number of sources, each contributing small amounts to the overall increase in output per person. (In passing, observe that Denison's measure—output per person employed—does not correspond precisely to the standard definition of productivity, namely, output per labor *hour*. However the two measures are very closely related, and the term "productivity" is also applied sometimes to output per *person* employed.)

The second column of Table 18-1 shows Denison's attempt to explain why output per person employed remained stagnant in the period from 1973 to 1981. The most important conclusion here is that Denison's "explanations" don't explain most of the slowdown. In fact, he explains only a third of the deterioration, leaving a large unexplained residual (1.8%, at the bottom of the last column). The reasons for the poor performance during this period remain something of a mystery, although the slowdown in research and development (R&D) and the increase in the price of oil may be more important than Denison estimated.

In the early 1980s, productivity increased more rapidly than during the period from 1973 to 1981. This raises the question of whether we have begun a new period of rapidly increasing productivity. At present, there is not enough information for a firm conclusion. Although productivity increased rapidly in 1983–1984, this was at least partly due to the effects of the business cycle, and may not represent an improvement in the underlying trend.

Since the Second World War, output per person in the United States has grown at about the same rate as in the United Kingdom, and more slowly than in most other major industrial countries, such as France, Japan, and West Germany. One reason for the more rapid growth abroad is that investment in these other countries has generally been a larger share of GNP. Other countries also have the advantage of copying U.S. technology. However, the U.S. technological lead is not so great as it once was, and therefore borrowed technology should give foreign countries a smaller advantage in the future than in the past. Traditionally, R&D expenditures have been a larger percent of GNP in the United States than in the other major industrialized countries. However, U.S. expenditures slowed down in the late 1960s and early 1970s, while expenditures grew in some other countries—most notably, West Germany and Japan. Now these two countries spend about as great a percentage of their GNP on R&D as does the United States (Figure 18-5 in the textbook).

Variations in productivity and growth in recent decades have drawn attention to a fundamental question: Why grow? There are obvious advantages to growth—it makes possible a higher standard of living in the future. But growth also has costs: (1) lower present consumption, as productive resources are diverted away from consumer goods and toward capital formation; (2) leisure foregone (rather than growing so fast, we could take more leisure); and (3) damage to the environment. The faster we grow, the more rapidly we create waste products, and the more rapidly we use our natural resources. However, as we will explain in Chapter 28, the relationship between pollution and economic growth is not necessarily close. It is possible to produce more goods, while at the same time paying more attention to the control of pollution.

The concept of an "optimal population" is considered briefly in this chapter. One idea is that the best population size would be one where real income per capita is at a maximum. However, this idea is not based on very strong foundations, because it is based on the implicit view that additional lives are undesirable if they depress the average standard of living even a little. There is nothing in economics which provides an answer to the question of whether one life is worth more than two lives at a lower per capita income.

Attitudes toward growth have changed in recent decades. The Kennedy-Johnson administrations actively sought to promote growth as a way to raise general living standards, reduce poverty, and keep ahead of the Russians. In the 1970s, the growth objective attracted less support, as people became more concerned over the speed with which we were using our natural resources. The Reagan administration has revived growth as a principal economic objective.

The growth policy of the Reagan administration is sometimes known as "supply-side" economics. One objective is to increase aggregate supply, and thus ease the inflation-unemployment dilemma discussed in Chapter 16. One way of increasing supply is to sharpen incentives by reducing taxes. This was one of the ideas behind the tax cuts enacted in 1981, which were also motivated by the desire to "get the government off the backs of the people." The Reagan administration put a high priority on limiting the role of government in the economy.

One of the theoretical supports for tax cuts was the Laffer Curve. Arthur Laffer argued that tax cuts would lead to increases, not decreases, in government revenues. Thus, a tax cut would be costless: It would benefit the public, without costing the government any revenues. The ballooning of government deficits in recent years suggests that this view is too optimistic.

Some economists argue that it is desirable for the government to have an industrial policy—to direct investment into important industries and help them in other ways. One problem with such proposals is that they often encompass two quite different ideas, namely that the government should help (1) new, high-technology industries with high profits and good growth prospects; and (2) declining industries with low profits and poor prospects.

Important Terms: Match the Columns

Match the term in the first column with the corresponding phrase in the second column. But before you do so, write out your own definition of the term in the first column.

_____ 1. Average productivity of labor
_____ 2. Technological improvement
_____ 3. Economies of scale
_____ 4. A cost of investment and growth
_____ 5. Supply-side economics
_____ 6. Laffer curve
_____ 7. Industrial policy
_____ 8. Lemon socialism
_____ 9. Crowding out

a. This emphasizes tax cuts as a way of encouraging saving, investment, and growth
b. The negative effects on investment, resulting from high interest rates caused by government deficits
c. The direction of investment into specific sectors, and the assistance of these sectors in other ways
d. Government ownership and support of declining industries
e. What exists if an increase of all inputs by 100% leads to an increase of more than 100% in output
f. Inventions and better methods of production
g. Foregone current consumption
h. This shows relationship between tax rates and tax revenues
i. Q/L

True-False

T F   1. If the labor force grows at a rapid rate, this will act as a drag on productivity.
T F   2. If the labor force grows at a rapid rate, this will act as a drag on the growth of output.
T F   3. Since 1929, the average length of the work week has increased, and this has contributed to U.S. economic growth.
T F   4. Between 1973 and 1981, output per person grew more slowly than it had previously, but Denison was unable to explain most of the slowdown.
T F   5. As the economy moves into a recession, output declines, and so does the rate of increase of productivity.
T F   6. The optimal population is the largest that can be maintained at more than subsistence incomes.
T F   7. The goal of economic growth has been emphasized by the Kennedy and Reagan administrations.
T F   8. According to Laffer, higher tax rates would cause a reduction in the government's tax revenues.
T F   9. As we would predict on the basis of the Laffer curve, tax revenues in the United States have increased since the tax cuts of 1981, and the budget has swung from deficit to surplus.
T F 10. Advocates of a new industrial policy usually recommend an across-the-board cut in tariffs.

Multiple Choice

1. When the number of labor hours increases very rapidly, the most likely effect is:
   a. a slow increase in productivity
   b. a very rapid increase in productivity
   c. a very slow increase in total output
   d. no change in output, since workers have less capital
   e. a decline in output, since workers have less capital

2. Between 1981 and 1984, productivity in the United States:
   a. increased more rapidly than at any other time in the past 100 years
   b. increased less rapidly than at any other time in the past 100 years
   c. increased more rapidly than during the period from 1973 to 1981
   d. increased less rapidly than during the period from 1973 to 1981
   e. actually declined

3. One of the topics studied by Denison was the change in the quality of the labor force, as measured by education. Denison concluded that the education of the U.S. labor force has:
   a. improved, and this improvement contributed as much to productivity as the increase in machinery and other physical capital
   b. improved, although this improvement contributed less to productivity than the increase in machinery and other physical capital
   c. deteriorated, since SAT scores have fallen
   d. deteriorated, since literacy levels have declined
   e. deteriorated, at least during the 1970s, since labor productivity deteriorated during that decade

4. National output fluctuates during the business cycle, and so does labor productivity. Specifically, when compared to the long-run average increase, labor productivity during a recession increases:
   a. more slowly, since the average worker has less capital to work with
   b. more slowly, since employers are reluctant to lay off skilled workers, and they accordingly keep underemployed workers on the job
   c. more rapidly, since the average worker has more capital to work with when other employees are laid off
   d. more rapidly, since the threat of layoff encourages workers to work harder
   e. more rapidly, since competitive pressures intensify

5. If we compare U.S. performance with that of France, West Germany, and Japan in the period from 1950 to 1980, we find that U.S. output per person grew:
   a. more slowly than in the other countries, while the rate of investment in the United States was also low
   b. more slowly than in the other countries, even though the rate of investment in the United States was high
   c. at very close to the average rate of the other industrial countries
   d. more rapidly than in the other countries, while the rate of investment in the United States was also rapid
   e. more rapidly than in the other countries, even though the rate of investment in the United States was low

6. Consider an economy in which output *per capita* grows at 2% per year, while population grows at 1.5% per year. Then growth in real GNP is approximately what percent per year?
   a. $2/1.5 = 1.33$ **d.** $1.5 \times 2 = 3$
   b. 1.5   **e.** $1.5 + 2 = 3.5$
   c. 2

7. The tax reductions enacted in 1981 are sometimes spoken of as "supply-side" cuts because:
   a. only the taxpayers who increased their supply of goods were allowed to benefit
   b. an important motive was to stimulate investment and growth
   c. they were designed to stimulate the supply of leisure
   d. they were designed to stimulate the growth of the government sector, and hence overall growth
   e. they were designed to stimulate the growth of the government sector, and hence stimulate saving

8. If a "supply-side" tax cut is successful in shifting the aggregate supply curve to the right, it will:
   a. result in more inflation, more output, and more unemployment
   b. result in more inflation, more output, and less unemployment
   c. result in more inflation, less output, and more unemployment
   d. result in more inflation, less output, and less unemployment
   e. make it easier to suppress inflation without causing unemployment

9. The Laffer curve was intended to show that it might be possible to:
   a. increase net exports without causing inflation
   b. increase net exports and growth at the same time
   c. cut taxes without causing unemployment
   d. cut taxes without causing a reduction in government revenues
   e. cut taxes without causing a reduction in government spending

10. Supply-side economists differ from Keynesian economists in what major way? Supply-side economists are likely to:
   a. emphasize *fiscal* policies, whereas Keynesian economists emphasize *monetary* policy
   b. favor *cuts* in tax rates to stimulate the economy, whereas Keynesian economists favor tax *increases* to stimulate the economy
   c. favor *increases* in government spending to stimulate the economy, whereas Keynesian economists favor *cuts* in government spending to stimulate the economy
   d. believe that cuts in tax rates will *increase* tax revenues, whereas Keynesian economists believe that lower tax rates lead to *lower* revenues
   e. believe that a rightward shift in the aggregate supply curve will *reduce* inflationary pressures, whereas Keynesian economists believe that it will *increase* inflation

11. Critics of supply-side economics argue that a decrease in tax rates may cause a *decrease* rather than an increase in investment and growth, because it will lead to:

    a. an increase in saving, and this will cause a recession because of the "paradox of thrift"

    b. bigger government deficits and higher interest rates, which will discourage investment

    c. bigger government deficits, which will lead to a recession

    d. lower government deficits, which will lead to a recession

    e. lemon socialism

12. Proponents of an industrial policy suggest that the government:

    a. encourage investment in "winning" industries, thus promoting growth

    b. discourage investment in "losing" industries, such as steel, since there is no future in such industries

    c. encourage investment in grain farming, in order to restore America's ability to feed the world

    d. avoid "lemon socialism" by discouraging investment in the citrus industry

    e. all of the above

Exercises

1a. Denison found that, during the period from 1948 to 1973, the increase in output per worker could be attributed to the following four sources (in addition to the unexplained residual, due partly to technological improvement): (1) _____, (2) _____, (3) _____, and (4) _____.

1b. Over this period, a drag on productivity was attributable to _____.

1c. Denison found that he could not explain most of the slowdown in the period from 1973 to 1981. He may have underestimated the effects of (1) _____ and (2) _____.

2. A more rapid rate of increase in population leads to a [more, less] rapid rate of growth of output. It generally acts as a [stimulus to, drag on] productivity, because the average worker has less _____ to work with. However, this effect may be offset, or more than offset, by economies of _____, which act to [increase, decrease] productivity as the size of the economy grows.

3. In Figure 18-1, curves L_1 and L_2 are two alternative Laffer curves. The tax rate in 1980 is illustrated as t_1. According to Laffer, we were at point _____ on curve _____ in 1980, where a cut in the tax rate would cause [an increase, a decrease] in tax revenues. According to Laffer's critics, we were at point _____ on curve _____ in 1980, where a cut in the tax rate would cause [an increase, a decrease] in tax revenues.

FIGURE 18-1

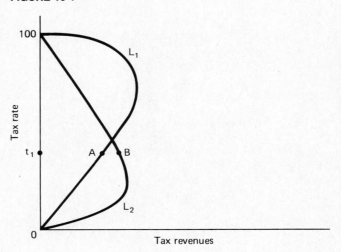

Essay Questions

1. Since 1966, labor hours (L) increased at a much faster rate than between 1919 and 1966 (Figure 18-1 in the textbook). How do you explain this rapid increase? Would you expect a rapid increase in the next decade? What do you think explains the *inverse* relationship between the growth in labor input and the increase in labor productivity? On the basis of these answers, do you have any predictions about what will happen to labor productivity in the next decade? How about the rate of growth of output? Are you confident regarding your last two answers? Why or why not?

2. Recall the "measure of economic welfare" (MEW) introduced in Chapter 7. If this, rather than GNP, were used to measure economic growth and productivity, how would the historical record in Figure 18-1 in the textbook be affected? How would the costs of economic growth be affected? How do your answers depend on how leisure is treated in MEW?

3. What is the simplest concept of an "optimal" population? Do you agree that such a population would be optimal? Why or why not? Do you think that the U.S. government should adopt policies to achieve this population size? Why or why not? What about China? India?

4. Suppose that you were made the head of a government planning organization, to assist industries as part of a national industrial policy. Would you favor assisting new, high-tech industries, or declining industries, or both? Or perhaps neither of these, but some other group of industries? (If so, explain how you would choose your favored industries.) Explain what problems you might encounter in picking industries for assistance, and the problems which might result from your policies.

Answers

Important Terms: 1 i 2 f 3 e 4 g 5 a 6 h 7 c 8 d 9 b

True-False: 1 T 2 F 3F 4 T 5 T 6 F 7 T 8 T 9 F 10 F

Multiple Choice: 1 a 2 c 3 a 4 b 5 a 6 e 7 b 8 e 9 d 10 d 11 b 12 a

Exercises: **1a.** better-educated labor force, increase in physical capita, economies of scale, improved allocation of resources. **1b.** short workweek. **1c.** slowdown in R&D, higher oil prices. **2.** more, drag on, capital, scale, increase. **3.** B, L_2, increase, A, L_1, decrease

Across

2. this occurs when depreciation exceeds gross investment
6. leisure
7. part of the foot
8. fluctuation in economic activity (2 words)
11. won't he _____ learn?
12. epoch
13. country with rapid economic growth
16. a Nobel prizewinner (see inside cover of text)
17. a major source of innovation (abbrev.)
19. study of the environment
24. Q/L
25. pull
26. without this, there would be no production
28. there are many of these in Shakespeare's plays
29. form of capital
32. a national business organization (abbrev.)
33. bright
34. the most important single contributor to the increase in productivity, according to Denison

Down

1. where bright ideas pay off
2. a Nobel prizewinner (see inside cover of text)
3. they develop the SAT exams (abbrev.)
4. help! (abbrev.)
5. important contributor to growth
9. lots of water
10. important for banks
14. on, in, or near
15. helps workers to produce
18. student of productivity and growth
20. product
21. southern cousin of Russians
22. slowed in 1970s
23. Laffer's side
27. rave
30. a cause of slowdown of 1970s
31. above

CHAPTER 19

FIXED OR FLEXIBLE EXCHANGE RATES?

MAJOR PURPOSE

The major purpose of this chapter is to explain the relationship between *international payments* and *macroeconomic policy*. This relationship depends to a considerable extent on the exchange rate system. Under the old *gold standard*, inflows and outflows of gold were a major reason for changes in the money stock, aggregate demand, prices, and unemployment. Changes in aggregate demand which resulted from gold flows were not necessarily best for the domestic economy. A deficit country might go through a painful *deflationary process*, with high unemployment. Under the International Monetary Fund (IMF) system, exchange rates were *pegged*, but a deficit country could escape the need for a painful deflation by devaluing its currency. The present system of *flexible exchange rates* provides countries with a *greater degree of independence* to follow the aggregate demand policies they think best for their domestic economies. However, problems can still be created by the relationship between domestic policies and international transactions. Large U.S. government deficits, combined with monetary restraint, have led to high interest rates, a rise in the dollar on the international exchanges, and to severe competitive problems for a number of basic U.S. industries, such as autos and steel.

Learning Objectives

After you have studied this chapter in the textbook and study guide, you should be able to:

Identify three sources of demand for a country's currency on the foreign exchange markets, and three sources of supply

Describe four options open to a government when the demand or supply for its currency shifts

Explain why intervention in the exchange market does not provide a permanent solution to disequilibrium in the foreign exchange market

Describe the relationship between the gold stock and the money stock under the gold standard

Describe the mechanism of adjustment under the gold standard, and explain why it was "automatic"

Explain the two major shortcomings of the gold standard

Describe how the "adjustable peg" worked

Explain the problems of adjustment, liquidity, and confidence, and describe how they are interrelated

Explain the advantages and disadvantages of flexible exchange rates

Explain the ways in which sharp movements in the dollar have caused problems for the United States

HIGHLIGHTS OF CHAPTER

This chapter deals with the issue of whether a government should regulate the country's exchange rate, and, if so, how. The topic is developed by looking at three historical exchange-rate arrangements: the *gold standard* of the nineteenth and early twentieth centuries; the *pegged-but-adjustable* exchange-rate system of 1945–1971; and the recent system of *flexible* or *floating* exchange rates. As a preliminary topic, the chapter explains the foreign exchange market.

The Foreign Exchange Market

International trade differs from domestic trade for two main reasons: (1) International trade must overcome barriers such as tariffs and (2) international trade involves two or more currencies (national monies). As a result of the second complication, international trade leads to transactions in the *foreign exchange market*, where one national currency is bought in exchange for another.

Exchange rates are determined in the foreign exchange market. The demand for, say, Canadian dollars, arises when people offer foreign currencies in order to buy Canadian dollars. They want the Canadian dollars in order to buy (1) Canada's exports of goods, such as automobiles and newsprint; (2) Canadian services, such as hotel accommodations for tourists; and (3) Canadian assets, such as Canadian government bonds or Canadian nickel mines. On the other side of the market, the supply of Canadian dollars arises when people offer Canadian dollars in order to buy foreign currencies. Canadians use foreign currencies to buy (1) imports of goods; (2) imports of services; and (3) foreign assets.

An *exchange rate* is the price of one currency in terms of another. An exchange rate may be quoted either way. For example, $1 U.S. = $1.25 Can. is the same as $1 Can. = $0.80 U.S. To verify this, multiply each side of the first equation by four-fifths.

An equilibrium exchange rate is one at which the quantity of currency supplied is equal to the quantity demanded. When demand for a country's currency decreases (the demand curve shifts to the left), the government has four options:

1. Buy the surplus quantity of the home currency at the existing exchange rate, in order to prevent the exchange rate from changing.

2. Decrease the supply of the home currency by direct actions, such as increasing tariffs or limiting the foreign assets that citizens are permitted to acquire.

3. Decrease the supply and increase the demand for the country's currency by more restrictive monetary and fiscal policies. By restraining aggregate demand, such policies will keep prices and incomes down, thereby reducing imports and stimulating exports.

4. Let the price of the currency fall to its new equilibrium.

Option 1 is only a temporary expedient. If the shift in demand is permanent, a country will run out of foreign exchange reserves if it relies solely on option 1.

The Gold Standard

The gold standard is an example of a *fixed* exchange-rate system—that is, a system which fixes the exchange rates within narrow limits. If, for example, the pound is worth 4.86 times as much gold as the U.S. dollar, then nobody will pay much more than $4.86 for a pound, or sell it for much less.

Under the gold standard, there was an *automatic adjustment mechanism* ensuring that there would not be large, persistent international imbalances, with one country ending up with all the gold and the others having none. Specifically, a country losing gold had an *automatic* decrease in its money stock for two reasons: (1) Gold itself was one form of money; when gold coins left the country, the money was directly reduced. (2) Gold was also a bank reserve. When banks had smaller gold reserves, their ability to make loans was restricted. As we saw in Chapter 12, the ability of banks to make loans helps to determine the money stock.

The decline in the money stock was the first step in the adjustment process. The remaining steps were as follows: As the money supply fell, aggregate demand, incomes, and prices fell in the deficit country. This made the country's goods more competitive on world markets, and its trade balance therefore improved. This process was aided by an automatic increase in money and inflation in the surplus countries. With prices rising in the surplus countries, it was even easier for the deficit countries to compete. This process—involving changes in the *relative prices* of the goods of the deficit and surplus countries—tended to continue until balance of payments deficits and surpluses were eliminated and gold flows stopped.

Observe that the gold system worked through changes in domestic demand—that is, option 3 in the previous section. However, even though the gold standard worked automatically to eliminate surpluses and deficits, it had two *major* defects:

1. The automatic mechanism could be very costly for a country with a payments deficit because the monetary contraction could cause large-scale unemployment. On the other side, inflationary pressures could be generated in the surplus countries. That is, there could be a *conflict* between the policies needed for a stable domestic prosperity and the monetary changes needed to bring about balance-of-payments adjustment.

2. The gold standard could lead to *very unstable* conditions, particularly if there was a run on the gold reserves of banks. This point was explained in detail in Chapter 13.

The Adjustable Peg, 1945–1971

Under the adjustable peg system:

1. The United States pegged the price of its currency to gold, at the price of $35 per ounce.

2. Other countries intervened in their foreign exchange markets as necessary, to keep the exchange rate within 1% of an official "par value."

3. Countries with temporary balance-of-payments deficits kept their exchange rates stable by selling reserves on the foreign exchange markets. Countries with temporary balance-of-payments surpluses kept their exchange rates stable by buying foreign currencies, thus increasing their foreign exchange reserves.

4. Countries facing a long-term, "fundamental" disequilibrium were to change their official par values. The change in exchange rates would affect the prices of their goods on international markets, and help to eliminate international deficits or surpluses.

There were three major problems with the adjustable peg system:

1. It was not clear how to distinguish between a "fundamental" disequilibrium and a "temporary" disequilibrium.

2. If a government tried to hold its exchange rate close to the official par when speculators believed that there was a fundamental disequilibrium, speculators often made large profits at the government's expense. For example, when a country had a large balance-of-payments deficit, speculators would sell its currency in large quantities. The government would have to use its reserves of foreign exchange to buy up the excess supply of its currency, in order to maintain the peg. As reserves dwindled, this strategy became less and less tenable, and the government was forced to devalue. Speculators were able to benefit by selling high before the devaluation, and buying low after the devaluation. The government, however, lost: It bought high and sold low.

3. The position of the U.S. dollar was precarious. If the United States maintained a strong international payments position, with a surplus, then other countries would not be able to acquire dollars to add to their reserves. But if the United States ran a large deficit—thereby providing other countries with the sizable quantity of dollars they wanted to add to their reserves—then doubts would arise about the ability of the United States to keep the dollar convertible into gold. There would be an incentive for foreign governments to ask the United States for gold in exchange for dollars. In other words, there would be a "run" on U.S. gold reserves. This in fact happened in 1971, leading to a U.S. decision to

suspend convertibility of the dollar into gold—that is, the U.S. government was no longer committed to sell gold in exchange for dollars at a fixed price of $35 per ounce. The crisis atmosphere of 1971–1973 led to the breakdown of the pegged exchange-rate system, and the move to flexible exchange rates.

Flexible Exchange Rates

A flexible exchange rate is allowed to change in response to changes in the demand and supply for foreign currencies. Flexible exchange rates have a number of advantages:

1. When pegged exchange rates break down, flexible rates may be the only feasible option. The lack of a good alternative may be the strongest argument for flexible exchange rates.

2. They permit fiscal and monetary policies to be directed primarily toward the important goal of stabilizing the domestic economy, rather than toward maintaining the exchange rate.

3. A country following stable domestic policies is insulated from foreign inflation (the *virtuous circle*).

The major disadvantages are:

1. Changes in exchange rates may disrupt international trade and investment.

2. Many of the large fluctuations in exchange rates since 1973 appear to have served no useful purpose; they have not been necessary to eliminate fundamental disequilibria.

3. With flexible exchange rates, domestic monetary and fiscal policies are no longer constrained by the discipline needed to keep exchange rates pegged.

4. Depreciation of the currency adds to domestic inflation. A country can fall into a *vicious circle* of depreciation-inflation-depreciation-inflation.

Because of these disadvantages, some of the Western European nations set up the European Monetary System, which provides for pegged rates among their currencies. However, there is more flexibility in this system than in the earlier system of pegged rates. For example, rates do not have to be kept so close to the official value.

Recent Developments

The U.S. dollar has fluctuated widely since 1973. Between 1976 and 1978, as inflation accelerated in the United States, the dollar fell sharply on the exchange markets. Fearing that the country was falling into a vicious circle, the administration moved toward more restrained domestic policies.

Between 1980 and the beginning of 1985, the dollar moved much higher on the exchange markets. Large foreign purchases of U.S. assets were the major reason. The high price of the dollar made U.S. goods more expensive to foreigners, and made foreign goods cheaper to Americans buying with dollars. As a result, U.S. industry had difficulty exporting, and faced severe competition from imports into the domestic market.

One reason for foreign purchase of U.S. assets was the high level of U.S. interest rates, which in turn was partly attributable to large U.S. government deficits. Recall the discussion in Chapter 14 of how the government's deficits caused a rise in the exchange value of the dollar and a trade deficit.

High interest rates in the U.S. and elsewhere added to the severity of the debt crisis faced by a number of developing countries.

Important Terms: Match the Columns

Match the term in the first column with the corresponding phrase in the second column. But before you do so, write out your own definition of the term in the first column.

_____ 1. Foreign exchange
_____ 2. Exchange rate
_____ 3. Deficit in international payments
_____ 4. Par value
_____ 5. Fundamental disequilibrium
_____ 6. Foreign exchange reserves
_____ 7. Devaluation
_____ 8. Depreciation
_____ 9. Speculate
_____ 10. SDR
_____ 11. Dirty float

a. Reduction in the par value of a currency
b. A new reserve, introduced by IMF
c. Buy something in anticipation of a price rise
d. Occurs when governments intervene to influence price of currency
e. Money of another country
f. Officially chosen exchange rate
g. Price of one currency in terms of another
h. Government's holdings of foreign currency
i. Exists when foreign expenditures exceed foreign receipts
j. Reason for devaluation
k. Fall in the market price of a currency

True-False

T F 1. When the Japanese buy Saudi Arabian oil, this creates a supply of yen
T F 2. If the United States cuts its tariffs, this will lead to an increase in imports and an increase in the supply of dollars on the world market
T F 3. The gold standard was *automatic*; it would work without government intervention. This means that it was an example of a clean float.
T F 4. Under the gold standard, a country was expected to change its par value in the event of a fundamental disequilibrium
T F 5. Under the pegged system of the IMF, a country was expected to change its par value in the event of a fundamental disequilibrium
T F 6. One of the problems with the IMF system was that if the United States ran international surpluses, the supply of dollars to add to other countries' reserves would dry up
T F 7. Under a pegged exchange rate system, when foreign exchange speculators make profits, governments lose
T F 8. The IMF creates new SDRs by open market purchases of the bonds of national governments
T F 9. With a pegged exchange rate, sales of reserves are a good way to deal with international deficits, in both the short run and the long
T F 10. Even some of the oil exporters have had problems in making payments on their international debts

Multiple Choice

1. Which of the following is a source of demand for the U.S. dollar on the foreign exchange markets?
   a. purchases of foreign currencies by the Federal Reserve
   b. U.S. demand for foreign goods
   c. U.S. demand for foreign services
   d. U.S. investment in foreign countries
   e. foreign demand for U.S. exports

2. Which of the following leads to a decline in the demand for British pounds on the foreign exchange markets?
   a. a decrease in British purchases of German chemicals
   b. an increase in the number of U.S. tourists in Britain

c. a switch by U.S. consumers from British to Japanese cars

d. an increase in U.S. purchases of British cars

e. an increase in British sales of textiles to the United States

3. Under the old gold standard system, an inflow of gold into the United States caused what sequence of events?

    a. an increase in the U.S. money stock, an increase in the U.S. price level, and an increase in U.S. exports

    b. an increase in the U.S. money stock, an increase in the U.S. price level, and an increase in U.S. imports

    c. an increase in the U.S. money stock, an increase in the U.S. price level, and an increase in spending by foreign visitors to the United States

    d. an increase in the U.S. money stock, an increase in the U.S. price level, and an increse in gold mining in the United States

    e. an increase in the U.S. money stock, an increase in the budget deficits of the U.S. government, and an increase in U.S. imports of goods

4. Under the old gold standard, a country faced a *conflict* between the policies needed for domestic stability and those needed for international adjustment when:

    a. it was losing gold and was in a recession

    b. it was gaining gold and was in a recession

    c. its prices were rising and its tariffs were also rising

    d. its unemployment rate was high

    e. its inflation rate was high

5. In a world of n countries, how many independent exchange rates are there?

    a. n **d.** $2n$

    b. $n - 1$ **e.** n^2

    c. $n/2$

6. From time to time, speculation was a major problem under the adjustable peg system of the early IMF. The major cause of severe speculation was

    a. the wildly fluctuating price of government securities

    b. the wildly fluctuating price of gold

    c. the wild upward and downward movements in the price of oil

    d. speculators would win if the par value were changed, but would not lose much if the par value were held

    e. speculators would win if the IMF made loans to a country to help it maintain the par value of its currency

7. Suppose that, on the foreign exchanges, $1 = 3 DM, while $1 = 12 francs. The exchange rate between the DM and the franc will then be:

    a. 1 DM = 36 francs   **d.** 1 franc = 4 DM

    b. 1 DM = 4 francs   **e.** 1 franc = 36 DM

    c. 1 DM = 1 franc

8. Suppose that a British machine costs £400,000, while the exchange rate is £1 = $2.00. Then the price of that machine, in dollars, is:

    a. $800,000   **d.** $200,000

    b. $600,000   **e.** $100,000

    c. $400,000

9. Under the IMF system of adjustable pegs, one problem was that of "self-fulfilling expectations." This meant that:

    a. when countries expected to have surpluses, they in fact had them

b. when countries expected to have deficits, they in fact had them

c. when officials expected to avoid a devaluation, they usually succeeded, because of the power of positive thinking

d. when speculators thought that a currency might be devalued, they sold it, increasing the probability that it would in fact have to be devalued

e. when speculators thought that a currency might be devalued, they bought it, increasing the probability that it would in fact have to be devalued

10. The "*n*th" country problem arose under the IMF system because:

    a. it was not understood by those at Bretton Woods

    b. not all countries became members of the IMF, and the nonmembers made the system less stable

    c. not all countries became members of the IMF, and the nonmembers held dollars as their principal reserve

    d. not all countries became members of the IMF, and the nonmembers held gold as their principal reserve

    e. there can be only n-1 independent exchange rates in an n-country world

11. A "dirty float" is called "dirty" because:

    a. it is unfair to foreign countries

    b. it is unfair to exporters

    c. it is unfair to importers

    d. it is not "clean;" that is, the central bank intervenes in exchange markets to influence exchange rates

    e. it is not "clean;" that is, the central bank departs from the rule of aiming for a steady growth in the money stock

12. Under a flexible exchange-rate system, which of the following would be a "vicious circle" for the United States?

    a. U.S. inflation causes an appreciation of the dollar on the exchange markets, which causes higher U.S. inflation, which causes more appreciation of the dollar

    b. U.S. inflation causes a depreciation of the dollar on the exchange markets, which causes higher U.S. inflation, which causes more depreciation of the dollar

    c. higher U.S. interest rates lead to a depreciation of the dollar, which causes even higher interest rates

    d. lower U.S. interest rates lead to an appreciation of the dollar, which causes even lower interest rates

    e. lower U.S. interest rates lead to an appreciation of the dollar, which causes U.S. interest rates to rebound sharply

13. Suppose that the price of the U.S. dollar rises on the foreign exchange markets. This will:

    a. encourage U.S. exports, and slow down inflation in the United States

    b. discourage U.S. exports, and make inflation worse in the United States

    c. discourage U.S. exports, and slow down inflation in the United States

    d. encourage U.S. exports, and make inflation worse in the United States

    e. encourage U.S. exports, and ease the U.S. problem of unemployment

14. Which of the following discourage exports of U.S. goods, and encourage imports of foreign goods into the United States:

    a. U.S. inflation and depreciation of the dollar

    b. foreign inflation and a depreciation of the dollar

    c. U.S. inflation and an appreciation of the dollar

    d. foreign inflation and an appreciation of the dollar

    e. a depreciation of the dollar, and an appreciation of foreign currencies

15. U.S. macroeconomic policies contributed to the sharp rise in the exchange value of the U.S. dollar between 1980 and 1984. Specifically:

    a. expansive monetary and fiscal policies made U.S. inflation higher, and this strengthened the dollar

    b. the combination of government deficits and monetary restraint resulted in high interest rates, which encouraged foreigners to buy U.S. assets

    c. the combination of government surpluses and monetary restraint resulted in high interest rates, which encouraged foreigners to buy U.S. assets

    d. the combination of government surpluses and monetary restraint resulted in low interest rates, which encouraged investment in the United States

    e. the combination of government deficits and monetary restraint resulted in low interest rates, which encouraged investment in the United States

Exercises

1. The data in Table 19-1 describe the demand and supply of pounds in the foreign exchange market. Plot the demand and supply curves in Figure 19-1, and label the demand curve D_1.

    a. The equilibrium exchange rate is \$_____ per pound, or £_____ per dollar. The equilibrium quantity of pounds sold is £_____ million, in exchange for \$_____ million.

Table 19-1

Exchange rate ($ per £)	Amount demanded (millions of £)	Amount supplied (millions of £)
1.25	100	40
1.50	90	50
1.75	80	60
2.00	70	70
2.25	60	80
2.50	50	90
2.75	40	100

    b. Suppose now that the demand for pounds decreases by £20 million at each exchange rate. Plot the new demand curve, and label it D_2. The new equilibrium exchange rate is \$_____ per pound. The equilibrium quantity of pounds sold is now £_____ million, in exchange for \$_____

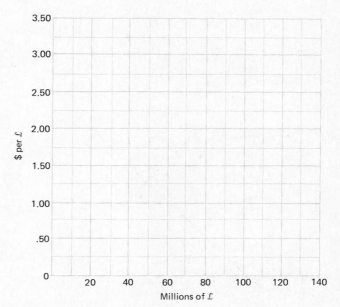

FIGURE 19-1

million. If the exchange rate were held fixed by the British government at its *previous* equilibrium (in part *a*), Britain would now have a balance of payments (surplus, deficit) of £_____ million; that is, \$_____ million.

Essay Questions

1. Suppose that, under the adjustable peg, the British government announced that it was going to devalue the pound by 10% in 1 week. How would this affect the demand and/or supply of pounds today? What would happen to the British government's holdings of dollar reserves? Would there be much risk in speculating today in the market for pounds? Why or why not? Would the government in fact be able to wait for a week before devaluing? Why or why not?

2. In early 1969, there was a public controversy between the German central bank (which wanted to raise the par value of the DM) and the German government (which didn't). What effect do you think this had on exchange markets? Why do you think the central bank took the position that it did? Why do you think the government took the position that it did?

3. How does the gold standard impose a "discipline" upon central banks and governments? What are the advantages of such discipline? The disadvantages? Is there a similar discipline with a pegged-but-adjustable rate? Why or why not? Is there discipline with a floating rate? Why or why not?

4. Explain how a country might fall into a "vicious circle." Now suppose that the world has only two countries, and they are approximately the same size. If one country is in a "vicious circle," will the other country also be in a "vicious circle," or will it be in a "virtuous circle?" Why?

5. Many people believe that there is a relationship between the two large U.S. deficits of the early 1980s— the U.S. government deficits, and the U.S. deficit in international trade. How might one cause the other?

Answers

Important Terms: 1 e 2 g 3 i 4 f 5 j 6 h 7 a 8 k 9 c 10 b 11 d
True-False: 1 T 2 T 3 F 4 F 5 T 6 T 7 T 8 F 9 F 10 T
Multiple Choice: 1 e 2 c 3 b 4 a 5 b 6 d 7 b 8 a 9 d 10 e 11 d 12 b 13 c 14 c 15 b
Exercises: **1a.** $2, £0.50, £70 m, $140 m. **1b.** $1.75, £60 m, $105 m, deficit, £20 m, $40 m.
Figure 19-1 completed:

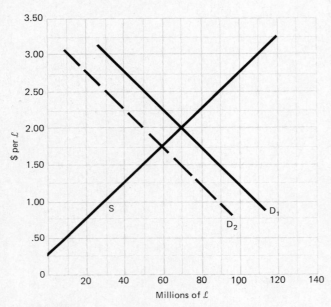

FIGURE 19-1

Across

1. get this by begging
3. 100 centimes
6. European country (abbrev.)
8. international organization of western hemisphere (abbrev.)
10. rate between currencies
12. part of SDR basket (abbrev.)
13. once, the key reserve
14. in the case that
15. I've got a yen to go there
20. problem with a pegged rate (2 words)
21. exchange rate system
24. fastener for clothing
25. the key currency
27. European auto company (abbrev.)
28. small European country (abbrev.)
29. in an emergency, do this
33. paper gold (abbrev.)
34. declaration that one will speak the truth
35. in early 1980s, dollar did this, almost
36. divided Asian country
37. U.S. position in the pegged exchange rate system
38. Middle East country

Down

2. Greek letter
3. type of disequilibrium
4. negative
5. stock market expression
7. U.S. dollar is the _____ currency
9. international financial organization (abbrev.)
11. for example (abbrev.)
12. type of float
16. losing presidential candidate, 1936
17. with pegged exchange rate, may pay to do this
18. once, the key currency
19. Japanese currency
22. a multinational oil company (abbrev.)
23. total reserves
26. an inconvertible currency
27. pig
30. ill-gotten gain
31. take _____!
32. smell

PART FIVE

MICROECONOMICS:

IS OUR OUTPUT PRODUCED EFFICIENTLY?

CHAPTER 20

DEMAND AND SUPPLY:

THE CONCEPT OF ELASTICITY

MAJOR PURPOSE

In this chapter, we begin the detailed study of micro-economics by picking up the supply and demand curves developed in Chapter 4. In that earlier analysis, we saw how a demand curve describes how buyers increase their purchases of a product if its price falls. For some products, this response by buyers will be very strong; for others it may be weak. To illustrate, visualize two demand curves with different slopes that pass through the same point. The flatter one describes buyers who are sensitive to price; they buy much more when price falls. On the other hand, the steeper demand curve describes buyers who are less responsive to price; the amount they buy changes relatively little as price falls. In this chapter we develop a measure—called the *elasticity of demand*—to describe this responsiveness of buyers to price.

A similar concept—*supply elasticity*—is developed to measure the responsiveness of sellers to price. An important question is then addressed: Why are demand and supply highly elastic in some cases, but inelastic in others? Finally, this chapter includes illustrations of how important elasticity may be in answering policy questions such as, Who bears the burden of a tax on a product—the buyers or sellers? and Why do U.S. farmers suffer from such chronic problems that economic recoveries sometimes leave them behind?

Learning Objectives

After you have studied this chapter in the textbook and the study guide, you should be able to:

Define elasticity of demand and elasticity of supply

Compare the elasticity of two demand curves that pass through the same point, showing why the flatter one is more elastic, and explain why slope and elasticity are not exactly the same when curves do not pass through the same point

Describe how a move to a lower point on a demand curve may increase or decrease the total revenue received by sellers from buyers, depending on the elasticity of demand

List four factors that increase the elasticity of demand for a good

List three factors that increase the elasticity of supply for a good

Explain how a commodity tax will affect buyers and sellers of a good, and why the group that is most sensitive to price (most elastic in its response to a price change) will be able to push the burden of the tax onto the other group

Describe the special problems of agriculture, and show how the concept of elasticity can throw light on these problems

Explain how increases in agricultural productivity have affected farm price

Describe the role income elasticity plays in determining the long-run price of agricultural goods

HIGHLIGHTS OF CHAPTER

In developing demand curves in Chapter 4, it was argued that they slope downward to the right. However, little was said about how steep or flat they might be; or more precisely, about how responsive buyers might be to a change in price. Similarly, in developing supply curves, little was said about how responsive sellers might be. For many problems that can be analyzed with supply and demand curves, it is important to have a simple and handy description of this sensitivity of buyers or sellers to price. Elasticity is such a measure.

Elasticity of Demand

This is defined as

$$\text{Elasticity of demand} = \frac{\% \text{ change in quantity demanded}}{\% \text{ change in price}}$$

To illustrate this formula, suppose that, as a result of a shift in the supply of a good to the right, equilibrium moves downward to the right along the demand curve. With the decrease in the per unit price (the denominator above), there is an increase in the amount demanded (the numerator). If these two are equal—that is, if the price and the quantity demanded change at the same rate, then the elasticity of demand in the equation above is equal to 1. Moreover, the *total* payment buyers make to sellers does not change. To see why this is so, suppose that when the price P paid by buyers falls by 1%, the quantity Q that they purchase rises at the same rate. Then the decrease in P is offset by the increase in Q, and there is no change in P times Q, the total payment made by buyers. This is the first conclusion: When the elasticity of demand is 1, there is no change in the total payment by buyers—that is, in the total revenue received by sellers.

Now suppose buyers are *more responsive* to a price change—as in panel *a* of Figure 20-1 of the text, where the quantity they demand increases by 60% (from 1,000 to 1,600 units) when the price falls by 20% (from $10 to $8). In this case, demand elasticity exceeds 1 in the equation above, and there is an *increase* in PQ, the total revenue received by sellers from buyers. In this case, demand is described as "elastic."

In panel *b* of that same diagram, buyers are *less responsive* to a price change: The quantity demanded increases by only 10% when the price falls by 20%. This is the unresponsive, inelastic case; the elasticity ratio in the equation above is less than 1, and there is a *decrease* in the total revenue received by sellers. Before you leave Figure 20-1 in the text, it is essential that you are comfortable with the way elasticity and total revenue are related.

In that diagram, slope and elasticity seem to be closely related: The flatter curve in panel *a* is the more elastic. Is this generally true? The answer is yes—but

only if the two curves being compared pass through the same point. (In Figure 20-1, the common point is E_1.) You should be sure you can recognize cases—such as the one shown in Figure 20-3 in the text—where a flatter curve is *not* more elastic.

Elasticity of Supply

This can also be calculated, using a ratio like the one in the equation above. The only difference is the obvious one—quantity demanded must be replaced with quantity supplied.

$$\text{Elasticity of supply} = \frac{\% \text{ change in quantity supplied}}{\% \text{ change in price}}$$

Whereas elasticity of demand has an important "total revenue" interpretation, elasticity of supply does not. The reason is that a move upward and to the right on *any* supply curve—regardless of its elasticity—will increase total revenue. The one simple interpretation of elasticity of supply is this: If a straight-line supply curve passes through the origin, it has an elasticity of supply of 1.

What Determines Demand and Supply Elasticity?

Demand elasticity tends to be greater if (1) the product is a luxury rather than a necessity, (2) it is a large item in purchasers' budgets rather than a small one, (3) it is easy for buyers to replace it with substitutes in consumption, and (4) we are considering the long-run, rather than the short-run, demand. The elasticity of supply tends to be greater if (1) the commodity can be inexpensively stored—that is, if it is not perishable and has low storage costs; (2) it is easy for users to replace with substitutes in production; and (3) we are considering the long-run, rather than the short-run, supply.

One of the most important of these influences on both supply and demand is time—the short run versus the long run. The reason is simple: If people—whether they are consumers or producers—are given a longer time to adjust to a change in price, they will be able to do more adjusting than if they are only given a short time.

Using Elasticity to Analyze the Burden of a Tax

The first important application of the concept of elasticity is in analyzing whether buyers or sellers bear the burden of a commodity tax. The conclusion from this analysis is important because it applies to any marketplace where two groups face each other, with buyers on the one hand and sellers on the other. The "inelastic" group that can't back away from the market but must complete the transaction almost without regard to price will bear more of the burden of a new tax or any other similar disturbance than will the more "elastic group" that is prepared to resist a price change by backing away from the market.

Using Elasticity to Analyze the Special Problems of Agriculture

For many food products there is (1) a highly inelastic demand curve; (2) a highly inelastic supply curve (at least in the short run); (3) large year-to-year fluctuations in the short-run supply curve, depending upon the state of the weather, and therefore on the harvest from one year to the next; (4) a great deal of technological change in recent decades which has produced large shifts to the right in the supply curve; and (5) relatively smaller shifts to the right in the demand curve, because as income increases over time, the public's spending on food doesn't increase as fast. (There is a low-income elasticity of demand, defined as the percentage change in the quantity demanded divided by the percentage change in *income*.)

In combination, influences (1) and (3) above have created large fluctuations in price. You can see this by drawing a very inelastic demand curve and shifting the supply curve back and forth. Notice how any shift in the supply curve changes price dramatically because demand is inelastic. To confirm this conclusion, draw an elastic demand curve instead, and show how exactly the same shifts in supply result in less change in price.

Moreover, influences (1) and (3) generate large fluctuations not only in farm price, but also in the income (that is, the revenue) received by farmers. Inelastic demand means that as price falls, farmers' income falls; as price rises, so does farm income. The change in farm price becomes a dominant influence over farm income.

As a background to all this, influences (4) and (5) have contributed to a long-run downward trend in agricultural prices, because they have caused the supply curve to shift to the right by more than the demand curve. Note, however, that some observers think that influence (4) will be less important in the future; according to this view, the future will bring smaller shifts to the right in supply. Be sure you can show in a diagram how a slowdown in the rightward shift in supply could reverse the downward trend in prices.

Important Terms: Match the Columns

Match the term in the first column with the corresponding phrase in the second column. But before you do so, write out your own definition of the term in the first column.

_____ **1.** Total revenue
_____ **2.** Elasticity of demand
_____ **3.** Elasticity of supply
_____ **4.** Income elasticity of demand
_____ **5.** Cross elasticity of demand
_____ **6.** Unit elasticity of demand
_____ **7.** Joint products

a. A measure of how strongly the quantity demanded responds to a change in income. It is defined as the percentage change in quantity demanded divided by the percentage change in income.

b. The percentage change in quantity supplied divided by the percentage change in price, as equilibrium moves from one point to another on a supply curve.

c. The amount of money received by sellers of a product. This also equals the amount of money spent by buyers of the product.

d. A measure of the effect the price of good Y has on the demand for good X. It is defined as the percentage change in the quantity of X divided by the percentage change in the price of Y. This is positive if X and Y are substitutes, and negative if they are complements.

e. The percentage change in quantity demanded divided by the percentage change in price, as equilibrium moves from one point to another on a demand curve.

f. Two products that result from one production process. To illustrate, beef and hides result from the production of beef.

g. When the percentage change in the quantity demanded is equal to the percentage change in price.

True-False

T F **1.** A move to a new lower equilibrium on an elastic demand curve means that total revenue falls.

T F **2.** A straight-line demand curve has the same elasticity at each point on the curve.

T F **3.** If the elasticity of demand is 1, then a 1% change in price will lead to a greater than 1% change in the quantity demanded.

T F   **4.** Arc elasticity of demand is defined as

$$\frac{\text{Change in quantity demanded/average quantity demanded}}{\text{Change in price/average price}}$$

T F   **5.** Elasticity of demand describes how responsive buyers are to a change in price, while elasticity of supply describes how responsive sellers are.

T F   **6.** If short-run demand elasticity is 1, then in the long run, demand will be inelastic.

T F   **7.** The government intervenes in agriculture markets to prevent prices from rising above a specified level.

T F   **8.** If the elasticity of supply of agricultural goods were 1, then an increase in demand would not affect price.

T F   **9.** The past downward trend in farm prices (relative to other prices) has occurred because improvements in farm technology have shifted the supply curve to the right more rapidly than the demand curve has been shifting.

T F   **10.** Because agricultural prices tend to be very stable in the short run, the only price problem in agriculture has been a long-term downward trend.

T F   **11.** When the government is stockpiling wheat, its price is higher than it would otherwise be.

Multiple Choice

1. If people reduce their consumption of coffee by very little, even when its price skyrockets, we can conclude that:
  a. supply is elastic
  b. supply is inelastic   **d.** demand is inelastic
  c. demand is elastic   **e.** demand has unit elasticity

2. If the elasticity of demand is greater than 1, then a 10% reduction in price will result in:
  a. no change in quantity demanded
  b. an increase of less than 10% in the quantity demanded
  c. a decrease of less than 10% in the quantity demanded
  d. a decrease of 10% in the quantity demanded
  e. an increase of more than 10% in the quantity demanded

3. The income elasticity of demand is the percentage change in:
  a. quantity demanded divided by the percentage change in price
  b. income demanded divided by the percentage change in price
  c. price divided by the percentage change in quantity demanded
  d. quantity demanded divided by the percentage change in income
  e. income divided by the percentage change in price

4. If the elasticity of supply is 3, then a 1% increase in price will:
  a. reduce the quantity supplied by 3%
  b. increase the quantity supplied by 3%
  c. increase the quantity supplied by 1%
  d. triple the quantity supplied
  e. reduce the quantity supplied by one-third

5. A move to a new, higher-price equilibrium on a supply curve means that total revenue:
  a. will not change
  b. may rise or remain unchanged   **d.** must fall
  c. may fall or remain unchanged   **e.** must rise

6. If the price of X goes from $1.50 per dozen to $2.50 per dozen, and suppliers are willing to increase from 9,000 to 11,000 the amount they offer for sale, then the arc elasticity of supply is:
  a. 0.10
  b. 0.4   **d.** 2.5
  c. 0.8   **e.** 4.0

7. In the long run, the elasticity of demand for foreign travel is high because:
  a. it is a necessity
  b. it is a luxury
  c. airliners can easily switch from transporting goods to transporting people
  d. travel has no substitutes in consumption
  e. travel has no substitutes in production

8. A technological change that shifts the supply curve to the right will cause total revenue to:
  a. rise if demand is elastic
  b. fall if demand is elastic
  c. rise if demand is inelastic
  d. rise if the elasticity of demand is 1
  e. fall if the elasticity of demand is 1

9. The burden of a commodity tax is born entirely by buyers:
  a. in any case
  b. if supply has unit elasticity
  c. if demand has unit elasticity
  d. if demand has infinite elasticity
  e. if demand has zero elasticity

10. A bumper crop will lower farm income:
  a. regardless of demand and supply elasticity
  b. if demand is elastic
  c. if demand is inelastic
  d. if demand and supply have equal elasticity
  e. if demand elasticity is infinite

11. Improvements in agricultural productivity tend to:
  a. raise farm prices and income
  b. lower farm prices
  c. raise farm prices, but lower farm income
  d. have no effect on farm prices
  e. have no effect on farm income

12. The base period in farm parity calculations is:

a. 1900–1904 **d.** 1920–1924
b. 1910–1914 **e.** 1930–1934
c. 1914–1920

13. Some people believe that long-run food prices will rise because:

   a. farmers will stay on the land, rather than taking jobs in the city

   b. the risk of drought in foreign countries will be eliminated

   c. population growth will be reduced in developing countries

   d. the supply curve will shift more rapidly to the right than the demand curve

   e. the supply curve will shift less rapidly to the right than the demand curve

14. Relative to other prices, farm prices have been:

   a. stable in the short run, with a long-term upward trend

   b. stable in the short run, with a long-term downward trend

   c. unstable in the short run, with neither an upward nor a downward long-term trend

   d. unstable in the short run, with a long-term downward trend

   e. unstable in the short run, with a long-term upward trend

15. Increased productivity at IBM has led to:

   a. a cut in its prices and profits

   b. an increase in its prices and profits

   c. an increase in its prices, and a cut in its profits

   d. a cut in its prices, and an increase in its profits

   e. a cut in its prices, and no change in its profits

Exercises

1a. If equilibrium is at A in Figure 20-1, total revenue is area _____, which is $_____. Total revenue at point B is area _____, that is, $_____. D_1 is [elastic, inelastic, unit elastic] because, as price falls, total revenue [increases, decreases]. To be more precise, we can calculate the elasticity of D_1 from the formula

$$\frac{\% \text{ change in } \underline{\hspace{1cm}}}{\% \text{ change in } \underline{\hspace{1cm}}} = \frac{\underline{\hspace{1cm}}\%}{\underline{\hspace{1cm}}\%} =$$

FIGURE 20-1

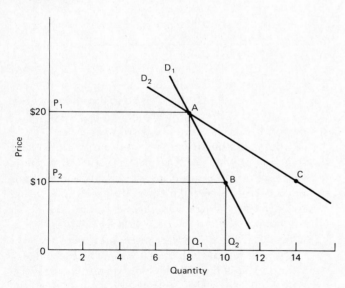

1b. D_2 is [more, less] elastic than D_1. We know this because the percentage change in price between A and C is (more than, less than, the same as) the percentage change in price between A and B, while the percentage change in quantity between A and C is (more than, less than, the same as) the percentage change in quantity between A and B.

2. Draw in a supply curve through point A and mark it S_1. Draw in another supply curve through point B and mark it S_2. Mark the point where S_2 cuts D_2 as F. If supply is initially at S_1, and it shifts to S_2, then the change in price is greater if demand is $[D_1, D_2]$; that is, the change in price resulting from a shift in supply is greater if demand is [more, less] elastic.

3a. In Figure 20-2, supply curve S_1 is [elastic, inelastic, unit elastic] because it _____. If price rises from P_1 to P_2, then the equilibrium on S_1 moves from point _____ to point _____. On the other hand, for supply curve S_2, this change in price would move equilibrium from point _____ to _____. The quantity response to this change in price is [greater, less] for S_2 than for S_1. S_2 is therefore [more, less] elastic than S_1. It is [true, not true] that if two supply curves pass through the same point—such as A—the flatter one is the more elastic. This conclusion is [the same as, quite different

FIGURE 20-2

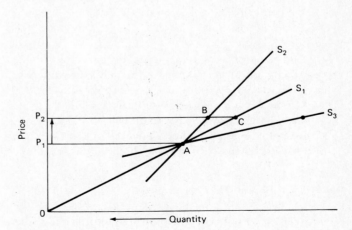

from] the one we arrived at in comparing slopes of demand curves. In general, if any straight line supply curve such as S_2 cuts the *quantity* axis, it is [elastic, inelastic].

3b. Now consider S_3. As price rises from P_1 to P_2, the quantity response is [greater, less] than for S_1. S_3 is therefore [more, less] elastic than S_1. It is still [true, not true] that if two supply curves pass through the same point—such as A —the flatter one is the more elastic. In general, if any straight line supply curve like S_3 cuts the *price* axis, it is [elastic, inelastic].

4. Draw in a demand curve through point A and mark it D_1. Draw in another demand curve through point B and mark it D_2. Mark the point where D_2 cuts S_1 as F. If demand is initially at D_1, and it shifts to D_2, then the change in price is greater if supply is [S_1, S_2]; that is, the change in price resulting from a shift in demand is greater if supply is [more, less] elastic.

5a. The data in Table 20-1 describe hypothetical demand and supply curves for apples. Plot these curves in Figure 20-3 and mark them S and D. Mark the equilibrium as point A, where the price of apples is $_____ per bushel, and the equilibrium quantity is _____ million bushels. Suppose the government sets a price floor at $19, making it illegal to sell apples at a price below this. Mark the new equilibrium in Figure 20-3 as B, and draw in an arrow showing the excess [demand, supply]. Mark this arrow BC.

Table 20-1

Price per bushel	Millions of bushels demanded	Millions of bushels supplied
$ 5	25	5
10	20	10
15	15	15
20	10	20
25	5	25

5b. If we compare points A and C we find that the percentage change in price is approximately _____. The percentage change in quantity that sellers would like to supply is approximately _____; therefore, the elasticity of supply is _____.

6a. Suppose now that the government cancels its price floor, and instead requires the sellers of apples to pay a sales tax of $10 per bushel. When the buyers now pay $15 per bushel, the sellers get to keep only $_____ per bushel after they pay the $10 per bushel tax. Thus, according to Table 20-1, they will supply _____ million bushels. Fill in the rest of Table 20-2.

Essay Questions

1. At the end of the chapter highlights section, the following general rule is given: The smaller the elasticity

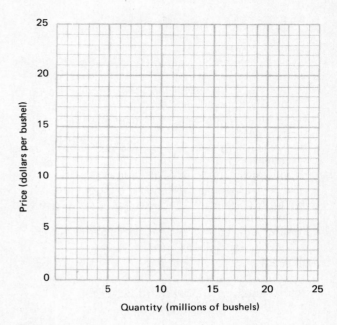

FIGURE 20-3

Table 20-2

(1) Price per bushel paid by demanders (including tax)	(2) Amount per bushel received by sellers	(3) Millions of bushels supplied
$10	$ 0	0
15	_____	_____
20	_____	_____
25	_____	_____

6b. Plot the new supply curve in Figure 20-3 and mark it S'. The new equilibrium price (paid by demanders) is $_____, and the new equilibrium quantity is _____. Of the $10 per bushel paid in sales tax, sellers are paying $_____, and buyers are paying $_____.

7. Draw a straight-line demand curve D' passing through point A which is more elastic than D. If this new demand curve were to replace the old demand curve, the equilibrium price *before* the imposition of the tax would be [higher, lower, no different], and the equilibrium quantity before the tax would be [higher, lower, no different]. The equilibrium price after the tax would be [higher, lower, no different] than with the old demand curve, and the equilibrium quantity would be [less, more, no different]. With the new demand curve, the amount of tax paid by buyers would be [more, less], and the amount paid by suppliers would be [more, less] than with the old demand curve.

of supply or demand, the larger the changes in equilibrium prices resulting from a shift in the other curve. Is it possible to state a similar rule with respect to equilibrium quantities? (Hint: See Figures 20-1 and 2 above.)

2. The U.S. government will not allow a huge U.S. bank (like Continental Illinois) or a huge auto company (like Chrysler) to go bankrupt, but it will allow farmers or other small businesses to go bankrupt. Is this government policy fair? Can it be justified on some other grounds?

3. Why might farmers sometimes hope for poor crops? (Hint: Refer to Box 20-2 in the textbook.) Which would result in the highest price of corn in Iowa: (a) A drought everywhere except in that state, (b) a drought everywhere except in the United States, (c) a drought everywhere except in North America, or (d) a drought nowhere. Explain.

4. (The next two questions are more difficult.) If you were a monopolist (a single seller) and you discovered that the demand for your product was inelastic, would you want to raise its price or lower it? Why?

5. It has been argued that stores issue trading stamps to discriminate against people who cannot be bothered collecting, licking, and redeeming the stamps. These people end up paying a higher price for their purchases than those who use the stamps, because only the users receive a "discount" in the form of the items they get with the stamps. Suppose you were the owner of a large chain of stores and you wanted to engage in this kind of price discrimination (that is, raise the price to nonusers of stamps, and lower it to users). What would happen to your total revenue if the demand by users of stamps were elastic and the demand by nonusers were inelastic? What would happen to your total revenue if the demand by users were inelastic and the demand by nonusers were elastic?

Answers

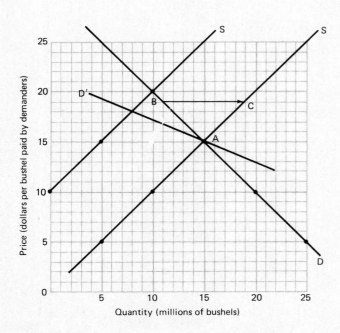

Table 20-2 completed:

(1)	(2)	(3)
$10	$ 0	0
15	5	5
20	10	10
25	15	15

6b. $20, 10, $5, $5.   **7.** no different, no different, lower, less, less, more.

CHAPTER 21

DEMAND

MAJOR PURPOSE

In the last chapter, we measured elasticity of demand and elasticity of supply, and we saw how important they are in analyzing policy problems. In this chapter, we get down to the fundamentals of demand; we examine the foundations of the demand curve. (In the next two chapters, the fundamentals of supply will be similarly examined.)

Three other major objectives in this chapter are (1) to analyze how the consumer facing a given price arrives at equilibrium, (2) to examine and measure how much the consumer benefits when the price of a product falls, and (3) to consider the other costs, in addition to price, that are incurred when someone purchases a good or service.

Learning Objectives

After you have studied this chapter in the textbook and the study guide, you should be able to:

Show how the market demand curve is constructed by adding up the individual demand curves

Define marginal benefit

Explain the principle of diminishing marginal utility (diminishing marginal benefit)

Describe the condition that must be fulfilled for a consumer to be in equilibrium

Use Adam Smith's champagne/water paradox to explain the importance of total utility as well as marginal utility

Use the demand curve to measure how consumers lose when price rises, citing two reasons for this loss

Explain how this measure of damage to the consumer can be used, along with the concept of elasticity from the previous chapter, to analyze the effect, for example, of a Florida freeze. How are all parties—citrus growers, consumers, and the nation as a whole—affected?

Show why purchasers must take into account not only price, but also transactions costs, including search (information) costs

Explain why search costs include not only out-of-pocket costs, but also time costs, and why time costs are also important in using a product

HIGHLIGHTS OF CHAPTER

The first fundamental characteristic of the demand curve that must be recognized is an obvious one: A market demand curve is simply the sum of all the individual demand curves. This is illustrated in Figure 21-1 in the textbook. In turning to the other characteristics of demand, we begin by examining the demand curve of one individual consumer.

Interpreting a Demand Curve

Underlying each individual demand curve are the two basic concepts introduced in Chapter 2—scarcity and choice. Thus the consumer can be viewed as choosing between two scarce goods, such as apples and cherries. This choice is described in Box 21-1 in the textbook and the Appendix to this chapter. Another view is that the consumer chooses between apples and *all* other goods—that is, between apples and money, since money is the means of acquiring all other goods. This is the choice that is described by the demand curve for apples, which tells us how much money the consumer is willing to give up to buy one box of apples, how much more to buy a second box, and so on.

Notice that here we are taking a different approach to the demand curve. In previous chapters, we have viewed the demand curve as telling us, *at each given price*, how many boxes of apples the buyer would purchase. The answer is given by each of the *horizontal* arrows in Figure 21-2a of the textbook. Now, we are viewing the demand curve as telling us, *at each given quantity*, how much money the consumer is willing to pay per box for that quantity of apples—as shown by the *vertical* arrows in panel *b* of that diagram.

Willingness to pay is typically a good indicator of how highly the consumer values each additional box of apples—that is, willingness to pay measures the *marginal benefit (marginal utility)* of apples. The more a consumer buys, the less marginal utility is derived from another box. In other words, the further to the right the consumer goes in making more and more purchases in Figure 21-2b, the shorter these vertical arrows of marginal utility become. This is why the demand curve for apples slopes downward to the right. In simplest terms, the more apples you eat, the less interested you become in eating any more. Formally stated, this is the *law of diminishing marginal utility*, which states that as more and more of any product is acquired, *eventually* the utility (or benefit) provided by one more unit must fall.

Consumer Equilibrium

With this background, the equilibrium of the consumer is now easily described. Because the marginal benefit of the first box of apples—as shown by the first arrow in Figure 21-3 of the textbook—is higher than the market price of $6, the consumer buys that box. For the same reason, the consumer buys a second box, a third, and so on. Purchases cease when the marginal benefit of another box falls to the level of price. (Beyond that, where marginal benefit has fallen below price, further purchases are obviously not justified.) This then provides an important conclusion: In equilibrium, the consumer purchases up to the point where the marginal benefit of a product equals its price.

How the Consumer Is Affected by a Change in Price

Figure 21-3 in the text also shows the concept of consumer surplus. In purchasing the first box of apples, the consumer enjoys a $4 surplus; the individual is willing to pay $10 for that box of apples, but it only costs $6. Similarly, there is a $3 surplus on the next box, and so on. The consumer purchasing five boxes acquires a surplus equal to all these arrows above the $6 price line, that is, the surplus is equal to the area of triangle FEP. Thus consumer surplus is the area of the triangle to the northwest of the point of equilibrium on the demand curve.

In Figure 21-5 of the text, these concepts are used to show how much the consumer benefits from a price reduction. At original price P and equilibrium at E, the consumer surplus is area FEP. When the price falls to $2 and equilibrium moves to E_2, the consumer surplus is area FE_2P_2, for an increase of PEE_2P_2—the area enclosed to the left of the demand curve between the old and new price. This is the consumer benefit if the price falls from P to P_2—or, of course, the consumer loss, if the price rises from P_2 to P.

Application of the Theory

This measure of consumer loss from a price increase is applied in Figure 21-6 in the textbook to the case of the typical Florida freeze that has made citrus scarce and has driven up its price. It is shown that the consumer loss must exceed any conceivable gain to producers and thus result in an overall loss to society as a whole. (Producers did gain from the crop loss in this case, because demand was inelastic; that is, the increase in price more than compensated for their reduced sales. However, in cases of elastic demand, producers would lose.)

This example also illustrates an important fallacy of composition—that is, the fallacy of arguing that what applies to an individual also applies to all individuals taken together. An individual farmer whose own crops are damaged is worse off because of a freeze. But, taken together, all farmers may benefit.

Costs to the Consumer in Addition to Price

The price of a good is not the only cost to a buyer. In addition, the buyer may also face *transaction costs*.

These may include dealer or brokerage fees in making the actual purchase, plus any *search costs* (information costs) that must be undertaken. Search costs are the costs incurred in making an intelligent purchasing decision. They may include out-of-pocket costs of buying publications that compare products, plus the "time costs" involved in studying these publications. There are also time costs in using products once they are pur-chased. If your new car turns out to be a lemon, you will incur a lot of time costs in taking it back and forth for repair. Thus if your time is worth a great deal, you are more likely to buy a reliable car that minimizes this time cost. In general, it is important in any purchasing decision to consider not only price, but all of these other costs as well.

Important Terms: Match the Columns

Match the term in the first column with the corresponding phrase in the second column. But before you do so, write out your own definition of the term in the first column.

_____ 1. Total benefit (total utility)
_____ 2. Marginal benefit (marginal utility)
_____ 3. Substitution effect
_____ 4. Income effect
_____ 5. Law of diminishing marginal utility
_____ 6. Consumer equilibrium
_____ 7. Consumer surplus
_____ 8. Search cost (information cost)
_____ 9. Time cost
_____ 10. Transactions costs

a. The additional satisfaction derived from one more unit of a product
b. When the price of a good falls, this is the increase in sales that occurs because the purchaser's real income has risen
c. When the price of a good falls, this is the increase in sales that occurs because this good has become less expensive relative to other goods
d. A situation in which the marginal benefit of each good just equals its cost
e. The difference between the amount that a consumer would be willing to pay for a good and the amount that actually is paid for it
f. As more and more of a good is consumed, a point is eventually reached where marginal utility begins to decline.
g. The time and money spent in collecting the information necessary to make an informed purchase
h. The total satisfaction derived from a product
i. All costs (except price) associated with buying or selling anything, including search costs and other costs such as fees or commissions
j. The time spent shopping for a good and using it

True-False

T F 1. If marginal benefit has fallen below the price of a good, the consumer has bought too much.
T F 2. If a consumer's purchase of a good is less than the equilibrium amount, marginal benefit will still be greater than the price of the good.
T F 3. The reason why a demand curve slopes down is that ultimately each consumer's marginal utility falls as the individual consumes more.
T F 4. Consumer surplus is the difference between what people would be willing to pay for a good, and what they, in fact, do pay.
T F 5. A Florida freeze would not result in any overall loss to the nation if the elasticity of demand were equal to 1.
T F 6. If drought damages the wheat crop, producers gain exactly what consumer lose.
T F 7. Time-saving devices are more prevalent in low-wage countries than high-wage countries.

Multiple Choice

1. The market demand for a good is the:
   a. vertical sum of the individual demands
   b. average of the individual demands
   c. horizontal sum of the individual demands

d. vertical product of the individual demands

e. horizontal product of the individual demands

2. The market demand curve has:

a. less slope than the individual demand curves

b. more slope than the individual demand curves

c. more slope or less; you can't tell in general

d. the same slope as the individual demand curves

e. more slope, if the individual demand curves are elastic

3. According to the substitution effect, a fall in the price of apples results in:

a. an increase in the purchases of apples because other goods have become cheap relative to apples

b. an increase in the purchases of apples because apples have become less expensive relative to other goods

c. a decrease in the purchases of apples because apples have become less expensive relative to other goods

d. a decrease in the purchase of apples because the buyer's real income has risen

e. an increase in the purchases of apples because the buyer's real income has risen

4. A consumer will continue to purchase a good until its:

a. marginal benefit falls to zero

b. marginal benefit falls to the level of its price

c. total benefit falls to the level of its price

d. total benefit falls to zero

e. total benefit rises to the level of its price

5. The amount of a good that a consumer purchases should depend on its:

a. marginal benefit only

b. search cost only

c. price only

d. price and search cost only

e. marginal benefit, search cost, and price

6. According to the law of diminishing marginal utility:

a. the utility from another unit can never rise

b. marginal utility must always fall

c. marginal utility must always be negative

d. marginal utility must rise at first, but eventually it may fall

e. marginal utility may rise at first, but eventually it must fall

7. If water and champagne had the same upward-sloping supply curve:

a. they would certainly sell for the same price

b. they would be likely to sell for the same price

c. champagne would be more expensive

d. water would be more expensive

e. no prediction could be made about their prices

8. If we know only the selling price of a perfectly competitive good, then we know:

a. the total benefit it provides

b. the total cost of producing it

c. its total cost and total benefit

d. the marginal benefit it provides

e. none of the above

9. If price increases, there is:

a. a gain to the consumer equal to the area to the left of the demand curve between the old price and the new price

b. a loss to the consumer equal to the area to the left of the demand curve between the old price and the new price

c. a loss to the consumer equal to the area to the left of the supply curve between the old price and the new price

d. a gain to the consumer equal to the area to the left of the supply curve between the old price and the new price

e. no effect on the consumer

10. Consumer surplus is a "triangle" with two sides being:

a. the vertical axis and the horizontal axis

b. the horizontal axis and the price line

c. the horizontal axis and the demand curve

d. the vertical axis and the price line

e. none of the above

11. In which case do consumers enjoy the least consumer surplus? (Assume in each case that they face the same price and purchase the same quantity.)

a. when demand elasticity is 1

b. when demand is highly inelastic

c. when demand is highly elastic

d. when supply elasticity is 1

e. when supply is highly elastic

12. If drought damages the wheat crop:

a. consumers lose, producers benefit, and the nation overall benefits

b. consumers lose, producers lose, and the nation overall loses

c. consumers and the nation lose; producers may benefit or lose

d. producers and the nation lose; consumers benefit

e. producers and the nation lose; consumers may benefit or lose

13. The more willing the public is to bear search costs:

a. the more variation there will be in price quoted by sellers

b. the less variation there will be in price quoted by sellers

c. the higher will be the price quoted by sellers

d. the greater the overcharging by wholesalers and retailers

e. the greater the overcharging by retailers, but not wholesalers

14. Time costs are:

a. greater in a high-income country, which is one reason why less reliable cars are purchased there

b. greater in a high-income country, which is one reason why more expensive and reliable cars are purchased there

c. less in a high-income country, which is one reason why more expensive and reliable cars are purchased there

d. less in a high-income country, which is one reason why less expensive and reliable cars are purchased there

e. less in a high-income country, but this doesn't affect the cars that are purchased there

15. A consumer buying two goods will be in equilibrium if:
  a. the ratio of the marginal utilities of these goods is greater than their price ratio
  b. the ratio of the marginal utilities of these goods is less than their price ratio
  c. the ratio of the marginal utilities of these goods is equal to 1
  d. the ratio of the marginal utilities of these goods is equal to their price ratio
  e. some other condition is met; the price ratio is irrelevant

Exercises

1a. If the price for the product shown in Figure 21-1 below is $7, then _____ units will be purchased, because this is the quantity where marginal benefit, as given by the height of the _____ curve, is equal to _____. There are two interpretations of any point such as R on an individual's demand curve. The first is that R indicates the *quantity* that will be purchased at a certain price—in this case $7. This interpretation is shown by arrow _____. The second is that R indicates, at a given quantity, the maximum *price* that the buyer is willing to pay for the marginal unit—in this case the 100th unit. This second interpretation is shown by arrow _____. Since this arrow indicates how much the consumer will pay to acquire that 100th unit, it measures the value the consumer puts on that unit—that is, the [total value of all 100 units, marginal benefit of that 100th unit].

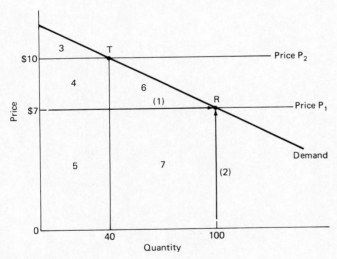

FIGURE 21-1

1b. The total benefit the consumer gets from all 100 units purchased is area _____, which is the sum of all the [horizontal, vertical] marginal benefit arrows like

_____ enclosed beneath the _____ curve throughout the range of quantities between _____ and _____. However, this purchase costs the consumer area _____, which is the quantity of _____ units multiplied by the $_____ price. Therefore, the *net* benefit to the consumer of this purchase is area _____, which is sometimes called _____.

2. If price increases to $10, the new equilibrium is at _____, where the quantity purchased is _____ units. The demand curve between R and T is [elastic, inelastic] because the % change in quantity is [less, more] than the % change in price. The total benefit from this smaller purchase is area _____. However, the cost is area _____, which is the quantity of _____ units times the $_____ price. Therefore, the *net* benefit to the purchaser when price is $10 is area _____.

3a. Since the net benefit to the purchaser when the price was $7 was area _____, and that benefit was reduced to area _____ when the price rose to $10, the burden of this price increase on the consumer is area _____, which is the area enclosed to the [left, right] of the _____ curve between the old price and the new price.

3b. Let's look at this from another point of view. Because price has risen, the consumer is buying _____ units less. The total benefit the consumer used to get on these units—and has now lost—is area _____. However, the consumer is no longer incurring the cost, shown by area _____, of purchasing these units, since they are no longer being bought. Therefore, the *net* loss of the consumer on these units that are no longer purchased is area _____. In addition, the consumer is hurt because of the greater amount that has to be paid on the first 40 units (that *continue* to be purchased). The higher cost to the consumer on these units is area _____, which is the $_____ price increase times those 40 units.

Thus, in summary, we confirm that the loss to the consumer because of the price increase is area _____. This is made up of a loss of area _____, because purchases are reduced, plus a loss of area _____, because of the higher price that must be paid on purchases that continue to be made.

Essay Questions

1. People derive more benefit from the water in the world than they do from all the diamonds in the world. Yet diamonds cost far more than water. Would diamonds be more expensive than water if the two had the same supply curve and were thus equally scarce? Explain your answer.

2. To judge by the amount of time spent, most people seem to derive more utility from watching television than from going to movies. Yet they will pay $4 or $5 to go to a movie, when they could stay home and watch television for nothing. Can you explain this?

3. When Henry Ford invented the mass production of automobiles, what effect do you suppose this had on the typical marginal benefit schedule for horse-drawn carriages? What do you suppose it did to the price and sales of horse-drawn carriages?

4. Heroin addicts find that the more they consume, the more they want. Does this contradict or illustrate diminishing marginal utility? Can you use this heroin example to illustrate the law of diminishing marginal utility?

Answers

Important Terms: **1** h **2** a **3** c **4** b **5** f **6** d **7** e **8** g **9** j **10** i
True-False: **1** T **2** T **3** T **4** T **5** F **6** F **7** F
Multiple Choice: **1** c **2** a **3** b **4** b **5** e **6** e **7** d **8** d **9** b **10** d **11** c **12** c **13** b **14** b **15** d
Exercises: **1a.** 100, demand, price, (1), (2), marginal benefit of that 100th unit. **1b.** 3 + 4 + 5 + 6 + 7, vertical, (2), demand, zero, 100, 5 + 7, 100, $7, 3 + 4 + 6, consumer surplus. **2.** T, 40, elastic, more, 3 + 4 + 5, 4 + 5, 40, $10, 3. **3a.** 3 + 4 + 6, 3, 4 + 6, left, demand. **3b.** 60, 6 + 7, 7, 6, 4, $3, 6 + 4, 6, 4.

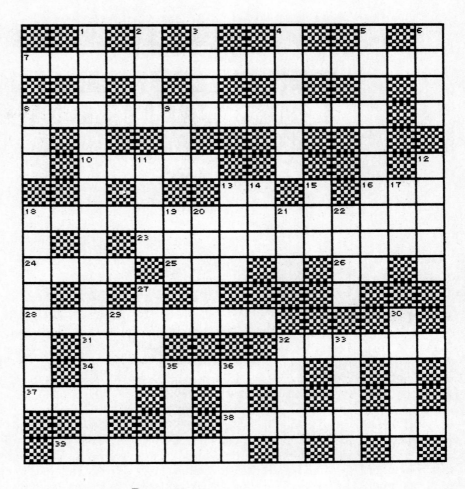

Across

7. benefit of consumers in excess of what they pay
8. beef and leather provide an example of _____ _____ (2 words)
10. laissez _____
13. indefinite article
16. a means of travel
18. benefit from consuming one more unit (2 words)
23. when the price of one increases, the demand for the other increases
24. where people skate
25. sound of disgust
26. 1st person, possessive
28. unresponsive to a change in price
31. bounder
32. an important economic objective is to reduce this
34. price is likely to be _____ when both demand and supply are inelastic
37. member of one of the British Houses of Parliament
38. fundamental reason for study of economics
39. if demand is elastic, total _____ increases when price is reduced

Down

1. this joins all points that provide equal satisfaction (2 words)
2. oxidized iron
3. close
4. area just outside a city
5. measure of how much quantity responds to a change in price
6. a continent
8. what an unemployed person wants
9. official price of a currency under pegged exchange rate system
11. part of the eye
12. an appointment of lovers to meet
13. in addition
14. a fruit covered with a woody shell
15. very successful movie or song
17. devoured
18. the _____ tax rate is the tax rate on additional income
19. central idea
20. all around
21. game without a winner
22. a small piece
27. passing fashions
29. one of the factors of production
30. one of the objectives of economic policy
32. this is used in producing many manufactured goods
33. low business activity
35. ripped
36. the _____ year is the year from which price changes are measured

CHAPTER 22

COSTS AND PERFECTLY COMPETITIVE SUPPLY:

THE SHORT RUN

MAJOR PURPOSE

In the last chapter we saw how a demand curve reflects the desire of buyers to acquire a good. In this chapter, our attention turns to supply. It will be shown that a supply curve reflects the marginal cost of producing a good. Specifically, just as you can visualize a whole set of marginal benefit bars enclosed below a demand curve, you can also visualize a whole set of marginal cost bars enclosed below a supply curve. To establish this important conclusion, we examine the cost curves facing a firm, and analyze a profit-maximizing firm's short-run response to various market prices. At each price, the firm will supply a quantity determined by its marginal cost curve (provided its variable costs are covered). Therefore supply reflects marginal cost.

We also show how the economist's definition of a firm's cost is far broader than an accountant's. For an economist, costs include not only the out-of-pocket costs that accountants take into account, but also implicit costs such as the opportunity costs of the owner's time and capital invested in the firm. Because the opportunity cost of capital—that is, normal profit—is included by an economist in calculating a firm's costs, any additional (excess or economic) profit is a return that can be earned in this industry above and beyond the return that can be earned elsewhere. Therefore, it is an incentive for more resources to move into the industry.

Learning Objectives

After you have studied this chapter in the textbook and the study guide, you should be able to:

Explain why, in the short run, some costs are fixed and some are variable, while in the long run all costs are variable

Define total, variable, fixed, and marginal costs; also average cost, average variable cost, and average fixed cost

Explain the law of (eventually) diminishing returns, and why this law means that marginal costs must eventually rise

Show why the equilibrium condition "marginal revenue = marginal cost" must be satisfied by any profit-maximizing firm

Show, as one specific case of the general theorem above, that "price = marginal cost" is the condition for profit maximization by a firm in perfect competition

Explain, using a diagram, why a firm's average cost curve is cut, at its minimum point, by its marginal cost curve

Demonstrate why the short-run supply curve of a perfectly competitive firm is its marginal cost curve (above its average variable cost curve)

Explain the difference between accounting costs and economic costs, and why opportunity costs must be included in economic costs

Explain why an economist defines costs to include normal profit, but not excess profit

HIGHLIGHTS OF CHAPTER

In our examination in this chapter of what underlies the cost curve—just as in our parallel examination in the last chapter of what underlies demand—we assume that rational self-interest is pursued. Specifically, in this chapter, we assume that producers supply the quantity of a good that will maximize their profit.

In this chapter, we focus on the short run—the period in which the firm cannot change the amount of plant and equipment it is using. In the next chapter, we turn to the long run, when the firm *is* able to vary the amount of capital and equipment it uses.

An important concept in this chapter is marginal cost MC—the cost of producing one more unit of output. If we graph MC, it must eventually rise, because of the law of (eventually) diminishing returns.

Given the firm's MC and other cost schedules, the question is: How much will the firm supply at any given price? The rule for *any* profit maximizing firm is to produce until MC = marginal revenue MR, where MR is the additional revenue earned from producing one more unit of output.

This general rule—that a firm will produce until MC = MR—can be stated in an alternative way for a perfectly competitive firm. The reason is that such a firm takes the price of its output as given. Therefore, its MR is just the price that it faces. For example, if it sells apples for a price P = $2 a basket, then each additional basket provides $2 of extra revenue MR. Because its MR = P, the profit-maximizing rule for a perfectly competitive firm can be stated thus: It continues to produce until MC = P. Thus at any given price, the firm will supply a quantity of output that can be read off its MC curve; in other words, the quantity supplied depends on the firm's MC curve. Be sure that you fully understand Figure 22–3 in the textbook. This is the diagram that most clearly demonstrates why the firm will produce until MC = P; and why, therefore the firm's supply curve reflects its marginal costs.

In defining the firm's supply, there is one more important consideration. Price must be above a certain minimum level, or the firm won't supply anything at all. This minimum level is the price that will generate enough revenue to cover the firm's variable costs; more specifically, price must be at least as high as the firm's "shutdown point" on its average variable cost (AVC) curve—that is, point K in Figure 22-5 in the textbook. As long as price is at least this high, then in the short run, the firm will supply this product. This is true, even if the price is still below the "break-even point" (H in the same diagram) where the firm is just barely able to cover its total cost, including both its variable costs *and* its fixed costs. Even though a firm operating between these two points is incurring a loss, it is still able to cover its variable costs and have at least something left over to cover part of its fixed costs. Therefore, it is better to continue to operate than to close down altogether. (If it closes down, it would be worse off: It would be unable to cover *any* of its fixed costs.) It should be emphasized that this analysis applies only to the short run when the firm cannot escape its fixed costs. However, in the long run it can escape these fixed costs, and it will do so. At any price below its break-even point, it will close down. Thus, our more precise conclusion is this: In the short run, the perfectly competitive firm's supply curve will be that part of its MC schedule lying above the minimum "shutdown" point on its AVC schedule. However, in the long run, the minimum price necessary to keep the firm in business will be at its break-even, rather than its shutdown, point.

The final important topic covered in this chapter is the difference between economic costs and accounting cost. While the accountant looks only at explicit, out-of-pocket costs, the economist also considers implicit costs, such as the opportunity costs of the owner of a firm. This opportunity cost includes the salary the owner could have earned in another job, and the interest income or dividends that the owner could have earned by investing his or her capital elsewhere. This alternative possible income on capital is called the firm's normal profit; it is the amount that is necessary to keep capital in that firm. Because economists thus include normal profit as a cost, when they speak of "profit" they mean excess profit—that is, additional profit above and beyond normal profit. Such above-normal or excess profit is important for the operation of the market system, because whenever it exists, it acts as a signal to attract resources into that industry.

Important Terms: Match the Columns

Match the term in the first column with the corresponding phrase in the second column. But before you do so, write out your own definition of the term in the first column.

_____ 1. Short run
_____ 2. Long run
_____ 3. Short-run production function
_____ 4. Marginal product
_____ 5. Law of (eventually) diminishing returns

a. The return an input could earn in its best alternative use
b. The sum of both fixed and variable costs
c. The increase in total revenue from the sale of one more unit. In perfect competition, this is the same as market price.

_____ 6. Fixed costs
_____ 7. Variable costs
_____ 8. Total cost
_____ 9. Average cost
_____ 10. Marginal cost
_____ 11. Marginal revenue
_____ 12. Break-even point
_____ 13. Shutdown point
_____ 14. Opportunity cost
_____ 15. Economic cost
_____ 16. Normal profit
_____ 17. Economic profit
_____ 18. Long-run production function
_____ 19. Economies of scale
_____ 20. Perfect competition

d. The point at which the marginal cost curve intersects the average variable cost curve. If the price falls below this, the firm will cease operating even in the short run.

e. The time period over which the firm's capital stock is variable.

f. The relationship between the amount of variable factors used and the amount of output that can be produced, when the amount of capital is constant

g. Explicit accounting costs, plus the implicit opportunity costs that are considered by economists but not by accountants

h. Total revenue minus economic cost; a return in addition to normal profit

i. The income that could be earned if capital were to be invested elsewhere. Economists view this item as a cost because it is the opportunity cost of the firm's capital.

j. The point at which the marginal cost curve intersects the average cost curve, and the firm makes a zero profit

k. Total cost per unit

l. The increase in total cost when output is increased by 1 unit

m. The time period over which the firm cannot vary its capital stock

n. The relationship that shows the maximum output that can be produced with various combinations of all the different inputs

o. All costs that change with output in the short run

p. The additional output the firm can produce by hiring one more unit of a factor

q. Costs that do not vary as output increases; also called *overhead* or *sunk* costs

r. Description of costs if doubling all inputs more than doubles the firm's output. This typically means that the long-run average cost curve is falling.

s. If more of a factor is employed while other factors are held constant, the marginal product of that factor must eventually fall.

t. A market in which there is freedom of entry and so many buyers and sellers of a standardized product that none has any influence over price

True-False

T F   1. If output is zero, variable costs are zero

T F   2. When marginal cost is more than average cost, then average cost must be rising.

T F   3. The law of diminishing returns states that the marginal product of any factor must eventually fall if other factors are held constant.

T F   4. The law of diminishing returns is unrealistic because it implies that we could feed the world from our back garden.

T F   5. Marginal revenue is total revenue less the cost that results when one more unit is produced.

T F   6. If a competitive firm is producing slightly less than the profit-maximizing amount, then price is greater than marginal cost.

T F   7. In the short run, the firm stops producing whenever price falls below its minimum average cost.

T F   8. When existing firms earn economic profit, then that industry is attractive for new firms.

T F   9. Economic profit is the profit that remains after account is taken of all explicit and implicit costs, including normal profit.

T F   10. If a firm is operating at capacity—that is, with a completely inelastic supply (MC) curve—then an increase in market price will result in no increase in its total revenue or output.

Multiple Choice

1. An example of a variable cost is:
   a. wage payments
   b. rental payments on a long-term lease
   c. interest payments on a mortgage
   d. depreciation costs
   e. all of the above

2. As output increases in the short run:
   a. fixed costs increase, but variable costs do not
   b. fixed costs decrease, but variable costs do not
   c. fixed costs and variable costs change
   d. neither fixed costs nor variable costs change
   e. variable costs increase, but fixed costs do not

3. As output increases in the short run:
   a. fixed cost falls
   b. fixed cost rises
   c. fixed cost has less and less influence on average cost
   d. fixed costs has more and more influence on average cost
   e. average fixed cost rises

4. A firm's costs are related in the following way:
   a. Average cost AC cuts marginal cost MC at the minimum point of MC.
   b. Average cost AC cuts average variable cost AVC at the minimum point of AVC.
   c. MC cuts AC at the minimum point of AC.
   d. MC cuts AC where the price line intersects AC.
   e. AVC cuts AC at the minimum point of AC.

5. If total costs are rising, then marginal cost must be:
   a. rising
   b. falling
   c. positive
   d. negative
   e. zero

6. The law of diminishing returns means that, as output increases in the short run:
   a. fixed cost will eventually fall
   b. fixed cost will eventually rise
   c. marginal costs will eventually rise
   d. marginal costs will eventually fall
   e. marginal costs will eventually become constant

7. In the long-run decisions of a firm:
   a. employment of labor is held constant, while its use of capital is allowed to increase
   b. employment of labor is held constant, while its use of capital is allowed to decrease
   c. use of capital is held constant, while its employment of labor is allowed to vary
   d. both are allowed to vary
   e. neither is allowed to vary

8. If a firm's fixed cost is $100, and its total cost is $200 to produce 1 unit and $310 to produce 2, then the marginal cost of the second unit is:
   a. $100
   b. $110
   c. $200
   d. $210
   e. $310

9. If a firm's fixed cost is $100, and its total cost is $200 to produce 1 unit, and $310 to produce 2, the firm is:
   a. already facing diminishing returns
   b. not yet facing diminishing returns
   c. not yet facing constant returns
   d. already facing increasing returns
   e. facing constant returns

10. The competitive firm's short-run supply curve is that part of its short-run marginal cost curve that lies above its:
    a. average cost curve
    b. average variable cost curve
    c. average fixed cost curve
    d. total cost curve
    e. fixed cost curve

11. The shutdown point is:
    a. the minimum point on the average cost curve
    b. the minimum point on the average variable cost curve
    c. the minimum point on the marginal cost curve
    d. the minimum point on the average fixed cost curve
    e. the point where marginal cost cuts the average fixed cost curve

12. If a perfectly competitive firm is producing more than the profit-maximizing amount, then price must be:
    a. above marginal cost
    b. equal to marginal cost
    c. below marginal cost
    d. below average variable cost
    e. equal to average variable cost

13. In the short run, the break-even point is:
    a. at the intersection of the marginal cost curve and the average fixed cost curve
    b. below the intersection of the marginal cost curve and the average fixed cost curve
    c. the same as the shutdown point
    d. above the shutdown point
    e. below the shutdown point

14. If a firm's total cost and total revenue curves (TC and TR) are plotted, the firm maximizes its profit where:
    a. its TC cuts its TR from above
    b. its TC cuts its TR from below
    c. its TC is parallel to, and above its TR
    d. its TC is parallel to, and below its TR
    e. its TC is horizontal

15. The opportunity cost of an input is:
    a. the most it could earn in the least attractive alternative use
    b. the least it could earn in its least attractive alternative use
    c. the most it could earn in its most attractive alternative use
    d. the least it could earn in its most attractive alternative use
    e. (a) or (d)

16. In defining costs:
    a. economists take implicit opportunity costs into account because they are an out-of-pocket cash cost
    b. economists take implicit opportunity costs into account, but accountants often do not
    c. accountants take implicit opportunity costs into account, but economists often do not
    d. both take implicit opportunity costs into account
    e. neither take implicit opportunity costs into account

Exercises

1a. If the price is P_1 in Figure 22-1 below, the quantity supplied will be _____, total revenue will be area _____, average cost will be _____, and multiplying this by the number of units sold yields a total cost of area _____. Thus economic profit will be area _____.

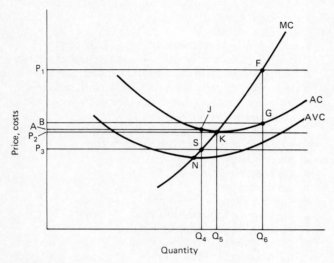

FIGURE 22-1

1b. Alternatively, we can arrive at this same profit by noting that the firm's average revenue is its price P_1, its average cost is _____, and therefore its average profit is _____. Multiplying this by its quantity of output yields its total profit of area _____.

1c. If the price is P_2, the firm will supply quantity _____, total revenue will be _____, average cost will be _____, total cost will be _____, and economic profit will be _____. Therefore, the [break-even, shutdown] point is _____.

1d. If the price is P_3, the firm will supply _____, total revenue will be _____, average cost will be _____, and total cost will be _____. Therefore, total economic [profit, loss] will be _____. If price stays at P_3, then the firm will continue to operate in the _____ run, but not in the _____ run. Despite its loss, it makes this short-run decision because price P_3 is still above the firm's [shutdown, break-even] point at _____. Another way of viewing this decision is that the firm is operating above its [MC, AC, AVC] curve. Therefore, it can more than cover its _____ costs and thus have some left over partly to cover its _____ costs. Shade in and mark for future reference the firm's profit when its price (in this case P_1) is above the minimum point K on its AC curve, and its loss when its price (in this case P_3) is below K.

2. Fill in a table similar to Table 22-6 in the textbook, showing how an accountant and an economist would describe the costs and profit of Mark Laporte, who owns and operates a farm. His total revenue in this particular year is $180,000. His expenses include $27,000 he pays to hire farm labor, $12,000 for fertilizer and seed, $10,000 he pays to rent an adjacent farm, and $20,000 for gasoline and other supplies. Although his accountant tells him that, relative to his neighbors, he's extremely successful, he sometimes considers giving up farming to take a job managing a farm supply business nearby where he has been offered a $65,000 salary. If he did so, he would sell his farm and invest the proceeds in government bonds that would yield a $62,000 per year interest income.

What is his accounting profit and his economic profit? Assuming that he finds farming and managing the farm supply business equally attractive, what would you recommend that he do? Why?

3a. (An introduction to Chapter 23.) Table 22-1 below shows two short-run production functions for a firm that uses only two factors: labor and capital. Each production function describes the amounts of labor the firm would need to produce various amounts of output. The left panel shows the short-run production function if the firm has 20 units of capital; the right panel shows its short-run production function if it has 40 units of capital.

The cost of labor to the firm is $500 per unit, and the cost of capital is $250 per unit. Thus, producing, say,

Table 22-1
TWO SHORT-RUN PRODUCTION FUNCTIONS

20 units of capital			40 units of capital		
Output	Capital	Labor required	Output	Capital	Labor required
0	20	0	0	40	0
1	20	8	1	40	7
2	20	14	2	40	12
3	20	28	3	40	20
4	20	45	4	40	30
5	20	65	5	40	46
6	20	90	6	40	66

Table 22-2
COSTS CALCULATED FROM THE TWO SHORT-RUN PRODUCTION FUNCTIONS IN TABLE 22-1, GIVEN A WAGE OF $500

Out-put	Total cost	Fixed cost	Variable cost	Average cost	Average variable cost	Marginal cost	Total cost	Fixed cost	Variable cost	Average cost	Average variable cost	Marginal cost
0				——	——	0				——	——	0
1												
2												
3	19,000	5,000	14,000	6,333	4,667							
4												
5												
6												

3 units of output with 20 units of capital costs a total of $19,000; that is, $5,000 in fixed costs (20 units of capital at $250 per unit) plus $14,000 in variable costs (28 units of labor at a $500 per unit wage rate). This $19,000 is entered in Table 22-2 above. Fill in the rest of this table.

Essay Questions

1. Draw a U-shaped average cost curve. Then draw in the corresponding MC curve and finally the AVC curve. In red show the new curves after a cost-cutting technological innovation. What effect does this have on the firm's supply curve?

2. In Figure 22-2b in the text, the marginal product curve cuts the average product curve at the highest point on the average product curve. Explain why this must be

3b. If the firm is making a long-run decision and wishes to produce 2 units of output, how much capital should it acquire—20 units or 40? Why?

3c. Answer question (3b) if the firm wishes to produce 5 units of output.

so, using an argument similar to the one used to establish that the MC curve intersects the AC at the lowest point on the AC curve.

3. "In the short run, a perfectly competitive firm will not produce at any point where its average cost is still falling." Do you agree? Why or why not?

4. Are either normal profit or economic profit—or both—included in costs? Explain why.

Answers

Important Terms: 1 m 2 e 3 f 4 p 5 s 6 q 7 o 8 b 9 k 10 l 11 c 12 j 13 d 14 a 15 g 16 i 17 h 18 n 19 r 20 t

True-False: 1 T 2 T 3 T 4 F 5 F 6 T 7 F 8 T 9 T 10 F

Multiple Choice: 1 a 2 e 3 c 4 c 5 c 6 c 7 d 8 b 9 a 10 b 11 b 12 c 13 d 14 d 15 c 16 b

Exercises: **1a.** Q_6, P_1FQ_6O, B, BGQ_6O, P_1FGB. **1b.** B, BP_1, P_1FGB. **1c.** Q_5, P_2KQ_5O, P_2, P_2KQ_5O, zero, break-even, K. **1d.** Q_4, P_3SQ_4O, A, AJQ_4O, loss, $AJSP_3$, short, long, shutdown, N, AVC, variable, fixed. **2.** The table you derive should look like this:

Costs and profits, evaluated by:					
1. An accountant			**2. An economist**		
Total revenue		$180,000	Total revenue		$180,000
			Costs:		
Costs:			Explicit:		
Labor	27,000		Labor	27,000	
Fertilizer, seed	12,000		Fertilizer, seed	12,000	
Rent	10,000		Rent	10,000	
Gas, etc.	20,000		Gas, etc.	20,000	
Total costs		69,000	Implicit		
			Owner's salary	65,000	
			Normal profit	62,000	
			Total costs		196,000
Accounting profit		111,000	Economic (above-normal) profit		− 16,000

His best course of action is to sell the farm, buy bonds with the proceeds, and take the other job, since he is now earning $16,000 less in farming than he could if he followed this alternative course of action. That is, his *economic* loss in farming is $16,000; his $111,000 of accounting income is $16,000 less than his opportunity cost of $65,000 + $62,000 = $127,000.

3a. Table 22-2 completed:

Table 22-2

Out-put	Total cost	Fixed cost	Variable cost	Average cost	Average variable cost	Marginal cost	Total cost	Fixed cost	Variable cost	Average cost	Average variable cost	Maginal cost
0	5,000	5,000	0	_____	_____	0	10,000	10,000	0	_____	_____	0
1	9,000	5,000	4,000	9,000	4,000	4,000	13,500	10,000	3,500	13,500	3,500	3,500
2	12,000	5,000	7,000	6,000	3,500	3,000	16,000	10,000	6,000	8,000	3,000	2,500
3	19,000	5,000	14,000	6,333	4,667	7,000	20,000	10,000	10,000	6,667	3,333	4,000
4	27,500	5,000	22,500	6,875	5,625	8,500	25,000	10,000	15,000	6,250	3,750	5,000
5	37,500	5,000	32,500	7,500	6,500	10,000	33,000	10,000	23,000	6,600	4,600	8,000
6	50,000	5,000	45,000	8,333	7,500	12,500	43,000	10,000	33,000	7,167	5,500	10,000

3b. 20 units, its average cost will be $6,000, rather than $8,000.　**3c.** 40 units, its average cost will be $6,600, rather than $7,500.

CHAPTER 23

COSTS AND PERFECTLY COMPETITIVE SUPPLY:

THE LONG RUN

MAJOR PURPOSES

Our major objective in this chapter is to examine costs in the long run and show how they differ from costs in the short run. In the previous chapter, we described costs and supply in the short run. In the long run, the firm can vary not only its labor input, but also those factors of production, such as capital, that are fixed in the short run. Thus, in the long run, *all* costs become variable. The first topic in ths chapter is to show how the long-run average cost curve (LAC) is related to the short-run average costs curves (SAC). There is a whole family of these SAC curves, one for each specific level of plant and equipment; and the LAC is the "envelope curve" that encloses all these SAC curves from below. With the LAC curve, we can illustrate economies of scale; these exist when the LAC has a downward slope.

With this description of long-run costs in hand, the next question is, How much will be supplied? To some degree, the answer to this question depends on the type of market; for example, a perfectly competitive firm and a monopolist will sell different quantities of output, even though these firms may have the same costs. In this chapter we continue to assume perfect competition, where there is such a large number of buyers and sellers of a standardized product that none can affect its price, and there is free entry of new producers. This last condition is important. It means that the long-run adjustment of a perfectly competitive industry includes not only an adjustment of output by *existing* firms, but also a change in the number of firms. For example, in such a market an increase in demand initially results in a short-run increase in price and profit that attracts new firms into the industry. This in turn increases supply and causes price to fall back part or all of the way to its original level. If it falls back only part way, the resulting long-run price increase provides original producers with an increase in profit. This benefit to *producers* can be read off a *supply* curve in much the same way as the effect of a price change on *buyers* can be read off a *demand* curve.

Learning Objectives

After you have studied this chapter in the textbook and the study guide, you should be able to:

Show in a diagram how long-run and short-run average costs curves are related to each other by an envelope relationship

Define economies of scale and diminishing returns, clearly distinguishing between the two, and explain why a firm may face both

Define perfect competition, explaining each of the three important requirements

Analyze the effect of the entry of new firms on an industry's supply

Describe how an industry adjusts to an increase in demand, clearly distinguishing between the short-run increase in price, and the long-term drift in that price back down towards its original level as new firms enter the industry

Distinguish between case A, where, in the long run, price falls all the way back to its original level and case B, where it falls back only part way

Explain the underlying conditions that give rise to each of these two cases

Restate this analysis—for both case A and case B— to describe what happens when demand *decreases*, rather than increases

Define producer surplus, explaining why it changes as price changes

Show how the benefit to producers from a price increase can be read off a supply curve, in much the same way that the loss to consumers can be read off a demand curve

HIGHLIGHTS OF CHAPTER

In the short run, labor is variable but capital is fixed. However, in the long run, *both* labor and capital are variable. The capital in an industry can increase because (1) existing firms decide to install more capital, and (2) new firms enter. This second issue—the entry of new firms—is discussed later in this chapter. We begin with a discussion of the first issue: In the long run, how much capital should a firm install?

Describing this decision by a firm requires knowledge of its cost curves, and Figure 23-2 in the text shows how a firm's long-run average cost curve (LAC) can be derived from its short-run average cost curves (SAC). (Each of its SAC curves applies to a specific amount of capital.) That Figure shows that the firm's LAC curve is the envelope curve enclosing all the SAC curves from below. It shows how a firm will produce any specified level of output—say, q_5 in that figure—by selecting the lowest cost combination of labor and capital. Specifically, the firm minimizes its average cost of producing q_5 at point S by selecting capital stock D. (SAC_D, of course, is the short-run average cost curve that applies if the firm has capital stock D.) Alternatively, if the firm wished to produce output q_4, it would do so at minimum average cost by producing at R using capital stock C. Thus the LAC "planning curve" tells the firm what its minimum average cost will be when, in the long run, it is free to select *any* capital stock.

This then sets the stage for comparing two important economic phenomena: economies of scale and the law of (eventually) diminishing returns. Economies of scale exist when a 10% increase in output requires less than a 10% increase in all inputs. In this situation, the cost of producing each unit of output falls as output increases (provided that input prices are stable). Thus, LAC slopes downward and to the right. An important conclusion follows: When there are economies of scale, the LAC slopes downward.

Figure 23-3 shows how a firm facing economies of scale—with a downward-sloping LAC—can also be facing diminishing returns. The reason is that diminishing returns occur when the *short-run* marginal cost curve SMC rises. Although economies of scale refer to falling costs (specifically, a downward sloping LAC) and diminishing returns refer to rising costs (an upward-sloping marginal cost curve) the two are not in contradiction. Diminishing returns apply to the short run, when the firm cannot change its capital stock, while economies of scale apply to the long run, when the firm *can* change its capital stock. To see this in more detail in Figure 23-3, note that in the short run, the firm cannot change its fixed capital stock A. Increasing only its labor results in rising marginal cost (SMC_A)— that is, diminishing returns. However, in the long run, when the firm can vary

both labor *and* capital, it operates on LAC. Because this is falling, the firm enjoys economies of scale.

In describing a firm's costs, we haven't had to specify the sort of market in which it is operating. Our description above equally well describes the costs of a firm producing in perfect competition or in any other sort of a market. However, the next obvious question— What quantity of output will be supplied?—*cannot* be answered without specifying the market form. In the text, the market is assumed to be perfectly competitive, and a more complete definition of this market form is now required. So far it has been defined as a market in which there are so many buyers and sellers that none can influence price. Now we emphasize that the product must be standarized, and add another important condition: There must be no barriers to the entry of new firms.

This now sets the stage for addressing the question, 'What is the long-run supply curve of a perfectly competitive industry?' To answer that, it is necessary to consider two cases.

Case A (Figure 23-5 in the Text): Long-Run Supply Is Completely Elastic

Suppose that new firms can produce at the same cost as old firms. (For this to happen, inputs acquired by new firms would have to be as productive as those used by existing firms, and the industry would have to be small enough so that new firms can purchase inputs without bidding up their price.) In such circumstances, an increase in demand for this industry's output can, in the long run, be met entirely by new firms entering the industry and selling at the same cost and price as old firms. Since supply is increasing without any increase in price, the long-run supply is completely elastic.

It is true that when demand initially increases, price does rise *in the short run*, before new firms can enter. It is this increase in price and hence profit to existing firms that provides the incentive for new firms to enter the industry. As new firms enter, supply shifts to the right. As a result, profit for new entrants is reduced. This process continues until price falls back all the way to its original level and there is no incentive left for new firms to enter.

Case B (Figure 23-7 in the Text): A Rising Long-Run Supply Curve

In this case, price does not fall all the way to its original level, because as the number of firms in the industry increases, costs rise. This may happen because new firms can not purchase inputs without bidding up their price, or because these firms cannot acquire inputs of the same quality as those used by existing firms. (For example, new entrants into farming may find that the only available land is less productive.) Because new firms are incurring higher costs, their profits will disappear *before* price falls all the way back to its original level. With no further incentive for more firms to enter, there will be a new equilibrium at a higher price than its original level. Thus, in this case, the long-run supply curve slopes up, as does S_L in Figure 23-7.

How Producers Are Affected by a Price Change

In case B above, rising costs limit entry of new firms. But these rising costs also result in a higher price that benefits producers who are already in the industry. For example, the original farmers on the most productive land enjoy an increase in price and therefore profit. This gain for producers is measured by noting that,

because this industry is producing more, its costs have increased—as shown in area 2 in Figure 23-8. However, revenue of the industry has gone up even more, by area 2 plus 3. Therefore area 3 represents the new gain to producers from the increase in price. Note how this is the area to the left of the supply curve between the old and new price—just as the effect on consumers of a change in price was measured in Chapter 21 as the area to the left of the *demand* curve between the old price and the new price. With this description of the impact of a price change on both producers and consumers in hand, we are in a strong position to analyze how markets work in the next few chapters.

Important Terms: Match the Columns

Match the term in the first column with the corresponding phrase in the second column. But before you do so, write out your own definition of the term in the first column.

_____ 1. Short run
_____ 2. Long run
_____ 3. Short-run production function
_____ 4. Law of (eventually) diminishing returns
_____ 5. Long-run production function
_____ 6. Economies of scale
_____ 7. Perfect competition

a. A market where there are no barriers to entry, and there are so many buyers and sellers of a standardized product that none has any influence over its price
b. The time period during which the capital stock is variable
c. The table or graph showing the maximum output that can be produced with various combinations of inputs
d. If more of one factor is employed while all other factors are held constant, the marginal product of that factor must eventually fall.
e. The relationship between the amount of variable factors used and the amount of output that can be produced, when the amount of capital is constant
f. Doubling all inputs more than doubles the firm's output, and implies a falling average cost curve (provided that input prices are stable).
g. The time period during which the firm cannot vary its capital stock

True-False

T F 1. Diseconomies of scale exist if a 15% increase in output requires a 16% increase in all inputs.
T F 2. It is not possible for a firm to be facing diminishing returns if its long-run average cost curve is falling.
T F 3. In the long run, there are no variable costs.
T F 4. The law of eventually diminishing returns describes a short-run situation in which labor varies but fixed factors do not.
T F 5. An increase in demand for a perfectly competitive good will result in a short-run increase in the output and profit of existing firms.
T F 6. If new entrants to an industry can obtain the same quality of inputs as existing firms, and inputs are available at stable prices, then the long-run industry supply will be upward-sloping.
T F 7. The industry long-run supply curve will be horizontal if any number of new firms can enter and produce at the same cost as existing firms.
T F *8. A graph of a production function is made up of a whole set of isoquants that show how the firm's output increases as it uses more inputs.
T F *9. Whereas each indifference curve of a consumer represents a *specific number* of units of satisfaction, each isoquant in a production function represents only a "higher" or "lower" level of output.

T F   **10.** The short-run production function is a row from the long-run production function table.
T F   **11.** The long-run production function shows the minimum output that can be produced with each combination of inputs.

*Based upon material from the appendix of your textbook.

Multiple Choice

1. If there are economies of scale:
  a. short-run average cost rises
  b. short-run average cost is constant
  c. short-run average cost falls
  d. long-run average cost falls
  e. long-run average cost rises

2. If there are diminishing returns:
  a. short-run marginal cost falls
  b. short-run marginal cost rises
  c. short-run marginal cost is constant
  d. long-run marginal cost falls
  e. long-run marginal cost is constant

3. Fixed costs are:
  a. fixed only in the short run
  b. fixed only in the long run
  c. fixed in both the long run and the short run
  d. fixed in neither the long nor the short run
  e. variable in the short run

4. A profit-maximizing firm may be willing to produce at a loss:
  a. in the short run, but not the long run
  b. in the long run, but not the short run
  c. in neither the long run nor the short run
  d. in both the short run and the long run
  e. in the long run, provided there are no variable costs

5. In the long run, a firm has to decide on:
  a. how much plant and equipment it uses, but not how much labor
  b. how much plant it uses, but not how much equipment and labor
  c. how much equipment and labor it uses, but not how much plant
  d. how much labor it uses, but not how much plant and equipment
  e. how much of all three it uses

6. A firm's long-run average cost curve is the envelope of its short-run:
  a. marginal cost curves
  b. fixed cost curves
  c. average variable cost curves
  d. average cost curves
  e. total cost curves

7. If an industry is perfectly competitive, then:
  a. there are barriers to entry that keep new competitors out and the product is standardized
  b. the product is not standardized, and there are barriers to entry
  c. the product is standardized, and there are no barriers to entry
  d. the product is not standardized, and there are no barriers to entry
  e. the government must license all firms in this industry

8. If demand decreases in a perfectly competitive industry, then:
  a. price will rise in the short run and fall in the long run
  b. price will rise in the short run and rise further in the long run
  c. price will fall in the short run and fall further in the long run
  d. price will fall in the short run and rise back toward the original price in the long run
  e. price will fall in the short run and therefore remain constant at that level

9. Suppose that demand has increased in a perfectly competitive industry and that each firm has moved to a new short-run equilibrium. Then, *in the further process of long-run adjustment*, the individual firm will face:
  a. falling price and decreasing profit
  b. falling price and increasing profit
  c. falling price and constant profit
  d. increasing price and decreasing profit
  e. increasing price and increasing profit

10. If price rises and output increases, then the benefit for the producer is:
  a. the increase in the firm's revenue, plus the increase in its costs
  b. the increase in the firm's revenue, minus the increase in its costs
  c. the increase in the firm's revenue
  d. the increase in the firm's costs, minus the increase in its revenue
  e. the decrease in the firm's costs

11. If price falls, then:
  a. producers benefit by the area to the left of the supply curve between the old price and the new price
  b. producers benefit by the area to the left of the demand curve between the old price and the new price
  c. producers are worse off by the area to the left of the demand curve between the old price and the new price
  d. producers are worse off by the area to the left of the supply curve between the old price and the new price
  e. there is no effect on producers

*12. In reading a long-run production function table, any evidence of:
  a. economies of scale would be found along a row, with diminishing returns along a diagonal
  b. economies of scale would be found along a diagonal, with diminishing returns along a row
  c. both economies of scale and diminishing returns would be found along a row
  d. both economies of scale and diminishing returns would be found along a diagonal
  e. economies of scale would be found along a column

13. Long-run equilibrium for the firm will occur where:
  a. an isoquant of the long-run production function is tangent to an equal-cost line
  b. an isoquant of the short-run production function is tangent to an equal-cost line
  c. an isoquant of the long-run production function intersects an equal-cost line
  d. an isoquant of the short-run production function intersects an equal-cost line
  e. an indifference curve is tangent to an equal-cost line

*Based upon material from the appendix of your textbook.

Exercises

1. Table 23-1 below presents average cost figures for four of the large number of plant sizes that a firm can select in the long run. (Note that plants B and C have costs similar to those you calculated for the two plants in Table 22-2.). In Figure 23-1, graph the four average cost curves. Label them A, B, C, D, and mark the minimum point of each M_A, M_B, M_C, and M_D. Sketch in a rough long-run average cost curve (LAC) for this firm. Does it pass through all the minimum points? In particular, does it pass through M_A and M_D? Through M_C? Why?

2. Table 23-2 describes a firm's long-run costs. In particular, column 3 shows its envelope curve LAC. Fill in the missing parts of the table. When the price of its output is \$70, the firm's long-run profit-maximizing output is _____, and its profit is _____. When the price is \$85, the firm's profit-maximizing output is _____, and its profit is _____.

When price rises from \$70 to \$85, its profit [increases, decreases] by _____.

3. In Figure 23-2, if price is P_1, the total revenue of the perfectly competitive industry is _____. If price falls to P_2, its total revenue is _____, for a [decrease, increase] in revenue of _____. However, this is partially offset by a decrease in _____ of _____. Therefore, the reduction in profit is _____.

4. In Figure 23-3, when D_1 decreases to D_2 in panel *b*, price falls from _____ to _____ as the short-run equilibrium of the industry shifts from _____ to

Table 23-1

| Output | Average cost, if fixed cost is: | | | |
| | \$2,000 | \$5,000 | \$10,000 | \$15,000 |
	Plant A	Plant B	Plant C	Plant D
1	\$ 7,100	\$9,000	\$13,500	\$13,900
2	6,700	7,000	8,000	8,500
3	6,800	6,300	6,700	6,900
4	8,000	6,900	6,200	6,600
5	9,600	7,600	6,600	6,500
6	12,000	8,700	7,200	6,600

FIGURE 23-1

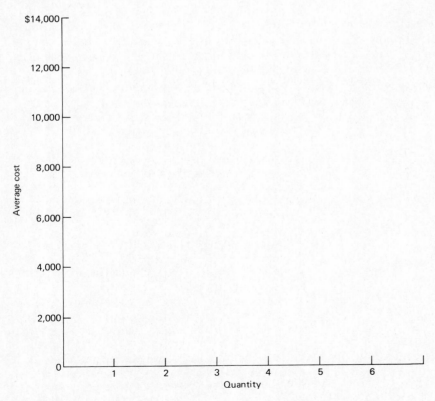

Table 23-2
A FIRM'S LONG-RUN COSTS

Output	Total cost	Average cost (LAC)	Marginal cost	Total revenue if price equals $70	Economic profit if price equals $70	Total revenue if price equals $85	Economic profit if price equals $85
1	$120		$120				
2	150						
3	200						
4	270						
5	350						
6	440						

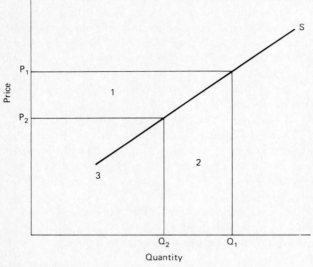

FIGURE 23-2

_____. Each firm in panel *a* responds by moving along its supply curve from _____ to _____. Each firm now has a [profit, loss] of _____. As firms therefore [enter, leave] the industry, the industry supply in panel *b* shifts from _____ to _____, and industry equilibrium moves from _____ to _____. The initial 30% leftward shift in demand has been offset by a _____% shift in supply, and price [moves to, returns to] P_1. Long-run supply is constructed by joining all points such as _____ and _____. It is [completely elastic, unit elastic, inelastic].

FIGURE 23-3

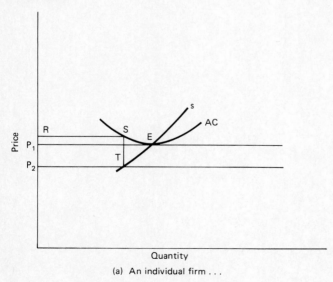

(a) An individual firm . . .

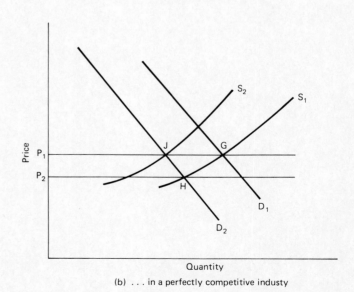

(b) . . . in a perfectly competitive industy

Essay Questions

1. "If a firm's overhead costs increase by, say, 20% because of an increase in its property taxes, its output will not be affected." Evaluate this statement, clearly distinguishing between the short run and the long run.

2. Do you agree with the following statement? Explain why. "If a firm producing 1000 units of output is on its long-run average cost curve, then the combination of capital and labor that it is using costs less than any alternative combination which could be used to produce 1000 units of output." Illustrate your answer with a diagram, showing two or three of the other combinations.

3. "The law of diminishing returns ensures a dismal economic future, because it tells us that as the labor force grows, it will eventually produce a lower and lower marginal product." Do you agree? Why or why not?

4. During a period in which population and income are rising rapidly, the price of good X remains constant. How would you explain this?

5. Would you expect the short run to be longer for a typing service or a steel company? Explain.

6. "If demand for a perfectly competitive product shifts downward, price must fall." Do you agree? Explain, clearly distinguishing between the long run and the short run.

Answers

Important Terms **1** g **2** b **3** e **4** d **5** c **6** f **7** a
True-False: **1** T **2** F **3** F **4** T **5** T **6** F **7** T **8** T **9** F **10** T **11** F
Multiple Choice: **1** d **2** b **3** a **4** a **5** e **6** d **7** c **8** d **9** a **10** b **11** d **12** b **13** a
Exercises: **1.** no, no, yes, because M_C is the lowest minimum value.
Figure 23-1 completed:

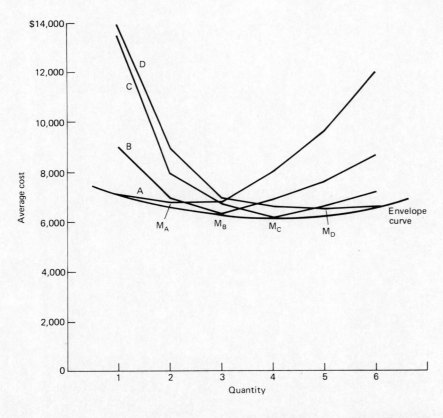

2. Table 23-2 completed:

Table 23-2

Output	Total cost	Average cost (LAC)	Marginal cost	Total revenue if P = \$70	Profit if P = \$70	Total revenue if P = \$85	Profit if P = \$85
1	\$120	\$120	\$120	\$ 70	\$−50	\$ 85	\$−35
2	150	75	30	140	−10	170	20
3	200	66⅔	50	210	10	255	55
4	270	67½	70	280	10	340	70
5	350	70	80	350	0	425	75
6	440	73⅓	90	420	−20	510	70

4, \$10, 5, \$75, increases, \$65.   **3.** 1 + 2 + 3, 3, decrease, 1 + 2, costs, 2, 1.   **4.** P_1, P_2, G. H, E, T, loss, $RSTP_2$, leave, S_1, S_2, H, J, 30%, returns to, G, J, completely elastic.

Across

1, 5. When you know these, you can calculate marginal costs
7. head of a corporation (abbrev.)
9. be (1st person)
11. in the past
13. the amount in input could earn in its best alternative use (2 words)
15. this grows in a damp, cool place
16. The U.S. government has had a large deficit in its _____
18. first name of President Carter's Secretary of State (abbrev.)
19. a business organization (abbrev.)
21, 23. the relationship of the long-run cost curve to a series of short-run cost curves
25. at this point, losses equal fixed costs
26. sign of affection
29. third "person"
30. overrun and inhabit
34. the sum of fixed and variable costs (2 words)
37. this elasticity is measured between two points on a curve
38. compulsive saver
39. more than a few
42. to maximize profits, a firm equates this with marginal cost (2 words)
44. with this type of floating exchange rate, governments don't accumulate foreign exchange reserves

Down

1. forbid, prohibit
2. get a return or reward
3. what Navy wants to do to the West Point football team
4. a reason why there are gains from specialization (3 words)
5. expenses
6. systematic statement of principles or propositions
8. a barrier to _____ reduces competition
10. things are dead around there
12. please don't chew this in class!
14. be (3rd person)
16. at the _____ even point, profits are zero
17. a number
18. thin rope
19. sever
20. when night falls, so does this
22. go to see
23. hints, signals
24. expression of a choice
27. German concentration camp
28. a size of type
31. economists consider this type of profit to be a cost
32. main character in a 1983 movie
33. elasticity of demand and supply determines who bears the _____ of a sales tax
35. an agency of the U.S. government (abbrev.)
36. this type of cost does not affect marginal cost
40. an important part of President Roosevelt's recovery program (abbrev.)
41. Japanese currency
42. manuscript (abbrev.)
43. a southern state (abbrev.)

CHAPTER 24

PERFECT COMPETITION AND ECONOMIC EFFICIENCY

MAJOR PURPOSE

The primary objective in this chapter is to demonstrate that, under certain conditions, a perfectly competitive market provides an efficient outcome. This is critical because it becomes a point of reference that allows us, in later chapters, to show clearly why many other forms of market are *not* efficient. Thus perfect competition must be studied carefully, even though it doesn't describe a large part of the economy; most products are produced in some other type of market. Nonetheless, many agricultural markets *are* perfectly competitive, and these are used in this chapter to illustrate how the perfect competition model can be applied to analyze policy problems.

Learning Objectives

After you have studied this chapter in the textbook and the study guide, you should be able to:

Explain why the condition "marginal cost to society = marginal benefit to society" is necessary for allocative efficiency

Explain why perfect competition results in allocative efficiency when there are no externalities

Show how perfect competition tends to promote technical efficiency

Demonstrate, in a diagram similar to Figure 24-3 in the text, that a deadweight loss to society results if either more or less than the efficient quantity of output is produced

Explain why perfect competition tends to promote dynamic efficiency in certain ways; but why, in some other ways, other types of market may provide greater dynamic efficiency

Show not only the great virtues of a perfectly competitive market, but also its limitations—in particular, explain why an efficient outcome is not necessarily best

Explain why speculation sometimes benefits society, and why it sometimes damages society

Demonstrate why government agricultural price supports increase efficiency if they *stabilize* price, but reduce efficiency if they *raise* price

Explain how such price supports transfer income among various groups—and, in particular, identify the costs they impose on consumers and taxpayers

HIGHLIGHTS OF CHAPTER

You sometimes hear it said that we should learn to cooperate more with each other than than compete. But the economist will say that, on the contrary, competition is often the best method of ensuring harmony. This is the message of Adam Smith's "invisible hand," as described in Chapter 1. In pursuing our own self-interest, each of us is led by market forces—as if by an invisible hand—to promote the interests of others as well. In this chapter we show how effectively this can happen through the operation of perfectly competitive markets. We also show that, despite their efficiency, these markets do have some shortcomings.

Perfect Competition and Allocative Efficiency

The core idea of this chapter is that, under certain conditions, perfectly competitive markets produce an efficient outcome. Consider first the concept of allocative efficiency, defined in Chapter 1. This requires that the marginal social cost of any activity be equal to its marginal social benefit—otherwise, a net gain can be acquired by changing the level of that activity. For example, if the marginal benefit of producing wheat is less than its marginal cost—that is, if the benefit of 1 more bushel of wheat exceeds its cost—then there is a *net* benefit from producing that bushel. The output of wheat should be increased. Moreover, it should continue to be increased until marginal benefit and cost *are* equal. Only then will the incentive for increasing output disappear; this output is efficient.

Under perfect competition, output is generally efficient because marginal social benefit (MB_S) and marginal social cost (MC_S) are equalized. The reason is that under perfect competition, supply equals demand. Supply reflects the marginal cost of producers, and demand reflects the marginal benefit to consumers. Therefore the equality of supply and demand means that the marginal cost of producers is equal to the marginal benefit to consumers. Provided these are the only benefits and costs—as carefully assumed in equations 24-1 and 24-2 of the text—it follows that the marginal cost to society is equal to the marginal benefit to society, and an efficient outcome results. Thus, in a perfectly competitive market, the pursuit by producers and consumers of their own *private* interest promotes the interest of society.

Figure 24-2 is particularly useful in clarifying this. In panel *a*, consumers pursue their self interest by responding as perfectly competitive price takers to the $10 market price. In panel *b*, perfectly competitive producers pursue *their* self-interest by also responding as price takers to the same $10 market price; and the result in panel *c* is an efficient outcome for society as a whole. We emphasize that this occurs in perfect competition, because both producers and consumers are price takers who respond to the same market price.

In succeeding chapters we will examine markets that, for one reason or another, are not efficient. One possible reason is that producers are not perfectly competitive price takers. A second reason is that consumers are not perfectly competitive price takers. A third reason is that consumers are not the only ones to benefit from a good; there are benefits that go to others in society as well. (When you buy home improvements, the benefits go not only to you, but also to your neighbors.) The fourth possible reason is that producers are not the only ones who face a cost when a good is produced. (Those living downstream face a cost when a chemical producer dumps waste into a river.) Note that, in each case, inefficiency arises because of the violation of one of the key assumptions underlying the efficient, perfectly competitive model.

Perfect Competition and Other Kinds of Efficiency

Perfect competition also tends to promote technical efficiency. Technically inefficient firms that are operating above their AC curves, aren't likely to survive competition with technically efficient firms that are operating *on* their AC curves.

The situation is different with respect to dynamic efficiency. Discovering innovations that generate economic growth is usually very expensive. The perfectly competitive firm is too small to be able to afford such expenditures. Nor does it have the incentive; a farmer who discovers a new strain of wheat would find that most of the benefit would go to the millions of other farmers.

Other Reservations about Perfect Competition

Efficiency isn't everything. There are problems that the perfectly competitive market doesn't solve. One is how the nation's income should be distributed. Perfect competition may not provide the best answer. The reason is that for every possible distribution of income there is a different perfectly competitive equilibrium. While each is efficient, the economist has no objective way of deciding which of these efficient outcomes is "best." This is an important point: Make sure you can explain it using Figures 24-1 and 24-6 in the textbook.

Another possible drawback of a perfect competitive market is that it may be subject to severe fluctuations in price and quantity—especially when production decisions must be based on price expectations far into the future. In the case of the hog cycle, the text shows how the expectation that future price will be the same as today's price leads to cyclical fluctuations in price and quantity. The text also describes how this problem may be reduced by private speculators or by government price-stabilization schemes. For example, if private speculators make accurate forecasts they will tend to iron out fluctuations in the market. They do this by buying when there is an oversupply (and thus keeping price from falling even more) and by selling when there is a scarcity (and thereby keeping the price from rising even higher).

A speculator who succeeds in this strategy will not only make a personal profit, but will also benefit society by helping to iron out the instability in this market. On the other hand, a speculator who gets it wrong—for example, one who buys when it is cheap and is forced to sell when it is even cheaper—will lose money and will damage society as well. But such individuals typically go out of business. (Another type of speculation that is damaging to the public interest is the attempt to corner a market in order to raise price.)

Farm Programs

Ideally, a government price support policy can be viewed as playing the same socially desireable role that speculators play that is, stabilizing price by buying when the item is in oversupply, and selling when it is scarce. In practice, it's not that simple. Just as speculators damage society when they err in their predictions, so too can the government. (Some would say that this problem is more serious for a government, since its decisions are typically made by those without experience or talent in predicting the future.) Government price support policies are also complicated because they are often used, not just to stabilize price, but also to raise it. In this case, farmers respond to an artificially high price by increasing their output above the efficient level, and the result is a triangular efficiency loss of the kind shown in Figure 24-3a in the text. Both this triangular efficiency loss from "producing too much" and the corresponding efficiency loss from "producing too little" in panel b of the same table are critical for you to understand and be able to reproduce. They will frequently reappear in the following chapters.

Important Terms: Match the Columns

Match the term in the first column with the corresponding phrase in the second column. But before you do so, write out your own definition of the term in the first column.

_____ **1.** Allocative efficiency
_____ **2.** Efficiency loss
_____ **3.** Speculation
_____ **4.** Cornering a market
_____ **5.** Pareto optimum
_____ **6.** Pareto improvement
_____ **7.** Deficiency payments

a. The activity of buying and selling commodities with a view to profiting from future price changes. In perfectly competitive commodity markets, this tends to stabilize prices if forecasts are reasonably good

b. Per bushel subsidy paid to farmer to raise price received to a specified target level

c. Buying up enough of a commodity to become the single (or at least dominant) holder, and thus acquire the power to resell at a higher price

d. A situation in which it is impossible to make anyone better off without making someone else worse off

e. The loss from producing an amount that is not efficient

f. Any change that benefits someone, without making anyone else worse off

g. Running an activity at a level where marginal social cost equals marginal social benefit

True-False

T F **1.** Perfect competition guarantees an efficient solution.
T F **2.** For a good with external benefits, marginal benefit to buyers is less than marginal social benefit.
T F **3.** The typical firm in perfect competition must strive to eliminate technical inefficiency because it could be driven out of business otherwise.
T F **4.** For each distribution of income, there is a different efficient solution.
T F **5.** The best possible distribution of income is the only distribution that can lead to an efficient outcome.
T F **6.** The greater the cost of storing a good, the greater will be the gap in its price between 2 years.
T F **7.** If the government's surplus stock of food keeps growing over time, then the government has been raising farm prices.
T F **8.** U.S. farm price supports provide a subsidy that is larger in dollar terms to the poor farmer than to the rich farmer.

T F   ***9.** Producers maximize their income by producing at a point of tangency between their production possibilities curve and the highest income line they can reach.

T F   **10.** The payments-in-kind (PIK) policy has been a supply management program.

*Based upon material from the appendix of your textbook.

Multiple Choice

1. In a perfectly competitive market where supply equals demand, the marginal benefit of each consumer will:
  a. be greater than the marginal cost of each producer
  b. be equal to the marginal cost of each producer
  c. be less than the average variable cost of each producer
  d. be less than the average fixed cost of each producer
  e. none of the above

2. A perfectly competitive market generates an efficient outcome if all but one of the following conditions holds. Which of the conditions below does *not* hold?
  a. Social costs are the same as private costs.
  b. Social benefits are the same as private benefits.
  c. Consumers equate marginal benefit and price.
  d. Producers equate marginal cost and price.
  e. Consumers equate marginal benefit and total cost.

3. If more than the efficient output is being produced, then:
  a. marginal social benefit MB_s is equal to marginal social cost MC_s
  b. MB_s is less than MC_s
  c. MB_s is more than MC_s
  d. MB_s is zero
  e. MC_s is zero

4. To be efficient, a perfectly competitive market requires that:
  a. benefits from the good are widely dispersed among buyers and nonbuyers
  b. all benefits of the good go to its purchasers, with none going to others
  c. costs of the good are borne by all producers and some nonproducers
  d. all costs of the good are borne by nonproducers
  e. costs of the good are borne by all members of society

5. If a firm is prevented from entering an industry because of failure to obtain a government license, then:
  a. the industry demand curve will overstate the marginal benefit to society
  b. the industry demand curve will understate the marginal benefit to society
  c. the industry supply curve will overstate the marginal cost to society
  d. the industry supply curve will understate the marginal cost to society
  e. (a) and (d)

6. In a perfectly competitive market:
  a. price is a rationing device that determines which buyers will acquire a good, and which sellers will produce it
  b. price is a rationing device that determines only which buyers will acquire a good
  c. price determines only which sellers will produce a good
  d. price determines neither which sellers will produce a

good, nor which buyers will acquire it: price only determines how wealthy sellers will be
  e. none of the above

7. Perfect competition is superior to monopoly in terms of:
  a. dynamic efficiency, but not necessarily allocative efficiency
  b. allocative efficiency, but not necessarily dynamic efficiency
  c. allocative efficiency, but not technical efficiency
  d. dynamic and technical efficiency
  e. dynamic and allocative efficiency

8. It is sometimes argued that perfect competition is inferior to other market forms in creating innovation because:
  a. a small firm has lots of funds, but doesn't have an incentive to spend them on R&D, since it would gain only a small share of the benefits
  b. a typical small firm doesn't have funds to finance larger R&D expenditures, although it has the incentive
  c. a small firm has neither the funds nor the incentive to spend them on R&D.
  d. a small firm has both the funds and the incentive to spend them on R&D, but it is just mismanaged
  e. a small firm knows that once it has created an innovation, the government will now allow it to be widely applied

9. If we are initially in an efficient, perfectly competitive equilibrium, and we take income from Smith and give it to Jones, then:
  a. the quantities of goods that each will acquire will remain unchanged
  b. there will be a move to a new, efficient equilibrium where Smith acquires fewer goods, and Jones more
  c. there will be a move to a new, efficient equilibrium where Jones acquires fewer goods, and Smith more
  d. there will be a move to a new, inefficient equilibrium where Smith acquires fewer goods, and Jones more
  e. there will be a move to a new, inefficient equilibrium where Jones acquires fewer goods, and Smith more

10. If the price in a hog cycle is:
  a. low this year, then there will be decreased production, and price will be even lower next year
  b. low this year, then there will be increased production, and price will be even lower next year
  c. high this year, then there will be reduced production, and price will be even higher next year
  d. high this year, then there will be increased production, and price will be even higher next year
  e. high this year, then there will be increased production, and price will be lower next year

11. In a market with only a few sellers (where some have influence over price), which of the following efficiency conditions for perfect competition is *violated*?
  a. There are costs of a product to others than producers.

b. There are benefits of a product to others than buyers.

c. Sellers equate their marginal cost and price.

d. Buyers equate their marginal benefit and price.

e. None of the above.

12. Speculation will be most effective in moderating a hog cycle if:

a. speculators buy pork when it is cheap and sell it when it is dear

b. speculators sell pork when it is cheap and buy it when it is dear

c. speculators buy pork when it is cheap and buy it again when it is dear

d. speculators sell pork when it is cheap and sell it again when it is dear

e. speculators lose money on the transaction

13. Suppose speculators buy in the first year and sell in the second. Then:

a. if price is higher in the second year, this speculation results in an efficiency loss for society, but a profit for speculators

b. if price is higher in the second year, this speculation results in an efficiency gain for society, but a loss for speculators

c. if price is lower in the second year, this speculation results in an efficiency loss for society, and a loss for speculators

d. if price is lower in the second year, this speculation results in an efficiency loss for society, but a profit for speculators

e. if price is lower in the second year, this speculation results in an efficiency gain for society, but a loss for speculators

14. Speculation that stabilizes price and quantity:

a. is beneficial to society because goods are moved from a year of glut to a year of scarcity when they are valued more highly

b. is beneficial to society because goods are moved from a year of scarcity to a year of glut when they are valued more highly

c. is damaging to society because goods are moved from a year of glut to a year of scarcity when they are valued more highly

d. is damaging to society for other reasons; supplies are *not* moved from one year to another

e. has no effect on society

15. When the government supports farm price above its free-market level:

a. there is an efficiency gain and a transfer from farmers to taxpayers

b. there is an efficiency gain and a transfer from taxpayers to farmers

c. there is an efficiency gain and no transfer

d. there is an efficiency loss and a transfer from taxpayers to farmers

e. there is an efficiency loss and a transfer from farmers to taxpayers

*16. A supply management program by the government:

a. is a policy that combines a price support with deficiency payments

b. reduces farmers' supply by providing them with an incentive to cut back their output

c. reduces farmers' supply by providing them with an incentive to produce more, but hold back most of what they produce

d. increases farmers' supply by providing them with an incentive to produce more

e. holds farmers' supply constant by providing them with an incentive not to change their output

*Based upon material from the appendix of your textbook.

Exercises

1. Figure 24-1 shows the supply and demand for a particular grade of wheat in a particular year in a perfectly competitive market in Chicago.

a. The equilibrium price is _____, and the equilibrium quantity is _____. Now suppose that the government, instead of allowing the market to operate freely, buys all the wheat directly from the farmers, offering them a guaranteed price of P_2. The amount that will then be supplied will be _____. As a result of this government intervention, producers realize a [gain, loss] of area _____. Shade in this area in the diagram.

b. Suppose that the government, after buying this wheat, now sells it all on the market for whatever price it will fetch. This price will be _____. As a result of this government intervention, consumers realize a [gain, loss] of area _____. Shade in this area in the diagram.

FIGURE 24-1

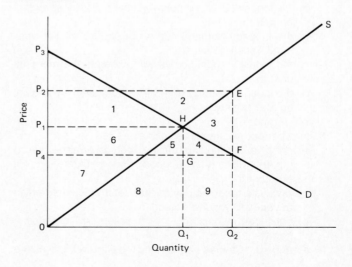

c. If we just consider these effects on consumers and producers (the two shaded areas), we would conclude that there is a net [gain, loss] to the economy as a result of the government's intervention. However, the government has made a [gain, loss] on these wheat dealings which the taxpayers must pay for. The total amount that the government paid for the wheat is _____ and the total revenue that the government received for selling the wheat is _____. Therefore the loss to the government (i.e., the taxpayers) is _____. If this is taken into account, we conclude that the government's action results in a net [gain, loss] to the economy of area _____.

d. Alternatively we could have even more easily arrived at this conclusion by noting that the government's action raised output from the perfectly competitive amount _____ to the amount _____, thus resulting in an efficiency loss measured by the triangle _____.

2. The purpose of this exercise is to demonstrate the social benefit that can be produced by the existence of markets. Figures 24-2 and 24-3 represent the markets for a manufactured good in Florida and Texas.

a. Suppose that initially there was no trade between the two states; that is, no market in which people from one state could trade with people from the other. Then the equilibrium price in

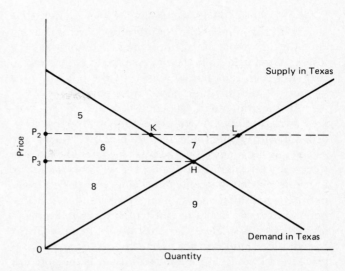

FIGURE 24-3

Florida would be _____, and the equilibrium price in Texas would be _____.

b. Next, suppose that a group of traders organized a market in which Texans could trade with Floridians. Suppose that there were no transportation costs or any other kind of cost to separate the market of the two states. Then there would in fact be only one market that included both states. A single equilibrium price would be established such that the total amount supplied in the two states was just equal to the amount demanded in the two states. (Suppose that no other states are involved.) Therefore, the excess of supply over demand in one state must equal the shortfall in the other. In Figure 24-2 and 24-3 the equilibrium price is _____. At that price Florida has an excess [demand, supply] of _____. This is an equilibrium price because the excess [supply, demand] of Texas is _____, which is equal to the excess [supply, demand] of Florida.

c. As a result of trade between the two states, consumers in Florida have realized a [gain, loss] of _____, and producers in Florida are [worse, better] off by _____; therefore, the net [benefit, loss] to Florida is _____.

d. Consumers in Texas have realized a [gain, loss] of _____, and producers in Texas are [better, worse] off by _____. Therefore, the overall [gain, loss] to Texas is _____.

These two triangles provide estimates of the gains to the two states from creating a market in this good.

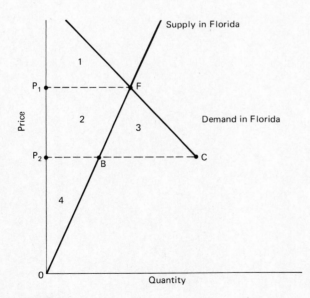

FIGURE 24-2

Essay Questions

1. In exercise 2 immediately above, who would be the winners and who would be the losers from the opening up of trade between the two states? What sort of arguments do you suppose the losers might propose in favor of a government prohibition of such trade? How could these arguments be countered? Can you imagine any way in which the winners might compensate the losers? Would the total gain in each state be enough so that after such compensation everybody could end up a winner. Would this then be a Pareto improvement?

2. According to the economist's theory of how markets work, butchers provide the public with meat in an economically efficient manner, not because they hate to see people go hungry, but because they are interested in their own incomes. In this chapter we have seen that butchers produce the efficient quantity in perfect competition where there are so many buyers and sellers that none can affect price. But is it true if there is a monopoly—that is, a single seller with power to raise price? Specifically, suppose there is a monopolist who raises price from P_1 to P_2 in Figure 24-1 above. Is the outcome then an efficient one? Explain your answer.

3. Argue the case that perfect competition tends to promote at least two different kinds of efficiency.

4. Apply the analysis of this chapter to show in a diagram the triangular efficiency loss from a rent-control policy.

5. Earlier we stated that the demand and supply of a product are defined in terms of a certain time and certain place. What is the "place," that is, the geographical extent of the market for the firms supplying the following items? (*a*) Pastries, (*b*) haircuts, and (*c*) copper.

6. The text gave reasons why a perfectly competitive firm would not engage in much R&D expenditure. Is the same true of advertising expenditure? Explain why. Do you think it might make sense for all perfect competitors in an industry to form as association to advertise their product?

Answers

Important Terms: 1 g 2 e 3 a 4 c 5 d 6 f 7 b
True-False: 1 F 2 T 3 T 4 T 5 F 6 T 7 T 8 F 9 T 10 T
Multiple Choice: 1 b 2 e 3 b 4 b 5 c 6 a 7 b 8 c 9 b 10 e 11 c 12 a 13 c 14 a 15 d 16 b
Exercises: **1a.** P_1, Q_1, Q_2, gain, 1 + 2. **1b.** P_4, gain, 4 + 5 + 6. **1c.** gain, loss, 1 + 2 + 3 + 4 + 5 + 6 + 7 + 8 + 9, 7 + 8 + 9, 1 + 2 + 3 + 4 + 5 + 6, loss, 3. **1d.** Q_1, Q_2, 3. **2a.** P_1, P_3. **2b.** P_2, demand, *BC*, supply, *KL*, demand. **2c.** gain, 2 + 3, worse, 2, benefit, 3. **2d.** loss, 6, better, 6 + 7, gain, 7.

CHAPTER 25

MONOPOLY

MAJOR PURPOSE

We have now completed our analysis of one extreme of the market spectrum—perfect competition, where there is free entry and so many buyers and sellers that none can influence price. Our focus now turns to the other extreme: monopoly, where a single seller not only can influence price, but can actually *determine* it, subject only to demand conditions. The following questions will be addressed: Under what conditions does monopoly arise? How does the monopolist's price and quantity compare with the perfect competitor's? How efficient is monopoly? What are the government's methods of controlling monopoly? Are there conditions under which a monopoly should be free not just to set its price, but to go beyond this to set several prices that discriminate among buyers?

Learning Objectives

After you have studied this chapter in the textbook and the study guide, you should be able to:

Explain four reasons why monopolies exist

Describe the cost conditions that lead to a natural monopoly, and explain how, in these circumstances, competition will eliminate all firms but one

Show why a monopolist's demand and marginal revenue are quite different from a perfect competitor's

Explain why a monopoly can select its profit-maximizing output by equating its marginal cost and marginal revenue

Demonstrate the alternative method of selecting this output by maximizing the rectangle defined between the firm's average cost and demand curves

Show why a monopoly produces too low a level of output to achieve allocative efficiency

Explain why the appropriate government policy towards collusive monopoly is to break it up or prevent it from being formed in the first place

Demonstrate why marginal cost pricing is the appropriate government policy towards natural monopoly, provided it is feasible; and why, if it is not feasible, average cost pricing or government ownership are possible alternative policies

Show why, in very special circumstances, price discrimination by a monopolist may benefit all concerned—both the producer and consumers of the product

HIGHLIGHTS OF CHAPTER

The key questions are discussed below.

Why Does Monopoly Exist?

Monopolies exist for any or all of the following reasons: (1) the monopoly may possess something valuable that is not available to a potential competitor (for example, some talent, property, or patent); (2) government may have created the monopoly by making competition illegal, as in the case of certain kinds of public transportation; (3) there may be a natural monopoly; or (4) the existing sellers may have colluded—that is, agreed to act in cooperation rather than competition.

The case of natural monopoly is perhaps the most important. It exists whenever there are economies of scale through a wide range—that is, whenever a firm has an average cost curve that continues to fall until its output becomes about large enough to satisfy the entire industry demand. (See panel *b* in Figure 25-1 in the textbook.)

How Does a Monopoly Maximize Its Profit, and How Do Its Price and Output Compare with a Perfect Competitor's?

A monopoly, just like a perfectly competitive firm, maximizes profit by choosing the level of output where its marginal revenue (MR) equals its marginal cost (MC). But whereas the perfect competitor's MR equals the market price, the monoply's MR is less than the market price; that is, its MR curve lies below its demand curve. This is because the perfect competitor faces a horizontal demand curve. When the firm sells one more unit the price stays the same; thus the firm's extra revenue MR is just the market price. Compare this to a monopoly, which faces a demand curve that slopes downward to the right. When this firm sells one more unit, the price *doesn't* stay the same. It falls. Thus the monopoly's extra revenue (MR) is the price that it receives from selling the extra unit, *minus* the loss it incurs because selling this extra unit lowers the price it receives for all the *other* units.

Since the monopoly's MR curve lies below its demand curve, it intersects the MC curve at a smaller output, as you can see in Figure 25-6b in the textbook; under perfect competition, output is 170,000, but under monopoly it is only 100,000 units. Thus, the monopoly exploits its advantage by reducing its output. By making the product scarce, it is able to raise price—from P_1 to P_2 in that diagram.

Like the perfectly competitive firm, the monopoly produces where MR = MC only if it is able to cover its costs. This requires that the demand curve overlap the AC curve; that is, the demand curve must not be always below the AC curve.

Is Monopoly Efficient?

The efficient output is the one under perfect competition, where supply (MC) equals demand (the marginal benefit of this good). When competitors collude to form a monopoly, output is reduced because the new monopoly is equating MC, not with demand, but instead with MR which is *below* demand. Because this reduces output below the efficient, perfectly competitive level, monopoly is inefficient. This is the main disadvantage of monopoly. But a complete verdict on any particular monopoly is not possible without also taking into account other factors such as the technical inefficiency that may exist because there is no competition to force the monopoly to fight rising costs. It is also necessary to take into account the transfer of income from consumers to the monopoly that results from the monopoly's higher price. Strictly speaking, we can't be sure whether this transfer is desirable or undesirable, because there is no objective way of comparing one person's gain with another's loss. However, it is often reasonable to assume that these transfer effects cancel; that is, each dollar transferred is valued as highly by the person losing it as the person receiving it. If this assumption is reasonable, then the efficiency losses of monopoly imply a welfare loss.

What Should Government Policy Be Toward Monopoly?

To answer this question, it is first necessary to specify what sort of monopoly is being considered. If it is a *collusive monopoly* of firms that would otherwise be highly competitive, then the solution is to break up the monopoly—or better still, prevent it from being formed in the first place. This is a problem of antitrust policy that is discussed in Chapter 27. On the other hand, if it is a *natural monopoly* because of extended economies of scale, then breaking it up is no longer a simple solution. The reason is that this policy would create smaller-volume firms and thus raise costs of production, and this would impose an unnecessary cost on society. The preferred approach in this case is to leave the firm as a monopoly and continue to benefit from its relatively low costs of production; at the same time, impose a government policy that forces the monopoly to act as though it were a price-taking perfect competitor. That is, take away its market power to raise its price by imposing a ceiling on that price.

The question is, At what level should that price be set? The simple answer is *marginal cost pricing* shown in Figure 25-7 in the text: Set the price at the efficient level where the marginal cost of producing this good (MC) equals the marginal benefit it provides—that is, the market demand.

Unfortunately, in many instances this policy is not feasible because forcing the price down this much would turn the monopoly into a money-loser, and drive it out of business in the long run. This is the case which is examined in Box 25-2, where the government would have to supplement marginal cost pricing with whatever subsidy would be necessary to keep the firm in business; or equivalently, put the firm under government ownership and subsidize its operations in this way. A final alternative which is often used is *average cost pricing*: Instead of driving the price all the way down to the level required by marginal cost pricing, drive it down only partway—specifically, to the level where demand intersects *average* cost rather than marginal cost. Because price equals average cost, the firm breaks even. It is *not* turned into a money-loser, and the problem of going out of business does not arise.

However, since price is reduced only partway, monopoly inefficiency is only reduced partway; it is not eliminated. There is also a problem which applies not only to average cost pricing, but also to marginal cost pricing—and indeed to any government policy to control natural monopoly. Firms lack adequate incentive to keep costs down: If their costs rise, they know that the government-administered price will rise, because price is tied in some way to (marginal or average) costs.

Price Discrimination

So far we have assumed that the monopoly charges a single price to all consumers. But the firm will usually find it more profitable if it can charge different customers different prices—that is, if it can charge a higher price to customers who are willing and able to pay. If the monopoly is profitable in any case, then there is no reason to allow the firm to do this. However, such a pricing policy by a monopoly may be beneficial if the firm would not otherwise exist. In that case, allowing the firm to discriminate might not only allow the firm to cover its costs, but also provide a benefit to consumers who would not otherwise be able to buy this product.

Important Terms: Match the Columns

Match the term in the first column with the corresponding phrase in the second column. But before you do so, write out your own definition of the term in the first column.

_F_ **1.** Natural monopoly
_C/H_ **2.** Market power
_H_ **3.** Marginal revenue
_D_ **4.** Price discrimination
_G_ **5.** Marginal cost pricing
_B_ **6.** Theory of the second best
_E/C_ **7.** Average cost pricing
_A_ **8.** Marketing association

a. An agency set up by firms to raise the price of their product
b. The theory of what constitutes an efficient level of output in one industry when, due to monopoly or for other reasons, the level of output in other industries is not efficient
c. The policy of regulating a monopoly's price by setting it at the level where the firm's average cost curve intersects the market demand curve
d. The ability of a seller or buyer to influence price
e. The practice of charging different prices to different customers for the same good. This is one method a monopoly may use to increase its profits
f. A situation in which there are economies of scale (falling average costs) over such an extended range of output that one firm can produce the total quantity sold at a lower average cost than could two or more firms
g. The policy of regulating a monopoly's price by setting it at the level where the firm's marginal cost curve intersects the market demand curve
h. The additional revenue from selling one more unit of output

True-False

T **F** **1.** Monopoly exists when there is only one buyer even if there are many sellers.
T F **2.** Very heavy overhead costs tend to make average costs fall further as output increases.
T **F** **3.** An unregulated profit-maximizing monopoly will set a price where marginal cost intersects the demand curve.
T **F** **4.** Oligopoly—a market dominated by a few sellers—is very rare compared to monopoly.
T **F** **5.** A profit-maximizing monopolist will set a price above marginal cost.
T **F** **6.** One cannot be certain that monopoly, with its efficiency loss, is damaging to society without taking into account the monopoly transfer of income.

T F   **7.** A likely disadvantage of breaking up a natural monopoly is that it will raise costs of production.

T F   **8.** One problem with government ownership or price regulation of a monopoly is this: Once the firm knows that the government will ensure that its costs are covered, the firm will have a reduced incentive to keep its costs down.

T F   **9.** If marginal cost pricing is feasible, it will eliminate the efficiency loss from a monopoly.

Multiple Choice

1. An example of a monopoly is:
 a. the auto industry, while an example of an oligopoly is the steel industry
 b. the auto industry, while an example of an oligopoly is the local natural gas supplier
 c. the steel industry, while an example of an oligopoly is the local natural gas supplier
 d. the local natural gas supplier, while an example of an oligopoly is wheat production
 e. the local natural gas supplier, while an example of an oligopoly is the auto industry

2. A firm's minimum cost is $30, achievable at 1,000 units of output. This firm will be a natural monopoly if the quantity demanded at a $30 price is about:
 a. 1 million units   **d.** 2,000 units
 b. 100,000 units   **e.** 1,000 units
 c. 10,000 units

3. Economists define market power as:
 a. the ability of a firm to influence federal antipollution legislation
 b. the ability of a firm to influence tax legislation in its home state
 c. the ability of consumers to purchase imports rather than domestically produced goods
 d. the ability of a firm to influence Supreme Court decisions
 e. none of the above

4. A monopoly's marginal revenue is:
 a. always positive
 b. always above average cost
 c. equal to the height of its demand curve
 d. less than the height of its demand curve
 e. greater than the height of its demand curve

5. Which of the following faces a completely elastic demand?
 a. IBM
 b. an individual wheat farmer
 c. General Motors
 d. Ford
 e. an urban transit company that is not subject to government price regulation

6. The demand facing a monopoly is:
 a. the same as the total market demand
 b. to the right of total market demand
 c. to the left of total market demand
 d. completely elastic
 e. more elastic than the total market demand

7. Market power is the ability of a firm to:
 a. shift its demand curve to the left
 b. shift its demand curve to the right
 c. adjust to a given market price

 d. influence market price
 e. shift its cost curves

8. An unregulated monopoly is inefficient because it equates:
 a. marginal cost with demand rather than with marginal revenue
 b. marginal revenue with demand rather than with marginal cost
 c. marginal revenue with average cost rather than with marginal cost
 d. average cost with demand rather than with marginal revenue
 e. marginal cost with marginal revenue rather than with demand

9. If the monopolist is producing more than the profit-maximizing amount, then:
 a. marginal revenue will exceed price
 b. marginal cost will exceed price
 c. marginal cost will exceed marginal revenue
 d. average cost will exceed price
 e. marginal revenue will exceed average cost

10. If a perfectly competitive industry is monopolized, the result is:
 a. higher output and lower price
 b. higher output and the same price
 c. higher output and higher price
 d. lower output and higher price
 e. lower output and lower price

11. Monopoly typically results in:
 a. allocative efficiency   **d.** (a) and (b)
 b. technical inefficiency   **e.** (b) and (c)
 c. allocative inefficiency

12. When a regulatory agency controls a monopoly by marginal cost pricing, the monopoly's:
 a. price is reduced   **d.** level of efficiency remains
 b. output is reduced   the same
 c. profit is eliminated   **e.** all of the above

13. The theory of the second best tells us that monopolizing one industry in an economy where monopoly exists elsewhere will:
 a. reduce efficiency
 b. increase efficiency
 c. have no effect on efficiency
 d. have an uncertain effect on efficiency
 e. have an uncertain effect on price in that industry

14. A government setting a price equal to a monopolist's MC is trying to induce the firm to:
 a. act like a perfect competitor by reducing output
 b. act like a perfect competitor by taking price as given
 c. produce to the point where above-normal profit finally disappears

d. produce to the point where normal profit disappears

e. reduce price while holding its output constant

15. A product is not being provided because the potential producer is a monopolist whose demand lies below its average cost curve AC. This problem may be solved by permitting the firm to discriminate and thus:

    a. at least cover its costs

    b. shift its demand above its marginal cost curve

    c. shift its demand above its average variable cost curve

    d. shift its AC curve down so it overlaps demand

    e. shift its demand above its AC curve

16. Economists use the assumption that firms seek to maximize profit because:

    a. its describes how many business decisions are made

    b. alternative plausible assumptions may not be specific enough to support a theory

c. alternative assumptions will generally not do a better overall job of describing business decision-making

d. all of the above

e. none of the above

*17. A government marketing agency that is introduced into a competitive industry will:

    a. typically set quotas to ensure that producers will increase their sales

    b. typically set quotas to ensure that producers will reduce their sales

    c. typically set quotas to ensure that producers will maintain their previous sales levels

    d. not set quotas, but will encourage producers to sell more

    e. encourage the entry of new firms

    *Based upon material from the appendix of your textbook.

Exercises

1a. If the monopoly shown in Figure 25-1 is unregulated, it will maximize profits by selecting output _____ where _____ equals _____ . The price it will quote is _____ , the highest price at which this output can be sold. Its profit will be _____ for each of the _____ units it sells, that is, a total profit of area _____ . An alternative view of its decision is that it selects the point _____ on the _____ curve that maximizes this profit rectangle. The efficiency loss is _____ .

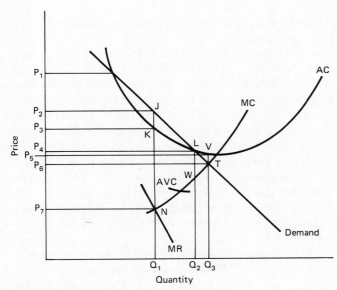

FIGURE 25-1

1b. A government regulatory agency that uses marginal cost pricing will set price equal to _____ . The firm will respond in the short run by producing output _____ because this is where its _____ curve cuts this price line _____ . However, in the *long run*, the firm

would produce an output of _____ because at equilibrium *T* it is operating at a [profit, loss] of _____ . To keep it in business the government would have to [provide a subsidy, impose a tax] of _____ . This policy would [reduce, increase, eliminate] the previous efficiency loss of _____ ; that is, it would improve efficiency by _____ .

1c. If the agency were instead to use average cost pricing, it would set price at _____ . The monopolist would produce output _____ and earn a profit of _____ . The subsidy now necessary to keep this firm in business would be _____ . This policy would reduce the efficiency loss from the original JTN to _____ ; that is, it would improve efficiency by _____ . Compared to marginal cost pricing, this average cost pricing policy improves efficiency [more, less]; but it avoids the government problem of having to [subsidize, tax] this firm.

1d. With either form of regulation, the monopoly is forced to act like [a perfect competitor, an oligopolist, a natural monopolist] facing a fixed price.

2. A monopoly has the demand and total cost figures shown in Table 25-1. Fill in this table, ignoring for now the last three columns.

    a. The monopoly's fixed cost is _____ . It will choose to produce a level of output equal to _____ and charge a price equal to _____ . Its maximum attainable profit is _____ .

    b. Suppose that, in an attempt to capture some of this monopoly's profits for the taxpayer's benefit, the government imposes a lump-sum tax of $5. This tax may be regarded by the monopoly as a fixed cost, because it must be paid no matter how much output is produced. After the imposition of this tax, the monopoly's fixed cost is _____ . Fill in the third-to-the-last column (1) indicating the monopoly's after-tax profit. After

Table 25-1

P	Quantity demanded	Total revenue	Marginal revenue	Total cost	Average cost	Marginal cost	Profit	(1) Net profit with lump-sum tax	(2) Net total revenue with excise tax	(3) Net profit with excise tax
$10	0	$0	$0	$ 2	$___	$0	$	$	$	$
8	1	8		3						
6	2			6						
4	3			11						
2	4			18						

imposition of the tax, the monopoly will choose to produce an amount of output equal to _____ and to charge a price equal to _____. Its maximum attainable after-tax profit will be _____.

c. Suppose that instead of the lump-sum tax, the government decides to impose a 50% excise tax on the monopoly. In other words, the monopoly must now pay the government 50% of its total revenue. In this case, the monopoly's fixed cost is _____. Fill in the second-to-the-last column (2), showing the monopoly's after-tax total revenue, and the last column (3), showing its after-

tax profit. In this case, the monopoly will choose to produce an amount of output equal to _____ and to charge a price equal to _____. Its maximum attainable after-tax profit will be _____. The amount of excise tax collected from this monopoly will be _____.

d. From the point of view of economic efficiency the [lump-sum, excise] tax is preferable. From the point of view of maximizing the amount of tax revenue collected from the monopoly, the [lump-sum, excise] tax is preferable.

Essay Questions

1. Are economies of scale a barrier to entry? Explain. Is IBM a monopoly? A perfect competitor? Or in a dominant position somewhere in between? Do you think economies of scale give it an advantage over potential competitors?

2. Compare a monopoly and a perfectly competitive firm in terms of their (a) demand and marginal revenue schedules, (b) their market power, (c) their efficiency, and (d) the appropriate government policy in dealing with each.

3. "Allowing a monopolist to charge some of his customers more than others is not appropriate because it is unfair to those who have to pay the higher price." Evaluate this statement. Are there any circumstances in which those who pay the higher price could actually benefit?

4. Suppose that the only two firms in an industry are considering a merger that would result in a reduction in costs of production through the elimination of wasteful duplication. Is it possible to argue that this action could increase efficiency? If so, how? Might it *decrease* efficiency? If so, how?

5. It has been argued by some that the American Medical Association is a collusive monopoly, because it restricts the output of medical services by controlling the

licensing of medical schools. How does this restriction affect the income of doctors and therefore the cost of medical services? What unfavorable consequences might there be if the government were to try to reduce this cost by allowing completely free entry into the medical profession—that is, allowing anyone, with or without training, to practice medicine? In view of this, (a) defend the position that the medical profession's collusive monopoly has been beneficial to the economy, and (b) defend the position that the monopoly has been harmful.

6. A perfectly competitive firm can sell all it wants at the existing price. Can a monopoly do that? If it tried to, what would happen? Does that mean that a monopoly is more constrained in its decision making than a perfect competitor?

7. Recall our discussion of the elasticity of demand from Chapter 20. If a monopoly's demand function is elastic, then what happens to its total revenue as its output increases? In this case, what can be said about the monopoly's marginal revenue? If the market demand is inelastic, what can be said about the monopolist's marginal revenue? In view of this, explain why a monopoly that has discovered that its demand curve is inelastic would want to change its output.

Answers

Important Terms: 1 f 2 d 3 h 4 e 5 g 6 b 7 c 8 a
True-False: 1 F 2 T 3 F 4 F 5 T 6 T 7 T 8 T 9 T
Multiple Choice: 1 e 2 e 3 e 4 d 5 b 6 a 7 d 8 e 9 c 10 d 11 e 12 a 13 d 14 b 15 a 16 d 17 b
Exercises: **1a.** Q_1, MC, MR, P_2, JK (or P_2P_3), Q_1, P_2JKP_3, J, demand, JNT. **1b.** P_6, Q_3, MC, P_6, zero, loss, P_5VTP_6, provide a subsidy, P_5VTP_6, JNT, JNT. **1c.** P_4, Q_2, zero, zero, LWT, JLWN, less, subsidize. **1d.** a perfect competitor.
2. Table 25-1 completed:

Table 25-1 completed

Price	Quantity demanded	Total revenue	Marginal revenue	Total cost	Average cost	Marginal cost	Profit	(1)	(2)	(3)
$10	0	$ 0	$ 0	$ 2	$—	$0	$ −2	$ −7	$0	$ −2
8	1	8	8	3	3	1	5	0	4	1
6	2	12	4	6	3	3	6	1	6	0
4	3	12	0	11	3⅔	5	1	−4	6	−5
2	4	8	−4	18	4½	7	−10	−15	4	−14

2a. $2, 2, $6, $6. **2b.** $7, 2, $6, $1. **2c.** $2, 1, $8, $1, $4. **2d.** lump-sum, lump-sum.

Across

1, 3. If perfect competition is to be efficient, this must equal the benefit to consumers

6. a curve frequently used in mathematics (abbrev.)

7. an early marginalist (see inside cover of text)

9. certainly not new

11. an element (abbrev.)

12. a famous quantity theorist (see inside cover of text)

13. a winner of Nobel prize in Economics (see inside cover of text)

14. misfortunes

17. to maximize profits, firm equalizes this and marginal cost (2 words)

19. a state in the Old South (abbrev.)

20. expensive

23. muse of history

24. industry with only one seller

26. above, and touching

27. large body of water

28. final part

29. with perfect competition, this is what every buyer and every seller is (2 words)

32. if the elasticity of demand is _____, total revenue remains constant when the price changes

33. an international organization for labor (abbrev.)

34, 35. the increase in variable costs when one more unit is produced

Down

1. buy or sell in the hope of profiting from a change in price

2. business owned by a group of consumers or producers (abbrev.)

3. Treasury _____ are short-term liabilities of the U.S. government

4. finish

5. this exists when we get the most out of our productive efforts

6, 21. for an efficient solution, this must equal social benefit

8. Chairman of Council of Economic Advisers, 1972–74

10. an illegal source of market power

15. natural log (abbrev.)

16. the best we can do when there are immutable imperfections in a market (2 words)

18. one of the two Germanies (abbrev.)

20. a type of efficiency

22. this is what a highly progressive income tax would do to the rich

24. "L'etat, c'est _____."

25. one of the four phases of the business cycle

29. the senior dance

30. rock that juts out

31. I (Latin)

CHAPTER 26

MARKETS BETWEEN MONOPOLY AND PERFECT COMPETITION

MAJOR PURPOSE

The last two chapters have described the two extremes in the spectrum of markets: perfect competition, where there are so many sellers that none has any influence over price; and monopoly, where the single firm is free to set any price it chooses, since it has no competitors to worry about. (A monopoly is restrained only by consumer demand and the possibility of government intervention.) Most American industries do not conform to either of these two extremes, but lie somewhere between, where individual firms have *some* influence over price. The objective in this chapter is to analyze two of the market forms that lie within this intermediate range. The first is *oligopoly*, a market dominated by a few sellers, in which in the absence of government intervention, there is a strong incentive for firms to collude in order to act like a monopolist and raise price. The most prominent example of such collusive behavior is described in this chapter: the Organization of Petroleum Exporting Countries (OPEC), which raised oil price by more than 10 times in less than a decade. The second market form analyzed in this chapter is *monopolistic competition* in which—as in perfect competition—there are a large number of sellers and free entry into the market. However, it differs from perfect competition because each firm produces a differentiated product, and this gives each firm some small degree of influence over price.

Learning Objectives

After you have studied this chapter in the textbook and the study guide, you should be able to:

Clearly distinguish between monopoly, oligopoly, monopolistic competition, and perfect competition

Give two reasons why oligopoly may arise

Explain why oligopolists have an incentive to collude, and the effect such collusion will have on efficiency

Explain why the OPEC countries were able to collude to raise the price of oil during the 1970s without imposing production quotas, and why they were forced into trying to set formal production quotas in the 1980s

Describe the kinked demand curve with a diagram

Explain why the kinked demand curve would discourage an oligopolist from changing price frequently

Explain the concept of price leadership, how it relates to the analysis of kinked demand, and why it is often viewed as "tacit collusion"

Give three examples of nonprice competition

Describe why economies of scale and advertising create barriers to entry

Summarize the arguments for and against advertising

Explain why the run-of-the-mill firm earns no above-normal profits in the long run in monopolistic competition, and why this market form is not necessarily inefficient, even though fewer firms could produce the same output at lower costs

HIGHLIGHTS OF CHAPTER

In discussing oligopoly and monopolistic competition—two of the "imperfectly competitive" market forms that lie between monopoly and perfect competition—our focus will be on the principles that govern business decision making in each case, and whether or not the outcome is efficient.

Oligopoly

How many sellers is "a few"? The smaller the number of sellers, the greater the market power (the influence over price) that can be exercised by each firm. Thus the first task is to define the degree of concentration of each industry. This is traditionally measured by the proportion of the industry's output made by the four largest firms. (An alternative measure, called the *Herfindahl index*, is described in Box 26-1 in the textbook. While it is slightly more complicated, it has the desirable feature of taking into account the output of all the firms in the industry—not just the four largest.)

An oligopoly can arise because an industry is a "natural oligopoly" in which the lowest-cost way of satisfying market demand is with a small number of firms. Alternatively, firms may combine or grow large, not because of cost conditions, but instead because they seek to acquire market power.

Because there are few clear-cut principles governing the behavior of oligopolists, the theoretical analysis is not as straightforward for oligopoly as it is for other market forms. But the following points are important:

1. There is a tendency for oligopolists to collude—that is, to act like a monopolist and raise price so as to maximize the total profits of the industry. To maintain the high price, each colluding firm is required to restrict its output to a certain quota level. This reduction in output leads to the same sort of efficiency loss as in the case of monopoly. However, it is precisely this reduction in the output of each firm that creates a tendency for collusive arrangements to break down; each firm is asked to reduce its output when it has an incentive to produce *more*. The reason the individual firm in an oligopoly would like to produce more is that, at its restricted level of output, the firm's marginal cost is still below its price. Therefore, it has an incentive to increase its output, if it can get away with such cheating. But if firms do cheat by producing more than their quota of output, the high price cannot be maintained, and the collusive arrangement comes apart.

2. When the oligopolistic firm chooses its price and output, it must take into account the possible reaction of its rivals—something that need not even be considered by the monopolist (with no rivals) or the perfectly competitive firm (whose rivals don't even notice what it's doing). This sort of complicated decision making is what makes the theory of oligopoly so interesting and difficult.

3. Oligopolistic firms sometimes face a *kinked demand curve*. If one firm raises its price, its rivals won't. Instead they'll hope to capture some of its sales. But if the firm lowers its price, its rivals will follow suit to avoid being undersold. In such circumstances, the firm is facing the kinked demand shown in Figure 26-7 in the textbook, and it will not want to change its price from the kinked level unless underlying cost conditions change substantially. While this theory is controversial as an explanation of how firms behave, it is very useful in making clear the issues that firms must deal with in making their decisions. For example, the kinked demand analysis in Figure 26-7 can be modified slightly to explain Cournot-Nash equilibrium in Box 26-3 in the textbook, or to explain price leadership.

4. In an industry with price leadership, one firm takes on the role of being the leader in announcing a price change, on the understanding that other firms will follow. This sort of "gentlemen's agreement" has often been criticized as a collusive arrangement, with the price leader setting the price at about the level that a monopolist would select. However, it is only "tacit collusion" because there is no communication between the firms, and it is therefore very difficult or impossible to prove that collusion has taken place. (Selling at the same price is not proof of collusion because, after all, that is what perfectly competitive firms do.)

5. Oligopolists who wish to avoid potentially destructive price competition have other options, in addition to tacit collusion in the form of price leadership. They can attempt to increase their market share by various forms of nonprice competition, such as product differentiation or advertising. Advertising in particular is controversial. On the one hand, it may involve wasteful competition, distort people's values, and mislead consumers. On the other hand, it may make consumers better informed and help to promote product quality by making firms fearful of losing the goodwill that they achieve through advertising. Moreover, it provides financial support for the media.

6. Oligopolists often succeed in erecting barriers to entry against new competitors. One such barrier is advertising which creates a favorable image of an existing firm that is difficult for new firms to overcome. But the most important barrier to entry may be economies of scale that leave room for only a few low-cost firms in the industry.

OPEC: An Example of Oligopoly Collusion

In many ways, the most interesting and far-reaching example of a collusive oligopoly has been the Organization of Petroleum Exporting Countries (OPEC). This collusive arrangement succeeded in quadrupling oil prices in 1973–1974, and again doubling them in 1979–1980. This was even more remarkable because during the 1970s OPEC had none of the restrictive quotas on output that are typically required to keep price up and ensure that the collusive arrangement won't come apart. There were several reasons for this, some of which are detailed Box 26-2 in the textbook. However, the most important was that the Saudi Arabians were the dominant producers of world-traded oil, and for many years they could keep the price up by restricting just their *own* very large output.

Why were the Saudis willing to do this? One reason was that, unlike some other OPEC members, such as Nigeria or Indonesia, they did not have a large population to support. Therefore, they could afford to keep their "black gold" in the ground. Moreover, because of their extremely large reserves, they were prepared to make short-term sacrifices in order to provide more assurance of a stable and healthy oil market in the long run. However, their power to keep price up was limited: By the early 1980s, the Saudis' production had been so far reduced in the attempt to maintain price, that they could no longer bear the lion's share of the burden. Their requirement that other OPEC producers would have to share this burden more equally led to the attempts to set up and enforce production quotas on all OPEC members. But by 1985, it was difficult to see how the high price of oil could be maintained. OPEC members could scarcely agree any longer on quotas, let alone abide by them. World oil demand was increasingly being satisfied by countries such as Mexico and the U.K., which were not even members of OPEC. And the Saudis

had pretty well exhausted their ability to support price by making further production cuts. Indeed, their production had already been reduced from a capacity level of over 10 million barrels per day to less than 3 million.

Monopolistic Competition

Whereas oligopoly, if unrestrained, often leads to a collusive outcome close to that of monopoly, the outcome in the case of monopolistic competition is closer to the other extreme of perfect competition. In monopolistic competition, as in perfect competition, there is a large number of firms. There is also free entry of firms into the industry, which means that any short-run excess profit for the run-of-the-mill firm will be eliminated in the long run. The important difference between the two market forms is this: Under monopolistic competition, a firm produces a differentiated product and therefore faces a downward-sloping demand curve. Under perfect competition, the firm produces a standardized product and faces a completely horizontal demand curve. Because the sloping demand curve gives a firm in monopolistic competition some influence over price, the firm quotes a higher price, and therefore produces a smaller output than a perfectly competitive firm that cannot raise its price. This restricted output suggests that monopolistic competition is inefficient, but this is not necessarily the case. Lower output by each firm means more firms are satisfying total market demand. Thus the consumer can choose from a wider range of differentiated products. This wider choice may more than make up for the disadvantage of lower output by each firm.

Important Terms: Match the Columns

Match the term in the first column with the corresponding phrase in the second column. But before you do so, write out your own definition of the term in the first column.

_____ **1.** Oligopoly
_____ **2.** Concentration ratio
_____ **3.** Natural oligopoly
_____ **4.** Product differentiation
_____ **5.** Cartel
_____ **6.** OPEC
_____ **7.** Kinked demand curve
_____ **8.** Price leadership
_____ **9.** Barrier to entry
_____ **10.** Monopolistic competition

a. The practice in some oligopolistic industries of having one firm announce its price change first, on the unspoken understanding that other firms will follow suit

b. The ability of each firm to distinguish its product from those of its rivals. Such distinctions may be real or imagined.

c. A market dominated by only a few sellers

d. A market in which there is (1) a large number of firms, (2) free entry of new ones, and (3) differentiated products. The demand curve facing each seller is quite elastic, but not completely so.

e. The proportion of an industry's output by the four largest firms (or, using an alternative measure, by the eight largest firms)

f. Anything that makes it difficult for new firms to enter an industry to compete against existing firms

g. A formal agreement among firms to collude in order to set prices and/or determine market shares

h. An industry in which total market demand can be satisfied at lowest cost by a few firms

i. The demand curve that will face an oligopolist if its rivals will follow it if it cuts its price, but will not follow it if it increases its price

j. The Organization of Petroleum Exporting Countries

True-False

T F **1.** The concentration ratio is relatively low in the auto industry.

T F **2.** Colluding firms in a cartel typically have an incentive to cheat by producing less than their quotas.

T F **3.** All cartels, regardless of where they may exist, are illegal.

T F **4.** A large firm acting as a price leader may decide not to retaliate against a small firm that has cut price, for fear that this may initiate a price war with other large firms.

T F **5.** Price leadership may be a disguised method of collusion.

T F **6.** The kinked demand curve arises mainly in monopolistic competition.

T F **7.** The theory of the kinked demand curve doesn't predict the price where the kink will occur.

T F **8.** All barriers to entry take the form of economies of scale.

T F **9.** Monopolistic competition is similar in many respects to perfect competition; but one important difference is that the product is differentiated.

T F **10.** Because consumers like variety, we cannot conclude that monopllistic competition is inefficient.

Multiple Choice

1. A firm's minimum cost is $10, achievable at 20,000 units of output. The industry will be perfectly competitive if the total quantity demanded of this product at a $10 price is:
- **a.** 1 million units
- **b.** 100,000 units
- **c.** 40,000 units
- **d.** 20,000 units
- **e.** 10,000 units

2. If oligopolistic firms collude to raise price:
- **a.** each benefits, while there is an overall loss to the economy as a whole
- **b.** the price leader benefits, while the other firms and the economy as a whole lose
- **c.** each firm and the economy as a whole benefit
- **d.** each firm benefits, while the economy as a whole is not affected
- **e.** each firm and the economy as a whole lose

3. General Motors is a:
- **a.** monopolist
- **b.** duopolist
- **c.** oligopolist
- **d.** monopolistic competitor
- **e.** perfect competitor

4. A high concentration ratio in an industry typically indicates that:
- **a.** the dominant firms in the industry have a great deal of market power
- **b.** no firms in the industry have much market power
- **c.** no firms in the industry have any market power
- **d.** the industry is monopolistically competitive
- **e.** the industry is perfectly competitive

5. Between 1980 and 1985, U.S. industry became:
- **a.** less competitive, because of the decline in international trade
- **b.** more competitive, because of the decline in international trade
- **c.** less competitive, because of the growth in international trade
- **d.** more competitive, because of the growth of international trade
- **e.** more competitive, despite the decline in international trade

6. The biggest surprise about OPEC is that it:
- **a.** survived for many years without a formal set of production quotas
- **b.** did not increase the price of oil when it had an opportunity to do so in 1973–1974
- **c.** has made no further price increases since its spectacular success in 1973–1974
- **d.** has been able to prevent any price reduction since 1973
- **e.** includes only countries from the Middle East

7. The success of the OPEC cartel in the 1970s and early 1980s was in substantial part due to:
- **a.** strong cultural ties among the member countries
- **b.** the strong sense of political unity among the member countries
- **c.** close social ties among the member countries
- **d.** all of the above
- **e.** the willingness of the Saudis to cut back their production

8. If all firms sell at the same price:
- **a.** there must be price leadership
- **b.** there must be some other form of collusion
- **c.** the industry must be perfectly competitive
- **d.** the industry must be an oligopoly
- **e.** none of the above

9. The growing importance of international trade has:

a. made U.S. firms more competitive
b. made U.S. firms less competitive
c. not affected the competitiveness of U.S. firms
d. made domestic concentration ratios more meaningful
e. (b) and (d)

10. The kinked demand curve:
a. helps to explain why oligopoly price has some degree of stability
b. leaves unanswered the question of how price is established in the first place
c. is based on the assumption that if a firm lowers its price, its competitors will follow
d. is based on the assumption that if a firm raises its price, its competitors won't follow
e. all of the above

11. Which of the following is *not* true about advertising?
a. It may involve waste.
b. It may mislead consumers.
c. It provides financial support for the media.
d. It may help to promote product quality by making firms fearful of losing goodwill.
e. It is sometimes undertaken by single firms in a perfectly competitive market.

12. In monopolistic competition:
a. there is a standardized product, just as in perfect competition

b. there is a standardized product, unlike the differentiated product in perfect competition
c. entry of new firms is restricted, unlike the free entry that exists in perfect competition
d. entry of new firms is restricted, just as in perfect competition
e. there is a large number of sellers, just as in perfect competition

13. In monopolistic competition:
a. there are very few sellers
b. it is impossible for new firms to enter the market
c. each firm sells a differentiated product
d. all of the above
e. none of the above

14. In a contestable market:
a. there is a single firm which can act as a monopolist
b. there is no free entry
c. the potential entry of new firms increases the market power of the existing firm
d. the potential entry of new firms has no effect on the market power of the existing firm
e. if there is a single firm, it cannot act as though it is a monopolist

Exercises

1a. In Figure 26-1, D represents the total market demand for an industry, with MR_I being the marginal revenue curve that corresponds to D. (For *any* demand curve, there exists a marginal revenue curve.) MC_A and AC_A are the cost curves for firm A, one of the five identical firms in this industry. Draw in the marginal cost curve *for the industry*, and label it MC_I. Label point R, where MC_I and D intersect, and point S, where MC_I and MR_I intersect. Label as Q the point directly above S on the demand curve.

If these firms act like perfect competitors and take price as given, then MC_I becomes the industry [demand, supply] curve, and the industry equilibrium is at point _____. _____ units are sold at price _____, with each firm earning a profit of _____.

1b. Now suppose that these firms collude to maximize their collective profit, which they will do by equating MC_I and _____, at an output of _____ units. They will sell this output for price _____. That is, the industry will select its profit-maximizing point _____ on the

FIGURE 26-1

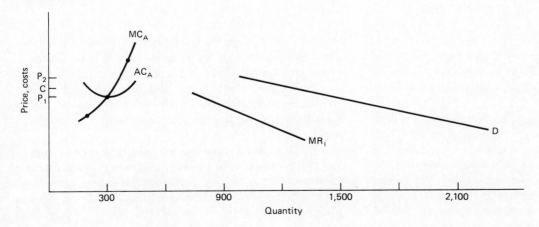

demand curve D. Since industry output has been reduced by one-third (from 1,500 to 1,000 units), the output of each individual firm, such as A, must be reduced by the same proportion, from 300 units to _____. Draw in point T, which is the equilibrium for firm A, where this firm is now selling 200 units at a price P_2. Label as V the point on AC_A directly below T. Shade in the new profit area _____ of firm A.

By colluding, these five firms have each [increased, decreased] their profit from _____ to _____. At the same time, the nation as a whole has [lost, gained] because of the efficiency [loss, gain] of area _____ that results because output has been [reduced, increased] to the [efficient, inefficient] level of _____ units from the [efficient, inefficient] level of _____ units where the marginal benefit to society shown by curve _____ equals the marginal cost to society shown by curve _____.

2. Figure 26-2 shows an oligopoly which—along with all its rivals—is currently charging price P and producing quantity Q. This firm faces the kinked demand curve that consists of the segment of D_A *above* the existing price P and the segment of D_B *below* the price P. The respective marginal revenue curves are MR_A and MR_B.

    a. If the firm increases its output to more than Q, it faces demand curve _____, and its MR curve is therefore [MR_A, MR_B]. But if it decreases its output to less than Q, if faces demand curve _____, and its MR curve is therefore [MR_A, MR_B]. Therefore, its complete MR curve is [MR_A, MR_B, $WXYZ$].

    b. If its MC is MC_1, then it will charge a price that is [more than, less than, the same as] P, and it will choose a quantity that is [more than, less than, the same as] Q.

    c. If its MC is MC_2, then it will charge a price that is [more than, less than, the same as] P and it will choose a quantity that is [more than, less than, the same as] Q.

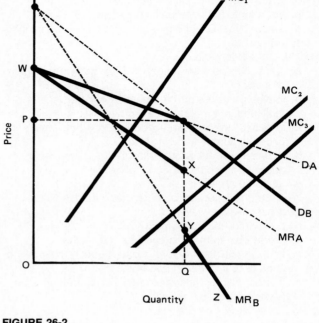

FIGURE 26-2

    d. If its MC is MC_3, then it will charge a price that is [more than, less than, the same as] P and it will choose a quantity that is [more than, less than, the same as] Q.

    e. If its MC is MC_2, we now see from a different point of view why the kinked demand curve results in a stable price. If MC_2 shifts up, but still intersects the horizontal segment XY, then the firm will [raise, lower, leave unchanged] the price. Alternatively, if MC_2 shifts down, still intersecting XY, the firm will [raise, lower, leave unchanged] the price. In other words, marginal cost can shift up or down within the range _____, without affecting price at all.

Essay Questions

1. Will firms in an industry with a high concentration ratio be more or less likely to engage in collusive activity than those in an industry with a low concentration ratio? Why?

2. Oligopoly is a market with a few sellers. But how many is a few? Does it matter if there are 4 or 14? Why? To be specific, compare the situation of an individual U.S. firm if (*a*) it has only three U.S. competitors with (*b*) a situation in which it has the same three U.S. competitors, plus two Japanese competitors, four European competitors, and two other foreign competitors. Would the U.S. firm have the same market power in either case? Would the U.S. firms be equally able to collude, tacitly or explicitly?

3. Explain why a group of oligopolists might have trouble establishing a collusive price agreement, and then have trouble keeping the agreement from coming apart.

4. It is often argued that advertising increases sales, and this permits lower prices to consumers. Explain the circumstances in which this could occur. Also explain the circumstances in which advertising would *increase* prices to consumers.

5. What industry characteristics distinguish oligopoly from monopoly? From perfect competition?

6. Explain some of the techniques oligopolists use to avoid price competition.

7. "If the two firms have identical cost curves, then in the long run, the perfectly competitive firm will produce at lower cost than the firm in monopolistic competition." Explain why you agree or disagree. Explain why this sort of an argument may or may not be used to establish that monopolistic competition is inefficient.

8. "Monopoly and perfect competition are both single-price industries. But in monopolistic competition, there are many prices." Explain why you agree or disagree.

9. Firms in monopolistic competition have some influence over price. Why don't they use this influence to raise price above average costs and therefore make an above-normal profit in the long run?

Answers

Important Terms: 1 c 2 e 3 h 4 b 5 g 6 j 7 i 8 a 9 f 10 d
True-False: 1 F 2 F 3 F 4 T 5 T 6 F 7 T 8 F 9 T 10 T
Multiple Choice: 1 a 2 a 3 c 4 a 5 d 6 a 7 e 8 e 9 a 10 e 11 e 12 e 13 c 14 e
Exercises: **1a.** supply, R, 1,500, P_1, zero. **1b.** MR_I, 1,000, P_2, Q, 200, P_2TVC, increased, zero, the shaded area, lost, loss, QSR, reduced, inefficient, 1,000, efficient, 1,500, D, MC_I.
Figure 26-1 completed:

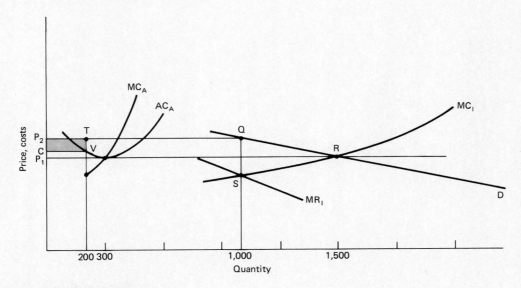

FIGURE 26-1 completed

2a. D_B, MR_B, D_A, MR_A, $WXYZ$. **2b.** more than, less than. **2c.** the same as, the same as. **2d.** less than, more than.
2e. leave unchanged, leave unchanged, XY.

PART SIX

ECONOMIC EFFICIENCY:

ISSUES OF OUR TIME

HOW MUCH SHOULD THE GOVERNMENT REGULATE BUSINESS?

MAJOR PURPOSE

This chapter begins Part 6, in which a number of markets are examined to see how well they work. When they don't work well, what sort of government intervention is appropriate? For example, Chapter 27 describes government antitrust intervention when there is a threat by firms to collude in order to restrain trade or monopolize an industry. Chapter 27, and more particularly Chapter 28, demonstrates how a free market may do an inadequate job of protecting health, safety, and the environment, and how the government is justified in intervening to provide such protection. Government intervention is also sometimes justified to prevent our resources from too rapid depletion (Chapter 29) and to provide public goods that free markets fail to provide (Chapter 30). Finally, the last two chapters in Part 6 (Chapters 31 and 32) deal with the great debate: What are the gains from international trade, and should the government intervene to restrict that trade? Although there are some situations in which such intervention is justified, the broad conclusion is that, with some exceptions, international markets work reasonably well, and there has been too much government intervention in this area in the past.

Chapter 27, to which we now turn, deals with government regulation of business. Such regulation can be divided into three categories:

1. Antitrust laws that prevent collusion and other restraints on trade. While such laws are necessary, their application will be critically evaluated by posing such questions as; Should firms be broken up without regard to the possible effect on costs of production?

2. Regulation of a naturally competitive industry, such as trucking and the airlines, where government regulation in the past has not removed restraints on trade, but instead has created them. Government intervention of this form has often been hard to justify, and is now being phased out with the deregulation of some of these industries.

3. Quality-of-life intervention by the government to protect our health, safety, and the environment. This chapter and the next will demonstrate why such government intervention is justified, but why such intervention often takes an unnecessarily costly form.

Learning Objectives

After you have studied this chapter in the textbook and the study guide, you should be able to:

Identify and briefly describe the three legislative acts that form the cornerstone of federal antitrust policy

Explain why it may be advantageous to have large-size firms, and why antitrust action to break them up involves costs as well as benefits

Show how economic efficiency may be promoted if the government on the one hand allows *natural* monopolies to exist (subject to price regulation), while on the other hand it uses antitrust policies to break up collusive monopolies

Give several reasons why "market-structure" regulation tends to be in the interest of the firms being regulated, rather than in the interest of consumers or the nation as a whole

Explain the two important reasons why it is feasible for a government agency to cartelize an industry, but why it is not possible for a private group of producers to do so

Explain how former Civil Aeronautics Board (CAB) regulations affected the interests of (1) the established airlines, (2) the nation as a whole, (3) passengers on heavily traveled trunk routes, and (4) passengers on small-city routes. In explaining (3) and (4), use the concept of cross-subsidization.

Demonstrate the extent to which benefit-cost analysis can be used to evaluate quality-of-life regulations on health, safety, and the environment

Explain why benefit-cost analysis involves many problems; for example, this approach often requires us to attach a value to a human life

Demonstrate why government policy becomes inconsistent, with too few lives saved, if a value is *not* placed on a human life

HIGHLIGHTS OF CHAPTER

This chapter focuses on several ways in which the government regulates business.

Antitrust Laws

The first category of regulation consists of antitrust laws. The main laws that underlie the government's antitrust policy are (1) the Sherman Antitrust Act (1890), which made collusion illegal; (2) the Clayton Act (1914), which banned, for example, interlocking corporate directorates, corporate takeovers that would lessen competition, and contracts that force a buyer to purchase a firm's entire product line or nothing at all; and (3) the Federal Trade Commission (FTC) Act (1914), which established the FTC to prevent "unfair competition." The text also briefly describes the Capper-Volstead Act (1922), the Robinson-Patman Act (1936), and the Miller-Tydings Act (1937), to illustrate how some government laws can have a perverse effect, in the sense that they encourage, rather than reduce restraints on trade.

The primary objective of antitrust legislation is to reduce restraints on trade and the abuse of market power by monopoly and oligopoly firms. The main tactic in pursuing this objective has been to enact and enforce legislation designed to limit the size of enterprises by breaking up large firms, and by preventing them from being formed in the first place. However, such a policy carries a cost, because size has advantages:

1. Large firms can *better afford* the expenditures on research and development (R&D) which generate growth and technological improvements. Large firms also have more *incentive* to undertake R&D expenditures, because their large market share allows them to capture a large share of the benefits from any new technique or product they may develop. For example, if GM develops a superior engine, it will acquire millions of dollars of benefits from this in its huge sale of cars, so GM can justify this sort of R&D. However, a Kansas farmer can't justify a similar R&D expenditure to develop a better strain of wheat; the benefits to him would be limited to a few thousand dollars, while the millions of dollars of additional benefit would be spread among thousands of wheat farmers.

2. Because of economies of scale, large firms may enjoy lower costs per unit than smaller firms; this point was demonstrated in the case of natural monopoly in Chapter 25.

Since economies of scale can be important, a good policy for promoting efficiency is not to break up natural monopolies, with their cost advantages. Instead, they should be allowed to exist—subject to price regulation that forces them to act like perfect competitors, taking price as given. Such a price policy will reduce or eliminate the efficiency loss that would otherwise occur under such a monopoly. (To review this point, see Figures 25-5 and 25-7 in the text.) At the same time, antitrust policy could be used to break up other monopolies where there is little or no cost advantage in continued large size. While this is a reasonable approach, it is far from perfect. One reason is the problems that are encountered in imposing price regulation on a natural monopoly. (See Chapter 25, and Appendix 25-B.) If these problems are judged to be more serious than the cost advantages the monopoly gets from economies of scale, it may make sense to break up the firm.

In addition to splitting large firms up into many smaller competitors, antitrust policy encourages competition in other ways as well. For example, it restricts cutthroat competition—that is, pricing below costs in order to drive competitors out of business. The problem with trying to deal with cutthroat competition is that it is never clear whether a firm is setting its price below costs because it is trying to cut the throats of its competitors, or because it is just trying desperately to make sales in a weak market—perhaps in the face of stiff foreign competition. (Moreover, remember that even under perfect competition, as firm might continue to operate with price less than average cost as long as the firm is covering its average variable cost. This is scarcely setting a cutthroat price. Instead the firm is just accepting an unfavorable price that's dictated by the market.)

3. A third antitrust objective is to prevent firms from colluding to "cartelize" an otherwise competitive industry. But collusion, like cutthroat competition, is difficult to establish in the courts. For example, the fact that all firms in an industry are charging the same price doesn't prove that there has been a conspiracy to fix prices, because uniformity of price occurs in a perfectly competitive market in which there is no collusion whatsoever.

Market-Structure Regulation of Price and Entry

The text discusses this kind of regulation mainly in terms of the example of the airlines industry, which used to be regulated by the Civil Aeronautics Board (CAB). Now that this industry has been deregulated—and the CAB has disappeared—it is clear that this industry is not a natural monopoly. It is naturally a much more competitive industry and was made noncompetitive when the CAB cartelized it.

The CAB did this by restricting entry into particular air routes, and by regulating price at a level that was favorable for the airlines. Such cartelization of an industry was far easier for a government agency than it would have been for a group of private producers because (1) any policies of a government agency, such as the CAB, are exempt from antitrust action, and (2) when the CAB set prices backed up by the force of law, this eliminated the problem that so often destabilizes other kinds of cartels—namely, the problem of firms cheating by cutting their price. Airlines didn't cut their price because this would have been illegal.

What were the overall effects of CAB regulation? First, it reduced efficiency by raising price and thus reducing the total amount of air travel. Second, its decisions were not taken in the interest of the flying public, but instead were in the interests of the airlines that benefitted from the high price. There was also a "cross-subsidization" transfer from the passengers on the longer trunk routes between big cities to small-city travelers. That is, the CAB required the airlines to provide small-city service, even in cases where it was not profitable; in compensation, the CAB allowed the airlines to cover their losses by charging a higher price on their profitable trunk routes.

In 1978, Congress passed the Airline Deregulation Act, empowering the CAB to dismantle its regulations and open the industry up to competition. (Of course,

safety regulation remained, administered by the Federal Aviation Administration.) As expected, the immediate effect of deregulation was to reduce price and increase quantity (number of passengers). It also resulted in severe financial difficulties for many of the airlines not efficient enough to survive the intensified competition. Finally, it drew into the industry many new firms whose entry had previously been prohibited by the CAB.

Unfortunately, Congress did not quite provide economists with a controlled experiment. As deregulation was taking place, jet fuel prices doubled, and a recession curbed the demand for air travel. Thus it was not clear how much of the financial plight of some of the airlines was due to deregulation and how much was due to these other factors.

Quality-of-Life Regulation

This differs from market-structure regulation in two major ways. First, whereas a market-structure agency such as the CAB imposes regulations on only one industry, quality-of-life regulatory agencies—such as the Environmental Protection Agency—impose regulations across *all* industries. *Second*, quality-of-life regulations are not imposed in the interest of the firms being regulated, as is often the case with market- structure regulation. Instead, complying with such regulation often imposes a substantial cost on business.

In this section of the chapter, one of the most important issues for you to study is how benefit-cost analysis may be used to evaluate quality-of-life regulations. Regulations to make air cleaner, jobs safer, and cars more reliable obviously have significant benefits, in terms of improving the health and safety of the population and saving lives. But quality-of-life regulations may also have significant costs. One of the most important principles to be learned in a first course in economics is that any policy with a very large benefit is not *necessarily* worth undertaking; its benefit must exceed its cost. The purpose of benefit-cost analysis is to perform just such a test.

One might expect that whenever policymakers are considering a new regulation, they would perform such a benefit-cost analysis. Unfortunately this is not always the case. In some recent legislation, it is expressly stated that regulations must be enforced *regardless of their costs*.

If we take a benefit-cost approach to analyse a proposed new quality-of-life regulation, costs must first be estimated. This is not an easy task, because costs of regulation fall in three categories: (1) the salaries and other operating costs of the agencies that administer the regulations; (2) the costs incurred by the firms in complying with the regulations, and (3) the efficiency costs of the regulation. The last category includes such items as the time delays because producers have to comply with regulations before selling new products; and the costs because some business ventures are not undertaken due to the regulatory paperwork that would be involved.

While it is difficult to estimate these *costs*, even greater problems are encountered in estimating the *benefits* of quality-of-life regulation. For example, one of the benefits of such regulation is the saving of lives—and no one wants to put a value on a human life. It is far easier to say that the value of a life is infinite, and leave it at that. But that's not how we value our lives. We all take some small risk with our lives whenever we take a trip in a plane—or, for that matter, an even bigger risk when we travel by car. We don't sit at home and avoid the risk, as we would if we truly believed our lives had an infinite value. But while it's easy to argue that the value of a life is less than infinite, it's very difficult to be more specific. For attempts to do so, see Box 27-4 in the textbook.

Even if the complete information necessary for a full benefit-cost test is not available, it is still possible to make government policy more effective using fragmentary information. To use an example cited in the text, a regulation limiting coke-oven emissions has been saving lives at an estimated cost of over $4 million per life. Alternatively, lives could be saved at a cost of only about $100,000 each by building more railroad overpasses. Obviously, we should switch to this policy; if we did, we could save a fortune. Or, to put the same point more appropriately, we could use our limited funds to save far more lives.

Finally, benefit-cost analysis raises broader problems. For example, one would expect that the Reagan administration's requirement that regulations pass a benefit-cost test would be a major step forward in getting a more appropriate evaluation of government policies. Not so, say critics, who charge that this is just a way of blocking desirable regulations where full information on benefits and costs is not yet available.

Important Terms: Match the Columns

Match the term in the first column with the corresponding phrase in the second column. But before you do so, write out your own definition of the term in the first column.

_____ 1. Cutthroat competition
_____ 2. Price leadership
_____ 3. Interlocking directorate
_____ 4. Tying contract
_____ 5. Fair trade contract
_____ 6. Horizontal merger
_____ 7. Vertical merger
_____ 8. Conglomerate merger
_____ 9. Natural monopoly regulation
_____ 10. Market-structure regulation
_____ 11. Quality-of-life regulation
_____ 12. Cross-subsidization
_____ 13. Benefit-cost analysis
_____ 14. Benefit-cost test

a. Charging one group of customers more in order to finance service (which would not otherwise be available) to another group of customers
b. The union of firms in the same competing activity
c. Fixing by a manufacturer of the price that retail stores can charge for its product
d. The requirement that the benefits of a program be at least as great as its costs
e. The practice in some oligopolistic industries of having one firm announce its price changes first, on the understanding that other firms will follow suit. Such a practice is sometimes suspected of being a form of "tacit" or silent collusion, in which the initial firm sets approximately the same price that a cartel would set.
f. The union of firms in unrelated activities. This almost happened when American Express, a credit card firm, tried to take over McGraw-Hill, the company that publishes this textbook.
g. A contract which requires purchasers to buy other items in a seller's line in order to get the items they really want (sometimes called *full-line forcing*)
h. The situation that exists when a director sits on a board of two or more competing firms
i. Regulation of the price and entry conditions in a naturally more competitive industry, such as the nation's trucking firms
j. Estimating and comparing the benefits and costs of a program
k. Pricing below costs in order to drive competitors out of business
l. The union of a firm and its supplier. This happened, for example, when the shoe retailer T. R. Kinney merged with the shoe manufacturer Brown Shoe Co.

m. Setting the price that can be charged by a natural monopoly such as an electric power company or a telephone company

n. Regulation of health, safety, working conditions, and the environment

True-False

T F **1.** Both criminal and civil antitrust suits can be brought against a firm.

T F **2.** Antitrust action that splits up a natural monopoly will lead to lower average costs of production

T F **3.** Full-line forcing is the requirement that purchasers buy a whole line of items in order to get the one they really want. It was prohibited by the Clayton Act in 1914.

T F **4.** So long as the acquiring firm offers to buy the target firm's stock, the management of a target firm will support the merger.

T F **5.** There has been a recent increase in the price of local phone service, and a drop in the price of long-distance service where competition has increased.

T F **6.** Airline regulation kept airline fares down for the consumer. It was only when regulations were relaxed in the late 1970s that airline fares rose dramatically.

T F **7.** Under cross-subsidization, the price to one group is raised so that better service or reduced price can be provided to another group.

T F **8.** Benefit-cost analysis is designed to ensure that the total benefits of a policy will at least equal its total costs.

T F **9.** Costs cannot exceed benefits for any environmental or safety regulation.

T F **10.** It makes no sense to impose coke oven regulations that cost more than $4 million for each life saved, while we are not building the railroad overpasses that could save lives for far less than $1 million each.

T F **11.** The Environmental Protection Agency has not been able to impose regulations unless they have been able to pass a benefit-cost test.

Multiple Choice

1. In recent years, the market power of large U.S. corporations has:
  a. decreased because of the growth of foreign competition
  b. decreased because of the decline of foreign competition
  c. increased because of the growth of foreign competition
  d. increased because of the decline of foreign competition
  e. been unaffected by changes in foreign competition

2. Government antitrust action resulted in:
  a. a breakup of IBM, but not AT&T
  b. a breakup of AT&T, but not IBM
  c. a breakup of neither
  d. a breakup of both
  e. a merger of the two

3. The increasing strength of foreign competition makes antitrust action against large U.S. firms:
  a. illegal
  b. more necessary
  c. less necessary
  d. neither more nor less necessary
  e. more necessary in some respects, but less in others

4. Interlocking directorates occur:
  a. when directors are forced to sit on the boards of several noncompeting companies
  b. when a director is on the board of several competing firms

  c. when directors are forced to hold stock in several noncompeting companies
  d. when directors trade inside information
  e. when a director of one company is involved in a takeover bid for another company

5. The Celler-Kafauver Antimerger Act:
  a. prevented a firm from purchasing the physical assets of another firm, if this would "substantially lessen competition"
  b. prevented a firm from taking over another firm by purchasing its common stock, if this would "substantially lessen competition"
  c. prohibited tying contracts
  d. prohibited full-line forcing
  e. legalized interlocking directorates

6. The Clayton Act:
  a. legalized interlocking directorates and full-line forcing
  b. made interlocking directorates and full-line forcing illegal
  c. prohibited one firm from taking over another by purchasing its common stock if this would "substantially lessen competition"
  d. (a) and (c)
  e. (b) and (c)

7. A merger of a firm and its supplier is called:
  a. a vertical merger d. a direct merger
  b. a horizontal merger e. an indirect merger
  c. a conglomerate merger

8. Between 1950 and 1980—that is, in the 30 years prior to

the Reagan administration—the authorities exercised substantial restraint over:
- **a.** conglomerate and vertical mergers, but were far less restrictive with horizontal mergers
- **b.** conglomerate and horizontal mergers, but were far less restrictive with vertical mergers
- **c.** vertical and horizontal mergers, but were far less restrictive with conglomerate mergers
- **d.** conglomerate mergers, but were far less restrictive with vertical and horizontal mergers
- **e.** horizontal mergers, but were far less restrictive with vertical and conglomerate mergers

9. In any takeover bid by firm A for firm B:
- **a.** the management and stockholders of B are almost certain to welcome the bid
- **b.** the management and stockholders of B are almost certain to oppose the bid
- **c.** the managers may oppose it, while the stockholders welcome it
- **d.** the managers of firm A typically employ their golden parachutes
- **e.** firm A usually regards firm B as a black knight

10. Greenmail is:
- **a.** the premium paid by a target firm to buy its own stock from a shark
- **b.** the premium paid by a shark to buy its own stock from a target company
- **c.** the price reduction a private firm enjoys when it buys its own stock from a shark
- **d.** the price reduction a shark has to accept when it sells the target firm's stock
- **e.** none of the above

11. In attempting to organize a cartel:
- **a.** a government agency is immune from antitrust prosecution, but a private group of producers is not
- **b.** a private group is immune from antitrust prosecution, but a government agency is not
- **c.** both groups are subject to antitrust prosecution
- **d.** neither group is subject to antitrust prosecution, because the antitrust laws don't cover cartels
- **e.** neither group is subject to antitrust prosecution, because the cartels do not fall under FTC jurisdiction

12. Before deregulation, the CAB conferred a net gain upon:

- **a.** the established airlines and the nation as a whole
- **b.** the nation, but not the established airlines
- **c.** the established airlines, but not the nation
- **d.** neither the established airlines nor the nation
- **e.** potential new airlines and the economy as a whole

13. Regulation of the airlines by the Civil Aeronautics Board:
- **a.** encouraged competition by restricting the entry of new firms
- **b.** encouraged competition by allowing the entry of new firms
- **c.** discouraged competition by allowing the entry of new firms
- **d.** discouraged competition by restricting the entry of new firms
- **e.** had no effect on competition because it prevented new firms from flying on existing routes

14. In controlling the release of new drugs:
- **a.** there is a cost of delay, for further testing, but no benefit of delay
- **b.** there is a benefit from delay, but no cost
- **c.** there is neither a benefit nor a cost from delay, because health is a noneconomic issue
- **d.** there is a cost and benefit of delay; the cost is that lives may be lost because a lifesaving drug can't be used yet
- **e.** there is a cost and benefit of delay, but neither can be specified

15. With the growth of regulation in the 1960s and 1970s, economic decision making shifted:
- **a.** toward the market and away from the courts
- **b.** away from the courts
- **c.** away from the regulatory agencies
- **d.** away from the market and toward the courts and regulatory agencies
- **e.** away from the market, the courts, and the regulatory agencies

16. In their daily decisions, most people implicitly value their own lives as worth:
- **a.** an infinite amount
- **b.** zero
- **c.** about half their current year's income
- **d.** some value between (a) and (c)
- **e.** some value between (b) and (c)

Exercises

1a. Suppose that the total cost for a firm producing widgets equals the fixed cost of $2 million plus a variable cost equal to $4 for every widget produced. Thus the marginal cost of producing widgets is always [constant, increasing, decreasing], and average cost is always [constant, increasing, decreasing]. The widget industry is a _____.

1b. Suppose this firm is being regulated using marginal cost pricing. Then its price would be $_____. Suppose the firm sells 2 million units at this price. Its cost per unit would be $_____, and its loss per unit would be $_____. Therefore, the taxpayer would have

to pay a total subsidy of $_____ to keep the firm in operation.

1c. If the industry were broken up into two separate firms, each with the same cost structure as before, and each firm were to produce half of this quantity, then the cost per unit would be _____, which is [more than, less than, the same as] before. The loss per unit would be $_____, which is [higher, lower, no different] than before. Therefore, the total subsidy required to keep the industry alive would be [higher, lower, no different] than before. Specifically, the total subsidy paid to both firms would be $_____.

1d. After this monopoly is broken up and all necessary subsidies are paid, the firms would [gain, lose, be unaffected], the consumers would [gain, lose, be unaffected], and the taxpayers would [gain, lose, be unaffected]. Thus the nation as a whole would [gain, lose, be unaffected]. What important principle is illustrated by this hypothetical example? _____

_____

2. The Apex Company employs 2,000 individuals working on high-steel construction. The firm has to pay its labor force a $1,000 per person wage premium each year in order to attract workers who are willing to risk their lives. The risks on this job raise the mortality rate by 2/1000; that is, the chance a worker will be killed during a year is 2/1000 higher than in other jobs. The question is; Should the government introduce a safety regulation that will reduce the risk by 1/1000, if this regulation costs $1.5 million (including both government administration costs and the compliance cost by the firm)?

To answer this, we need to know the value of a human life. Because each worker is willing to take a 2/1000 chance of losing his life if he is paid $1,000 more, this means that he values his life at [$5 million, $500,000, $1,000, $500], which is his $_____ wage premium divided by the _____ increase in risk.

Although this can't be predicted precisely in advance, the *expectation* is that this regulation would be expected to save _____ lives, which is the _____ risk reduction from this regulation times the 2,000 workers employed. Since each worker values his life at $_____, the *benefit* of this regulation is $_____. This is [greater than, less than, the same as] the $1.5 million *cost* of the regulation. Thus, this regulation [passes, fails] this benefit-costs test, and it would be [introduced, rejected].

If its cost were $500,000, then it would [pass, fail] the benefit-cost test, and it should be [introduced, rejected].

Essay Questions

1. Discuss the benefits and costs of breaking up a natural monopoly. Do you think these benefits and costs were also present in the government's attempt to break up IBM?

2. "Giant companies such as IBM and General Motors still dominate the production of many goods. Thus our antitrust laws cannot have been effective." To what extent do you agree with this statement? Explain your position.

3. "Natural monopoly is one of the simplest areas of government decision making. Just set up an agency that will impose marginal cost pricing on the company." Do you agree? Explain.

4. "In restricting GM's use of its market power, the competition from Japanese auto companies has been far more effective than our antitrust laws." Do you agree? Explain your position.

5. Evaluate the following FTC ruling on mergers: ". . . proof of violation [of the antitrust laws] consists of . . . evidence showing that the acquiring firm's . . . over-all organization gives it a decisive advantage in efficiency over its small rivals." In the matter of Foremost Dairies, Inc., 60 FTC, 944, 1084 (1962).

6. Why do you suppose the unions representing truck drivers tried so hard to prevent the trucking industry from being deregulated?

7. Show why the value of human life may have to be taken into account in calculating the costs of regulation by the Federal Drug Administration, as well as the benefits of this regulation.

Answers

Important Terms: 1 k 2 e 3 h 4 g 5 c 6 b 7 l 8 f 9 m 10 i 11 n 12 a 13 j 14 d
True-False: 1 T 2 F 3 T 4 F 5 T 6 F 7 T 8 T 9 F 10 T 11 F
Multiple Choice: 1 a 2 b 3 c 4 b 5 a 6 e 7 a 8 c 9 c 10 a 11 a 12 c 13 d 14 d 15 d 16 d
Exercises: **1a.** constant, decreasing, natural monopoly. **1b.** $4, $5, $1, $2 million. **1c.** $6, more than, $2, higher, higher, $4 million. **1d.** be unaffected, be unaffected, lose, lose. From the point of view of efficiency, natural monopolies should be regulated rather than broken up. **2.** $500,000, $1,000, 2/1000, 2, 1/1000, $500,000, $1 million, less than, fails, rejected, pass, introduced.

Across

5, 7, 8. economies of scale and advertising can create these
13. U.S. soldier (abbrev.)
15. type of competition aimed at eliminating rivals
16. won't he _____ learn?
17. mad, fanatical
18, 21. a major objective of the firm
23. an academic degree
24. on the interior of
25. _____ policies are designed to limit market power
29. at one time, the foundation of the monetary system
30. estimated time of arrival (abbrev.)
31. one
32, 33. when this exists, there are economies of scale
35. goods from foreign countries
36. a source of technological improvement
38, 39. this type of analysis sometimes used to evaluate government regulations
40. an international organization whose purpose is to exercise market power (abbrev.)

Down

1. Lincoln's first name
2. this is greatest in a monopolized industry
3. one reason for the development of monopoly
4. government agency with antitrust responsibilities (abbrev.)
6. income from land or buildings
9. return on an investment
10. the concentration _____ measures the degree to which an industry is dominated by a few sellers
11. one of the major antitrust acts
12. a type of merger
14. citizen of a middle-eastern country
15. what students often do the night before the exam
19. this type of efficiency is generally reduced by monopoly
20. the same (Latin abbrev. used in scholarly references)
22. correct
25. smallest particle of an element
26. Keynes believed that the objective of balancing the budget every year represented a policy _____
27. remain
28. light brown
34. this organization became the CIA (abbrev.)
37. Much _____ about Nothing

CHAPTER 28

PROTECTING THE ENVIRONMENT IN A GROWING ECONOMY:

HOW SHOULD POLLUTION BE LIMITED?

MAJOR PURPOSE

Many people think that environmental pollution is simply a bad thing that should be prevented. They believe that it has nothing to do with economics, and such economic considerations as cost are irrelevant. Pollution, they contend, should be cleaned up, regardless of cost. The objective in this chapter is to show that pollution *is*, in fact, an economic problem—one that involves many of the principles that have already been developed in this book. Moreover, if economic considerations are ignored, pollution will be much more costly to control. Society will waste valuable resources in the cleanup effort. Or, to put the same point another way: Our limited available funds will give us far less improvement in the environment if we ignore costs.

The specific questions we will address in this chapter are:

1. What is pollution?
2. Why is it a problem that even a perfectly competitive market cannot deal with efficiently?
3. What principles should guide our antipollution policy?
4. What policies have actually been used in the United States, and how successful have they been?

Learning Objectives

After you have studied this chapter in the textbook and the study guide, you should be able to:

Identify the two major legislative acts designed to control pollution in the United States

Explain why pollution is an externality

Explain why perfect competition does not lead to efficiency when there is pollution or any other kind of external cost (such as congestion, analyzed in the Appendix to this chapter)

Measure the efficiency loss from pollution, in a diagram similar to Figure 28-2 in the textbook

Show why we cannot and should not attempt to eliminate pollution completely

Explain why the policy of imposing a physical limit on pollution can be a far more costly way of reducing it than imposing a tax on emissions

Show why a third option—imposing physical limits on pollution, but allowing the rights to be bought and sold—is as efficient as imposing a tax, and compare these two preferred policies in terms of their political feasibility and equity

Critically evaluate the policy of subsidizing pollution-control equipment

Provide detail on the past mistakes and future problems facing U.S. policymakers in cleaning up the environment

Explain how recycling reduces the pollution problem, and, as a favorable side effect, also reduces the problem of resource depletion that we will be studying in the next chapter

HIGHLIGHTS OF CHAPTER

Each of the four key questions listed above will be considered.

1. What Is Pollution?

Pollution is an external cost. It is a cost to society resulting from our economic activities of production and consumption. But this cost is external, because it isn't paid for by those responsible for it. For example, when smoke from a factory soils someone's clothes, the factory owner doesn't have to pay the cleaning bill.

2. A Failure of the Invisible Hand: Why Does a Perfectly Competitive Market Fail to Deal with the Pollution Problem?

When there is an externality like pollution, the "invisible hand" of a perfectly competitive, free market provides an inefficient outcome. The reason is that there is a violation of one of the conditions in Chapter 24 that allows perfect competition to deliver an economically efficient outcome. The condition that is violated is that the marginal cost to producers (MC) must be the same as the marginal cost to society (MC_S). This condition does not hold when there is an external cost such as pollution, because MC_S is *more* than MC. The difference between the two is the marginal external cost MC_E, as illustrated in Figure 28-1 in the textbook.

Efficiency requires that the marginal benefit to society (shown by the demand curve) be equal to the marginal cost to society MC_S. In Figure 28-2 of the textbook we see that this efficient outcome is at E_2. However this is *not* the equilibrium in a perfectly competitive free market. The reason is that, as always in such a market, supply reflects the cost facing producers. But this is only their private cost MC. The *external* cost of their actions is a cost they *don't* have to face. Because supply reflects private cost MC only, the perfectly competitive equality of demand and supply is at equilibrium E_1 rather than the efficient E_2. Thus perfect competition is inefficient; too much output of this polluting good is produced (Q_1 rather than the efficient output Q_2). The efficiency loss is measured by the red triangle in this figure. Be sure you can explain this triangle: For each of the units of "excess" output between Q_2 and Q_1, social cost MC_S exceeds benefit D. There is therefore a net cost involved in producing each of these units—with the sum of all these costs being the red triangle.

3. What Principles Should Guide Our AntiPollution Policy?

The above analysis suggests a simple way that the government can make a perfectly competitive market efficient: Impose a tax on polluting producers equal to the external cost they are creating; that is, impose tax r in Figure 28-2 in the text. This tax now becomes one of the costs producers have to face. In other words, the "external cost is now internalized," because it has now become one of the costs that producers have to pay. Since supply reflects the costs producers have to face, it now reflects both internal and external costs—that is, supply is now S_2. Now the perfectly competitive equilibrium of demand and supply is at the efficient point E_2. Thus, with this simple imposition of a tax, the perfectly competitive market does yield an efficient outome after all. Adam Smith's "invisible hand" does work, because, with this tax, the government is applying the appropriate pressure on the market.

Figure 28-2 in the text illustrates another important principle: Polluting output can be cut back "too much." Limiting it to Q_3 is even worse than a "hands-off" policy that would allow output to continue unrestricted at Q_1. (At Q_3, the efficiency loss FE_2G is even greater than the red efficiency loss at Q_1.)

4. Antipollution Policies: What Has the U.S. Experience Been?

The main policy of the government has not been to tax polluters, but has instead been to impose physical limits on pollution. Such limits are imposed under the Clean Air Act and the Water Pollution Control Act, and are enforced by the Environmental Protection Agency (EPA). The government has also relied upon another method—subsidizing the purchase of pollution-control equipment. On the whole, these programs have resulted in a substantial reduction in pollution. However, most economists believe that the programs have not reduced pollution in an efficient manner, for the following reasons:

1. The physical limits in some cases have been too restrictive and in other cases too loose, because the EPA has tended to disregard the cost of reducing pollution.

2. Even if the total physical limit were to be set correctly (for example, at Q_3 in Figure 28-3 of the text), allocating individual limits for individual polluters is a much more costly way of reducing pollution than is the imposition of a pollution tax. Under a pollution tax the firms that can cut back pollution at least expense would automatically cut back more; thus there would be a lower cost of reducing pollution. You should be able to demonstrate this in Figure 28-3. The least expensive way of cutting back pollution to Q_3 is to have the firms to the right of Q_3 cut out their pollution at a cost shown by, for example, the short red bar. But when physical limits are imposed, some of the reduction in pollution must be undertaken by firms to the left of Q_3 at the relatively high cost shown by, for example, the tall red bar. There is the same reduction in pollution, but it is achieved at an unnecessarily high cost. (For a detailed example, see exercise 5 below.)

Be sure you can demonstrate in Figure 28-3 in the

textbook not only why a physical limit on pollution is less efficient than a tax, but also why a physical limit becomes as efficient as a tax, *if* the government modifies this to a "tradeable permit" policy—that is, if the government issues a certain number of permits to pollute, and allows these permits to be freely bought and sold.

3. The simple policy of just imposing physical limits on polluting firms has encouraged many of them to engage the government in costly legal actions to try to gain exemption from the limits.

4. In some cases, the government has been forced to back down from its standards when firms claimed to be unable to meet them, and threatened widespread layoffs of their labor force.

5. The government has failed to ensure that the pollution-control equipment it has subsidized is used effectively.

6. This pollution-control equipment has, at best, provided an "end-of-pipe" solution that is often more costly than other solutions such as using "cleaner" inputs. (For example, less polluting western coal could be used in power plants.) Again, either a pollution tax or a system of tradeable permits would be a lower cost policy because it would give firms not only the incentive to cure pollution, but also the incentive to find the *least expensive* cure. (See exercise 6.)

In conclusion, the good news is that the government is beginning to move away from a policy of just imposing physical limits on polluters to the more efficient policy of issuing tradeable permits. By allowing polluters to buy and sell their rights to pollute, the government reduces cleanup costs by harnessing the power of the marketplace.

As a postscript we emphasize one more important idea in this chapter. Recycling can play a role in reducing the amount of pollution by using up polluting wastes (such as empty beer cans). Such a policy would also mean that we will need to extract fewer natural resources from our environment. If we produce new beer cans out of old ones, we won't need to mine as much bauxite (aluminum ore).

Important Terms: Match the Columns

Match the term in the first column with the corresponding phrase in the second column. But before you do so, write out your own definition of the term in the first column.

_____ **1.** Internal cost
_____ **2.** External cost
_____ **3.** Social cost
_____ **4.** The marginal cost of reducing pollution (MCR)
_____ **5.** Marginal cost of having pollution (MCP)
_____ **6.** "End-of-pipe" treatment
_____ **7.** Recycling

a. The cost of reducing pollution by one more unit
b. The cost that is paid by the producer (also called *private cost*)
c. The cost of having one more unit of pollution
d. The cost paid not by the producer (or consumer) of a good, but by someone else (also called *neighborhood cost* or *cost spillover*). Examples include costs of pollution and traffic congestion
e. The policy of removing pollutants just before they enter the environment. (Sometimes this is a more costly method of reducing pollution than the alternative of using cleaner fuels or different production processes that produce less pollution in the first place.)
f. The total cost to society, that is, the sum of internal and external costs
g. Using materials again rather than throwing them away, which can reduce pollution and preserve natural resources

True-False

T F   **1.** Restricting industrial growth is one of the best measures for controlling pollution.
T F   **2.** Inefficiency occurs if producers do not take external pollution costs into account.
T F   **3.** Marginal external cost equals marginal social cost minus marginal private cost.
T F   **4.** The main effort of the Environmental Protection Agency has been to collect the taxes that the government has imposed to discourage pollution.
T F   **5.** A pollution tax "internalizes and externality" because the producer is forced to face not only production costs, but also the external costs imposed on society.
T F   **6.** Without government intervention, the marginal cost of having pollution would be zero.
T F   **7.** Setting an arbitrary physical limit on pollution will always be better than doing nothing at all.

T F   **8.** The problem with pollution is that, in the absence of government intervention, firms view it as an internal cost.

T F   **9.** The Clean Air Act has sometimes been interpreted to mean that the air should not be allowed to deteriorate anywhere—even in states with no air pollution problem.

T F   **10.** We should continue to build more roads until all congestion is eliminated; that is, the external costs of taking any trip become zero.

Multiple Choice

1. An example of an externality being internalized occurs if:
   a. an export firm is required to raise the price of a good it is also selling in the home market
   b. an export firm is required to export less and sell more goods on the home market instead
   c. a producer is forced to pay a tax equal to the external cost his product imposes on society
   d. a producer is forced to pay a tax equal to the internal cost his product imposes
   e. a tax is imposed on the producer equal to the marginal social cost of the good

2. In a perfectly competitive market, the marginal benefit of a polluting good will equal its marginal social costs if:
   a. a tax is imposed on the good equal to its marginal external cost
   b. a tax is imposed on the good equal to its marginal internal cost
   c. a subsidy is provided equal to the marginal internal cost
   d. a subsidy is provided equal to the marginal external cost
   e. the government does not intervene with either a tax or subsidy

3. In a perfectly competitive market for a polluting good where the government is following a "hands-off policy":
   a. price will be higher than the efficient level
   b. price will be equal to the efficient level
   c. less than the efficient amount will be produced
   d. more than the efficient amount will be produced
   e. the efficient amount will be produced

4. In the face of external costs, efficiency can be achieved in a perfectly competitive market by setting a tax that is equal to:
   a. the marginal social cost of producing the good
   b. the marginal internal cost of producing the good
   c. the marginal external cost of producing the good
   d. the total social cost of producing the good
   e. the total internal cost of producing the good

5. Airplanes flying low over houses near airports cause "noise pollution." The most efficient policy to deal with this would be to:
   a. rely on the "invisible hand" to take care of the problem
   b. provide a subsidy to each airline depending on the total amount of noise it creates in the affected neighborhoods
   c. impose a tax on each airline depending on the total amount of noise it creates in the affected neighborhoods
   d. impose limits on the number of flights of each airline
   e. subsidize airlines that install noise-abatement devices

6. It has been estimated that pollution-control measures necessary to meet the U.S. cleanup standards set in the early 1970s would cost roughly:
   a. $4 to $6 million per year
   b. $40 to $60 million per year
   c. $400 to $600 million per year
   d. $4 to $6 billion per year
   e. $40 to $60 billion per year

7. As time passes, pollution becomes a more difficult problem to deal with because the marginal cost of reducing pollution (MCR):
   a. shifts to the left, while the marginal cost of pollution (MCP) is rising
   b. shifts to the right, while MCP is rising
   c. shifts to the right, while MCP is falling
   d. shifts to the left, while MCP is falling
   e. remains stable, while MCP is rising

8. An effluent fee is:
   a. any tax imposed on the wealthy
   b. a special tax on the wealthy who pollute
   c. a tax on each unit of pollution
   d. a subsidy provided to polluters to encourage them to use cleaner fuels
   e. a subsidy provided to polluters who install pollution-abatement equipment

9. Superfund is a multimillion-dollar program:
   a. to clean up ground pollution
   b. to clean up industrial air pollution
   c. to clean up air pollution from auto exhausts
   d. to publicize the dangers of pollution to the public
   e. to publicize the environmental benefits of the Environmental Protection Agency

10. If a physical limit is set on the amount of pollutants each firm can emit:
   a. there will be no change in the total nationwide amount of pollution
   b. there will be an increase in the total nationwide amount of pollution
   c. pollution will be cut back, but at a higher cost than necessary
   d. pollution will be cut back, at the minimum possible cost
   e. nothing can be said about the pollution that will result

11. The least-cost way of reducing pollution by an industry is to:
   a. encourage all firms to cut back their pollution by the same percentage
   b. force all firms to cut back their pollution by the same percentage
   c. let the firms with the highest profits cut back the most
   d. force the firms with the lowest profits to go out of business

e. provide an incentive for firms with the lowest cost of reducing pollution to make relatively large cutbacks

12. The government's policy of subsidizing the purchase of pollution control equipment can be criticized because it:
  a. places too great an emphasis on "end-of-pipe" treatment
  b. places too little emphasis on "end-of-pipe" treatment
  c. has led to an overemphasis by the government on how efficiently this machinery will subsequently be operated
  d. has been supported by inadequate short-term financing during its construction
  e. none of the above

13. A sag point is:
  a. a location where pollution does the least damage
  b. a location where pollution is particularly harmful

c. a location where pollution is heavy but not very damaging
d. the period before an election when unpopular pollution-control legislation cannot be passed
e. the period before an election when members of Congress are so exhausted that they will pass unpopular pollution-control legislation

14. In the face of a highway congestion, efficiency requires a:
  a. subsidy to drivers equal to the external cost of a trip
  b. subsidy to drivers equal to the internal cost of a trip
  c. toll or tax on drivers equal to the external cost of a trip
  d. toll or tax on drivers that will eliminate congestion entirely
  e. subsidy to drivers that will eliminate congestion entirely

Exercises

Figure 28-1 represents the market for a good that causes pollution.

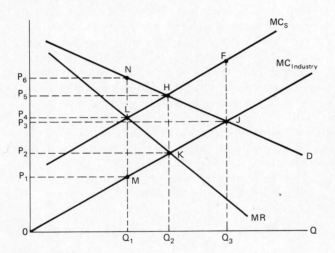

FIGURE 28-1

  a. If the market is perfectly competitive, output will be _____, market price will be _____, marginal social cost will be _____, and the marginal external cost will be _____.
  b. If the commodity produces no external benefits, then the *optimal* output is _____. This output would be attained under perfect competition if the producers were faced with a tax of _____ per unit. This would result in a market price of _____. Without this tax, the efficiency loss will be area _____.
  c. Suppose that these firms were able to collude to form a monopoly. Then the level of output (with no tax) would be _____, the market price would be _____, and the efficiency loss would be _____.

  d. Assume that the marginal external cost is a constant—i.e., that the lines MC_s and $MC_{industry}$ are parallel, with $LM = HK = FJ$. Now suppose that the government imposes the same tax on the monopolist that it earlier charged to the perfect competitors. In this case, the monopolist will produce an output of _____, it will charge price _____, and the efficiency [gain, loss] will be area _____. Thus a per unit tax on a polluting monopolist [will, will not] necessarily lead to greater efficiency.

2. If pollution is left uncontrolled in Figure 28-2 below, the amount of pollution will be _____. If the government imposes a tax T to reduce pollution, it will be cut back to _____. Those firms to the [right, left] of Q_1 will stop polluting, while those firms to the [right, left] of Q_1 will continue to pollute.

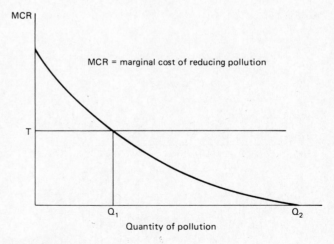

FIGURE 28-2

3. This problem requires Box 28-3 in the textbook.
  a. If MCP_1 in Figure 28-3 below is the marginal

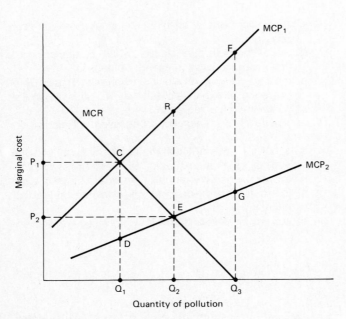

FIGURE 28-3

cost of having pollution and MCR is the marginal cost of reducing pollution, then, in the absence of any pollution tax, the quantity of pollution will be _____, MCR will be _____, and MCP will be _____. The economically efficient reduction in pollution is to quantity _____. This will result if firms are charged a tax of _____ per unit of pollution.

b. Now suppose that the marginal cost of having pollution is MCP$_2$ instead of MCP$_1$. Then the economically efficient amount of pollution is _____. This will result if firms are charged a tax of _____ per unit of pollution. The efficient

amount of pollution in this case is [more, less] because pollution is [more, less] damaging.

4. Now suppose that the marginal cost of having pollution is *really* MCP$_1$ but that the government makes a mistake and estimates it to be MCP$_2$. The government erroneously uses MCP$_2$ and sets the tax on pollution at _____. The resulting quantity of pollution is _____, which is [more, less] than the economically efficient amount. At this level of pollution, MCR is _____, and the true MCP is _____. There will be an efficiency [gain, loss] from the government's estimating error equal to area _____. Thus we [may, may not] conclude that, if the government underestimates the problem it will take inadequate action to counter it; that is, the government will set too low a pollution tax.

5a. The two lines in Figure 28-4 below show the marginal cost of reducing pollution MCR for two smoke-polluting firms (which are otherwise identical). Bars are added for detail. Reducing smoke pollution is less costly for firm [A, B]. Suppose that each firm is presently required by law to limit its output of smoke to 10 units, as shown by the dark vertical line. Both firms together generate 20 units of pollution. Now suppose that a government official decides, after reading this study guide, to impose a pollution tax instead of limiting each firm's smoke. If he sets the tax at $650 for each unit of smoke emitted, then firm A will [cut back, expand] its emissions to _____ units of smoke, and B will [cut back, expand) its emissions to _____ units. Both firms together generate [more, less, the same] pollution as before. The firm with the higher MCR has [increased, decreased] its pollution, and the one with the lower MCR has [increased, decreased] its pollution.

5b. Firm A's pollution-reduction costs have [increased, decreased] by _____, while firm B's pollution-

FIGURE 28-4

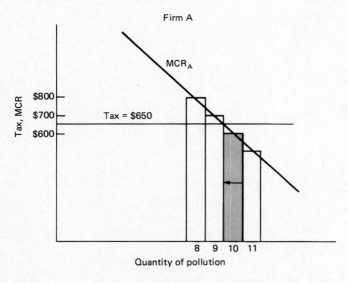

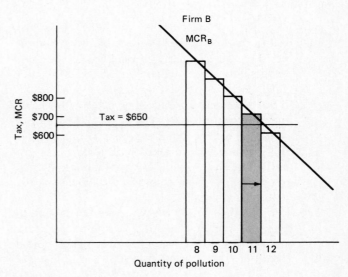

reduction costs have [increased, decreased] by _____. Thus the total pollution reduction costs of the two firms have [increased, decreased, stayed the same], while the total amount of pollution by the two firms has [increased, decreased, stayed the same]. Therefore, the tax is [more, less] efficient in keeping down costs than the previous limits on pollution.

6a. Suppose that a company can produce either a car that runs on gasoline or one that runs on a newly invented fuel which sells for the same price but which reduces the emission of pollutants by 50%. Unfortunately, the car using the new gasoline costs $200 more to construct. Suppose that, in all other respects, both cars perform equally well, so that consumers do not care which fuel a car uses; if given the choice, they will buy the car with the lower purchase price. Therefore, with no regulations, the car producer will build the car using [gasoline, new fuel].

Suppose that it is also possible to install an "end-of-pipe" pollution control device on all its cars, which also reduces emissions by 50% but costs $500. Again, suppose that consumers do not care whether or not a car has this device. Then the auto producer will build the car using [gasoline, new fuel], and [with, without] the device. The cars [will, will not] pollute the atmosphere; but the car companies don't take this into account because this is an [external, internal] cost.

6b. Now suppose that a government agency wants to cut back auto emissions by 50%, so it requires the

company to install the pollution-control device. The company will now build cars using [gasoline, new fuel], and with the device. The cost to society of this end-of-pipe reduction in pollution is $_____ per car.

Now suppose instead that the government just requires the auto producer to cut back the emissions from its cars by 50%, leaving it up to the company to decide how to do this. Then the cost to the company of complying with this requirement would be $_____ per car if it installed the device or $_____ per car if it switched to the new fuel. Therefore, it would choose the [device, new fuel]. In this case the cost to society of the reduction in pollution would be $_____ per car.

6c. In this example, the policy of telling the company *how* to reduce pollution is $_____ [more, less] costly per car than the policy of just telling them to do it and leaving all details to them. If instead the agency had told the company to do it by making cars that use the new fuel, the cost to society would have been [more than, less than, the same as] the cost of just telling them to do it. What general rule does this suggest about the relative cost of telling companies to comply compared with telling them exactly how to comply?

_____

_____

_____

Essay Questions

1. "One advantage of using taxes rather than physical limits to control pollution is that the former policy harnesses the forces of the marketplace to help find an efficient solution, whereas the latter policy does not." Do you agree or disagree? Explain your answer.

2. Explain why, in selecting the specific least-cost method of reducing pollution, private firms will do at least as good a job as government agencies, and often better.

3. Explain how the concept of an external cost (that is, a cost not borne by the decision-maker) is illustrated by the following example. When Napoleon, the founder of the conscription system, was told that a planned military operation would cost too many men, he replied: "That is nothing. The women produce more of them than I can use."

4. In recent years a large Canadian distillery has paid for the tickets to enable people to travel free on the Toronto subway system on New Year's Eve. Explain how this self-imposed tax has helped to promote economic efficiency by internalizing an external cost.

5. This problem is based on Box 28-2 in the textbook. Some economists maintain that all external costs are a result of society's failure to assign property rights to individuals. For example, if my factory pollutes the air above your house, then I am using a valuable commodity (namely, the air above your house) without having to pay for it. If our laws were changed so that anyone who owned a house also owned all the air above that house, then I would have to persuade you to sell me the right to use your air before I could pollute it. Explain how, if the law were changed in this way, the external cost—that is, the emission from my factory—would be internalized.

Suppose that I managed to persuade everyone in the neighborhood except you to sell me the right to pollute their air. Explain how that would put you in position to take undue advantage of me when we were bargaining over what price I should pay for the right to pollute your air. Can you think of any other problems that might arise if this "property right" solution to the problem of pollution were to be attempted?

Answers

Important Terms: 1 b 2 d 3 f 4 a 5 c 6 e 7 g

True-False: 1 F 2 T 3 T 4 F 5 T 6 F 7 F 8 F 9 T 10 F

Multiple Choice: 1 c 2 a 3 d 4 c 5 c 6 e 7 b 8 c 9 a 10 c 11 e 12 a 13 b 14 c

Exercises: **1a.** Q_3, P_3, Q_3F, JF. **1b.** Q_2, HK, P_5, HFJ. **1c.** Q_2, P_5, zero **1d.** Q_1, P_6, loss, NLH, will not. **2.** Q_2, Q_1, right, left. **3a.** Q_3, essentially zero, Q_3F, Q_1, P_1. **3b.** Q_2, P_2, more, less. **4.** P_2, Q_2, more, Q_2E, Q_2R, loss, CRE, may. **5a.** A, cut back, 9, expand, 11, the same, increased, decreased. **5b.** increased, $600, decreased, $700, decreased, stayed the same, more. **6a.** gasoline, gasoline, without, will, external. **6b.** gasoline, $500, $500, $200, new fuel, $200. **6c.** $300, more, the same, Telling them exactly how to comply will cost more unless the government happens to pick the least-cost method—in which case it doesn't matter.

CHAPTER 29

NATURAL RESOURCES:

ARE WE USING THEM AT THE RIGHT RATE?

MAJOR PURPOSE

In the last chapter, we saw that there was an external cost—in terms of damage to those living downstream—if chemicals are produced by a factory that dumps wastes into a river. The objective in this chapter is to use much of this same analysis to examine the external cost that is associated with resource extraction—namely, the cost to future generations because less of the resource will be available then. In this analysis, the question of who owns the resource is a critical one. If it is privately owned, then the owner will tend to take this future cost into account (since it's the owner's own resource that is being depleted) and decisions will therefore tend to be efficient. However, if the resource is common property (publicly owned), then those extracting the resource

have no reason to take the future into account. Because they tend to ignore the external cost to future generations, there is an inadequate conservation effort; an inefficiently large quantity of the resource is extracted.

In this chapter, we also return to the case study of oil, one of our most important natural resources. Earlier, in Chapter 26, we examined the attempt by OPEC to keep the world price of oil high; in this chapter, we examine the difficulties and inefficiencies introduced in the 1970s when the U.S. government kept the domestic price of oil low. Why did the government do this, and what was the effect of this policy on oil use? Finally, we examine alternative forms of energy, since these will determine how painful any shortage of oil may be to future generations.

Learning Objectives

After you have studied this chapter in the textbook and the study guide, you should be able to:

Describe the internal and external costs of extracting a common-property resource, and explain why both of these are internal costs if the resource is privately owned

Explain why a perfectly competitive market in a natural resource may be efficient if the resource is privately owned, but not if it is common property

Describe the maximum sustainable yield (Box 29-1 in the textbook) and explain why harvests involve no future costs if the population of a species is greater than this; and why problems arise if the population is harvested down to a level below this

Explain why simple projections of the use and availability of resources yield misleading predictions

Give three reasons why population growth continues to be rapid in less developed countries despite the scarcity of resources

Present the case in favor of economic growth, and the case against

Describe how the domestic price of oil was controlled before 1979, and some of the practical problems that were encountered

Explain the efficiency and transfer effects of decontrol—that is, of allowing the domestic price of oil to rise to the world price

Explain how such a price rise affected the amounts produced, consumed, and imported by Americans

Present the arguments for raising the domestic price of oil above the world price

Explain the advantages and disadvantages of each of the three major alternative sources of energy—natural gas, coal, and nuclear power

HIGHLIGHTS OF CHAPTER

Since no one owns the fish in the sea, they are a common-property resource, and provide a good illustration of one of the central issues in this chapter: Common-property resources are inadequately conserved in a free, perfectly competitive market. The reason is that fishing involves two costs: (1) the internal costs incurred by those who fish, such as the boats, nets, and labor, and (2) the external cost that falls on future generations because there is less of this resource available to them. If the resource is common property, fishing firms don't pay any attention to this second cost. Like the polluting firm that ignores its external cost—such as the damage its pollutants do to those living downstream or downwind—the fishing firm that ignores the external costs it is imposing on future generations will produce more than the efficient amount. (Its output decision is influenced by its internal costs, but not by the external costs it creates.)

Policies to Reduce Inefficiency in Resource Extraction

There are three possible ways to reduce inefficiency:

1. Set a physical limit on the catch. The problem with this approach is that it does not use the market mechanism. The government restricts the catch (perhaps by putting a limit on the size of nets or size of boats); and, as in the case of pollution discussed in the previous chapter, too severe a physical restriction may be worse than no restriction at all. The two alternative ways to increase efficiency *do* use the market mechanism.

2. Impose a tax or fishing fee on fishermen according to the number of fish they catch—specifically, impose a tax on them equal to the external costs they generate, just like the tax on polluting firms analyzed in the last chapter.

3. Create property rights; let the fish be privately owned. While this is not possible in the oceans or Great Lakes, it might be in inland lakes or ponds. (And it certainly is feasible for many other resources—such as timber—that are already privately owned.) Once the schools of fish are privately owned, the owners will take into account both the harvesting costs *and* the cost of having a reduced catch in the future. (It is their future catch that will be reduced.) Thus this future external cost is internalized once the resource is privately owned. Since the private owners will take all costs into account, the result is an efficient one. But it won't be equitable, unless the new owners are charged in some way for the asset (the fish) that they now own.

Special Problems of Nonrenewable Resources

Since schools of fish can eventually reproduce themselves, they are a *renewable* resource. On the other hand, there are other resources, such as coal, oil, or base metals, that are not renewable. The key questions with such resources are, Will we run out, and if so, when? And what can we do to prevent this? Simple projections of present trends point to an eventual doomsday, when rising population overtakes our limited resources. But such projections are oversimplified, because they do not allow for the adjustments that will take place as resources become scarce. One of the most important kinds of adjustment is this: As a resource becomes more scarce, it becomes more expensive; this, in turn, leads to (1) a substitution in production for the scarce resource by other factors that are more plentiful, (2) a substitution in consumption by goods that require less of the scarce resource, (3) induced innovation that economizes on these resources, and (4) a reduction in the rate of growth of population because raising children becomes costly as the price of resources rises. Some have criticized this last point by noting that in the less developed countries, population growth has continued even though most parents can't afford to have children. However, the experience of these countries can be explained by three special factors: (1) Poverty is so severe that people have children to provide them with support in their old age, (2) there are religious and social objections in these countries to birth control, and (3) their recent population growth is not just a reflection of birthrates, but also of falling *death* rates, due to dramatic advances in medical services; however, falling death rates cannot continue to have the impact on population that they have had in the past.

In addition to the question of whether our future growth will be severely restricted by resource scarcity (as the doomsday models predict) or whether growth can continue because adjustment mechanisms work well, there is another overriding question: Do we really want substantial economic growth? The traditional argument in favor of growth is that it helps to relieve unemployment, reduce poverty, and raise our incomes and those of our children. However, a number of arguments have recently been put forward *against* continued growth. For example, it has been pointed out that growth contributes to pollution and depletes our natural resources. The main difficulty with such antigrowth arguments is that restricting growth is not the best way to attack these problems. Much more progress is possible if we design policies—such as taxes on polluters or on those firms extracting resources—that deal directly and specifically with each of these problems. In the case of resources, it is important to ensure that they are being priced high enough to provide adequate conservation.

Oil

Recently, this resource has been priced well above the requirements of conservation. Under the influence of OPEC—and in particular, the Saudi Arabians—the world price of oil rose over 10 fold between 1973 and 1982. To provide some relief to oil users, the U.S. government instituted a policy of holding the domestic U.S. price down below the rapidly escalating world price. Full detail on the effects of this price ceiling—and the problems it raised—cannot be provided without a diagram, and you should be sure you have mastered Figure 29-6 in the text before proceeding. However, two of the broad effects of such a price ceiling can be sketched out:

1. There were winners and losers. The winners were oil users—from Sunday drivers to the giant power-generating companies and their customers—who benefited because the price of oil was kept down. However, this lower price hurt oil producers in the United States.

2. There were two efficiency losses, shown by the two shaded triangles in Figure 29-6 in the textbook. The first arose because the low price encouraged oil consumption, while the second arose because the low price discouraged domestic oil production.

To reduce the negative effects on production, the government added a twist to this policy and thus created a "blended price system." Under this system, the price of "new" currently produced oil was not kept down. It was allowed to rise to the world price. Thus domestic production of oil would not, it was hoped, be discouraged after all. On the other hand, the price of "old" oil (that was already being produced, and would continue to be produced almost regardless of price) was still kept low. Finally, the price that oil buyers paid was a "blended" average of these various prices (including, in addition, the high world price of imported oil). Because U.S. oil users were paying the average of what these various kinds of oil cost, it was not necessary for the government to provide any subsidy of the kind typically required by a price control policy.

Unfortunately, however, it was an imperfect solution. Because it did not allow the domestic price paid by oil users to rise to the world price, U.S. consumption and hence imports of oil continued at a high level. In turn, this demand by the United States to buy oil on the world market allowed OPEC to keep the *world* price of oil rising. Paradoxically, the more that the United States tried to keep its domestic price below the world price, the greater was the upward pressure on the world price.

When this policy was phased out by Presidents Carter and Reagan, the U.S. domestic price rose to the world price, and U.S. oil consumption and therefore imports were correspondingly reduced. This falling U.S. purchase of oil was one of the reasons the world price began to fall.

Important Terms: Match the Columns

Match the term in the first column with the corresponding phrase in the second column. But before you do so, write out your own definition of the term in the first column.

_____ **1.** Reservation price
_____ **2.** Sustainable yield curve
_____ **3.** Maximum sustainable yield
_____ **4.** Induced innovation
_____ **5.** Renewable resource
_____ **6.** OPEC
_____ **7.** Blended price

a. The average of the low price of old oil and the higher price of imported and new oil
b. The curve relating the annual increase in a renewable resource (such as fish) to its population size. For any given population, this curve indicates the amount that can be extracted and still leave the population size constant.
c. The international cartel formed in 1965 that raised the world price of oil by more than 10 times between 1973 and 1982

d. The largest value on the sustainable yield curve. This is the largest amount of a renewable resource that can be extracted each year without reducing the population size.

e. The marginal cost of providing a resource. It includes (1) the cost of harvesting or extraction and (2) the amount necessary to compensate for the reduction in the resources available in the future.

f. The result when people turn their minds to finding substitutes for increasingly expensive resources

g. A resource that reproduces itself naturally (such as fish) or that reproduces itself with human assistance (such as timber)

True-False

T F 1. Under perfect competition, the rate of extraction of a privately owned resource is generally greater than the efficient rate.

T F 2. Those harvesting a common-property resource take into account only the harvesting cost—not the cost to society of having less of this resource available in the future.

T F 3. For a common-property resource, supply is determined by the marginal extraction cost only.

T F 4. A competitive equilibrium in the market for a privately owned natural resource is generally inefficient.

T F 5. If it were possible to tax those who fish for each fish caught, then in theory it would be possible to eliminate the efficiency loss that results because the oceans are not privately owned.

T F 6. An open border to fishermen from foreign countries would make the harvesting of fish more efficient, just as a border open to imports of foreign goods makes production within a country more efficient.

T F 7. Allowing the domestic price of oil to rise to the world price makes us more dependent on foreign supplies.

T F 8. A case can be made for keeping the U.S. domestic oil price at or below the world price, but no case can be made for keeping it higher.

Multiple Choice

1. In a perfectly competitive market, the last unit of a privately owned resource will be sold for:
  a. more than its reservation price
  b. less than its reservation price
  c. its reservation price
  d. more than its conservation price
  e. less than its conservation price

2. The height of the supply curve for a common-property resource reflects:
  a. the extraction cost
  b. compensation for the reduced amount available in the future
  c. the extraction cost less compensation for the reduced amount available in the future
  d. the extraction cost plus compensation for the reduced amount available in the future
  e. the extraction cost or compensation for the reduced amount available in the future, whichever is larger

3. Which of the following is a common-property resource?
  a. fish   **d.** coal
  b. timber on privately owned land **e.** copper
  c. an oil company's reserves

4. In analyzing resource use, the term "reservation price" means:

  a. the lowest bid a buyer will make in an auction
  b. the highest bid a buyer will pay in an auction
  c. the cost of harvesting or extracting a resource today
  d. the amount necessary to compensate for the reduced availability of the resource in the future
  e. (c) plus (d)

5. The reservation price of a resource will decrease if:
  a. the expected future cost of extracting the resource rises
  b. the expected future price of the resource rises
  c. the expected future price of the resource remains constant
  d. auction prices have remained constant
  e. auction prices have been rising

6. The creation of private property rights over what was previously a common-property resource:
  a. is not legal for the government to do
  b. would increase the efficiency of the extraction of the resource
  c. would decrease the efficiency of the extraction of the resource
  d. would have no effect on the extraction of the resource
  e. would freeze in the previous level of inefficiency in the extraction of the resource

7. The problem with doomsday models (that is, models that predict disaster because a growing population runs out of resources) is that typically:

    a. they are based on the assumption that current trends will continue long into the future

    b. they take inadequate account of the adjustments that will occur as resources become scarcer

    c. they take inadequate account of changing patterns of population growth as the population becomes larger

    d. all of the above

    e. none of the above

8. Which of the following is an argument commonly used in favor of economic growth?

    a. Unemployment is likely to be less severe in a rapidly growing economy.

    b. Faster economic growth helps to economize on scarce natural resources.

    c. Growth reduces pollution.

    d. Growth is necessary, or our children will run out of natural resources.

    e. Growth reduces congestion.

9. Which of the following is most important in explaining the increase in population in most less developed countries?

    a. the increase in the stock of natural resources relative to the labor force

    b. constant wages

    c. a change in the resource/capital ratio

    d. increasing wealth

    e. advances in medicine that have reduced the death rate

10. Between 1973 and 1982, the world price of oil rose from:

    a. less than $3 a barrel to $13 a barrel

    b. less than $3 a barrel to $23 a barrel

    c. less than $3 a barrel to over $30 a barrel

    d. $13 a barrel to $23 a barrel

    e. $13 a barrel to over $30 a barrel

11. The rapid increase in the price of oil in the 1970s:

    a. could be fully justified as a conservation measure

    b. could be partly justified as a conservation measure, but also reflected the exercise of monopoly power

    c. could not be justified, even in part, as a conservation measure

    d. represented a transfer from OPEC countries to oil importing countries

    e. discouraged U.S. conservation efforts

12. Which of the following is a valid reason for raising the domestic U.S. price of oil above the world price?

    a. It would increase OPEC revenues, and thus allow these countries to strengthen themselves militarily.

    b. It would encourage consumers to substitute oil for natural gas.

    c. It would make U.S. oil users take into account the cost of U.S. vulnerability to a cutoff of oil supplies from the Middle East.

    d. (b) and (c)

    e. None of the above.

13. Keeping the domestic price of oil below the world price:

    a. encouraged production and consumption

    b. discouraged production and consumption

    c. discouraged consumption and encouraged production

    d. encouraged consumption and discouraged production

    e. encouraged consumption, but had no effect on production

14. Under the "blended oil price" policy of the 1970s, which was highest?

    a. the price received by sellers of old oil

    b. the price received by sellers of new oil

    c. the price paid by buyers of oil

    d. none of the above because these prices were all the same

    e. the policy was so confused that there was no way of telling

15. The fact that a significant reduction of U.S. demand might depress the world price of oil is a point in favor of having a domestic price:

    a. below the world price

    b. equal to the world price

    c. above the world price

    d. either above or below, depending upon the elasticity of domestic demand

    e. either above or below, depending upon the elasticity of domestic supply

16. Before 1979, controls kept the domestic price very low on:

    a. new oil   **d.** neither new nor old oil

    b. old oil   **e.** oil whose age could not

    c. both new and old oil   be determined

17. Which of the following contributed to the slowdown of the nuclear power industry in the 1970s?

    a. concern over how to dispose of radioactive wastes

    b. concern over the possible proliferation of nuclear weapons

    c. the fear of accidents, such as the one at Three Mile Island

    d. higher-than-expected plant costs

    e. all of the above

Exercises

1a. Figure 29-1 depicts a perfectly competitive market for a natural resource. The demand curve is D, the marginal cost of extraction is the height of the curve labeled S, and the reservation price is the height of the curve labeled S'. The socially efficient quantity (assuming no external benefits) is _____, and this quantity will be demanded if the price is _____. If the resource is privately owned, the price will be _____, the quantity extracted will be _____, and the size of the efficiency loss will be _____.

1b. If the resource is not privately owned, the price will be _____, the quantity extracted will be _____,

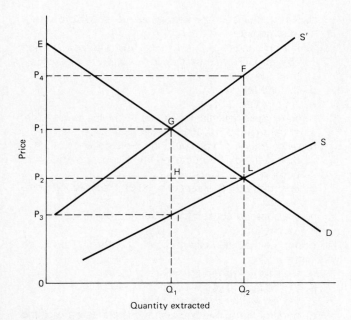

FIGURE 29-1

and the size of the efficiency loss will be _____ . The efficiency loss could be eliminated by a [tax, subsidy] on extraction equal to _____ per unit.

2a. In Figure 29-2, D represents the demand curve for a common-property resource sold in a perfectly competitive market. The internal cost of extracting this resource is the height of S, while the external cost is the vertical distance between S and S'. The equilibrium price is _____ , and quantity extracted is _____ . The efficiency loss is _____ , because the efficiency equilibrium is at point _____ , where price is _____ and the quantity extracted is _____ .

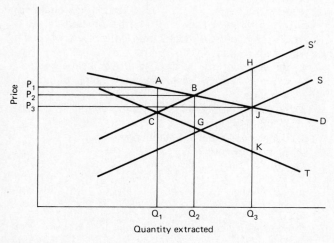

FIGURE 29-2

2b. Now suppose that the resource is given to a monopoly. Its marginal revenue will be the line _____ ; it will extract a quantity equal to _____ , and set a price

equal to _____ . The size of the efficiency loss will be _____ . Since this efficiency loss is [greater than, less than] the original efficiency loss _____ , it means that monopolizing this industry has [increased, reduced] efficiency. The reason is that the efficiency loss from monopoly is, in this case, more than offset by the efficiency gain that results from changing the resources from [public to private, private to public] ownership.

This is one example of a "conserving monopolist" who increases efficiency. However, a conserving monopolist may *reduce* efficiency. To illustrate, redraw this diagram so that the efficiency loss under the monopoly is greater than the original efficiency loss. (Hint: Make the demand curve less elastic. Also draw S' closer to S; this reduces the advantage of private ownership.)

3a. In Figure 29-3, a controlled price of P_1 is imposed on the domestic oil market. Domestic production is _____ , consumption is _____ , and [exports, imports] are _____ . Because importers have to buy oil at the high world price P_2 and sell it domestically for only P_1, the government must compensate them by paying them a subsidy of _____ per barrel, times the _____ barrel they are importing, for a total government subsidy payment of area _____ .

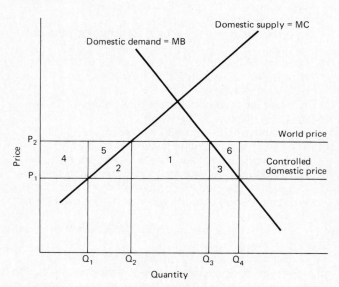

FIGURE 29-3

3b. When this price control is removed, price becomes _____ , domestic production [increases, decreases] to _____ , and domestic consumption [increases, decreases] to _____ . [Imports, Exports] consequently [increase, decrease] to _____ . Consumers [gain, lose] area _____ , while producers [gain, lose] area _____ , and the government [gains, loses] area _____ , the [subsidy, tax] it no longer has to [pay, impose].

3c. When all these gains and losses are taken into account, the *net* [gain, loss] from decontrolling price is _____. This can be broken down into its two components: (1) The efficiency gain of area _____, because consumers are no longer buying oil they value at less than its true cost (the world price), and (2) the efficiency gain of area _____, because domestic firms are now producing oil for less than it previously cost to import. At the same time, there has been a transfer from consumers to _____ and _____.

Essay Questions

1. Explain how the problem of an excessive use of a common-property resource is similar to the problem of environmental pollution. To deal with each of these problems, the government sometimes considers quantity restraints. Explain why you think these policies are effective or ineffective in dealing with each of these problems.

2. How does private ownership help to eliminate the inefficiency that exists when a resource is publicly owned (common property)? Would inefficiency be eliminated just as well if ownership were given to a single owner who then had a monopoly? What new problems might be created by allowing the resource to be monopolized? (Hint: See exercise 2 above.)

3. "One of the shortcomings of the market mechanism is that private business interests are concerned, not with the future, but instead with how much profit they can earn right now. We need the government to regulate the rate of extraction of natural resources to protect future generations from being deprived of their rightful share of resources." Do you agree or disagree? Why?

4. (This problem is based on Box 29-1 in the textbook.) "If the population of a species is initially greater than the point of maximum sustainable yield, and if firms are now harvesting at a rate just large enough to maintain a constant size of population, then by increasing the rate of extraction they can harvest more now and more in the future." Explain this statement, using a diagram similar to Figure 29-2. If the cost of extraction is zero, what is the opportunity cost of raising the rate of extraction in this situation? Is this a case of being able to get something for nothing?

5. Suppose that scientists working on nuclear fusion make a major breakthrough, which means that the economic break-even point in fusion energy will be reached by 1990.

a. What would you expect the effects (if any) to be on the world price of oil (1) now, and (2) in 1990?

b. What would you expect the effect (if any) to be on the U.S. price of natural gas (1) now, and (2) in 1990?

c. How would your answers to question (a) change if the discoveries will lead in 1990 only to the energy break-even point rather than the economic break-even point?

6. "It is not fair for our oil companies to make excess profits on the oil they produce and sell to us within the United States simply because halfway around the globe, OPEC has raised the world price. Oil companies in the United States should be forced to sell us the oil we need at a more reasonable price." Which U.S. policy in the 1970s was guided by this sort of philosophy? Does it make sense to you? Did this policy create problems? Explain.

7. The strict auto emission standards imposed by the EPA during the 1970s achieved their primary purpose of reducing pollution. But it had an unfavorable side effect because it increased our consumption of gasoline and thus damaged our attempts to conserve oil. Could the benefits of reduced pollution have been achieved without damaging the conservation effort if a policy of a higher oil price had been implemented instead? Explain.

8. "It is easier for governments to deal with the adverse transfer effects of allowing prices to rise than it is to deal with the adverse efficiency effects of preventing them from rising." Show how the U.S. experience with oil could be used to back up this statement.

9. Explain some of the external costs of producing and using oil. In your view, how do these costs compare with those arising from the production and use of natural gas? Coal? Nuclear fission?

Answers

Important Terms: 1 e 2 b 3 d 4 f 5 g 6 c 7 a
True-False: 1 F 2 T 3 T 4 F 5 T 6 F 7 F 8 F
Multiple Choice: 1 c 2 a 3 a 4 e 5 a 6 b 7 d 8 a 9 e 10 c 11 b 12 c 13 d 14 b 15 c 16 b 17 e
Exercises: **1a.** Q_1, P_1, P_1, Q_1, zero. **1b.** P_2, Q_2, GIL, tax, P_1P_3. **2a.** P_3, Q_3, HBJ, B, P_2, Q_2. **2b.** T, Q_1, P_1, ABC, less than, HBJ, increased, public to private. **3a.** Q_1, Q_4, imports, Q_1Q_4, P_1P_2, Q_1Q_4, 5 + 2 + 1 + 3 + 6. **3b.** P_2, increases, Q_2, decreases, Q_3, imports, decrease, Q_2Q_3, lose, 4 + 5 + 2 + 1 + 3, gain, 4 + 5, gains, 5 + 2 + 1 + 3 + 6, subsidy, pay. **3c.** gain, 5 + 6, 6, 5, producers, the government.

Across

1, 4. If a pasture or fishing area is owned in this manner, it may be overused

6. he was a student of Marxism (see inside cover of text)

7. a common type of harmful externality

8. an emission fee is one way to protect our _____

10. the _____ yield is the amount of a renewable resource (for example, fish) that can be harvested while still leaving the population constant

11. one way to reduce the pollution problem is to _____ waste

14. an economist famous for his writings on externalities and on macroeconomics (see inside cover of text)

16. famous hockey player

17. the efficient output occurs where the _____ social cost equals the _____ social benefit

18. what a doctor, lawyer, or teacher provides

19. what people do after studying for a long time

22, 24. one way of dealing with the problem of a scarce natural resource

25. major communications company (abbrev.)

26. in the direction of

Down

1. high prices encourage people to _____ scarce raw materials

2. if people have _____, they may use raw materials too quickly

3. arrest

4, 13. the creation of _____ _____ is one way to discourage the overuse of a natural resource

5. overfishing today creates an _____ cost which will be faced by future fishers

9. this, plus error, is a hard way to learn

10. private cost plus external cost equals _____ _____ (2 words)

12. mistake

14. our _____ is sometimes called "spaceship earth."

15. rock used in the construction of buildings

18. a place to keep money

20. major conglomerate (abbrev.)

21. South American city (abbrev.)

23. yes (Russian)

CHAPTER 30

PUBLIC GOODS:

WHAT SHOULD THE GOVERNMENT PROVIDE?

MAJOR PURPOSE

The last chapter dealt with external costs. In this chapter we use a parallel approach to analyze external benefits— that is, the benefits of a product that are enjoyed by others, above and beyond the internal benefits enjoyed by those who buy it. When external benefits exist, a free perfectly competitive market does not produce an efficient outcome. There is too little free-market production of such a good, just as there was too much production of a good with an external cost in the last chapter. The solution is to subsidize the good with the external benefits, just as the good with external costs was taxed in the last chapter.

A further objective of this chapter is to extend this analysis of external benefits to describe the concept of a public good. A flood-control dam is an example of a public good, because *no one* can be excluded from enjoying its benefits, regardless of who pays for it. Typically, with such a broad distribution of benefits, there are no specific individuals who play a significant enough role as users to be prepared to buy the good. So if it is to be provided at all, the government must purchase it. In this chapter, we describe the difficulties a government faces in trying to decide whether or not such a purchase is justified; and we also describe the more general problems that arise whenever the government provides the public with any good or service. Even when the private market fails, and a good must be provided by the government (if it is to be supplied at all) problems remain.

Learning Objectives

After you have studied this chapter in the textbook and the study guide, you should be able to:

Demonstrate why a free, perfectly competitive market provides less than the efficient amount of a good with external benefits

Measure, in a diagram like Figure 30-1 in the textbook, the efficiency loss resulting from the private provision of a good with external benefits

Show why efficiency requires a good to be subsidized by an amount equal to the marginal external benefit it provides (assuming that there are not high costs of administering the subsidy)

Define and explain the concept of a public good

Construct the marginal social benefit curve (1) for a public good, and (2) for a private good, making clear the difference between the two

Explain why the "free-rider" problem makes it difficult for the government to estimate the benefits of a public good simply by asking people how highly they value it

Give the reasons for believing that when the government provides a good or service—whether or not this is in response to a failure by the free market—major problems remain, such as the problems of bureaucracy; efficiency is still not guaranteed

Show why it may be necessary to view as a public good any wildlife species that is becoming extinct

Explain the concept of "option demand" and demonstrate its significance in dealing with such a wildlife species

HIGHLIGHTS OF CHAPTER

Why is there too little production of a good with an external benefit?

The Inefficiency of a Private Market when There Are External Benefits

A free, perfectly competitive market fails to produce enough of a product with an external benefit because the marginal cost of the product is equated to its marginal *private* benefit, rather than to its marginal *social* benefit. The reason is that, in deciding on their demand for the product, buyers look only at the *private* benefit it will provide them, and ignore the *external* benefit it will provide to others. With some of the benefit of the product thus being ignored, it is no surprise that too little is produced, as Figure 30-1 demonstrates. The appropriate government policy is to subsidize this product by the amount of the external benefit it provides (assuming there are not substantial costs in administering the subsidy). Such a subsidy will increase the demand for the product and thus increase its output to the efficient amount.

Public Goods

In the case of the products with an external benefit that we have been describing so far—such as gardening—you will receive an external benefit if your neighbor pays $100 for gardening services. But, of course, you will get an even larger benefit if you pay the $100 to have the gardening done on your lawn rather than on your neighbor's. Thus the benefits you get depend on who pays. A public good can be viewed as the extreme case of a good with an external benefit—where the amount of benefit that an individual gets is just as great if someone else buys as it is if he or she were to buy it. In other words, the individual cannot be excluded in any way from enjoying it. For example, you get the same benefit from cleaner air, whether or not you help to pay for antipollution measures. That is not true of a private good. You can't enjoy a movie or a restaurant meal unless you pay for it. This is the reason why the benefits of a private good are horizontally summed in Figure 30-2 in the textbook, while the benefits of a public good are *vertically* summed in Figure 30-3.

The Free-Rider Problem

If you will get the same benefit whether or not you help pay for a good, why not be a "free rider" and not pay at all (or pay as small a share as you can get away with)? The incentive for people to ride free raises problems for an entrepreneur who believes (let's suppose correctly) that the benefits people would get from a public good—such as flood-control dam—exceed its costs and it therefore should be built. How can it be financed, when everyone the entrepreneur asks to contribute to it tries to minimize that contribution by understating the benefits the dam would provide? In short, each individual has an incentive to be a free rider, enjoying the benefits of the dam without contributing to it. Since all individuals have this incentive to understate the benefits of the dam, it appears not to be justified, and does not get built.

Suppose the government, rather than a private entrepreneur, tries to evaluate the dam by asking people how highly they would value it. If they think they will be taxed according to their answer, they will understate. On the other hand, if they think their taxes won't be affected by the project, they will tend to *overstate* their benefit—as a means of slightly increasing the chance that the project will be undertaken. In this case, they have nothing to lose, since the cost *they* incur is not affected by their overevaluation.

An Alternative Approach by the Government

In view of the difficulties in trying to get people to answer accurately, the authorities generally reject the approach of asking people for their evaluation of a project. Instead they often use a "benefit-cost" analysis based on a completely different kind of information. To use the example in the text, they may estimate the benefit of a dam by examining how frequently floods have occurred without it, and the average crop loss. This approach may be superior, but it still involves major problems. For example, those who are running this analysis may have a vested interest in having the dam pass the benefit-cost test because they may hope to be employed in its construction. Or they may simply be trying to please their employer—a government that has promised this dam in the last election. They may therefore add benefits—perhaps at an inflated value—until these benefits exceed the costs, and the project is justified. Such an inflation of benefits may be easy, especially if one of the benefits of a flood-control project is to save lives. It is very difficult indeed to attach a dollar value to a human life. (Recall our discussion in Box 27-4 in the textbook.)

Other Problems with Government Expenditure Decisions

More generally, when decision making shifts from the private marketplace to the government—as indeed it must in the case of a public good which the private market fails to deliver—then a new set of special problems arises:

1. Typically, private firms stop producing goods if they are no longer profitable—or if they fail outright from the start—because these firms would lose money otherwise. On the other hand, government projects that are no longer justified are much more difficult to terminate for two reasons: (*a*) No politician wants to admit that a project may have been a mistake, for fear of losing the next election as a result, and (*b*) there is no natural check, like the bankruptcy of a private firm, to force termination of a government project.

2. Political votes are not as specific and frequent as the economic votes that people cast every day when they are deciding what to buy with their money. Thus private auto companies get a clear message of the models the public wants and does not want. Not so with public goods. It may be 2 or 4 years before the next election when the public can vote on how it likes or dislikes the dam and the other goods and services the government is providing. And even if people do approve of what the government is doing—and vote for it in the next election—it's hard to know whether the election victory is due to the dam the government has built, or its foreign policy or some other completely different issue. (Public opinion polls make this problem less severe, but don't remove it.)

3. Special interest groups can exert an inordinate influence on government decision making. If you have no particular interest in a dam in the Rocky Mountains, it probably doesn't pay you to oppose it, since it may add only a trivial 10 cents to your tax bill. But those directly affected in the area have a strong incentive to support it and lobby for its construction. Thus, a few large benefits concentrated in one area may *politically* outweigh many small, widely dispersed costs, even if the sum of all these small costs exceeds the benefits *economically*.

4. Politicians are mainly interested in projects with benefits that are obvious to the public and immediate. (If they don't have a payoff before the next election, it may be too late.) Thus politicians often do not take a long-term point of view; there is a tendency for much government effort to be centered on short-term decision making.

5. The job of implementing—and sometimes initiating—government policies is performed by a bureaucracy. There is a constant tendency for bureaus and their budgets to expand, in part because of the incentives for bureau chiefs to expand their personnel. Accordingly, bureaus tend to grow beyond the efficient size. This tendency is not checked by the threat of economic loss or bankruptcy that faces a private firm that overexpands.

Important Terms: Match the Columns

Match the term in the first column with the corresponding phrase in the second column. But before you do so, write out your own definition of the term in the first column.

_____ **1.** External (spillover) benefit
_____ **2.** Public good
_____ **3.** Internal private benefits
_____ **4.** Benefit-cost analysis
_____ **5.** Option demand
_____ **6.** Free riders
_____ **7.** Internalizing an externality

a. A good whose benefits are available to everyone, regardless of who pays for it
b. Forcing firms or individuals to face the external costs or benefits they are creating
c. The estimation of the dollar value of the costs and benefits that are likely to result from a particular government policy
d. Those who cannot be excluded from the benefits of a public good, even though they do not pay their share of its costs
e. The benefit derived from a good by those who do not buy it
f. The desire to have something, not because we want to enjoy it today, but because we may want to enjoy it in the future. This appears to be the nature of the demand for some public goods, such as the preservation of a particular wildlife species.

g. The benefits from a good derived by the purchaser. These are usually the only benefits that are considered by households and firms in making their purchasing decisions.

True-False

T F **1.** Internalizing externalities means that producers are forced to face any external costs of their actions; and buyers are allowed to enjoy any external benefits generated by their purchases.

T F **2.** One benefit of having the government provide public goods such as flood control dams is that these decisions are easily reversible.

T F **3.** The reason why private firms can't be relied on to produce a public good is that they would externalize the internal benefits.

T F **4.** The marginal social benefit curve of a public good can be constructed by vertically summing the individual demand curves.

T F **5.** You cannot be excluded from enjoying the benefits of a public good even if someone else pays for it.

T F **6.** It is generally more difficult to cut out an expenditure program in the private than in the public sector.

T F **7.** The public can be more specific in expressing its preferences for goods by voting in elections than by making purchases in the marketplace.

T F **8.** It may make sense to vote for a party that has promised to make a certain government expenditure, even though you don't want this expenditure at all.

T F **9.** Politicians prefer policies with costs that are obvious, and benefits that are obscure.

T F **10.** Government policy should ensure that no damage whatsoever occurs to the environment.

Multiple Choice

1. In producing two goods (one with an external benefit, the other with an external cost) a free, perfectly competitive market will generate:
   a. too much output of the good with the external benefit, and too little of the good with the external cost
   b. too little output of the good with the external benefit, and too much of the good with the external cost
   c. too little output of the good with the external benefit, and just the right amount of the good with the external cost
   d. too little of both
   e. too much of both

2. Which of the following comes closest to being a private good with no external benefits?
   a. national defense
   b. painting the outside of your house
   c. painting the inside of your house
   d. hiring a gardner
   e. the police force

3. If the government follows a "hands-off" policy, then the production of a perfectly competitive good with an external benefit will result in:
   a. marginal external benefit being greater than marginal social benefit
   b. marginal external benefit being equal to marginal social benefit
   c. marginal social cost being equal to marginal social benefit
   d. marginal social cost being greater than marginal social benefit

   e. marginal social cost being less than marginal social benefit

4. If a good has an external benefit, the government can ensure an efficient outcome by imposing a:
   a. tax equal to the external benefit
   b. tax greater than the external benefit
   c. subsidy equal to the external benefit
   d. subsidy less than the external benefit
   e. subsidy greater than the external benefit

5. If there are substantial administrative costs in subsidizing a good with an external benefit, the government should:
   a. tax it instead, to provide the same result
   b. subsidize the good regardless
   c. cancel the subsidy regardless
   d. cancel the subsidy if the efficiency gain it would produce is less than the administrative costs
   e. cancel the subsidy if the efficiency gain it would produce is greater than the administrative costs

6. The internal benefit of a good is the:
   a. benefit enjoyed by those who haven't purchased it
   b. benefit enjoyed by the individual who has purchased it
   c. benefit enjoyed by free riders
   d. benefit enjoyed by the government, even though the public has purchased it
   e. benefit enjoyed by the public, even though the government has purchased it

7. An example of internalizing an externality occurs when:
   a. a firm building a ski lift buys a restaurant at the bottom of the hill

b. a firm buys from a domestic supplier a good that it used to buy from abroad

c. a city government subsidizes exterior home improvements

d. (a) and (c)

e. (b) and (c)

8. In defining the marginal benefit to society of a public good:

a. the demand curves by individuals are horizontally summed

b. the demand curves by individuals are vertically summed

c. the demand curves by individuals are horizontally summed and then vertically summed

d. we use the same technique that was used to derive the market demand curve for a private good from the individual demand curves

e. we take the demand curve of the individual who is most eager and able to buy the good

9. With a public good:

a. anyone can participate in the benefits except the actual purchaser

b. everyone can participate in the benefits including the actual purchaser

c. no one participates in the benefits except the purchaser

d. only free riders participate in the benefits

e. free riders are prevented from participating in the benefits

10. Estimates the government collects from individuals on how highly they value public projects tend to be unreliable because:

a. if people feel they will be taxed according to the value they state, they will tend to understate

b. if people feel they will be taxed according to the value they state, they will tend to overstate

c. if people feel they will not be taxed according to the value they state, they will tend to overstate

d. if people feel they will not be taxed according to the value they state, they will tend to understate

e. (a) and (c)

11. A free rider is someone:

a. who cannot be excluded from enjoying the benefits of a project even though this individual has paid nothing to cover its costs

b. who is trying to encourage the government to continue its transportation subsidies

c. who can be excluded from enjoying the benefits of a project

d. who is trying to discourage the government from continuing its transportation subsidies

e. who has paid more than a fair share of the costs

12. Benefit-cost analysis often involves the following problem:

a. Questionable projects that have been promised in an election campaign may be justified by exaggerating benefits.

b. Questionable projects that have been promised in an election campaign may be justified by underestimating costs.

c. It is very difficult to place a value on a human life.

d. Projects may be evaluated by those with a conflict of interest—for example, engineers who may eventually be employed in building the projects.

e. All of the above.

13. Typically, a government bureau that is a monopoly will produce:

a. too much output, while a private monopoly will produce too little

b. too little output, just like a private monopoly

c. too much output, just like a private monopoly

d. the right amount of output, while a private monopoly will produce too little

e. too little output, just like a private oligopoly

14. A species of wildlife in the wilderness:

a. cannot die out unless it is adversely affected by human action

b. will die out if it is left unprotected

c. may die out if it is left unprotected

d. will be prevented from dying out by free-market forces

e. should not be protected by the government because of option demand

Exercises

1. Figure 30-1 shows the supply curve S and demand curve D for a perfectly competitive good that provides external benefits. Assume for now that there are no external costs of producing this good, and ignore MC_S.

a. In an unregulated market, the quantity that is produced is _____, and the market price is _____. If the marginal social benefit curve is MB_S, then the economically efficient quantity is _____, and the marginal external benefit is _____.

b. The efficiency loss from relying upon the private market for the provision of this good is _____.

The government could eliminate this efficiency loss by offering a per unit [subsidy, tax] of _____ to the producers of this good.

c. Now suppose that the good involves external costs as well as external benefits. Let the curve labeled MC_S represent the marginal social cost of producing the good. Then the efficient amount of production of the good is _____. At that level of production, the marginal external cost would be _____, and the marginal external benefit would be _____. With no tax or subsidy, the private market would produce [more, less] than the economically efficient amount, and the efficiency loss would be _____. This effi-

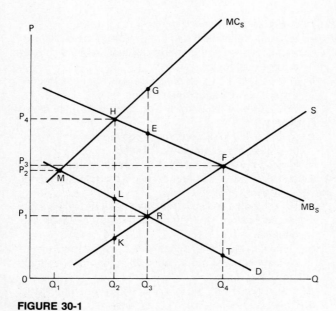

FIGURE 30-1

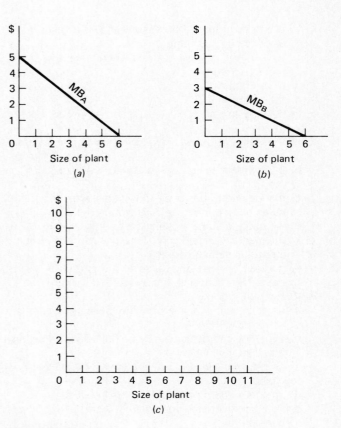

FIGURE 30-2

ciency loss could be eliminated if the government were to [tax, subsidize] the production of the good by _____ per unit.

2. Figure 30-2 shows the marginal private benefit MB_A and MB_B that individuals A and B receive from a public good (a waste-treatment plant). In Figure 30-2c show the marginal social benefit, assuming that A and B are the only members of society affected by the project.

3a. Suppose that there are 1,000 farmers affected by a proposed dam. Each of them would receive a benefit of $1,000. The social benefit of the dam is $_____. If the dam costs $500,000, it [is, is not] worth building.

3b. Suppose you are one of the farmers. The government tells you that it intends to tax farmers according to how much each says the dam will be worth to him or her. If you tell the truth, it will cost you $_____. If you say $2,000 it will cost you $_____. If you say no benefit it will cost you $_____. You will have an incentive to [understate, overstate, reveal accurately] how much it is worth to you. Other farmers [will, will not] have the same incentive to provide this sort of answer, so the dam [will certainly, may not] be built—an [efficient, inefficient] outcome.

3c. As another example, suppose that the same

1,000 farmers would get the same true benefits from the dam, but now suppose that the cost of building the dam is $1.5 million. In this case the dam [should, should not] be built. But suppose that now the government says that if it goes ahead with the dam it will tax the millions of inhabitants of your state a few cents each to finance it. Your taxes will be scarcely affected. The only question the government has is, Should it go ahead or not? That depends on how highly farmers value it. If the government goes ahead, you will have a net gain (value to you of the dam minus your new taxes) of _____. You will maximize your chances of getting this gain if you [understate, overstate, reveal accurately] your benefit, and thus [increase, decrease] the chance that the dam will be built. Other farmers [will, will not] have the same incentive to give the same sort of answer, so the dam [may, will certainly not] be built—an [efficient, inefficient] outcome.

Essay Questions

1. Explain carefully whether or not each of the following might be considered to be a good with an external benefit: (a) the United States Olympic team, (b) your telephone, (c) driver safety lessons, and (d) television programs.

2. If you ask people to reveal how much they would benefit from a public good, will they be unlikely to tell the truth? If you ask them to reveal how much they are being damaged by a good with an external cost, will they tell you the truth? Why or why not? How will their answer be affected if you tell them that the government is thinking of providing them with protection from this external cost, with this protection to be financed out of the government's general tax revenues?

3. Many industries pay lobbyists to influence regulatory agencies, congressional committees, and other government agencies and officials in Washington. These lobbyists spend a lot of time promoting the idea that their industry is a source of external benefits. Why would the firms in an industry pay lobbyists to do this?

4. Criticize the following statement: "The government should not be providing money for vaccination programs. If people are unwilling to pay the full cost without subsidy, then vaccinations fail the market test and should not be provided at all."

5. Explain why you agree or disagree with the following statement: "You can rely upon the government to provide you with the goods you want at a reasonable price just as much as you can rely upon private business firms. The reason is that the party in power wants you to be pleased with what it provides so that you will vote for it in the next election, just as a private business firm wants you to be pleased with what it provides so that you will buy the product again."

6. It has been argued that when the government spends more money, it provides a great deal of benefits to a small number of people and a very small cost to a large number of people (namely, taxpayers). Give an example. Why does a government judge that such a policy is in its interests? Will it necessarily be in the nation's economic interest?

Answers

Important Terms: 1 e 2 a 3 g 4 c 5 f 6 d 7 b
True-False: 1 T 2 F 3 F 4 T 5 T 6 F 7 F 8 T 9 F 10 F
Multiple Choice: 1 b 2 c 3 e 4 c 5 d 6 b 7 d 8 b 9 b 10 e 11 a 12 e 13 a 14 c
Exercises: **1a.** Q_3, P_1, Q_4, *TF*. **1b.** *EFR*, subsidy, *TF*. **1c.** Q_2, *KH*, *LH*, more, *HGE*, tax, *LK*. **2.** a straight line intersecting the vertical axis at \$8, and the horizontal axis at 6. **3a.** \$1 million, is. **3b.** \$1,000, \$2,000, 0, understate, will, may not, inefficient. **3c.** should not, almost \$1,000, overstate, increase, will, may, inefficient.

CHAPTER 31

WHAT ARE THE GAINS FROM INTERNATIONAL TRADE?

MAJOR PURPOSE

Americans in Kansas gain from *domestic* trade with other Americans in Minnesota and New York. Similarly, Americans gain from *international* trade with the Japanese and French. The reasons are the same in either case. Our purpose in this chapter is to examine the gains from trade from three broad sources: (1) increased competition, (2) economies of scale, and (3) comparative advantage. This chapter analyzes these three sources of gain in detail. It also identifies the winners and losers from trade. While winners outnumber losers, and the nation as a whole benefits from trade, some people are hurt. Their ability to organize themselves and apply political pressure is one of the big reasons why countries maintain restrictions on trade—restrictions that will be examined in the next chapter.

Learning Objectives

After you have studied this chapter in the textbook and the study guide, you should be able to:

Identify the three main sources of gain from international trade

Explain why trade increases competition in the domestic U.S. market and reduces the market power of U.S. producers, thus generating an efficiency gain

Explain why trade makes possible cost reductions because it provides opportunities to exploit economies of scale, with the result that income is increased and a wider variety of new products is available

Explain the difference between comparative advantage and absolute advantage

Explain why countries export those commodities in which they have a comparative advantage, and how comparative advantge is determined by opportunity costs

Explain the two respects in which international trade and technological change are similar, and the respects in which they are different

Measure diagrammatically the gains from international trade using a production possibilities curve as in Figure 31-4 in the textbook, or alternatively, using the supply and demand diagrams shown in Figures 31-6 and 31-7

Show the gain from trade in a supply-demand diagram by comparing the effect of trade on consumers with its effect on producers

Identify the winners and losers from international trade

HIGHLIGHTS OF CHAPTER

The two broad questions addressed in this chapter are, Why are there gains from trade? and Who are the winners and losers? First, consider why we gain from trade.

The Sources of Gain

Increased competition For domestic producers, there are two dramatic changes when trade is opened up. First, they face a much larger market; they can now sell to people anywhere in the world. Second, they now face many more competitors. Zenith no longer competes against RCA and other U.S. producers, it now also competes with an additional group of producers from Japan, Europe, and elsewhere. Because of increased competition, oligopolists such as Zenith and RCA lose much of their market power—their ability to influence price. Thus they move closer to perfect competition, with the increase in efficiency that this implies. Similarly a U.S. monopolist may, as a result of trade, find itself an oligopolist, with several foreign competitors; this industry also moves closer to perfect competition.

Economies of scale Without international trade, each country must be self-sufficient; it must therefore produce a wide variety of products in the small quantity necessary just to satisfy its own needs. With international trade, each country can specialize, producing only a few items in large volume and trading to get the rest. Often large volume means reduced cost; that is, there are economies of scale. And reduced cost means that we can produce and therefore consume more. In other words, our real income rises. It also rises because other countries are specializing and reducing their costs. Thus the products we trade for, as well as the goods we produce ourselves, fall in cost.

Not only are costs reduced; in addition, variety may be increased. For example, because of international trade, someone buying a car in the tiny European country of Liechtenstein can choose among Fords, Volkswagens, Datsuns, and many others that are produced elsewhere. Without international trade, consumers wouldn't have this choice. They would have to buy cars produced in Liechtenstein. But the market there is so small (the population is less than 30,000), that they would be lucky to have even one auto firm producing one model. There would be little or no variety.

Comparative advantage To understand comparative advantage, you must first understand absolute advantage. Table 31-3 in the textbook can be used to clarify the difference between the two. In the right-hand column of this table, we see that the United States has an absolute advantage in food because a U.S. worker can produce 3 units of food, whereas a worker in Europe can produce only 1. In other words, it only takes a third as many workers to produce food in the United States as in Europe. The *input requirement*—that is, the labor re-quirement—to produce food in the United States is lower than in Europe. (This is the definition of absolute advantage: a country has an absolute advantage in a good if the input requirement in that country is lower than that in other countries.)

The United States also has an absolute advantage in clothing. (A U.S. worker outproduces a European worker in clothing by 6 to 4, as shown in the first column of Table 31-3, just as a U.S. worker outproduces a European worker by 3 to 1 in food production.) Because the United States has an absolute advantage in producing both goods, absolute advantage cannot be the key to explaining which country will produce what. If it were the key, then the United States would produce both goods, and Europe neither—and that is inconsistent with the two-way trade we observe.

What then does determine the pattern of production and trade? The answer is: comparative advantage. But in which product does the United States have a comparative advantage? The answer is: food, because this is where the United States' absolute advantage is greater; a U.S. worker can outproduce a worker in Europe by 3 to 1 in food, but by only 6 to 4—that is, 3 to 2—in clothing. Because the United States has a comparative advantage in food, Europe has a comparative advantage in clothing; that's where Europe's absolute *dis*advantage is *least*.

Using a more formal definition, we say that the United States has a comparative advantage in food if it has a *lower opportunity cost* of producing food than Europe. This is indeed the case. In the second row of Table 31-3, we see the high opportunity cost of food in Europe. Since a worker who is now producing 1 unit of food could instead be producing 4 units of clothing, the opportunity cost (the alternative foregone) of producing that 1 unit of food is 4 units of clothing. Compare this to the lower opportunity cost of food in the United States, derived from the top row in this table: Since a U.S. worker who is now producing 3 units of food could instead be producing 6 units of clothing, the opportunity cost in the United States of each unit of food is 6/3 = 2 units of clothing. Because it has a lower opportunity cost of food than Europe, the United States has a comparative advantage in food, and will specialize in this. Similar calculations for clothing will show that Europe has a comparative advantage here. With specialization in their products of comparative advantage, the United States and Europe enjoy an overall gain, as is demonstrated in the calculations at the bottom of this table.

To sum up: Both absolute and comparative advantage refer to the cost of production. The difference is in how this cost is measured. For absolute advantage, cost is measured in terms of *inputs required*. For comparative advantage, cost is measured in terms of *outputs foregone*, that is, opportunity cost.

Here's an intuitive approach that may help you to

understand better the gains from trade. Trade is the way a country can inexpensively acquire the goods in which it does *not* have a comparative advantage. Why produce these goods at home—where their opportunity cost is high—when they can be purchased from another country where their opportunity cost is low?

This gain from trade is further illustrated using the production possibilities curve shown in Figure 31-4 in the textbook. The gain comes when a country uses trade to move from point *B* to point *D*. But you should be able to break down this move into its two components: (1) the move from *B* to *C*, as the country *specializes in food*, and (2) the move from *C* to *D*, when the country then *trades food for clothing*.

This production possibilities curve is also useful, as shown in Figure 31-5 in the textbook, where it is used to compare international trade and technological change. Both allow a country to consume a combination of goods lying beyond its *current* production possibility curve, and both can be the source of unemployment that may have to be endured in the short run in order to realize income gains in the long run.

Finally, the textbook also illustrates the gains from trade using familiar supply and demand diagrams. You should be able to understand clearly why the nation gains from unrestricted exports, as shown in Figure 31-6, and unrestricted imports, as shown in Figure 31-7. We gain on the export side because we sell goods abroad for more than it costs us to produce them (or more than we lose when we switch these goods away from domestic consumption). At the same time, we gain on the import side because we can buy imports for less than it would cost us to produce them inefficiently at home; and imports also allow us to increase our consumption of bargain-priced goods from abroad. For both exports and imports there is a triangular efficiency gain which you should be able to confirm by comparing the effects of trade on consumers and producers. This technique then allows you to fill in the details on the second key question in this chapter:

Who Are the Winners and Losers?

Since opening our borders to an import lowers the domestic price of this good, consumers win and domestic producers are damaged. On the export side, there is also a conflict between these two groups—although the roles are reversed: Producers win and consumers lose. Whenever trade policy is made for a specific industry, this conflict between consumers and producers arises. This must be understood before turning to the often-contentious issues on trade policy discussed in the next chapter.

Important Terms: Match the Columns

Match the term in the first column with the corresponding phrase in the second column. But before you do so, write out your own definition of the term in the first column.

_____ 1. Economies of scale
_____ 2. Comparative advantage
_____ 3. Opportunity cost
_____ 4. Absolute advantage
_____ 5. International specialization

a. Country A has this in good X if the opportunity cost of producing X is lower in country A than in any other country.
b. Each country concentrating on one product, or a small number of products, and acquiring the others through international trade.
c. Country B has this in good Y if Y can be produced with fewer inputs in country B than in any other country.
d. Falling average cost as output increases. This is one source of gain from international trade.
e. The quantity of good B that must be sacrificed in order to produce another unit of good A.

True-False

T F   1. No country can have a comparative advantage in everything.
T F   2. Comparative advantage ensures that U.S. exports of any good will equal U.S. imports of that same good.
T F   3. International trade tends to transform a natural oligopoly into a natural monopoly.
T F   4. Although each member country in the European Economic Community imposes tariffs in its trade with other member countries, it may trade freely with the rest of the world.
T F   5. If the United States has an absolute advantage in a good, then it will necessarily specialize in that good.
T F   6. If the United States has a lower opportunity cost of producing good X than any other country, then it has a comparative advantage in X.

T   F   7. While improved technology allows a country to consume more by moving to a higher production possibility curve, international trade allows a country to consume more without moving its production off its existing production possibilities curve.

T   F   8. Large U.S. exports of grains following droughts abroad in the early 1970s benefited U.S. farmers, hurt U.S. consumers, and resulted in an overall efficiency loss.

T   F   9. If a country exports oranges, then consumers of oranges in that country probably lose from international trade in oranges.

T   F   10. If a country imports oranges, then producers of oranges in that country probably gain from international trade in oranges.

Multiple Choice

1. Machinery is:
a. imported, but not exported by the United States
b. exported, but not imported by the United States
c. exported by the United States to Europe only
d. imported and exported by the United States
e. neither imported nor exported by the United States

2. Comparative advantage provides gains in:
a. domestic trade only
b. foreign trade only
c. domestic and foreign trade
d. neither domestic nor foreign trade
e. foreign trade, so long as countries do not have an absolute advantage

3. Which of the following is a possible result of international trade?
a. A natural monopoly in the domestic market may be transformed into a natural oligopoly in the world market.
b. A perfectly competitive industry may be turned into a natural oligopoly.
c. A natural oligopoly may be turned into a natural monopoly.
d. A perfectly competitive industry may be turned into a natural monopoly.
e. Large firms are able to exercise more market power because the size of the market is increased.

4. International trade increases domestic competition in terms of:
a. price
b. quality
c. design
d. the introduction of new products
e. all of the above

	Newsprint	Machinery
Output per U.S. worker	10	5
Output per Canadian worker	4	4

5. In the table above, Canada has:
a. an absolute advantage in machinery
b. a comparative advantage in machinery
c. an absolute advantage in newsprint
d. a comparative advantage in newsprint
e. a comparative advantage in neither

6. Under international trade we export those goods for which we have a relatively low:

a. materials cost
b. implicit cost
c. accounting cost
d. opportunity cost
e. overhead cost

7. The idea of comparative advantage was developed by:
a. Adam Smith
b. Karl Marx
c. David Ricardo
d. Alfred Marshall
e. John Maynard Keynes

8. If the United States has an absolute advantage in a good, then it:
a. may or may not export that good
b. will necessarily export that good
c. will necessarily avoid exporting that good
d. will necessarily import that good
e. will necessarily avoid importing that good

The next five questions are based on the table below. In this simple example, there are only the two goods shown, and labor is the only factor of production.

	Clothing	Food
Output per U.S. worker	6	3
Output per European worker	4	1

9. In the table above, international trade would induce the United States to import:
a. food
b. clothing
c. both
d. neither
e. one or the other; we can't say which

10. In the table above, the United States has an absolute advantage in:
a. both goods, and a comparative advantage in food
b. both goods, and a comparative advantage in clothing
c. both goods, and a comparative advantage in neither
d. neither good, but a comparative advantage in food
e. neither good, but a comparative advantage in clothing

11. In the table above, Europe has an absolute advantage in:
a. both goods, and a comparative advantage in food
b. both goods, and a comparative advantage in clothing
c. both goods, and a comparative advantage in neither
d. neither good, but a comparative advantage in food
e. neither good, but a comparative advantage in clothing

12. In the table above, Europe's opportunity cost of producing food is:
a. 3 units of clothing
b. 6/3 = 2 units of clothing
c. 6/4 = 1½ unit of clothing
d. 4 units of clothing
e. 3 units of food

13. If the lower right-hand number in the table above is changed from 1 to 2, then the United States has an absolute advantage in:

    a. both goods, and a comparative advantage in food
    b. both goods, and a comparative advantage in clothing
    c. both goods, and a comparative advantage in neither
    d. neither good, but a comparative advantage in food
    e. neither good, and a comparative advantage in neither

14. A nation's real income can be increased by:

    a. international trade, but not by improved technology
    b. improved technology, but not by international trade
    c. neither technology nor international trade
    d. both technology and international trade
    e. international trade, provided there is protection for competing domestic industries

15. International trade allows a nation to increase its income by:

    a. reaching a point beyond its production possibilities curve (PPC)
    b. reaching a point inside its PPC
    c. moving along its PPC to a point to the northwest and staying there

    d. moving along its PPC to a point to the southeast and staying there
    e. staying at the same point on its PPC

16. According to the theory of international trade:

    a. every U.S. citizen gains from international trade
    b. as a general rule, international trade in a good will benefit both producers and consumers of that good in the United States
    c. as a general rule, producers are damaged, but consumers gain from international trade
    d. as a general rule, neither consumers nor producers gain from international trade
    e. there is an efficiency gain to the United States from allowing international trade

17. The efficiency gain from the export of a good reflects a gain to:

    a. consumers, plus a gain to producers
    b. consumers, minus damage to producers
    c. producers, minus a loss to consumers
    d. producers only
    e. consumers only

Exercises

1. Suppose that Figures 31-1 and 31-2 represent the markets for shoes in England and Spain.

    a. Without international trade, the price in England would be _____, and the quantity produced in England would be _____; the price in Spain would be _____, and the quantity produced in Spain would be _____. With trade, price will [rise, fall] in England and [rise, fall] in Spain.

    b. With international trade the single price at which the total demand—that is, the English demand plus Spanish demand—equals the total supply is _____. At that price English demand equals _____, and English supply equals _____; Spanish demand equals _____, and Spanish supply equals _____. In this situation [Spain, England] will export _____ units of shoes. England has a comparative [advantage,

FIGURE 31-1

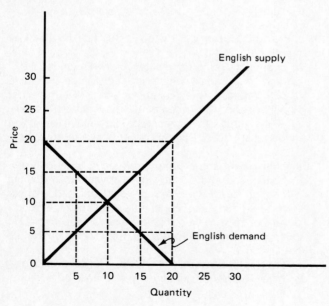

FIGURE 31-2

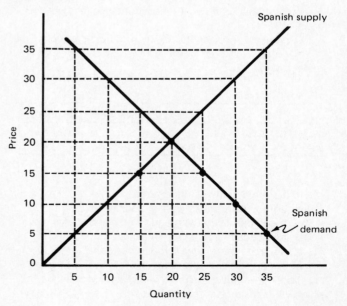

disadvantage] in shoes, as reflected by the [lower, higher] price and cost of shoes in England before trade.

2a. This exercise is designed to help you understand comparative advantage. In Table 31-1, suppose that for country A, each acre of land will produce 100 bushels of wheat or 30 bushels of corn, whereas for country B, each acre of land will produce 40 bushels of wheat or 20 bushels of corn. Suppose that each country has 4,000 acres. Fill in Table 31-1, giving the production possibilities for A and B.

2b. Plot the PPC for the two countries in Figure 31-3.

2c. Country _____ has an absolute advantage in producing corn; country _____ has an absolute advan-

tage in producing wheat; country _____ has a comparative advantage in producing corn; and country _____ has a comparative advantage in producing wheat. Suppose that, before trade, each country devotes half its land to each product. Then country B will produce and consume _____ bushels of wheat and _____ bushels of corn. Mark this on Figure 31-3. Also mark the production and consumption point for country A.

2d. Suppose that A and B were then to trade with each other at the price of 10 bushels of wheat for every 4 bushels of corn. (Note that this ratio of 10:4 is between A's pretrade domestic exchange ratio of 100:30 = 10:3 cited at the beginning of this question, and B's ratio of 40:20 = 10:5. Therefore, it is a rate of exchange that will make trade beneficial for both countries.) Let's see now

Table 31–1

A's production possibilities		B's production possibilities	
Thousands of bushels of wheat	Thousands of bushels of corn	Thousands of bushels of wheat	Thousands of bushels of corn
0		0	
100		40	
200		80	
300		120	
400		160	

FIGURE 31-3

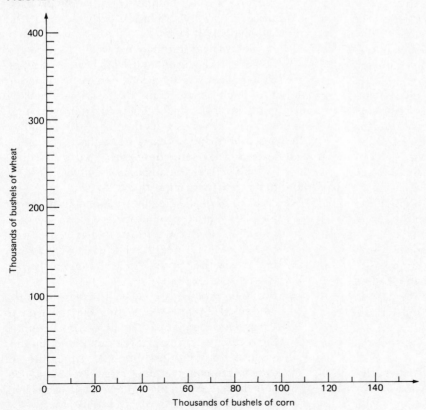

precisely why it's in B's interest to specialize in corn and purchase its wheat from A. If it does so, and devotes all its 4,000 acres to corn, B will produce _____ bushels of corn and _____ bushels of wheat. B then keeps the original 40,000 bushels of corn for its own consumption, and takes the additional 40,000 it has produced and sells this for _____ bushels of wheat. It is now able to consume the same 40,000 bushels of corn as before, and 20,000 [more, less] bushels of wheat. This 20,000 bushels of wheat represents its [gain, loss] from specialization and trade. Graph B's specialization and trade with arrows in Figure 31-3, clearly indicating B's gains from trade.

Now plot similar arrows for A in Figure 31-3 to show how this exchange also benefits A. (Hint: A moves to the northwest along its PPC in order to produce the 100,000 more bushels of wheat it needs to exchange with B. When it gives up this wheat to B, it acquires 40,000 bushels of corn for it; this trade moves it back to the southeast. The question is, Does A go back to its original point or to a point superior to it and thus also acquire a gain from trade?)

Note how the trade arrows from the two countries have the same length and slope. They must; each trade arrow describes the exchange of 100,000 bushels of wheat for 40,000 bushels of corn. The only difference in the two arrows is the direction in which they are pointing. (They must point in opposite directions, because an export for one country is an import for the other.) Note also that gains from trade arise because the two PPCs have different slopes, and it's therefore possible to have a mutually beneficial trade arrow with a slope in between. If the two PPCs had the same slope, then opportunity costs would be the same in both countries. Consequently, neither country would have a _____ advantage, and mutually beneficial trade would [be possible, not be possible]. We emphasize that we're concentrating here just on comparative advantage. Economies of scale also provide opportunities for mutually beneficial trade—but that's another story.

3. In Figure 31-4, D is the U.S. domestic demand curve for a perfectly competitive good.

a. Suppose initially that there is no international trade. Then the amount _____ will be produced, and the market price will equal _____. Suppose now that international trade is introduced, and that it results in a price equal to P_2. Then consumption of the good in the United States will be _____, production of the good in the United States will be _____, and the difference between these amounts will be _____, which will be the amount of the good that the United States [exports, imports].

b. As a result of allowing international trade in this good, U.S. producers are [better, worse] off by the amount _____, and U.S. consumers [gain,

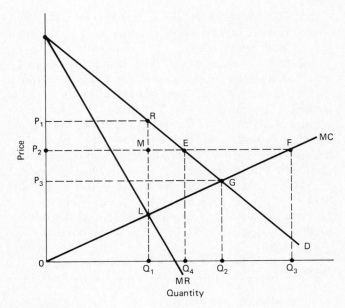

FIGURE 31-4

lose] the amount _____. Therefore, the net efficiency [gain, loss] to the United States equals _____.

c. Suppose next that there is no international trade in the good and that the market in the United States is an unregulated monopoly. Its marginal revenue will be the line _____. The monopolist will produce the amount _____ and will charge price _____. The efficiency [gain, loss] from monopoly will be _____.

Suppose now that international trade is introduced and that as a result the firm that used to have a monopoly in the United States is forced to behave as a perfect competitor. Suppose as before that with international trade the market price is P_2. Then consumption of the good in the United States will equal _____, production of the good in the United States will equal _____, and the difference between these two amounts equals _____, which will be the amount of the good that the United States [exports, imports].

d. As a result of allowing international trade in this good, the total revenue received by the producer in the United States has gone from _____ to _____, so the net gain in total revenue equals the rectangle _____, minus the rectangle _____.

e. But the producer's cost has increased by the four-sided figure _____; thus the net gain to the producer equals the triangle _____, minus the rectangle _____. At the same time, there is a consumer [gain, loss] of _____; thus the net gain to the country (the net gain to consumers plus the net gain to the producer) equals the area of the figure _____. Shade in this area.

f. In this case trade brings two efficiency gains: the standard gain from trade that results even in a world of perfect competition, shown by area _____, plus a gain because trade also ends monopoly abuse, as shown by area _____. Both gains make up the area _____, thus confirming our earlier conclusion.

g. Does this illustrate a special case in which it is possible for international trade in a specific commodity to benefit both the consumers and the producers of that commodity?

_____

Essay Questions

1. Who gains and who loses from a tariff that prohibits the import of a certain good? Do the gains outweigh the losses, or vice versa? Explain.

2. Looking ahead to the next chapter, can you think of any goods that we would not want to export, no matter how great the net economic benefits might be? (Hint: Americans now trade military aircraft and equipment with Canada, and this trade provides economic benefits to both countries. Would you recommend that the United States do the same with the Soviet Union?)

3. "One of the gains from international trade is that it induces firms to reduce or eliminate technical inefficiency." Is this true? Why? Did we miss this point, or was it covered under one of our three broad sources of gains from trade?

4. Why did the leaders of the United Auto Workers argue that the government should take steps to limit the number of autos imported into the United States? If you were one of these leaders, what would be your attitude toward a similar restriction on U.S. imports of steel? Why?

5. Why might trade between New York and Pennsylvania benefit both states? In your answer, you may want to define the concept of an "export to another state" and an "import from another state."

6. A recent slogan has been "Trade, not aid. If we reduce U.S. restrictions on imports from the less developed countries, they will benefit, and so will we." Do you agree or disagree? Explain why.

7. Can you name any goods produced in your state that have developed as a result of interstate specialization—that is, specialization between states? Any industries that have developed as a result of international specialization?

8. If the United States and Mexico have an approximate balance in their trade, which country is more dependent on that trade? Why?

9. "There is no trade in cement between the United States and Australia. The reason is that transport costs on so bulky and heavy an item more than cancel out the gains from trade." Explain this statement. Do you agree with it? Does that mean that transport costs influence trade patterns? Explain how high transport costs in a good may explain "cross-hauling"—for example, the export of cement from California *to* Mexico at the same time as cement is being imported into Texas *from* Mexico.

Answers

Important Terms: 1 d 2 a 3 e 4 c 5 b
True-False: 1 T 2 F 3 F 4 F 5 F 6 T 7 T 8 F 9 T 10 F
Multiple Choice: 1 d 2 c 3 a 4 e 5 b 6 d 7 c 8 a 9 b 10 a 11 e 12 d 13 c 14 d 15 a 16 e
17 c
Exercises: **1a.** $10, 10, $20, 20, rise, fall. **1b.** $15, 5, 15, 25, 15, England, 10, advantage, lower.
2a. Table 31–1 completed:

Table 31–1 completed

A		B	
Wheat	Corn	Wheat	Corn
0	120	0	80
100	90	40	60
200	60	80	40
300	30	120	20
400	0	160	0

2b. Figure 31-3 completed:

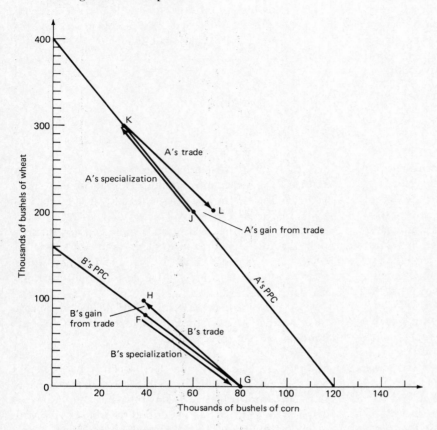

2c. A, A, B, A, 80,000, 40,000. **2d.** 80,000, zero, 100,000, more, gain, comparative, not be possible. **3a.** Q_2, P_3, Q_4, Q_3, Q_4Q_3, exports. **3b.** better, P_2FGP_3, lose, P_2EGP_3, gain, EGF. **3c.** MR, Q_1, P_1, loss, RGL, Q_4, Q_3, Q_4Q_3, exports. **3d.** P_1RQ_1O, P_2FQ_3O, MFQ_3Q_1, P_1RMP_2. **3e.** LFQ_3Q_1, MFL, P_1RMP_2, gain, P_1REP_2, $RLFE$. **3f.** EGF, RLG, $RLFE$. **3g.** yes.

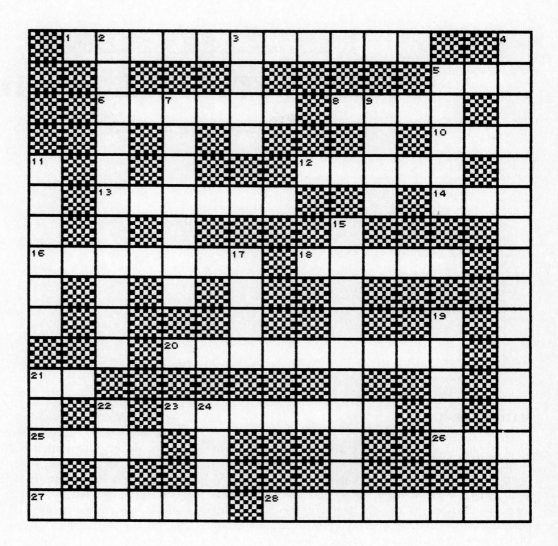

Across

1. this type of advantage is sufficient for mutually beneficial trade
5. a government agency that makes recommendations on trade policy (abbrev.)
6, 8. people cannot be prevented from enjoying this, even if they do not help to pay for it
10. thousands of years
12. a barrier to imports
13. another barrier to imports
14. total
16, 18. winner of Nobel prize; he studied the problems of majority rule
20. if all barriers to international commerce were removed, this would exist (2 words)
21. symbol for lead
23. he explained theory of comparative advantage
25. this product is both exported and imported by the United States
26. period of time made noteworthy by important events
27. the state of Denmark, according to Hamlet
28. this type of advantage is not necessary for mutually beneficial trade

Down

2, 22. this is measured by slope of production possibilities curve
3. _____ roads are a way of transporting heavy goods
4. major reason for gain from international or domestic trade (3 words)
5. often, these are more powerful than the sword
7. flattery, guff
9. a musical instrument
11, 21. this is reduced by competition from imports
15. because of these people, public goods won't be produced by the free market (2 words)
17. buy the labor of
19. a noted international trade theorist, winner of a Nobel prize
24. according to the _____ law of wages, population pressures would drive wages down to the subsistence level

CHAPTER 32

INTERNATIONAL TRADE:

POLICY DEBATES

MAJOR PURPOSE

Even though the gains from trade have been evident since the days of Adam Smith, and even though tariffs have been coming down dramatically over the last 50 years, many trade barriers still remain. We are still a long way from free trade. The primary objective of this chapter is to answer the question, How is it possible for these barriers to still exist? Can they, or can they not, be justified? We will also address a number of other important, and closely related questions: What have been the major developments that have moved us toward freer trade? As we have been moving two steps forward, what are the new barriers to trade that have been moving us one step back? Why does U.S. trade with Japan remain such a contentious issue? And how do the multinational corporations that span international borders fit into this picture?

Learning Objectives

After you have studied this chapter in the textbook and the study guide, you should be able to:

Explain the military and political reasons why trade barriers still exist

State three fallacious economic arguments for protection, explaining why they are fallacious

State five economic arguments for protection that contain some element of truth, and the difficulties with each of these arguments

Describe the multilateral liberalization of our trade over the last 50 years, with special reference to the major events of 1947, 1967, and 1979

Evaluate the European Economic Community (EEC) in terms of its benefits and costs to the Europeans, and the problems it raises for U.S. exporters

Describe the growth of nontariff barriers, and explain why they are particularly difficult to deal with

Explain the conflicts that have arisen in U.S.-Japanese trade

Give some of the reasons why companies go multinational

Evaluate multinational corporations (MNCs) in terms of their benefits and costs to the public at large

HIGHLIGHTS OF CHAPTER

The trade barriers that remain—and the new ones that have been introduced—have been defended by their supporters as "in the national interest." Do the arguments they use make sense?

Arguments for Protection

Much of the defense of trade barriers has little to do with economics. It is instead an appeal to military or political considerations.

The military reason for restricting trade is that weapons and some related goods are vital for our national defense. Under completely free trade, with all countries specializing in their comparative advantage, some military goods might be produced in foreign countries—some of them hostile. Since it would be unacceptable for the nation to find itself dependent on such sources of supply in time of crisis, the production of these goods is protected in the United States as a matter of national security. This military argument does make sense. The major problem it raises is that it is not clear where we should draw the line. Almost any industry can argue that its products are vital for national defense, in one way or another.

The other noneconomic reason for protection is political. The loss that results from allowing a good to be freely imported is felt very heavily by the few people who specialize in producing that good; in many cases, their jobs are threatened by the competition of imports. These people will often vote for a politician who promises to restrict such imports. As we saw in the last chapter, the damage to these losers from free trade will be more than offset by the benefits to the winners—all the people who are able to enjoy a wide variety of inexpensive imported goods. But these winners' benefits are widely dispersed over the public as a whole, with the benefit received by each individual being relatively small. Thus winners usually vote for other issues on which they feel more deeply, and the politician who proposes to restrict an import is often elected. Thus trade restrictions that make no economic sense are still introduced for political reasons.

Now let's turn to the *economic* arguments that have been used to try to justify protection. Some are fallacious, but some contain an element of truth:

1. "Buy American because it keeps our money at home. When we buy Korean goods we lose our money to Korea." This argument is fallacious. When we buy Korean goods our money eventually comes back when the Koreans buy *our* goods.

2. "We can't compete with cheap foreign labor." This argument is also fallacious. Labor in many foreign countries is less expensive because it is less productive. Our higher productivity means that, on average, we can compete with cheap foreign labor. We do particularly well in goods in which we have a comparative advantage (where our productivity advantage more than offsets our higher wage rate). We can't compete where we don't have a comparative advantage, where our productivity advantage does *not* offset our higher wage rate.

3. "Tariffs should be tailored to equalize costs at home and abroad." This too is a fallacious argument. According to the theory of comparative advantage, we gain from international trade because there are differences in costs between countries. Tailoring tariffs to eliminate these differences would eliminate trade, and all the gains it provides.

4. "If we buy steel from Pittsburgh rather than Japan, employment will rise in Pittsburgh rather than Japan." There is a grain of truth in this argument. Restricting imports of steel from Japan may stimulate employment in Pittsburgh, at least in the short run. However, there are two problems. First, Japan may retaliate with its own restrictions against our exports, and this will reduce U.S. employment. Thus we don't get employment gains after all. In short, we are following a "beggar-my-neighbor" policy that doesn't provide employment benefits, but results in shrinking trade and a loss of the gains from trade. Second, blocking out Japanese competition makes it more difficult to control costs and prices in U.S. industries. If U.S. workers don't feel that they have to compete with the Japanese, they will be less restrained in their wage demands. We saw in Chapter 31 that one of the gains from trade is that it makes our economy more competitive. We lose this gain whenever we protect our industries.

5. "Restricting trade will diversify a nation's economy." This may be true for some countries. Trade may lead a country to specialize in producing just a few goods. If world prices drop for these few goods, the country will suffer from having "put all its eggs in one basket." On the other hand, such heavy specialization will put it in a particularly favorable position if those prices rise; a prime example is the group of OPEC countries who export almost nothing but oil. But these arguments simply don't apply to the United States. A country this large will always produce such a large variety of goods that overspecialization will not be a serious concern.

6. "We need to protect our infant industries." This argument is sometimes valid. Without the protection of trade restrictions, some industries may never reach the size where they can realize the economies of scale necessary to compete in world markets. However, there are three difficulties with this argument: (*a*) Infant industries never seem to grow up. They typically continue to demand protection, and no government wants to lose votes by cutting the apron strings; (b) even if an industry were to grow up, it might still not be able to compete effectively; and (c) if the infant industry really does have a promising future, then why aren't private lenders willing to lend it enough money to survive until maturity?

7. "Restricting imports may reduce the price we have to pay for them." This may make sense if the United States buys so much of a good that a cutback in this demand (as a result of a U.S. import restriction) would reduce the world price. While this policy may work if it's applied to an import from a small trading partner, it won't work on a large partner like the European Economic Community. If the EEC sees the United States doing this, it can take the same attitude and restrict its purchase of a U.S. good. The price of that U.S. export will then fall. With the price of a U.S. import *and* a U.S. export both falling, the United States may not achieve any price advantage after all. Moreover, for both countries, the gains from trade will shrink.

8. "Restricting imports may reduce our vulnerability to a cutoff in foreign supplies." Cutbacks in oil supplies from OPEC countries in the 1970s made clear the force of this argument. But oil is special; for most other commodities, the risk of having our supply cut off is minimal: if one country stops selling to us, we can turn to other sources of supply.

History of Trade Policy

The history of trade policy in the western world since the depression of the 1930s has been one of falling tariffs. However, the fall has not been steady; it has been broken by temporary periods of tariff increase. The highlights of this history are illustrated in Figure 32-1 in the textbook. The most important events to remember are the following:

1. In 1947 the United States and 22 other countries signed the General Agreement on Tariffs and Trade (GATT), which set the stage for several rounds of multilateral negotiations to lower tariffs.

2. In the late 1950s the European Economic Community (EEC) was formed. It provided (a) free trade between all its members, (b) a common tariff against all goods coming in from outside the EEC, and (c) other measures of economic cooperation.

3. In 1967 the GATT countries completed the "Kennedy round" of negotiations by agreeing to cut their tariffs, on average, by about 35%. In the 1970s there was some backsliding; many countries began raising nontariff barriers (NTBs) such as import quotas. However, in 1979, the "Tokyo round" of negotiations was completed; this cut tariffs by about another third, and provided some relief from NTBs—although, unfortunately, only limited relief.

The Multinational Corporation (MNC)

The most important thing to understand about MNCs is why they exist. Why do companies go multinational, by setting up subsidiaries in foreign countries?

1. One incentive is to reduce transportation costs by producing goods in several countries, rather than producing them all in the United States and then shipping them abroad.

2. Because it operates in many different countries, an MNC is not so vulnerable to political pressure from any one. If the MNC feels that the government in one country is taxing it too heavily or imposing regulations that are too costly, it can switch some of its operations to other countries.

3. The MNC is in a good position to exploit economies of scale. For example, the technological improvements it discovers in one country can be transferred easily to its operations in other countries, reducing costs there.

4. One reason for producing goods in a foreign country rather than producing them in the United States and exporting them to that country is the existence of tariffs in the foreign country. For example, a number of U.S. companies have set up branch plants in Europe to produce there. The alternative of producing here and shipping to Europe instead would have been more expensive because of the European tariff they would have had to pay at the border.

The world economy has benefited from the development of MNCs in three ways:

1. It's in the interests of any profit-seeking MNC to locate each of its activities in the country that has a comparative advantage. Because MNCs thus help countries to "find comparative advantage," they assist in the realization of worldwide real income gains from trade. They also assist in the realization of real income gains from economies of scale.

2. MNCs have also helped to raise standards of living by quickly transmitting technological knowledge across borders.

3. By producing in many countries, MNCs have reduced the costs of transporting goods among those countries. For example, if a U.S. firm sets up a branch plant to produce and sell in Europe, the firm will no longer incur the transport costs of shipping this good from the United States to Europe.

However, many people think that the MNCs now have too much influence over governments. Scandals in which executives of Lockheed paid large bribes to government officials in other countries have illustrated the abuse of economic power by MNCs.

Important Terms: Match the Columns

Match the term in the first column with the corresponding phrase in the second column. But before you do so, write out your own definition of the term in the first column.

_____ 1. Tariff
_____ 2. Nontariff barrier (NTB)
_____ 3. Quota
_____ 4. Trade restriction
_____ 5. Protection
_____ 6. "Begger-my-neighbor" policy
_____ 7. Infant industry
_____ 8. Terms of trade
_____ 9. Bilateral negotiations
_____ 10. The General Agreement on Tariffs and Trade (GATT)
_____ 11. The European Economic Community (EEC)
_____ 12. Kennedy round
_____ 13. Tokyo round
_____ 14. Multinational corporation (MNC)
_____ 15. Multilateral negotiations

a. The common market in Europe formed in the late 1950s by Germany, France, Italy, Holland, Belgium, and Luxembourg, and later joined by other countries such as Britain and Denmark

b. The policy of imposing barriers to trade in order to shield domestic industries from foreign competition

c. Negotiations between only two countries

d. A tax imposed on imported goods as they enter a country

e. The series of multilateral GATT negotiations ending with the 1979 agreement to cut tariffs by about a third, and limit NTBs

f. An industry that has not yet reached the size at which it can capture sufficient economies of scale to compete in world markets

g. Any government regulation—other than a tariff—that restricts trade

h. A large corporation with its head office in one country and subsidiaries in other countries

i. A treaty signed in 1947 by the United States and 22 other countries calling for multilateral negotiations to reduce trade restrictions

j. The use of trade restrictions to reduce imports, increase domestic production, and therefore reduce unemployment. Such a policy transfers an unemployment problem to another country.

k. A limit on the number of units of a good that can be imported into a country

l. Negotiations between many countries

m. The series of multilateral negotiations between GATT countries in the 1960s that was concluded by the signing of a 1967 agreement to reduce tariffs by about a third

n. The price we receive for our exports, compared to the price we pay for our imports

o. Any tariff or nontariff barrier that impedes international trade

True-False

T F 1. When international trade is opened up in a good, the United States as a whole gains only if we end up exporting that good.

T F 2. The promotion of economic diversity is one argument for protection.

T F 3. If the United States were to increase restrictions on imported steel, this would tend to increase employment in Pittsburgh in the short run.

T F 4. After an infant industry has been supported by the government for a year or two, political pressure to remove the protection becomes almost irresistible.

T F 5. U.S. presidents have been more likely than the Congress to favor a policy of increasing trade barriers.

T F 6. Because wages in the United States are higher, it follows that costs of production are also higher—and this justifies protecting our goods from cheap foreign products.

T F 7. By restricting its imports, a country may be able to improve its terms of trade. But in practice this may be very difficult to accomplish because other trading countries are often powerful enough to retaliate.

T F 8. The major purpose of the GATT is to provide for bilateral negotiations in which countries will agree to lowering their tariffs.

T F 9. European auto tariffs reduce production in Europe by Ford and GM subsidiaries.

Multiple Choice

1. A policy of protecting essential defense industries:
   a. has been opposed by economists since the days of Adam Smith
   b. is sometimes abused by industries that contribute very little to national security but still try to use the defense argument to get protection
   c. is based on the expectation that such protection would increase real GNP
   d. is justified as a method of creating employment, but can't be justified in any other way
   e. all of the above

2. The strongest political pressure for a change in trade policy usually comes from:
   a. producers lobbying for import restrictions
   b. producers lobbying for export restrictions
   c. consumers lobbying for import restrictions
   d. consumers lobbying for export restrictions
   e. consumers lobbying for a reduction in trade restrictions

3. With free trade it is likely that the United States would:
   a. give up the production of industrial goods in order to concentrate on agricultural goods
   b. give up the production of agricultural goods in order to concentrate on industrial goods
   c. give up one industry (say, electrical machinery) in order to specialize in another (say, chemicals)
   d. give up the production of some items of electrical machinery in order to specialize in other items of electrical machinery and do the same in chemicals
   e. in both electrical equipment and chemicals, produce an even wider range of items than at present

4. A "beggar-my-neighbor" policy involves:
   a. encouraging the purchase of essential materials from abroad
   b. export controls to prevent the sale of our natural resources to foreign countries
   c. import restrictions designed to capture employment from foreign countries
   d. subsidies to encourage imports of foreign natural resources
   e. subsidies to encourage imports of foreign luxury goods

5. The infant-industry argument for protection makes sense if the infant industry:
   a. is able to compete against foreign firms now, but not in the future
   b. is not able to compete against foreign firms now, but will be able to in the future
   c. won't be able to compete now or in the future
   d. will be able to compete now and in the future
   e. won't be able to compete now; the future is irrelevant

6. "If I buy a radio from Taiwan, I get the radio and Taiwan gets the dollars. But if I buy a U.S.-built radio, I get the radio and the dollars stay here." This argument is:
   a. misleading because the Taiwanese don't keep the dollars they earn from us in trade; they eventually spend them on our goods
   b. misleading because the dollars I spend buying a U.S.-built radio also leave this country

   c. correct; this is why we should stop trading
   d. correct; we should trade only for political reasons
   e. true for radios, but not for most goods we import

7. Trade restrictions on a good are most likely to improve our terms of trade if:
   a. U.S. demand for the good is a significant part of world demand
   b. U.S. demand for the good is an insignificant part of world demand
   c. the U.S. industry is a natural monopoly
   d. the lower prices that result drive some of our own producers out of business
   e. the U.S. is already self-sufficient in this good

8. U.S. tariffs today are:
   a. higher than in the 1930s
   b. slightly lower than in the 1930s
   c. much lower than in the 1930s
   d. about the same as in the 1930s
   e. higher in most goods than in the 1930s, but lower in some

9. The formation of the European Economic Community:
   a. was one of the reasons for the severe scarcity of agricultural goods in the early 1980s
   b. has made it easier for Americans to compete against the French in the German market
   c. has made it more difficult for Americans to compete against the French in the German market
   d. has made it more difficult for Americans to compete against the Japanese in the German market
   e. has had no effect on Americans competing in the German market

10. The European Common Agricultural Program has:
    a. raised the price of U.S. farm exports
    b. not affected the price of U.S. farm exports
    c. increased the quantity of U.S. farm exports
    d. led to conflicts within the United States, but has reduced conflicts within Europe
    e. led to conflicts within Europe

11. In the early 1980s:
    a. a high value of the U.S. dollar made it difficult for U.S. firms to compete and increased the pressure for protection
    b. a high value of the U.S. dollar made it relatively easy for U.S. firms to compete and reduced the pressure for protection
    c. a low value of the U.S. dollar made it relatively easy for U.S. firms to compete and reduced the pressure for protection
    d. a low value of the U.S. dollar made it difficult for U.S. firms to compete and increased the pressure for protection
    e. a low value of the U.S. dollar made it relatively easy for U.S. firms to compete. This had no effect on the protectionist pressure at that time, which was building up for other reasons.

12. In the Kennedy round, participating countries cut their tariffs by about a third. In the Tokyo round that followed:
    a. almost no further progress was made
    b. no further progress was made

c. participating countries cut their remaining tariffs by about 10%

d. participating countries cut their remaining tariffs by roughly another one-third

e. participating countries cut their remaining tariffs by roughly two-thirds

13. In its 1984 trade with Japan alone, the United States had a:

a. deficit of almost $400 million

b. deficit of almost $4 billion

c. deficit of almost $40 billion

d. surplus of almost $40 billion

e. surplus of almost $400 million

14. When the U.S. government moved to prevent Western European subsidiaries of U.S. multinationals from exporting oil pipeline equipment to the U.S.S.R.:

a. European governments viewed this as a reasonable request, and encouraged the subsidiaries to comply

b. European governments viewed this as a serious compromise in their sovereignty; when they resisted, the U.S. action was withdrawn

c. European governments viewed this as a reasonable request, but for other reasons the United States withdrew this policy

d. European governments viewed this as a serious compromise in their sovereignty; despite their resistance, the U.S. policy is still in effect

e. European governments viewed this as a serious compromise in their sovereignty, and U.S. insistence on this policy led to a trade war

15. Nontariff barriers are:

a. designed solely to restrict trade

b. designed solely to improve health standards

c. designed solely for other nontrade reasons

d. sometimes designed to restrict trade, and sometimes designed to improve health standards; but in either case, they restrict trade

e. justified so long as they provide a benefit, regardless of their cost

Exercise

Parts of this exercise cover the same ground as the Appendix to the chapter. You will probably be able to do the exercise and find it helpful, even if you are not being asked to study the Appendix. However, if you get stuck, you can refer to the Appendix for help. In any case, first try to do the exercise on your own.

Figure 32-1 shows the domestic supply and demand for a good that is traded internationally.

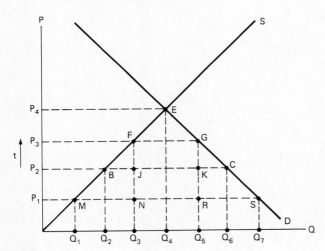

FIGURE 32-1

a. Without international trade the price would be _____, and the quantity produced would be _____. If international trade results in a price of P_2, then domestic production will be _____, domestic consumption will be _____, and the country will [import, export] the amount _____. As a result of this international trade,

the [gain, loss] to consumers is area _____, while producers are [better, worse] off by area _____. If we consider both producers and consumers, the effect of international trade on the nation, on balance, is an efficiency [gain, loss] of area _____.

b. Suppose that the government imposes a tariff on this good, shown by arrow t. Suppose that this has no effect on the world price of the good. Because of the tariff, the domestic price will rise to _____. (Importers who are willing to bring this good in for a price P_2 will need this higher price to compensate them for the tariff t that they now have to pay the government.) The quantity of imports will be _____. As a result of the tariff, consumers [gain, lose] area _____, while producers are [better, worse] off by area _____. Moreover, the government is now collecting a tariff t on quantity _____ of imports, _____, for a total revenue of area _____. Therefore, there is a net [gain, loss] to the nation from this tariff of areas _____.

c. Now suppose that, instead of this tariff t, the government imposes an import quota that restricts imports to the quantity FG. With imports of FG, P_2 [is, is not] an equilibrium price, because the demand for this good at price P_2 is [more than, less than] the domestic plus imported supply. Thus price will be [above, below] P_2. P_3 [is, is not] an equilibrium price because, with imports FG, the demand for this good at P_3 is [more than, less than, equal to] the domestic plus imported supply. Thus, this quota of FG is the quota equivalent of tariff _____, because both raise U.S. price by _____, and reduce imports to _____.

d. Because of the quota, the price in the domestic market will rise to _____, consumers will [gain, lose] area _____, and producers will [gain, lose] area _____. Suppose that the quota rights are held by foreigners exporting to the United States, with any of the benefits that a quota may provide going to them. The revenue the U.S. government gets from the imposition of this quota is _____. Therefore, the net effect on the nation of this quota is its effect on producers and consumers, which is a [gain, loss] of area _____.

e. When the U.S. government imposes an import quota, and gives away these quota rights to foreigners, then a quota will result in a [larger, smaller] amount of [gain, loss] to the United States than will an equivalent tariff. The additional [gain, loss] from the quota results because duty revenue is collected by the U.S. Treasury if there is a [tariff, quota], but is not collected if there is this type of [tariff, quota].

Essay Questions

1. The text argued that a country may improve its terms of trade by restricting imports. In 1973 the oil-producing countries of OPEC managed to improve their terms of trade by restricting their exports. Explain carefully what are the similarities and differences between the "terms of trade" argument for restricting imports and the "terms of trade" argument for restricting exports.

2. When a country is in a severe recession, the demand to reduce imports becomes stronger. Why? Critically evaluate such a proposal.

3. It is sometimes argued that trade restrictions protect our high standard of living from being eroded by competition from low-income countries. Evaluate this. Do trade restrictions maintain our standard of living or reduce it for the nation as a whole? For the industry that's being protected?

4. The watch industry, the chemical industry, the canned crab industry, and the lead pencil industry have all, at one time or another, used the national defense argument in seeking protection. Evaluate the claim of each.

5. Explain carefully how a tariff tends to reduce the benefits of international specialization.

6. Consider a tariff high enough not just to reduce, but to completely prevent, imports. How would it affect consumers? Producers? The nation as a whole? Would the U.S. Treasury collect any duty revenue from such a tariff? From a tariff that only *reduces* imports?

Answers

Important Terms: 1 d 2 g 3 k 4 o 5 b 6 j 7 f 8 n 9 c 10 i 11 a 12 m 13 e 14 h 15 l

True-False: 1 F 2 T 3 T 4 F 5 F 6 F 7 T 8 F 9 F

Multiple Choice: 1 b 2 a 3 d 4 c 5 b 6 a 7 a 8 c 9 c 10 e 11 a 12 d 13 c 14 b 15 d

Exercises: **a.** P_4, Q_4, Q_2, Q_6, import, BC, gain, P_4ECP_2, worse, P_4EBP_2, gain, EBC. **b.** P_3, FG, lose, P_3GCP_2, better, P_3FBP_2, FG, $FGKJ$, loss, FJB and GKC. **c.** is not, more than, above, is, equal to, t, t, FG. **d.** P_3, lose, P_3GCP_2, gain, P_3FBP_2, zero, loss, $FGCB$. **e.** larger, loss, loss, tariff, quota.

PART SEVEN

MICROECONOMICS:

HOW INCOME IS DISTRIBUTED

CHAPTER 33

WAGES IN A PERFECTLY COMPETITIVE ECONOMY

MAJOR PURPOSE

In this chapter, the objective is to use the familiar tools of supply and demand developed in earlier chapters to analyze how wages are determined in perfectly competitive labor markets. The labor market for a specific industry will be perfectly competitive if (1) workers are mobile and can move in and out of this industry, (2) there are so many buyers and sellers of labor service that none can affect the wage rate, and (3) labor is standardized, with all workers being equally productive. If these assumptions hold, and there is also perfect competition in the markets for products, then the labor demand by an industry reflects the marginal product of labor in that industry, and labor supply reflects the marginal product of labor in other industries. The conclusion that follows is that perfect competition yields an efficient outcome in a labor market, just as it did in a product market. Finally, a number of real-world complications in labor markets are recognized. For example, what happens when the government intervenes to set a minimum wage? What happens when the assumption of labor mobility—assumption (1) above—does not hold? Specifically, what happens when discrimination prevents blacks from entering jobs traditionally held by whites? These questions are addressed in this chapter. In the next chapter, assumption (2) above is relaxed in order to show the effects when workers form a union to raise wages—or employers form an association to lower wages. Finally in Chapter 35, assumption (3) is relaxed in order to analyze what happens when workers are not equally productive.

Learning Objectives

After you have studied this chapter in the textbook and the study guide, you should be able to:

Explain why, under perfect competition, the curve showing an industry's demand for labor is the same as the curve showing the marginal revenue product of labor

State two reasons why the labor demand curve might shift to the right

Illustrate how the labor demand curve can be used to show the total income of labor in an industry and the total income of other factors of production

Explain why the height of the labor supply curve for an industry reflects the opportunity cost of labor—that is, labor's wage and marginal product in other industries

Explain why perfect competition in the labor market typically results in an efficient wage and employment level

Measure diagrammatically the efficiency loss that results when a labor market is not perfectly competitive

Explain why one cannot necessarily jump from the conclusion that a perfectly competitive labor market is efficient, to the much stronger conclusion that a free, unregulated labor market is "best"

Explain the effects of a minimum wage in an otherwise perfectly competitive labor market, and its more favorable effects in a labor market that is not competitive
   Discuss the effects of discrimination in a labor market
   Describe and evaluate the concept of comparable worth

HIGHLIGHTS OF CHAPTER

As a first approximation, a wage can be viewed just like the price of any other good or service that is traded in the market. In this case, the service is labor, the demanders are employers, and the suppliers are workers.

The Demand for Labor

In defining its demand for labor, a firm begins with its *marginal physical product* (MPP). This schedule, shown in column 3 of Table 33-1 in the textbook, shows how the firm's output increases—in physical units—as it hires more labor. If markets for goods are perfectly competitive, we can multiply this increase in physical output by its price to calculate the additional *revenue* the firm receives as it hires more labor. This is called its *marginal revenue product* (MRP), and is shown in column 5 of Table 33-1. In a perfectly competitive economy, MRP will also be VMP, the value of the marginal product (or marginal product for short). However, if there is not perfect competition in goods' markets, MRP will be less than VMP (as illustrated in problem 33-3). It is very important that you be able to distinguish MPP, MRP and VMP. If necessary, work through Tables 33-1, 2 and 3 in the exercise below, in addition to Table 33-1 in the text.

The profit-maximizing firm will demand labor up to the point where the MRP is just equal to the wage rate W. The reason is that, if MRP were greater than W, the firm could increase its profits by hiring more workers; and if MRP were less than W, the firm could increase its profits by hiring fewer workers. Thus the MRP curve shows how much the firm will hire at each possible wage. In other words, the MRP curve is the firm's labor demand curve. (The argument here is essentially the same as the one used in Chapter 21 to show that the marginal benefit curve and the demand curve for an individual are the same.)

A firm's demand for labor schedule slopes down because of diminishing returns (recall this concept from Chapter 22). As a firm hires more and more labor (with other factors fixed), it eventually finds that the marginal physical product of labor—and therefore MRP—decreases. In other words, its demand for labor slopes downward.

There are several reasons why a firm's demand curve for labor might shift: (1) If the price of the firm's output falls, this will cause a downward shift in its MRP, and therefore its labor demand; and (2) if the firm's marginal physical product of labor shifts up, its MRP and

labor demand curve will also shift up. Such an upward shift might occur, for example, if the firm increases the amount of capital it employs; this would make labor physically more productive by providing it with more machinery to work with. Another example might be a technological improvement that allows a firm to get more physical output from its workers. (Often increased capital equipment and technological change come together, but it is possible for one to occur without the other.)

The market demand curve for labor is just the horizontal sum of the demand curves of all the individual hiring firms. Again, this is similar to the summation of the individual demand curves for a good discussed at the beginning of Chapter 21.

Before turning to the supply curve for labor, we pause briefly to consider a further important interpretation of labor demand.

How the Labor Demand Curve Shows the Distribution of Income

The total revenue of an industry is the sum of the MRPs of all workers employed in that industry. That is, in Figure 33-4 in the textbook, it is the sum of all the MRPs—such as bars *a* and *b* on the left—of all *N* workers in this industry. In total, this is areas 1 and 2 under the labor demand curve. Of this area representing total industry revenue, rectangular area 2 is labor income since it is the quantity of employment (the base of this rectangle) times the wage (the height of this rectangle). The rest—that is, area 1—goes to other factors of production, in the form of rent, interest and profit.

The Supply of Labor

The labor supply curve for an industry is derived much like the supply curve for a commodity in Chapter 22. The height of the labor supply curve indicates how much must be paid to attract one more worker into the industry. This is (roughly) the wage and marginal product of this worker in another industry. In other words, the height of the labor supply curve is the opportunity cost of an additional worker.

Is a Perfectly Competitive Labor Market Efficient?

Efficiency requires that labor be hired in an industry up to the point where its marginal benefit is just equal to its marginal costs. (If there are no externalities—as assumed here—then there is no difference between social and private benefits, and no difference between social and private costs.) The marginal benefit of labor is its marginal product in this industry, as given by the labor demand curve. The marginal cost of labor is its opportunity cost—that is, its marginal product elsewhere; this is given by its supply curve. Since supply and demand for labor are equated in a perfectly competitive labor market, the marginal cost of labor is equal to the marginal benefit of labor, and this market is therefore efficient.

When a labor market has been shifted away from a perfectly competitive equilibrium, there is an efficiency loss that can be measured by the triangle between the demand curve, the supply curve, and the vertical line at the actual quantity of employment. An example is provided in panel *b* of Figure 33-6 in the textbook. It should be emphasized again that this measure is valid only under the twin assumptions of (1) perfect competition, and (2) no externalities. If such triangular efficiency losses are not clear, you may wish to review the similar analysis that was used in Figure 24-3 to show efficiency losses in product markets.

Although a perfectly competitive labor market is efficient, it does not necessarily follow that a free, unregulated labor market is "best," for the following four reasons:

1. In an unregulated market, employers may discriminate against minorities, and thus violate the mobility assumption of perfect competition; labor is *not* free to move into such an industry. (This point will be considered in more detail in a moment.)

2. In an unregulated market, employers may have market power, thus violating another assumption of perfect competition.

3. There may be externalities.

4. Even if none of these problems arise—and an unregulated labor market is efficient—it may not be best because of the way it distributes income.

The Effect of a Minimum Wage

There are four effects when a minimum wage (above the existing equilibrium wage) is introduced into a perfectly competitive labor market:

1. Employment is reduced.

2. Reduced employment leads to an efficiency loss, similar to the red triangle in panel *c* of Figure 33-6. (The efficiency loss is even more than this if the minimum wage is imposed across all labor markets.)

3. Although the wage received by workers who are still employed in this industry rises, the wage of those who no longer have a job here falls (or disappears altogether). Therefore, on balance the overall effect on total labor income is uncertain.

4. The amount of income going to other factors of production will definitely decrease, because the higher wage that might be paid to labor will put a squeeze on these other incomes.

While these four effects can be predicted from our theory, there is another effect that experience has taught us: The unemployment created by minimum wage legislation falls most heavily on teenagers and nonwhites.

The important qualifications to this analysis include:

1. Even if the minimum wage raises total labor income, workers may not feel that they benefit overall from the change. Even though jobs pay better, they are harder to find; and employers paying a higher wage may no longer feel that they can afford the cost of on-the-job training that is so beneficial to workers.

2. The more industries covered by minimum wage legislation, the greater the unemployment it will create (the harder it is for an unemployed person to find a job elsewhere, because there are fewer and fewer of these "other jobs" available).

The Effects of Discrimination in the Labor Market

Figure 33-8 in the text shows the economic effects when employers discriminate by hiring blacks only for jobs with a low marginal product; the offensive moral and social dimensions are also recognized, even though they cannot be dealt with in this analysis.

When black workers are forced into jobs where they produce less, there is an efficiency loss roughly equal to the reduction in their output. Moreover, because they are less productive, blacks receive a lower wage. Thus the efficiency loss is essentially all borne by blacks. It is true that white workers benefit from a higher wage, due to the artificial scarcity of labor created in their part of the market because blacks are no longer able to work there. However, other factors of production lose, because their interest, rent and profit income is squeezed by the higher white wage. Since most other factors of production are owned by whites, it is not clear, on balance, whether whites benefit overall or lose. The one clear message is that discrimination imposes an efficiency loss on the economy, and most or all of it is borne by blacks.

About 15 years ago, it was estimated that black income in the United States was 25% to 40% below white income. While that gap initially appeared to be closing, by the early 1980s it was apparently widening again.

Comparable Worth

With equal pay for men and women in the *same* job now a widely accepted principle, the focus has shifted to the question, What should be done when men and women are in *different* but equally demanding jobs, and women are paid less? Should nurses be paid less than truck drivers? Proponents of comparable worth say no. If these jobs are judged comparable, in terms of the education, responsibility, skill, etc., that they require, then pay should be equalized. Moreover, several state and municipal governments are doing just that. However, critics are concerned because this policy requires that specific jobs be compared; and these comparisons will be based on subjective and arbitrary judgments by bureaucrats or judges who will be second-guessing labor markets. They will be imposing a detailed and complex system of wage controls that will leave many labor markets in a chronic condition of excess demand or supply. To this argument, the proponents of comparable worth reply: Relying on the market would allow discrimination to continue, and this is not acceptable.

Important Terms: Match the Columns

Match the term in the first column with the corresponding phrase in the second column. But before you do so, write out your own definition of the term in the first column.

_____ 1. Marginal physical product (MPP) of labor
_____ 2. Marginal revenue product (MRP) of labor
_____ 3. Opportunity cost of labor
_____ 4. Value of the marginal product (VMP) of labor
_____ 5. Transfer price of labor

a. The additional revenue that a firm can earn by hiring one more worker
b. The wage necessary to induce a worker to change jobs
c. The additional number of units of output that a firm can produce by hiring one more worker
d. The marginal product of labor in another industry
e. Marginal physical product of labor times the price of the employer's product

True-False

T F   1. A profit-maximizing firm that is operating in perfectly competitive labor and product markets will hire labor to the point where the value of the marginal product equals the wage rate.

T F   2. The demand for labor schedule shifts to the right whenever the marginal revenue product of labor schedule shifts to the right.

T F   3. If the marginal revenue product of labor is less than the wage, a perfectly competitive firm can increase its profits by hiring more labor.

T F   4. A minimum wage increases the income of some workers while decreasing the income of some others.

T F   5. Even if there is an external cost of employing labor, a perfectly competitive labor market will still be efficient.

T F   6. The marginal revenue product of labor is the amount the firm's revenue increases when it hires one more worker.

T F   7. The value of the marginal product of labor is the same as the marginal revenue product of labor, if the hiring firm is a monopolist in its product market.

T F   8. If the wage rate rises elsewhere in the economy, the wage and employment in a perfectly competitive industry will tend to rise.

T F   9. There is a greater efficiency loss if the minimum wage is applied just to one industry rather than to all industries.

Multiple Choice

1. The marginal physical product of labor:
   a. is based on the assumption that the use of all other factors is held constant as the employment of labor increases
   b. is based on the assumption that the use of all other factors increases by the same proportion as labor employment
   c. shows the additional revenue a firm can earn because it hires one more worker
   d. is set equal to the wage rate by an employer in equilibrium
   e. is the same as the value of the marginal product

2. A firm's demand curve for labor is the curve showing its:
   a. total physical product of labor
   b. average revenue product of labor
   c. marginal physical product of labor
   d. average physical product of labor
   e. marginal revenue product of labor

3. The demand for labor by a firm producing bolts shifts up in response to:

   a. a rise in the price of bolts
   b. a fall in the marginal product of labor in the bolt-making industry
   c. a downward shift in the demand for bolts
   d. a decrease in the stock of machinery in the industry
   e. a decrease in the stock of other investment equipment in the industry

4. A leftward shift in the labor supply schedule may be the result of:

   a. a rightward shift in the marginal revenue product of labor schedule
   b. a leftward shift in the marginal revenue product of labor schedule
   c. higher available wages in other industries
   d. a reduction in the marginal product of labor in other industries
   e. a falling opportunity cost of labor

5. If there is a perfectly competitive market for farm labor, and there is a fall in the price of grain and other farm outputs, then there will be:

   a. a shift to the left in the labor supply curve
   b. a shift to the left in the labor demand curve
   c. a higher wage and more employment
   d. a higher wage and less employment
   e. a lower wage and more employment

6. The value of the marginal product of labor is equal to the marginal revenue product of labor:

   a. always
   b. never
   c. only if the hiring firm is a monopolist in its product market
   d. only if the hiring firm is a perfect competitor in its product market
   e. only if the hiring firm is an oligopolist in its product market

7. The total area under an industry's demand for labor schedule to the left of the existing quantity of employment equals:

   a. the income received by other factors in the industry
   b. the total income of labor in the industry
   c. the total income of labor and all other factors in the industry
   d. total profits in the industry
   e. the marginal revenue received by the industry

8. In perfect competition, the division of income in an industry is measured from the equilibrium point on its labor demand curve in the following way:

   a. Labor receives the triangular area to the southeast of this point, while the triangular area to the northwest goes to other factors of production.
   b. Labor receives the rectangular area to the southwest of this point, while the triangular area to the northwest goes to other factors of production.
   c. Other factors of production receive the rectangular area to the southwest of this point, while the triangular area to the northwest goes to labor.
   d. Both the areas mentioned above go to labor; the income of other factors is shown on another diagram.

e. Both the areas mentioned above go to capital; the income of labor is shown on another diagram.

9. An increase in the price of houses (caused by an increase in the demand for houses) will result in:

   a. a shift to the right in the labor supply curve
   b. a lower wage, and increased employment
   c. a lower wage, and reduced employment
   d. a higher wage, and reduced employment
   e. a higher wage, and increased employment

10. In a perfectly competitive labor market for an industry, an increase in wages elsewhere in the economy will result in:

   a. a shift to the right in the labor supply curve
   b. an increase in wages and employment in this industry
   c. a decrease in wages and employment in this industry
   d. a decrease in wages, and an increase in employment in this industry
   e. an increase in wages, and a decrease in employment in this industry

11. In a perfectly competitive labor market for an industry, there will be an efficiency loss unless labor is hired up to the point where:

   a. the marginal product of labor in this industry exceeds its marginal product elsewhere
   b. the marginal product of labor in this industry is less than its marginal product elsewhere
   c. the marginal product of labor in this industry is equal to its marginal product elsewhere
   d. the opportunity cost of labor exceeds its marginal product in this industry
   e. the opportunity cost of labor is less than its marginal product in this industry

12. The unemployment created by minimum wage legislation is particularly severe among:

   a. all white workers   **d.** teenage blacks
   b. teenage whites   **e.** auto workers
   c. white-collar workers

13. A labor market is "color-blind" if:

   a. all employers ignore color in making hiring and firing decisions
   b. quotas exist which ensure that workers of one color will get a certain percentage of the jobs
   c. blacks are last hired, first fired
   d. blacks are first hired, last fired
   e. blacks are restricted to jobs with a low marginal product

14. The most likely result of discrimination against men in a perfectly competitive market for nurses' labor is:

   a. an increase in the income of male nurses
   b. an increase in the income of female nurses
   c. a decrease in the wages of female nurses
   d. an increase in the income of other factors
   e. a reduced supply of female nurses

15. If the government imposes a minimum wage above the prevailing wage in a perfectly competitive labor market:

   a. there will be an efficiency gain
   b. some but not all workers will benefit
   c. all workers taken together must benefit
   d. employment will increase
   e. employment won't change

16. The efficiency loss from discrimination in a perfectly competitive labor market:

a. is borne mostly by blacks, whose income is reduced
b. occurs because blacks are employed in more productive activities, while whites are in less
c. occurs because income is transferred from white labor to other factors of production
d. occurs because income is transferred from black labor to non-labor factors of production
e. occurs because the other factors of production are owned by outsiders

Exercises

Table 33-1

Number of workers	Total physical output	Marginal physical product of labor	Marginal revenue product (MRP) when price of output is $10 per unit	Marginal revenue product (MRP) when price of output is $15 per unit
0	0			
1	12			
2	19			
3	24			
4	28			
5	30			

1a. Fill in the missing data in Table 33-1 above for a hypothetical firm with a given stock of capital, and selling its output in a competitive market at a constant price.

If the wage rate is $55 per worker per day, then the firm will want to hire _____ workers if the price of its output is $10, and _____ workers when this price is $15.

1b. Fill in the missing data in Table 33-2 for another hypothetical firm, assuming that the wage it faces is $40 per worker per day and the price of its output is $5.

Table 33-2

Number of workers	Total physical output	Marginal physical product	Marginal revenue product
0	0	—	—
1		10	
2		9	
3		8	
4		7	
5		6	

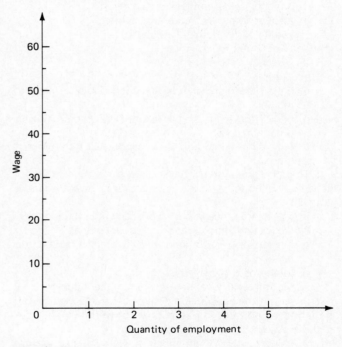

FIGURE 33-1

The firm will be willing to hire no more than _____ workers. With this amount of employment, the firm's total revenue will be _____, its total wage payment will be $_____, and the income of other factors will be _____.

Plot the labor demand schedule of this firm in Figure 33-1. Draw a horizontal line at the wage rate of $40 per worker per day. Label as 1 the area representing labor income. Label as 2 the area representing the income going to other factors.

2. Consider the firm in Table 33-3 which is *not* selling its output in a perfectly competitive market; it is not facing a given price for its product. (In column 4, the price of its product falls as it sells more and more.)

Fill in the missing items. Are the VMP and MRP the same? Why or why not?

Table 33-3

(1) Number of workers	(2) Total physical product	(3) Marginal physical product	(4) price of product	(5) Total revenue (col. 2 × 4)	(6) Marginal revenue product (MRP) (change in col. 5)	(7) Value of marginal product (VMP) (col. 3 × col. 4)
0						
1	16	16	$12	$192	$192	$192
2	31		11			
3	45		10			
4	58		9			
5	70		8			

3. Figure 33-2 depicts a perfectly competitive labor market with no externalities. The equilibrium wage rate is _____, and the equilibrium quantity of employment is _____. Suppose that a minimum wage of U is imposed. Then employment will be _____. Next, suppose that the minimum wage is H. Then employment will be _____, and the difference between demand and supply will be _____. Fill in Table 33-4.

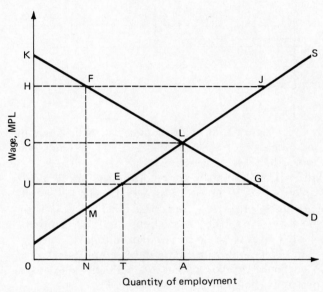

FIGURE 33-2

Table 33-4

	Efficiency loss is area:	Total labor income is area:	Income of other factors is area:
No minimum wage			
Minimum wage at U			
Minimum wage at H			

4a. Panel a in Figure 33-3 shows a perfectly competitive labor market in which there is no discrimination against women. The equilibrium wage rate is _____, and employment is _____; this is made up of N_M men and _____ women. The income of men is area _____, while women earn _____. The income of other factors of production is _____.

4b. Suppose now that there is discrimination against women, and N_F women are forced into the relatively unproductive market in panel b. Equilibrium in the main labor market in panel a now moves to point

_____. In this labor market, men earn an income of _____, while the earnings of other nonlabor factors of production change from original area _____ to _____, for an [increase, decrease] of _____.

4c. In the secondary, relatively unproductive labor market in panel b, equilibrium is at point _____, with _____ females employed at a wage of _____. Income of females is area _____, while the income of other factors in this market is _____.

4d. When we take $both$ markets into account, we conclude that female labor income [increases, decreases]

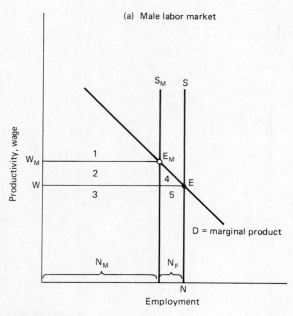

(a) Male labor market

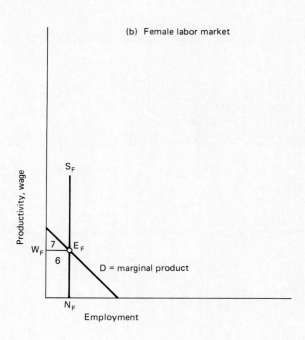

(b) Female labor market

FIGURE 33-3

by _____ as a result of discrimination; male labor income [increases, decreases] by _____; and nonlabor income [increases, decreases] by _____. There is a transfer [from, to] male workers [from, to] other factors of area _____. There is a loss overall—that is, an efficiency loss—of _____. Since this efficiency loss is the same as the [loss, gain] to [women, men], we can therefore say that it is borne by [women, men].

5. (This requires study of the text *and* Box 33-1 in the textbook.) A labor market in a perfectly competitive economy is shown in Figure 33-4.

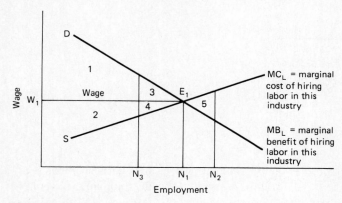

FIGURE 33-4

a. The marginal product of labor (VMP) in this industry is shown by the _____ curve, while the marginal product of labor elsewhere is shown by the _____ curve. The equilibrium is at _____, with wage _____ and employment of

_____ workers. At this equilibrium, employers have [maximized, minimized] their profit by hiring labor up to the point where its marginal benefit—that is, the marginal product of labor in this industry as shown by the _____ curve—is equal to the marginal cost the *employers* face, as shown by _____. At the same time, employees have [minimized, maximized] their own benefit by offering their labor up to the point where their marginal benefit, as shown by _____, is equal to their marginal cost, shown by _____. This marginal cost to employees is called a [substitute, opportunity] cost, because it represents their potential earnings in their [least, most] attractive alternative job.

b. If employment is at N_2, there is an efficiency [gain, loss] of area _____ because the N_2N_1 extra workers employed would have a [higher, lower] marginal product elsewhere—as shown by the _____ curve—than in this industry where their marginal product is shown by the _____ curve. On the other hand, if employment in this industry is at N_3, then there is an efficiency [gain, loss] because N_3N_1 workers should be employed in this industry, but are not. These workers would have marginal product here shown by the _____ curve compared to their [lower, higher] marginal product elsewhere, as shown by the height of the _____ curve. Only at an employment level of _____ can one or the other of these efficiency losses be avoided.

Essay Questions

1. "The labor demand schedule slopes down for the same reason that the demand curve for a consumer good slopes down." Explain to what extent this is or is not true.

2. List and explain some influences that could shift the labor supply curve for an industry. In each case, indicate in which direction the shift would occur.

3. Over the past 50 years, the number of domestic servants in the United States has fallen dramatically. Do you think this is because of the price and availability of laborsaving household appliances? Or is it due to rising wages in other occupations? Or do both factors play a role? Explain how each affects the supply and demand for domestic help.

4. Discuss the influences that affect the elasticity of demand for labor, by first reviewing the influences affecting the elasticity of demand for a consumer good discussed in Chapter 21 in the text.

5. How would the elasticity of the supply of labor in a particular market be affected by a decrease in the cost of moving from one city to another?

6. Would you expect labor market discrimination to be more of a problem in a perfectly competitive industry or in a monopolistic industry?

Answers

Important Terms: 1 c 2 a 3 d 4 e 5 b
True-False: 1 T 2 T 3 F 4 T 5 F 6 T 7 F 8 F 9 F
Multiple Choice: 1 a 2 e 3 a 4 c 5 b 6 d 7 c 8 b 9 e 10 e 11 c 12 d 13 a 14 b 15 b 16 a
Exercises
1a.

Table 33-1 completed:

W	O	MPP	MRP if P = $10	MRP if P = $15
0	0	—	—	—
1	12	12	120	180
2	19	7	70	105
3	24	5	50	75
4	28	4	40	60
5	30	2	20	30

2, 4.
1b.

Table 33-2 completed

Number of workers	Total physical output	MRP
0	0	—
1	10	$50
2	19	45
3	27	40
4	34	35
5	40	30

3, $135, $120, $15.

Figure 33-1 completed:

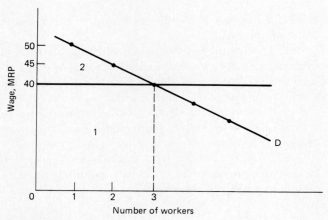

FIGURE 33-1

2.

Table 33-3 completed:

(1) Number of workers	(2) Total physical product	(3) Marginal physical product	(4) Price of product	(5) Total revenue (col. 2 × col. 4)	(6) Marginal revenue product (MRP) (change in col. 5)	(7) Value of marginal product (VMP) (col. 3 × col. 4)
0						
1	16	16	$12	$192	$192	$192
2	31	15	11	341	149	165
3	45	14	10	450	109	140
4	58	13	9	522	72	117
5	70	12	8	560	38	96

Not the same. In column 7, the VMP of the second worker is $165—that worker's marginal physical product (MPP) of 15, times the $11 price at which the firm sells its output. In column 6, the marginal revenue product (MRP) is less than this—namely, $149, because MRP takes account of something else that happens when the second worker is hired: To sell its larger output, the firm has to reduce its price by $1, from $12 to $11. Therefore, hiring the *second* worker means that the firm gets a $1 lower price for the 16 units of output of the *first* worker. For this reason, its revenue is $16 less. Note indeed that this $16 is the difference between the $165 VMP and the $149 MRP.

3. *C, A, A, N, FJ.*

Table 33-4 completed

Zero	OCLA	KLC
Zero	OCLA	KLC
FLM	OHFN	KFH

4a. W, N, N_F, 3, 5, 1 + 2 + 4.   4b. E_M, 2 + 3, 1 + 2 + 4, 1, decrease, 2 + 4.   4c. E_F, N_F, W_F, 6, 7.   4d. decreases, 5 − 6, increases, 2, decreases, 2 + 4 − 7, to, from, 2, (4 + 5) − (6 + 7), loss, women, women.   5a. D, S, E_1, W_1, N_1, maximized, D, $W_1 E_1$, maximized, $W_1 E_1$, S, opportunity, most.   5b. loss, 5, higher, S, D, loss, D, lower, S, N_1.

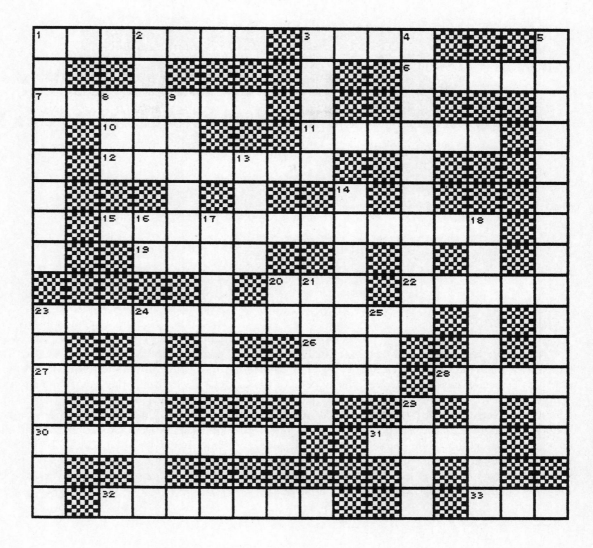

Across

1, 3. proponents say this raises the incomes of the poor; critics say it causes unemployment
6. gas commonly used as a refrigerant
7. he explained the idea of comparative advantage
10. historical period
11. a barrier to international trade
12. one of the arguments for the protection of domestic industry from foreign competition
15. Bastiat suggested that these people might object to the unfair competition from the sun
19. new (German, fem.)
20. a flying mammal
22. "The British are coming," Paul Revere _____
23. the key to rising living standards
26. tool for propelling a boat
27, 28. where this is low, a country has a comparative advantage
30. form an association of workers
31. this type of theory deals with conflicts
32. a third type of efficiency (in addition to allocative and technological efficiency)
33. he is associated with idea that, in aggregate, supply creates its own demand

Down

1, 23. in a perfectly competitive economy, the wage is equal to the value of this
2. picture
3. in an efficient economy, this is avoided
4. the goal of getting the most out of our productive efforts
5. one of the major arguments for tariffs (2 words)
8. ungentlemanly chap
9. do this to oil to produce gasoline
13. African river
14. he suggested that tariffs were equivalent to a "negative railway"
16. one
17. sweet, melodious
18. externalities
20. twice, doubly, involving two (prefix)
21. a good lawyer can often help clients to _____ taxes
24. industry with only two sellers
25. attempt
29. organization for negotiating over tariffs and other trade barriers (abbrev.)

CHAPTER 34

WAGES IN IMPERFECTLY COMPETITIVE LABOR MARKETS

MAJOR PURPOSE

The key objective in this chapter is to analyze what happens when labor markets are not perfectly competitive. Typically, the result is inefficiency, and this is compared with the efficient outcome when labor markets are perfectly competitive, as described in the last chapter. Elements of imperfect competition may appear on either side of the labor market. On the one side, workers may form a union which, as a monopoly (a single seller of labor services) is able to raise the wage rate. On the other side, employing firms may form a bargaining

association which, as a monopsony (a single buyer of labor services) is able to *lower* the wage rate. In either case, an inefficiently low amount of labor is hired. The interesting, and quite frequent, case of bilateral monopoly arises when there is a monopoly (a union) on the workers' side of the market, and a monopsony on the employer's side. Illustrations are provided to show how difficult and complicated wage bargaining can be in this case. In particular, special problems arise in any bargaining between a monopoly union of public service workers and their monopsony employer—the government.

Learning Objectives

After you have studied this chapter in the textbook and the study guide, you should be able to:

Describe how and why union membership changed in the various periods of U.S. labor history

Identify the laws that have been important in encouraging or deterring the U.S. labor movement, and state the major provisions of each

Show in a diagram the inefficiency that results when a union succeeds in raising wages in an otherwise perfectly competitive labor market

Explain the inefficiency that results when a union negotiates a featherbedding contract

Describe, on the other hand, the special ways that a union may improve efficiency

Show, in particular, how efficiency may be increased if a union is formed in a labor market that has previously been monopsonized

Analyze bilateral monopoly, where market power is held by a union on one side of the market, and by a single employer (or an employers' association) on the other

Explain why a strike may occur even though all parties lose from it

Show why there may be large internal *and* external costs if labor negotiations break down and a strike occurs

Identify three ways of averting an imminent strike

Explain the possible imbalance of bargaining power when a public service union negotiates with a government

State four reasons why workers get different wages

HIGHLIGHTS OF CHAPTER

The major topics covered in this chapter include (1) the history of the labor union movement in the United States; (2) the effects of introducing a union into an otherwise perfectly competitive labor market; (3) the effects of introducing a monopsony (a single buyer) into an otherwise perfectly competitive labor market; (4) a description of bilateral monopoly, where a monopoly union bargains with a monopsony employer; (5) the reasons why public service employees form a union, but the special problems that then arise; and (6) the reasons why wages aren't the same for all workers.

The History of the U.S. Labor Movement

Figure 34-1 in the textbook shows the three distinct periods in U.S. labor history:

1. Prior to 1935, union membership was very low. The key player during this period was the American Federation of Labor (AFL), a collection of craft unions— that is, unions that draw members from any industry, provided they have a common skill. In those early days, strikes were not an effective union tactic because employers could easily get a court injunction forcing workers back to their jobs. This practice was ended in 1932 by the Norris-LaGuardia Act, which limited injunctions to protecting property and preventing violence.

2. From 1935 to 1945 union membership grew rapidly, aided by two major events: (a) the founding in 1936 of the CIO, a collection of industrial unions (an industrial union draws its members from a single industry regardless of their skills), and (b) the Wagner Act of 1935, which made it clear that workers had the right to form a union, prohibited various unfair labor practices of employers, and established the National Labor Relations Board (NLRB) to prevent unfair labor practices and to settle disputes between unions.

3. In the period since 1945, union membership has steadily declined as a percentage of the labor force. During the years of World War II, which immediately preceded this last period, some people felt that unions had used their newly gained power irresponsibly, in strikes that were damaging to the war effort. As a result, the labor movement entered this post-1945 period facing some public hostility.

You should be familiar with two major labor laws that were passed during this third period. The first was the Taft-Hartley Act of 1947, which (1) outlawed closed shops in industries engaged in interstate commerce, (2) outlawed jurisdictional strikes, (3) outlawed the practice of checking off union dues unless workers agree in writing, (4) imposed restrictions on union leaders that forced them to be financially more responsible, (5) empowered the president to seek a court injunction forcing strikers to return to work for an 80-day "cooling-off" period if there were a strike that endangered national health or safety, and (6) recognized the right of states to enact "right to work laws" which made union shops illegal (section 14b). The other major law was the Landrum-Griffin Act of 1959, which imposed even more financial restrictions upon union leaders and strengthened the power of union members to challenge their leaders.

This third period of declining union membership extended into the early 1980s, when unions came under further pressures. These pressures included stronger— indeed sometimes illegal—management opposition; the severe recession of 1981–1982 and the threat by firms to move their plants to the less unionized southern states or abroad; and the strong action taken by President Reagan in firing air controllers and decertifying their union when they went out on an illegal strike.

The Effects of Unions

A union gives workers a voice in presenting grievances to their employer. It also negotiates with management to establish seniority rules and improve working conditions. These benefit not only the workers but also the employer who is able to offer more attractive jobs and therefore reduce quit rates.

But the main objectives of a union are to protect the jobs and raise the wages of its members. According to recent estimates, unionized workers get 10% higher wages than comparable nonunionized workers. If a union is established that raises the wage in a previously competitive labor market, there are three main effects: (1) There is a reduction in employment and in the income of workers who lose their jobs; (2) there is an increase in the wages and incomes of workers who still have jobs, with this increase coming at the expense of other factors of production; and (3) there is a triangular efficiency loss that can be measured by the usual geometric technique. Study Figure 34-2 in the textbook until you can demonstrate these three effects on your own.

Finally, a union tries to protect its members' jobs in three ways:

1. It may try to negotiate a shorter workweek. If there is unemployment, fewer hours per worker means more workers can get jobs.

2. It can press the government to restrict imports. In Chapter 32 we saw that this may indeed increase U.S. employment; however, on balance the net effect of such protection is unfavorable.

3. It can negotiate a featherbedding agreement. There are two main effects of introducing a featherbedding agreement into a previously competitive labor market with no externalities: (a) Employment in that market increases, and the job security of union members is maintained; and (b) there is an efficiency loss, not only because employment exceeds the efficient, perfectly competitive quantity, but also because workers are typically employed under such an agreement in useless jobs rather than jobs with some productivity. (An example of a useless job was the employment of railroad firemen on diesel locomotives that had no fire. This was a zero-productivity task—a classic case of featherbedding. This is much more costly than General Motor's 1984 agreement with the union to keep displaced workers on the payroll, since GM could still employ them in jobs with some productivity.)

This analysis so far of the efficiency losses that result from unions is overly harsh, because in some ways unions *improve* efficiency. First, by giving workers a voice, unions provide them with an alternative to quitting or being fired when a problem arises. Thus, they save unnecessary costs of labor turnover. Second, by improving working conditions they can reduce the tension between workers and employers, and thus create a more productive atmosphere. Third, a union's bargaining power may simply offset the bargaining power of monopsonist employers; in this case, a union may increase efficiency. (Remember that our earlier discussion of the efficiency losses from a union applies only if the labor market is perfectly competitive before the union is formed.)

Monopsony

As a single employer of labor, a monopsonistic firm tries to exploit its market power by reducing wages. If it succeeds—in an otherwise perfectly competitive labor market—the three main effects will be to (1) transfer income from labor to other factors of production; (2) reduce employment; and (3) create an efficiency loss. Study Figure 34-3 in the textbook until you can demonstrate these three effects on your own.

Bilateral Monopoly

In many labor markets, there is bilateral (two-sided) monopoly, with market power being held both by a union on the one side, and by a monopsonistic employer on the other. Unfortunately, this case is also the most difficult to analyze.

To illustrate, suppose a union is formed in a labor market where a monopsonist employer has been keeping the wage rate below the perfectly competitive level. In this case, the formation of the union may raise the wage back towards the perfectly competitive level. If this is the outcome, the union will be simply undoing some of the effects of the monopsony. Specifically, the union will (1) transfer income back from other factors of production to labor, (2) increase employment, and (3) reduce the efficiency loss from monopsony. Before reading further make sure you can illustrate these effects with a diagram similar to Figure 34-5 in the textbook.

However, the outcome is not this simple to predict, because there is no guarantee that a newly formed union will only raise wages *toward* the perfectly competitive level; it may raise wages beyond this. If this happens we can no longer be sure that the union will increase efficiency. This is the basic problem in analyzing bilateral monopoly: We don't know where the wage will be set. All we know for sure is that the wage will be somewhere between the high wage the union seeks, and the lower wage the monopsonistic employer seeks. At what point the wage will be determined within this range depends on the bargaining power of each side. This in turn depends partly on the ability of each to outlast the other in the event of a strike. Thus, the bargaining power of the union depends upon the size of the union's strike fund. The bargaining power of the employer depends upon its inventories of finished goods that it continues to sell during a strike.

Strikes

In a sense, everyone is damaged by a strike. The employer loses profits, and the labor force loses wages. Nevertheless, strikes do occur, because (1) each side may see a strike as a way of getting a more favorable wage rate than the other side's "final offer"; (2) each side may want to increase its future credibility and bargaining power by clearly demonstrating that it is prepared to allow a strike to take place; or (3) either side may make a bargaining mistake that prevents agreement from being reached before a strike deadline. (Nevertheless, the average U.S. worker spends less than 1 day a year on strike).

One reason why strikes pose an important issue for public policy is spillovers—that is, costs of strikes to people not involved in the bargaining. For example, a transit strike prevents people from getting to their jobs.

There are two main ways of averting a strike when the two sides are unable to reach agreement on their own:

1. The president may seek a Taft-Hartley injunction that forces workers back to their jobs. The Federal Mediation Service may then help to find an agreement during the cooling-off period.

2. Both sides may agree to voluntary arbitration, in which a third party decides upon a settlement that both sides agree in advance to accept. There are many collective bargaining agreements that contain provisions for voluntary arbitration as a means of resolving conflicts over the terms of the agreement.

Unions of Public Service Employees

Unions in the public sector raise problems because they have such a strong bargaining position, for the following reasons.

1. There are large spillover costs to the voting public when public servants such as transit workers or the police go on strike. Thus voters may exert great pressure on the government to settle the dispute.

2. Public servants know that, in the last analysis, the government will almost certainly be able to find *some* way of raising the funds necessary to pay a higher wage. The government can tax or borrow in a way that is not available to private employers.

3. A union has much greater bargaining power over a financially weak government than it would have over a financially weak private employer. The reason is that a strike won't force a government out of business, but it might drive a private employer bankrupt.

4. Because public service employees now constitute a large bloc of voters, politicians are reluctant to fight hard against their wage demands.

Because public servants have such a strong bargaining position, it is often suggested that they should not be allowed to strike, or even form a union. But this would raise a problem. If these workers cannot form a union, how can they defend themselves against a monopsonistic employer (the government). If not with a union, what else?

Wage Differences

Wage differences can exist for at least five different reasons: First, there may be *dynamic wage differentials*. When new job opportunities open up in an industry, wages must rise temporarily to attract workers from other industries. Eventually, the influx of new workers will bring the wages back down. Second, *compensating wage differentials* give workers more pay for especially hazardous or unpleasant jobs. Third, monopoly or monopsony power may be greater in some labor markets than in others. Fourth, barriers to entry can keep wages artificially high in some jobs, while discrimination keeps them low in others. Fifth, those with special talents and skills earn a higher wage because they are more productive, as we shall see in the next chapter.

Important Terms: Match the Columns

Match the term in the first column with the corresponding phrase in the second column. But before you do so, write out your own definition of the term in the first column.

_____ **1.** Seniority rules
_____ **2.** Industrial union
_____ **3.** Craft union
_____ **4.** Collective bargaining
_____ **5.** American Federation of Labor (AFL)
_____ **6.** National Labor Relations Act
_____ **7.** Congress of Industrial Organizations (CIO)
_____ **8.** Closed shop
_____ **9.** Union shop
_____ **10.** Open shop
_____ **11.** Right-to-work law
_____ **12.** Jurisdictional dispute
_____ **13.** Checking off
_____ **14.** Featherbedding
_____ **15.** Monopsonist
_____ **16.** Strike fund
_____ **17.** Injunction
_____ **18.** Mediation
_____ **19.** Arbitration
_____ **20.** Dynamic wage differentials
_____ **21.** Compensating wage differentials

a. A collection of industrial unions

b. A union whose members all belong to the same craft or profession, although they may work in different industries. Examples are the plumbers' and carpenters' unions.

c. The specification of a third party to suggest a compromise settlement in a labor dispute. The third party cannot make any binding recommendations.

d. Differences that may arise if labor views some jobs as less attractive than others. (Employers have to pay a higher wage to fill the unattractive jobs.)

e. Preference in sequencing of layoffs to those who have been longest on the job

f. A union whose members all work in the same industry, or group of industries, although they may belong to different crafts or professions. Examples are the United Auto Workers and the United Mine Workers.

g. Employing labor in superfluous jobs

h. A statute making closed ships or union shops illegal

i. A firm in which anyone hired by an employer must join the union within some specified period

j. Differences in wages that arise because of changing demand or supply conditions in the labor market. These differences tend to disappear over time as labor moves out of the relatively low wage jobs and into those that pay a relatively high wage.

k. A collection of craft unions, formed by Samuel Gompers

l. Negotiations between a union and an employer over wages, fringe benefits, hiring policies, job security, or working conditions

m. A court order compelling someone to refrain from a particular act, such as a strike

n. A firm in which an employer can hire only workers who are already union members

o. A sum of money owned by a union for the purpose of supporting its members while on strike

p. A single buyer

q. The practice of having employers collect union dues by deducting them from workers' paychecks

r. The Wagner Act of 1935

s. Conflict between unions over whose members will do specific jobs

t. A firm in which employees do not have to join a union

u. The specification of a third party to suggest a compromise settlement in labor dispute. The decision of the third party is binding upon both labor and management.

True-False

T F   1. Bilateral monopoly in the labor market means that employers are exercising monopsony power and labor is exercising monopoly power.

T F   2. An industrial union draws its members from *any* industry, provided they have a common skill (such as plumbing).

T F   3. The United Auto Workers is a craft union.

T F   4. Samuel Gompers's American Federation of Labor was an attempt to organize labor for a political class struggle, rather than for the pursuit of improved wages and working conditions.

T F   5. If wages are reduced below what they would be in perfect competition there will be a loss in efficiency.

T F   6. A monopolist in the labor market will seek to raise wages, while a monopsonist will seek to lower them.

T F   7. A union will tend to strike the financially weakest firm in the industry.

T F   8. A company producing perishable goods is typically more vulnerable to strike threats than one producing durable goods.

T F   9. The spillover cost of a strike must be less than the internal cost to the industry in which the strike occurs.

T F   10. Public service unions have recently been growing less rapidly than other unions.

T F   11. Compensating wage differentials would not exist if workers viewed all jobs as equally attractive.

Multiple Choice

1. When a union negotiates seniority rules, workers with seniority are typically:
   a. the first to be laid off, and the first to be rehired
   b. the first to be laid off, and the last to be rehired
   c. the last to be laid off, and the last to be rehired
   d. the last to be laid off, and the first to be rehired
   e. left unaffected in terms of being laid off or rehired

2. Craft unions draw their membership from:
   a. workers in companies that build pleasure boats
   b. workers in companies that build any boats
   c. all workers in a specific industry regardless of their skills
   d. all workers in a specific industry provided they have the same skill
   e. all workers from any industry provided they have the same skill

3. Which of the following provides the greatest barrier to entry into a work force?
   a. an open shop   d. the Taft-Hartley Act
   b. a closed shop   e. right-to-work legislation
   c. a union shop

4. If a firm can only hire workers who are already union members, it is described as:
   a. a constrained shop   d. an open shop
   b. a closed shop   e. a restricted shop
   c. a union shop

5. Which of the following is most likely to occur if a union is introduced into a previously competitive labor market with no externalities?
   a. Total income to labor will decrease.
   b. The income of some individual workers will increase.
   c. Employment in that market will increase.
   d. Incomes of nonlabor factors of production will increase.
   e. An efficiency gain will result.

6. Unionized workers in the United States are estimated to earn wages that are higher than comparable nonunionized workers by about:
   a. 10%   d. 55%
   b. 30%   e. 65%
   c. 42%

7. Unions came under pressure in the 1980s because of:

a. the threat by firms to move their plants abroad

b. management's stiffer opposition, occasionally in the form of the illegal firing of workers for union activities

c. the severe 1981–1982 recession

d. the threat of bankruptcies of employing firms

e. all of the above

8. Which of the following is the clearest example of featherbedding?

   a. seniority rules

   b. sexual harassment on the job

   c. firemen employed on diesel trains

   d. shorter workweeks

   e. the firing of technologically displaced workers

9. Unions may have beneficial effects on efficiency:

   a. by removing labor's collective voice and thus reducing distractions in the workplace

   b. by reducing communication between labor and management, and thus reducing distractions facing managers

   c. by increasing quit rates

   d. by reducing quit rates

   e. by increasing management's market power to raise wages

10. Which of the following is most likely to increase employment in an otherwise perfectly competitive labor market?

   a. the introduction of a union whose main effect is to raise wages

   b. collusion by employers to act together like a monopsonist

   c. an increase in the minimum wage

   d. the introduction of a closed shop

   e. featherbedding

11. A union's negotiating power will be increased most by:

   a. a large union strike fund

   b. a small union strike fund

   c. a right-to-work law

   d. large inventory holdings by the employer

   e. reduced tariff protection on the employer's output

12. In a labor market with a strong union, the creation of a monopsony bargaining association by employers tends to:

   a. raise wages even further

   b. lower wages

   c. transfer income from other factors of production to labor

   d. (a) and (c)

   e. none of the above

13. Baseball salaries before and after the players' escape from the reserve clause illustrate:

   a. how much unions can raise salaries

   b. how much unions can lower salaries

   c. how much monopsonists can raise salaries

   d. how much monopsonists can lower salaries

   e. the countervailing power of a union

14. In most labor negotiations:

   a. both sides start off close together, but they move farther and farther apart so that a strike results

   b. both sides start off close together, but they move farther and farther apart, so that there is no strike

   c. both sides start far apart, but they move closer together so that there is a strike

   d. both sides start off far apart, but they move closer together so that eventually there is a settlement instead of a strike

   e. one side sticks by its original offer, while the other makes all the concessions

15. Which of the following is *not* an example of a spillover cost of a strike?

   a. the lost output in the industry where the strike occurs

   b. the lost output in other industries that depend on this one for supplies

   c. the disruption of work when a transit strike stops people from getting to their jobs

   d. the disruption in firms that do business through the mails when postal workers go on strike

   e. the disruption of a nationwide sales conference of a chemical company when an airline goes on strike

Exercises

1a. In Figure 34-1, MC_L is supply, and MB_L is demand in a perfectly competitive labor market with no externalities. The equilibrium wage is _____, and the equilibrium quantity of employment is _____. In perfect competition the income of labor is area _____, and the income of other factors is area _____.

1b. Suppose now that a union is formed, which increases the wage to W_2. Then the quantity of employment will be _____, the income going to labor still in this industry will be _____, the income going to other factors will be _____, and the efficiency [gain, loss] will be _____.

1c. Now suppose that there is an external benefit from hiring labor in this activity. (To use the example cited in Chapter 33: Suppose that the workers being hired are musicians. They provide not only a direct benefit to their employer—the symphony orchestra—

FIGURE 34-1

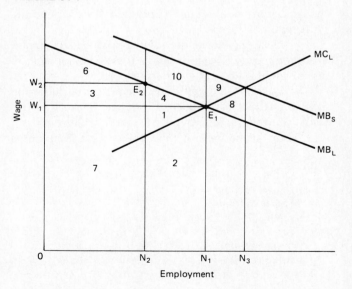

whenever they play in a concert, but also an external benefit because of their other contributions to the cultural life of the community.) Because of this external benefit, the marginal social benefit of labor is MB_S rather than just the employers' benefit MB_L. Then the efficient quantity of employment will be _____. In perfect competition the wage will be _____, the quantity of employment will be _____, and the efficiency [gain, loss] will be _____.

1d. With this externality, if a union is formed to raise wages to W_2, then the quantity of employment will equal _____, and the efficiency [gain, loss] will equal

_____.

2. In Figure 34-2, D represents the demand for labor, while area 1 represents the external cost of a strike.

If a strike occurs, the cost to labor—in terms of lost wages—is area _____, while the loss of income by other factors is area _____. This means that the total internal cost to all factors in this industry is _____. In addition, there is an [external, internal] cost of area _____. Therefore, the total cost to society of a strike in this industry is _____. The problem with a strike is that the labor and management participants in the negotiation only take into account [external, internal] costs _____. No account may be taken of the additional cost

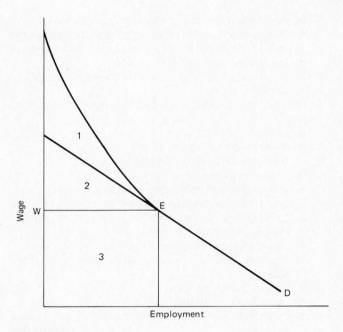

FIGURE 34-2

to other groups shown as _____. A Taft-Hartley [closed shop, injunction] may be viewed as a way of injecting the public interest into the negotiations.

Essay Questions

1. "Unions represent just one special form of monopoly, and should not be allowed to exist." What is your position on this? Explain why.

2. Do you think that unions help or hinder the attempt to achieve (*a*) stable prices and (*b*) an equitable distribution of income?

3. If there is no union on one side of the market to raise wages, and no collusion or association by employers on the other side of the market to lower wages, compare the bargaining position of the individual worker and the individual employer.

4. Describe the conditions under which an increase in the minimum wage may increase the amount of employment.

5. Describe the spillovers if each of the following went on strike: (*a*) municipal garbage workers (*b*) air traffic controllers, (*c*) city police, and (*d*) steelworkers.

6. In the summer of 1980, the orchestra members

of New York's Metropolitan Opera went on strike. Their union leaders thought they had a lot of bargaining power because of the opera's recent financial success. Why might this strengthen the union's bargaining power? Why might that bargaining power also have been strengthened by the knowledge that the opera would be receiving a large income from the nationally televised live performances that were to begin in the fall of 1980? After failing to reach agreement with the union, the management of the opera announced that the whole season would have to be canceled, and offered to refund the tickets already bought. Eventually, one more round of negotiations was undertaken, agreement was reached, and management announced that the season could proceed after all, but with fewer operas than planned. Do you suppose that the announcement of cancellation of the season helped to speed up a resolution of the strike? Why or why not?

Answers

Important Terms: **1** e **2** f **3** b **4** l **5** k **6** r **7** a **8** n **9** i **10** t **11** h **12** s **13** q **14** g **15** p **16** o **17** m **18** c **19** u **20** j **21** d

True-False: **1** T **2** F **3** F **4** F **5** T **6** T **7** F **8** T **9** F **10** F **11** T

Multiple Choice: **1** d **2** e **3** b **4** b **5** b **6** a **7** e **8** c **9** d **10** e **11** a **12** b **13** d **14** d **15** a

Exercises: **1a.** W_1, N_1, 7 + 1 + 2, 6 + 3 + 4. **1b.** N_2, 3 + 7, 6, loss, 1 + 4. **1c.** N_3, W_1, N_1, loss, 9. **1d.** N_2, loss, 1 + 4 + 9 + 10. **2.** 3, 2, 2 + 3, external, 1, 1 + 2 + 3, internal, 2 + 3, 1, injunction.

CHAPTER 35

OTHER INCOMES

MAJOR PURPOSE

In the previous two chapters, we analyzed labor income. The objective of this chapter is to analyze other forms of income—specifically, interest, profits, and rent. For example, in discussing interest rates, we see how they are determined by supply and demand in the market for loanable funds. This simple analysis is then extended to show the *efficiency* and *equity* effects when the government intervenes to impose a ceiling on interest rates.

While our initial emphasis in this chapter is on the income earned by physical capital, such as buildings and machinery, the focus later shifts to another important form of capital—human capital in the form of education and training. One form of human capital is a college education, and returns to such an investment are examined. Finally, this chapter analyzes rent—the return to a factor of production above its opportunity cost (that is, above the income it could earn in an alternative activity). Rent is earned not only by land, but also by any other highly productive factor. Examples include the rent earned by highly skilled baseball players or business executives.

Learning Objectives

After you have studied this chapter in the textbook and the study guide, you should be able to:

Explain the concepts of debt capital, equity capital, physical capital, and human capital

Explain how the demand for loanable funds is related to the marginal efficiency of investment schedule

Show in a diagram how an interest-rate ceiling imposed on a perfectly competitive market for loanable funds will affect efficiency and redistribute income

Explain why it is a fallacy to suppose that interest-rate ceilings necessarily help poor people

Compare an investment in human capital and an investment in physical capital

Describe the conditions under which investment in human capital could be less than the efficient amount, and the conditions under which it could be more than the efficient amount

Explain why it is difficult to measure the rate of return on human capital

Describe changes in the rate of return on human capital over the last two decades, and explain why these changes have occurred

Define rent and describe five examples

Explain why rent can be earned not only by land, but by any factor of production

Describe how rent is capitalized in the value of land and why this raises problems for any agricultural subsidy program that increases farm rents

Describe the basic roles played by factor prices in a market economy

HIGHLIGHTS OF CHAPTER

About one-quarter of national income in the United States goes to factors of production other than labor. This chapter examines how these other incomes—such as interest, profit, and rent—are determined.

The Rate of Interest

The rate of interest indicates how present goods may be converted into even more future goods, through "roundabout" methods of production. The interest rate may be viewed as a price—the price that equates the demand and supply of loanable funds. The demand for loanable funds is the marginal efficiency of investment schedule, already described in Chapter 12. The supply of loanable funds measures the willingness of savers to part with present income—that is, their willingness to defer present consumption until the future when the loan is repaid. The higher the rate of interest, the greater their reward.

In practice, there is not one rate of interest but many, because of differences in risk. The greater the risk that a borrower will be unable to repay a loan, the higher the rate of interest that this particular borrower will have to pay. Interest rates are also influenced by a number of other factors, such as the expectation of inflation and the length of term of the loan. In addition, the expectation of a change in future interest rates will affect today's interest rates.

An important policy question studied in this section is, What happens if the government imposes an interest-rate ceiling? If the market for loanable funds is perfectly competitive, there are likely to be four main effects of such a policy:

1. The public saves less because the interest reward for savings has been reduced. Consequently, fewer loans are made and there is less investment.
2. Because of inadequate investment, there is an efficiency loss, shown by the familiar triangle in Figure 35-3 in the textbook.
3. There is an additional efficiency loss, because investment funds must be rationed, and the borrowers who do succeed in acquiring the limited funds may not be those with the most profitable investment projects.
4. Income is transferred from lenders to those borrowers who are still able to acquire loans. (They now pay a lower interest rate.)

It is a fallacy to suppose that interest-rate ceilings necessarily help poor people. The people who benefit are the borrowers who get the limited funds at a bargain price. But these borrowers may be quite rich, while those who don't get funds may be poor.

Normal profits are earned by owners of equity capital. *Normal profit* is defined as the return that could be earned in an alternative investment—in this case, the interest the owner could have earned lending these funds out instead.

Human Capital

There are two main forms of investment in human capital: (1) formal education, and (2) apprenticeship, or on-the-job training.

There are three reasons why investment in human capital could be less than the efficient amount:

1. Minimum wage laws tend to discourage employers from providing on-the-job training, because many employers cannot afford to provide an unskilled worker with both the minimum wage and such training
2. Employers are reluctant to provide on-the- job training because trainees may quit and take their skills elsewhere.
3. There are external benefits from human capital. For example, when a highly educated scientist discovers a cure for a disease, it benefits the entire population. Because such external benefits are not taken into account by those making the decision to invest in human capital, this investment may fall short of the efficient level.

On the other hand, investment in human capital is encouraged by government subsidies to education. If these are substantial enough, then there may be *over*investment in human capital.

The concept of human capital also provides insight into the problem of discrimination. Workers will not be able to invest in human capital in the form of on-the-job training if they are discriminated against in employment that provides this training. Nor will they be able to provide their children with the best education if discrimination keeps their income low and/or prevents them from moving into good school districts. As a consequence, minority groups may continue, over generations, to acquire inadequate human capital. Thus they may now have low incomes, even if employers today do not discriminate.

Estimates indicate that the return graduates get from a college education fell between 1900 and 1940, and thereafter remained stable until 1970. Then it started to fall again, to the 5% to 9% range by the early 1980s. However, there is the prospect that, as we leave the population bulge of college graduates behind in the 1980s, the return to an education will start to increase. (Note that at recent rates of return, a college education is difficult to justify as an investment; the reason is that the returns to an education are in many cases below the returns earned on physical capital. Thus an education must in part be justified as a consumption good.)

In practice, arriving at any sort of precise estimate

of the returns to a college education are exceedingly difficult for a number of reasons. For example:

1. People with high incomes tend to have substantial education and considerable native ability. It's hard to sort out how much of their higher income is due to each.

2. Not all education is an investment; some of it is undoubtedly a consumption good.

3. Much of the return to education is in the form of a more satisfying job—and it is difficult to measure this effect.

Further complications arise if we wish to calculate the *social* return to education:

1. It is difficult to measure the external benefits of education. (How do you measure the benefits to society when a highly educated scientist discovers a new strain of wheat?)

2. It is difficult to tell if education has increased the productivity of graduates or simply given them a "credential" that raises their income.

Rent

Perhaps the most important thing to understand about rent is that it can be earned not only by land, but also by other factors of production. It is defined as the earnings of *any* factor above its opportunity cost. The textbook gives five examples of economic rent:

1. The return to agricultural land because of differences in quality

2. The return to urban land because of differences in location

3. The income from mineral deposits of high quality

4. Above-normal profits earned in an industry with barriers to entry

5. The return to an individual with a valuable talent or skill

A person's wage includes (1) a "basic wage" component, (2) a return to that individual's human capital, and (3) the rent on that person's special talents. This last item is rent so long as the opportunity cost for the individual is roughly the sum of the first two items.

The Role of Factor Prices

Factor prices do more than determine people's incomes. They also help to determine how much of each factor of production will be allocated to each task. For example, if labor becomes scarcer, and capital more plentiful, wages will rise and the returns to capital will fall. This encourages firms to substitute cheap capital for expensive labor. While this may be a painful process for the workers displaced by automated capital equipment, our experience since the early days of the industrial revolution is that these people get jobs elsewhere. And this historical process of substituting capital for labor has been the source of much of our economic progress.

Important Terms: Match the Columns

Match the term in the first column with the corresponding phrase in the second column. But before you do so, write out your own definition of the term in the first column.

_____ **1.** Debt capital
_____ **2.** Equity capital
_____ **3.** Human capital
_____ **4.** Physical capital
_____ **5.** Marginal efficiency of investment
_____ **6.** Time preference
_____ **7.** Roundabout production
_____ **8.** Affirmative action
_____ **9.** Economic rent
_____ **10.** Monopoly rent

a. Skills, training, and education of individuals that can be used for producing goods and services

b. The process of deferring the production of consumer goods, in favor of producing capital goods that can be used in the future to produce even more consumer goods

c. The above-normal profits accruing to any individual or business because of the possession of monopoly power

d. Funds that are lent to businesses (or others)

e. The schedule that ranks investments in terms of their percentage return

f. Funds that are provided when part or complete ownership of a business is purchased

g. A program designed to correct discrimination by favoring those who have difficulty competing today because of discrimination they have suffered in the past

h. A desire to consume now rather than in the future. This determines the supply curve for loanable funds.

i. The return to any factor of production in excess of its opportunity cost

j. The plant, machinery, and other forms of equipment that can be used for producing goods and services

True-False

T F 1. Capitalists as a group receive a larger share of U.S. national income than all workers.
T F 2. The greater the risk associated with a loan, the lower the interest rate will tend to be.
T F 3. An interest-rate ceiling benefits all those who wish to borrow.
T F 4. If a ceiling is imposed on the price of any good or service, then any necessary rationing of this good or service is likely to lead to an efficiency loss.
T F 5. Factor prices act as a screening device to help allocate factors of production.
T F 6. Human capital is like physical capital insofar as it represents an expenditure today that is expected to pay off in the future.
T F 7. The costs of a university education include more than living, tuition, and book costs.
T F 8. Studies indicate that the private rate of return to those acquiring a university education is the same as the social rate of return.
T F 9. Very little of John McEnroe's tennis income is rent.

Multiple Choice

1. What is the annual rate of return on a machine that costs $10,000 and generates enough sales over its 1-year lifetime to cover labor, materials, etc, plus $12,000?
   a. 120%
   b. 20%
   c. 12%
   d. 10%
   e. 2%

2. A company in a shaky financial position pays:
   a. a higher interest rate on its borrowing than it would if it were financially sound
   b. a lower interest rate on its borrowing than it would if it were financially sound
   c. the same interest rate on its borrowing as it would if it were financially sound
   d. a higher or lower rate, depending upon the rate of inflation
   e. a lower rate, because of the expectation of inflation

3. A rightward shift in the marginal efficiency of investment schedule is likely to:
   a. decrease the rate of interest and decrease the amount of loanable funds
   b. decrease the rate of interest and increase the amount of loanable funds
   c. increase the rate of interest and increase the amount of loanable funds
   d. increase the rate of interest and decrease the amount of loanable funds
   e. increase the rate of interest and leave the amount of loanable funds unchanged

4. An increase in wages will induce a firm to:
   a. hire more labor
   b. lower its prices
   c. use more laborsaving techniques
   d. use fewer laborsaving techniques
   e. produce more output

5. The income of a minority group is:
   a. increased by current discrimination, but reduced by past discrimination
   b. reduced by current discrimination, but increased by past discrimination
   c. reduced by current discrimination, but not affected by past discrimination
   d. not affected by either current or past discrimination
   e. reduced by both current and past discrimination

6. During the 1970s, the return to a college education:
   a. rose because of the increase in future income benefits
   b. rose because of the change in tuition costs
   c. fell because of falling tuition costs and future income benefits
   d. fell because of rising tuition costs and falling future income benefits
   e. did not change significantly

7. A high school education can be viewed as:
   a. a bad investment, because it yields a lower return than a college education
   b. a bad investment, even though it yields a higher return than a college education
   c. a bad investment, because it yields a lower return than physical capital
   d. a good investment, even though it yields the same return as a college education
   e. a good investment, because it yields a higher return than physical capital

8. In explaining why the private and social returns to a college education differ, we must take into account:
   a. external benefits of a college education
   b. government subsidies to college education
   c. benefits—such as screening benefits—that raise graduates' incomes but may not be a benefit to society
   d. all of the above
   e. none of the above

9. The income of the typical physician includes:
   a. rent on innate talents
   b. a return to human capital accumulated in medical school
   c. a return to human capital accumulated as an intern
   d. all of the above
   e. none of the above

10. For an economist, which of the following is *not* rent?
    a. an individual's potential earnings in an alternative occupation

b. the above-normal profit of a monopolist

c. earnings in excess of opportunity costs

d. the income from oil land that has no other use

e. the income from farm land that has no other use

Exercises

1a. Figure 35-1 shows a perfectly competitive market for loanable funds. The equilibrium rate of interest in this market is _____, and the equilibrium quantity of loans is _____. In a competitive equilibrium the interest income received by lenders would equal _____.

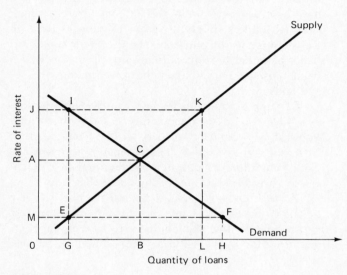

FIGURE 35–1

1b. If the government imposes an interest-rate ceiling at M, then the quantity of loans will be _____, the MEI will be _____, the excess demand for loans will be _____, the interest income received by lenders will be _____, and the size of the efficiency loss will probably be [more, less] than the area _____.

1c. If the interest ceiling is set at J, then the size of the efficiency loss will be _____.

2a. Figure 35-2 shows a perfectly competitive market for a factor of production, where D is the demand curve, and S_1 is the supply curve. In a competitive equilibrium, the factor price would be _____, and the quantity of employment of the factor would be _____. The income received by the owners of this factor would equal _____, and the income received by the owners of all other factors would equal _____.

2b. Now suppose that a tax is imposed on the owners of this factor, equal in amount to LE per unit of the factor that they are supplying. This would shift the supply curve up vertically by the amount LE, so that the after-tax supply curve is the one labeled S'_1. With the tax, the equilibrium price paid by the firms for the factor

will equal _____; the equilibrium price received, after tax, by the owners of the factor will equal _____; the after-tax income accruing to the owners of the factor will be _____; the amount of the tax collected will be _____; the income received by other factors will be _____; and the size of the efficiency loss will be _____.

2c. Now suppose that there is no tax; instead, suppose that supply shifts from S_1 to S_2. S_2 is [more, less] elastic than S_1. With supply curve S_2 the equilibrium factor price will be [no different, more, less] than with S_1, and the equilibrium quantity of employment of the factor will be [no different, more, less] than with S_1.

2d. With S_2 the same tax LE will shift the supply curve up to the one labeled S'_2. With the tax, the equilibrium price paid by the firms for the factor will be _____; the equilibrium price received, after tax, by the owners of the factor will equal _____; the quantity of employment of the factor will equal _____; the after-tax income accruing to the owners of the factor will equal _____; the amount of the tax collected will equal _____; the income received by other factors will equal _____; and the size of the efficiency loss will equal _____.

2e. If we consider the effects of a tax in the face of these two pretax supply curves S_1 and S_2, the one gener-

FIGURE 35–2

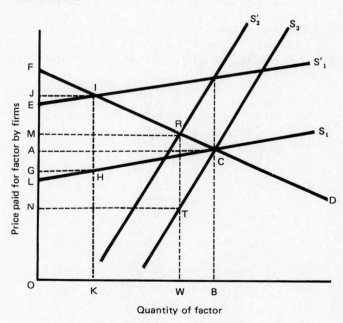

Quantity of factor

ating the greater tax revenue is $[S_1, S_2]$; the one that produces the smaller efficiency loss from the tax is $[S_1, S_2]$; the one generating the smaller reduction in employ-ment is $[S_1, S_2]$; the one generating the smaller reduction in the factor's after-tax income is $[S_1, S_2]$; and the one reducing other incomes the least is $[S_1, S_2]$.

Essay Questions

1. The discoverers of insulin, Banting and Best, did not become millionaires as a result of their discovery, despite the fact that it has probably saved millions of human lives. Explain what this means if we wish to compare the private and social rates of return to human capital.

2. Name several factors that determine the position of the MEI schedule, explaining in each case how the schedule would be affected, and in what direction, by an increase in that factor.

3. Show how the income of a surgeon is partly wages, partly return to human capital, and partly rent. Which of these components would be increased by the surgeon's efforts to develop more advanced surgical techniques? By the surgeon's honorary appointment to the Royal College of Surgeons? How would the rent component be affected if licensing requirements were relaxed to permit more people to practice surgery? Explain.

4. Most on-the-job training is job-specific. That is, the training is useful only for a particular job, such as selling insurance or operating a crane. Some on-the-job training is also firm-specific. That is, it involves "learning the ropes" of a particular firm's operations. Does the fact that workers may quit tend to discourage job-specific on-the-job training more or less than it does firm-specific on-the-job training? Explain.

5. As the interest rate rises, the price of bonds falls. (If necessary, review Box 13–1.) Bearing this in mind, show how an increase in the rate of interest affects potential lenders differently from those who have already lent money by purchasing bonds. Show also how it affects potential borrowers differently from the way it affects those who have already borrowed money by selling bonds.

6. Suppose that a factor had a totally inelastic supply. What would its opportunity cost be to society? Would it be accurate to classify all its income as rent? What can you say about the efficiency loss that would result from imposing a tax of a certain number of dollars on each firm for each unit of the factor that it uses?

7. The textbook sets out several reasons why it is difficult to measure the rate of return on investment in human capital. How many of these reasons also apply to measuring the rate of return on investment in physical capital?

Answers

Important Terms: 1 d 2 f 3 a 4 j 5 e 6 h 7 b 8 g 9 i 10 c
True-False: 1 F 2 F 3 F 4 T 5 T 6 T 7 T 8 F 9 F
Multiple Choice: 1 b 2 a 3 c 4 c 5 e 6 d 7 e 8 d 9 d 10 a
Exercises: **1a.** A, B, OACB. **1b.** G, J (or GI), EF (or GH), OMEG, more, ICE. **1c.** O. **2a.** A, B, OACB, FCA.
2b. J, G, OGHK, JIHG, FIJ, ICH. **2c.** less, no different, no different. **2d.** M, N, W, ONTW, NMRT, MFR, RCT. **2e.** S_2, S_2, S_2, S_2, S_2.

Across

1. price of land may equal this (2 words)
6. returns in excess of opportunity cost
9. an international organization of the Americas (abbrev.)
11, 12. the desire to have goods now rather than in the future
16. _____ Chi Minh
17. this person is responsible for the production of a newspaper or book
18. one of the factors of production
20. demand payment from
21. one of the authors teaches there (abbrev.)
22. hole in the ground
24. here (Fr.)
25. lyric poem
26. if used carelessly, resources can be _____
28. one
29. a woman's name
31. small piece
32. investment demand (abbrev.)
33. me (Fr.)
34, 36. an economist considers this as part of cost, but an accountant doesn't (2 words)
38. 3.14
39. a key to economic growth

Down

1. this increases as a result of investment
2. a British conservative
3. one cause of inequality
4. poke fun at
5. education is a form of _____ capital
7. out of harm's way
8. industry with only one seller
10. bitter, caustic
12. an advanced academic degree (abbrev.)
13. production with capital is sometimes spoken of as _____ production
14. this is partly consumption, and partly investment
15. a movie character
19. _____ Kapital, the chief work of Marx
23. a major reason for an increase in output
26. in a perfectly competitive economy, this equals the value of the marginal product of labor
27. a barrier to international trade
30. a major U.S. corporation (abbrev.)
35. small (prefix)
36. a progressive tax can change the division of the national "_____"
37. A U.S. government agency that regulates the railroads (abbrev.)

CHAPTER 36

INCOME INEQUALITY

MAJOR PURPOSES

In the three preceding chapters, we described how incomes are determined in our society. For example, some people have a higher income because of some innate talent or a large investment in human capital. Others may earn rent from land they own. Our first objective in this chapter is to summarize these economic reasons for differences in incomes, and complete that list with the additional reasons—such as just plain luck—that have not been dealt with in earlier chapters because they don't yield to economic analysis.

Our second objective is to examine the U.S. income distribution that results from all these influences. How much income inequality is there? This question is answered with a Lorenz curve from which information can be extracted on how much of the nation's income is earned by low-income Americans, and how much by high-income Americans. The conclusion is that a great deal of inequality exists.

The next question we address is, How effective are government programs of taxation and expenditure that have been introduced to reduce inequality? The answer is that some have been more effective than others.

This then provides the background for tackling one of the most difficult issues in economics—the normative question. How unequal *should* incomes be? While economists cannot answer that question in a definitive way, they can throw a great deal of light on this issue.

Learning Objectives

After you have studied this chapter in the textbook and the study guide, you should be able to:

Explain the reasons why some people have more income than others

Explain how the Lorenz curve is constructed and why it provides a good picture of the nation's income distribution

Explain why the Lorenz curve exaggerates the degree of inequality

Identify four government policies designed to make incomes more equal, and specify which of these is most successful in achieving this objective

Explain why the *direct* effects of policies designed to increase equality are at least partially offset by their negative *indirect* effects on incentives

Demonstrate why it cannot be claimed that a free market leads to a fair distribution of income

Show why complete equality of income is not necessarily fair; that is, show why equality is *not* the same as equity (fairness)

Explain two principles for comprising between the extremes of a free market and complete equality

Show why a conflict exists between equity and efficiency

HIGHLIGHTS OF CHAPTER

Four broad questions are addressed in this chapter:

1. Why is there income inequality?
2. How much income inequality exists in the United States?
3. How much of this inequality has been eliminated by government expenditures, transfers, and taxes?
4. How much inequality *should* there be?

Why Inequality?

There are at least eight reasons why some people may have more income than others: (1) their greater investment in human capital, (2) a rent earned on some innate ability, (3) greater financial wealth, either because they have inherited it or saved it, (4) greater market power due to membership in a union or possession of some other form of monopoly power, (5) a willingness to work harder or longer hours, (6) discrimination in their favor in the labor market, (7) good connections and other benefits of family background, and (8) just plain luck—being at the right place at the right time. To illustrate how costly it can be if you are in the right place at the wrong time, consider the classic complaint of the failing stock-market speculator: "I got all the decisions exactly right; it was just the timing I got wrong."

Which of these influences is most important? Professor Jacob Mincer's surprising reply is that 60% of the differences in income can be attributed to the first factor on this list—differences in human capital.

How Much Inequality Is There in the United States?

It goes without saying that the highest-income 20% of the U.S. population receives more income (before government taxes and expenditures) than the poorest 20%. But the question is, How *much* more? The remarkable answer: In excess of 100 times more. These and other similar comparisons are described, in Figure 36-1 in the text, by a Lorenz curve. This shows the percentage of the nation's income received by the poorest 20% of the population; and by the poorest 40%; and so on. If everyone had exactly the same income each year, then the Lorenz curve would be the 45° "complete-equality" line shown in Figure 36-1 in the text. In this case, the poorest 20% would get 20% of the nation's income; the poorest 40% would get 40% of the nation's income; and so on. This is not true for the U.S. Lorenz curve shown in this diagram. Its large bow indicates a substantial degree of inequality.

Actually, this overstates the case. Even if there were perfect equality, with all families receiving exactly the same *lifetime* income, there would still be some bow in the Lorenz curve, since it measures income at a single point in time. The reason is that some families would be at the height of their earning power. They would be

observed with far more income in a particular year than other younger families, who would be just beginning their careers at a low income.

How Much Do Government Expenditures and Taxes Reduce Inequality?

The Lorenz curve in Figure 36-2 in the text shows that government taxes and transfers reduce inequality by about a third. That is, the area between the complete inequality line and the Lorenz curve is reduced by a third. This reduction has been accomplished by four broad government programs:

1. *Social insurance*, such as unemployment insurance and social security. In reducing inequality, this is the most important category of government policies.
2. *Taxation*. Taxes generally reduce inequality, because most taxes fall more heavily on the rich than the poor.
3. *Cash transfers*, such as Aid to Families with Dependent Children.
4. *Transfers-in-kind*, such as food or medical services that are provided by the government. Taken together, transfers-in-kind and cash transfers are about as important in reducing inequality as taxation.

While these programs have the *direct* effect of reducing inequality, they also have an offsetting *indirect* effect. They *increase* inequality because they reduce the incentive for the poor to find and hold jobs. Furthermore, they reduce the incentive for families at all income levels to stay married. (When a family breaks up, its income is split between two families, lowering the income per family.)

What Is a "Fair" or "Equitable" Distribution of Income?

This question cannot be answered with complete certainty, because it is a normative question of "what ought to be," rather than a positive question of "what is." Nevertheless, most people would agree on two points:

1. The outcome of the free market has no special claim to being fair, because there is no way of justifying huge profits to monopolists. This is the problem of markets that are not perfectly competitive. But there are problems that go deeper than this. *Even if markets were perfectly competitive*, it would be difficult to argue that their outcome would necessarily be fair. The example in the text is of the individual who makes no effort or contribution to the nation's output, yet who receives a very high income because he owns inherited agricultural land. The only claim for perfect competition—and it's an important one—is that, in the absence of externalities, it provides an outcome that is *efficient*. But no claim can be made that this outcome is necessarily fair.

2. At the other extreme, complete equality of income would not be fair either, because some people work harder and longer than others, and some people have more dangerous or odious jobs than others. Most would agree that such people "deserve" a higher income. After reading this section, it is essential that you be able to explain why equality and equity are not the same. Equality means "being equal," while equity means "being fair."

With these two extremes—the free market's distribution of income and a completely equal distribution of income—being judged unacceptable, what is a reasonable compromise? The text suggests two guidelines:

1. Set equality of *opportunity* as our objective rather than equality of *reward*. View life as a race that should be fair, with all participants starting out together, although of course, not finishing that way. There should be no handicaps; for example, no one should be denied the opportunity of an education because of discrimination. But this doesn't mean that everyone should be awarded a college degree—that should depend on what people are able to do with their equal opportunity.

2. We should modify the rewards of the race. Some must finish last, but they should not be left in an impoverished state.

Perhaps the most important concept in this chapter is this: In striving for equity, it must never be forgotten that there is a *conflict between equity and efficiency*. To take the extreme case: If everyone were guaranteed an equal income, who would want to fight fires or work the long hours of the computer engineer? Equalizing the nation's income pie would reduce the size of that pie.

The ideas of Professor John Rawls discussed in Box 36-1 in the text are of considerable interest because for some time many people thought he had the solution to the problem of what the nation's income distribution should be. Rawls suggests that we imagine everyone to be in an "original position," in which no one knows what his or her particular income will be. Then ask what kind of income distribution reasonable people would choose from behind this "veil of ignorance." They would be choosing a distribution of income—that is, an "income ladder"—without knowing on which of the rungs they themselves would be located.

Rawls argues that in these circumstances, everyone would agree to his "difference principle": There should be complete equality in the distribution of income, *unless* there is an unequal distribution that leaves everyone better off. But he arrives at this conclusion by supposing that all the people who make this decision would figure that, with their luck, no matter what "income ladder" they might choose, they would end up on the lowest rung; so, they would choose an income distribution in which the lowest rung is as high as possible. In other words, they would use the *maximin principle* of choosing the distribution with the largest minimum income.

In this box, we give examples to show that Rawls's theory only applies to people who won't take a risk under *any* circumstances. Therefore it just doesn't apply to average Americans—let alone those who visit Las Vegas in search of risk. Thus Rawls did not answer the question of what our income distribution should be. To this question, there may never be a clear answer.

Important Terms: Match the Columns

Match the term in the first column with the corresponding phrase in the second column. But before you do so, write out your own definition of the term in the first column.

_____ **1.** Lorenz curve
_____ **2.** Complete equality line
_____ **3.** Social insurance
_____ **4.** Transfers-in-kind
_____ **5.** Original position (Box 36-1 in the textbook)
_____ **6.** Difference principle (Box 36-1 in the textbook)
_____ **7.** Maximin principle (Box 36–1 in the textbook)

a. This appears in the Lorenz curve diagram and has a 45° slope. The Lorenz curve would coincide with this only if all families received exactly the same income in the year of observation.

b. The theory that income should be equally distributed unless there is some other distribution that makes everyone better off.

c. This shows the percentage of national income that is received by the poorest 20% of families, by the poorest 40% of families, and so on.

d. It is in this location that Rawls would ask everyone to choose the best income distribution, without knowing what his or her position on that income scale will be.

e. Payments made by the government, which receives nothing in return. These payments are not in cash, but instead are in the form of goods or services such as food stamps or medical care.

f. Making the choice that maximizes the minimum value
g. Government programs that require employers and employees to contribute insurance premiums (such as unemployment insurance or social security premiums). The employees then receive benefits once they retire or become unemployed.

True-False

T F   **1.** The category of government expenditures that most shifts the Lorenz curve is transfers-in-kind.
T F   **2.** Government expenditures are more effective than taxes in reducing inequality.
T F   **3.** There was an increase in income equality during the first Reagan administration.
T F   **4.** If income is defined broadly to include both money and leisure, then fairness requires that those who take a lot of their income in one form (leisure) should get less in the other form (money).
T F   **5.** The only reason that complete equality is rejected as a target is that this division of the nation's income pie would shrink its overall size.
T F   **6.** Equity is a normative, rather than a positive, issue.
T F   **7.** Scientific evidence indicates that complete equality is the only fair way of distributing the nation's income.
T F   **8.** The provable virtues of a free, perfectly competitive market have to do with its equity—not its efficiency.
T F   **9.** Equity necessarily requires that everyone be paid the same income, regardless of how much and how hard he or she works.
T F   **10.** It is possible to have an absolutely fair competition, but a bad system of rewards.

Multiple Choice

1. How much of the nation's wealth is held by the poorest 20% of the population?
    a. 15%   **d.** 1%
    b. 12%   **e.** essentially none at all
    c. 3%

2. Research indicates that, in determining differences in income:
    a. the least important influence is wealth
    b. the least important influence is family background
    c. the most important influence is human capital
    d. the most important influence is luck
    e. the least important influence is human capital

3. The greater the degree of income inequality:
    a. the smaller the bow in the Lorenz currve (i.e., the closer the Lorenz curve is to the 45° line)
    b. the larger the bow in the Lorenz curve
    c. the steeper the initial slope of the Lorenz curve
    d. the higher the point the Lorenz curve eventually reaches
    e. none of the above

4. What percentage of the total U.S. income (before taxes and transfers) is earned by the lowest-income 20% of U.S. families?
    a. less than 1%   **d.** about 13%
    b. about 5%   **e.** about 15%
    c. about 10%

5. Because government taxes are:
    a. highly progressive, they are more effective than government expenditures in making incomes more equal

    b. highly progressive, they are less effective than government expenditures in making incomes more equal
    c. not highly progressive, they are less effective than government expenditures in making incomes more equal
    d. not highly progressive, they are more effective than government expenditures in making incomes more equal
    e. regressive, they are more effective than government expenditures in making incomes more equal

6. Putting an end to racial discrimination is likely to:
    a. increase the bow in the Lorenz curve
    b. decrease the bow in the Lorenz curve
    c. change the Lorenz curve so that its bow is above rather than below the 45° line
    d. make the Lorenz curve start from a different initial point
    e. make the Lorenz curve end at a different point

7. If some individuals acquire more and more human capital, while others do not, then this is likely to:
    a. increase the bow in the Lorenz curve
    b. decrease the bow in the Lorenz curve
    c. change the Lorenz curve so that its bow is above, rather than below, the 45° line
    d. make the Lorenz curve start from a different initial point
    e. make the Lorenz curve end at a different point

8. Bluestone and Harrison's main conclusion is that there has been:

a. a decrease in both high- and low-income jobs
b. a decrease in middle-income jobs, and an increase in low-income jobs
c. a decrease in middle-income jobs, and an increase in high-income jobs
d. an increase in both middle- and high-income jobs
e. an increase in middle-income jobs, and a decrease in low-income jobs

9. Unemployment insurance is an example of:
a. a progressive tax
b. a proportional tax
c. social insurance
d. privately administered insurance
e. transfers-in-kind

10. If we tried to pursue the goal of perfect equity, we would find that it would:
a. conflict with the goal of efficiency
b. complement the goal of efficiency
c. neither conflict with nor complement the goal of efficiency
d. conflict with or complement the goal of efficiency, depending upon the rate of inflation
e. expand the size of the national income pie

11. It is difficult to argue that the free market would do a completely equitable job of distributing income because:
a. the free market is often not perfectly competitive; some people raise their income through the exercise of market power
b. even if the free market were perfectly competitive, it would still often provide luxuries for the wealthy, without providing adequate necessities for the poor
c. the free market is efficient
d. (a) and (b)
e. none of the above

12. The most difficult concept for economists to pin down is:

a. efficiency gain
b. equity
c. equality
d. efficiency loss
e. inequality

13. A policy of trying to completely equalize incomes has been criticized because it would:
a. be inefficient
b. be unfair, because it would give people who work the same reward as those who do not
c. require a change in our present system of inheritance
d. shrink the national income pie
e. all of the above

14. John Rawls argues that income should be divided equally:
a. in all circumstances
b. in no circumstances
c. unless an unequal distribution benefits the majority
d. unless an unequal distribution benefits a large minority
e. unless an unequal distribution benefits everyone

15. During the first Reagan administration, 1981–1985, the shares of the nation's income distribution shifted somewhat. How?
a. There was a decrease in inequality in the income distribution, but an increase in poverty at the low end.
b. There was an increase in inequality, and a decrease in poverty.
c. There was a decrease in inequality, but no change in poverty.
d. There was an increase in inequality, and an increase in poverty.
e. There was a decrease in inequality, and a decrease in poverty.

Exercises

1. Table 36-1 gives the income distribution of a hypothetical economy, as in panel *a* of Table 36-1 in the textbook. In Table 36-2, fill in the cumulative income distribution.

Table 36-1

	Lowest 20%	Second 20%	Third 20%	Fourth 20%	Highest 20%
Percent of income	4	6	10	20	60

Table 36-2

	Lowest 20%	Second 20%	Third 20%	Fourth 20%	Highest 20%
Percent of income					

Plot the Lorenz curve in Figure 36-1, and label it L_1. Suppose that the government then taxes away half the income of every family in the top 20% of the income distribution and gives it in equal amounts to every family in the lowest 60% of the distribution. Fill in the resulting income distribution in Table 36-3 and the resulting cumulative income distribution in Table 36-4.

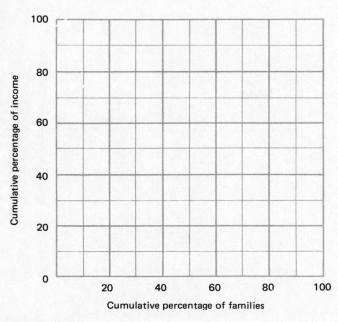

Cumulative percentage of income

Cumulative percentage of families

FIGURE 36–1

Table 36-3

	Lowest 20%	Second 20%	Third 20%	Fourth 20%	Highest 20%
Percent of income					

Table 36-4

	Lowest 20%	Second 20%	Third 20%	Fourth 20%	Highest 20%
Percent of income					

Plot the Lorenz curve for income after taxes and transfers in Figure 36-1 and label it L_2.

2. Consider the five following ways of distributing income among five families in an economy:

    a. Four families receive $1,100 per year each, and the fifth family receives $600 per year.

    b. Four families receive $500 per year each, and the fifth receives $3,000 per year.

    c. Each family receives $500 per year.

    d. Four families receive $1,100 per year each, and the fifth family receives $5,600.

    e. Four families receive $5,000 per year each, and the fifth receives nothing.

Fill in Table 36-5, giving the total national income according to each distribution.

Table 36-5

Total national distribution	Total national income
A	
B	
C	
D	
E	

Fill in Table 36-6 for each of the distributions, showing the cumulative percentages.

Table 36-6

		Lowest 20%	Lowest 40%	Lowest 60%	Lowest 80%	Total
Percentage of income	A					
	B					
	C					
	D					
	E					

Draw and label the Lorenz curve for each of these distributions in Figure 36-2.

Indicate in Table 36-7 the way that these distributions would be ranked according to Rawl's maximin criterion.

Table 36-7

Rank	Distribution
Best	
Second best	
Third best	
Fourth best	
Fifth best	

According to this ranking, does the best distribution have the largest total income? _____. Does it have the least inequality as measured by the Lorenz curve? _____.

The reason that egalitarians (those who believe in equal incomes) were disillusioned by Rawls is illustrated in Figure 36-2, where we see that Rawls [does, does not] recommend the "complete-equality" distribution _____. Instead, he recommends distribution _____,

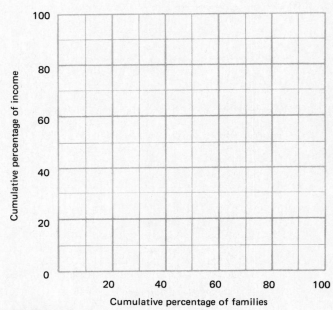

FIGURE 36–2

which is one of the [most, least] equal of the distributions.

Essay Questions

1. "With a problem as perplexing as determining the best income distribution for the nation, the best approach is a simple one that strikes right to the heart of the matter: Make all incomes equal. This is philosophically and morally the fair and just solution." Do you agree? Explain your position.

2. In your view, is it possible for an unequal income distribution to be equitable? Use examples to support your position.

3. Is it fair to allow John McEnroe to earn such a high income from doing something—playing tennis—that many others in the world enjoy?

4. In what way do you think the shape of the Lorenz curve would be affected by (a) an end to racial discrimination; (b) some individuals' acquiring more and more human capital, while others do not; (c) unemployment insurance; (d) a highly progressive tax; (e) a special new tax on wage income; and (f) a special new tax on incomes over $100,000?

5. Marxists believe in the principle, "To each according to his needs, from each according to his abilities." Do you agree or disagree? Why or why not? Do you think that this principle would lead to a straight-line Lorenz curve? Why or why not? Do you think that a government that tried to put this principle into effect would run into problems? Would it face a conflict between equity and efficiency?

Answers

Important Terms: 1 c 2 a 3 g 4 e 5 d 6 b 7 f
True-False: 1 F 2 T 3 F 4 T 5 F 6 T 7 F 8 F 9 F 10 T
Multiple Choice: 1 e 2 c 3 b 4 a 5 c 6 b 7 a 8 b 9 c 10 a 11 d 12 b 13 e 14 e 15 d
Exercises: 1. Table 36-2: 4, 10, 20, 40, 100. Table 36-3: 14, 16, 20, 20, 30. Table 36-4: 14, 30, 50, 70, 100.

Figure 36-1 completed:

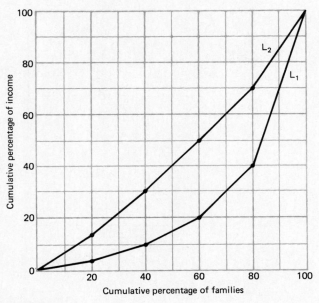

FIGURE 36–1

2.

Table 36-5 completed:

Total national distribution	Total national income
A	$ 4,600
B	$ 5,000
C	$ 2,500
D	$10,000
E	$20,000

Table 36-6 completed:

	Lowest 20%	Lowest 40%	Lowest 60%	Lowest 80%	Total
Percentage of income A	13	35	57	78	100
B	10	20	30	40	100
C	20	40	60	80	100
D	11	22	33	44	100
E	0	25	50	75	100

Table 36-7 completed:

Rank	Distribution
Best	D
Second best	A
Third best	B
Fourth best	C
Fifth best	E

No, no, does not, *C*, *D*, least.

Figure 36-2 completed:

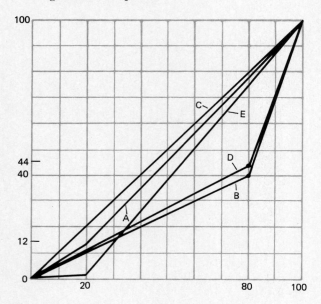

FIGURE 36–2

CHAPTER 37

GOVERNMENT POLICIES TO REDUCE INEQUALITY:

CAN WE SOLVE THE POVERTY PROBLEM?

MAJOR PURPOSE

The objective of this chapter is to evaluate what we are now doing—and what we might possibly do in the future—to alleviate the grinding effects of poverty on the poorest individuals in our population. Specifically, we will address three sets of questions:

1. How is the poverty line defined, and who are the poor below it?

2. What policies does the government now have in place to reduce poverty, and how successful have they been?

3. What income maintenance programs have been proposed to replace the present welfare system, and how likely is it that they would be successful?

Learning Objectives

After you have studied this chapter in the textbook and the study guide, you should be able to:

Describe how the poverty line is defined

Explain why, over long periods of time, our definition of the poverty line tends to drift up to a higher level of real income

State the factors that increase the likelihood of a family's being poor

Describe the government policies that attack the causes of poverty, and the policies that reduce its symptoms

Explain the difference between social insurance and welfare programs

Describe the problems with our present welfare system

Explain the concept of the implicit tax in a welfare program and why this is important in evaluating such programs

Critically evaluate the guaranteed minimum income proposal

Argue the case that income maintenance programs are the cure for poverty

Argue the opposite case that such programs are the cause of poverty

Describe how a negative income tax program would work

Explain the theoretical advantages of a negative income tax program

Explain why three objectives come into conflict when the government is trying to design a negative income tax: (1) to raise the minimum income to an acceptable level, (2) to increase the incentive to work, and (3) to keep the costs of the program from escalating

Describe the results of experimental studies on the negative income tax

Explain the pros and cons of a wage subsidy

HIGHLIGHTS OF CHAPTER

Here are the broad questions that are addressed in this chapter.

How Is the Poverty Line Defined?

The Department of Agriculture estimates the lowest possible cost of feeding a family with a diet that would be reasonably edible, and that would meet minimal nutrition standards. Since the poor spend about a third of their income on food, the poverty line is defined as 3 times the cost of this diet. In 1984 the poverty line was $10,610 for a family of four. This poverty line is adjusted every year to take account of inflation. It also drifts higher in real terms over long periods of time because our idea of what is barely acceptable tends to increase.

Who Are the Poor?

A family is more likely to be poor if it is (1) non-white, (2) from the south, (3) not well educated, (4) living in the core of a big city, or (5) fatherless. If a family falls into several of these categories, the chance it will be poor may rise dramatically.

What Are the Government Policies That Reduce Poverty?

Four kinds of government programs attack the *causes* of poverty, by helping the poor to earn more income: (1) policies that subsidize investment in human capital, such as free schooling and subsidies for training unemployed workers; (2) policies designed to reduce unemployment or disability, such as those that increase safety in the workplace; (3) policies, such as the Equal Pay Act of 1963 and the Civil Rights Act of 1964, that are designed to prevent discrimination in the labor market; and (4) other programs, such as WIN (Work Incentive Program) which subsidize the training and employment of people on welfare, and provide the day-care facilities for children that allow parents to take jobs.

There are two categories of programs that reduce the *symptoms* of poverty by providing income assistance:

1. *Social insurance programs*, such as social security, unemployment insurance, and medicare for the elderly. These programs have not been aimed specifically at the poverty problem since they provide benefits to all participants whether or not they are poor. Nevertheless, they still play an important role in reducing poverty.

2. *Welfare programs* have been designed specifically to alleviate poverty by providing benefits only to the poor. Examples are AFDC (Aid to Families with Dependent Children) and transfers-in-kind, such as food stamps, public housing, and medical services for the poor (medicaid).

How Successful Have Government Antipoverty Policies Been?

Over long periods during this century, poverty has been steadily and substantially reduced. However, in the decade of the 1970s, progress on this front essentially ended, and in the early 1980s the percentage of the nation in poverty increased. This recent experience does not prove that antipoverty programs have become ineffective. During this period, some of these programs were cut back, so one would expect that poverty would become more severe. The incidence of poverty also increased because of high unemployment.

Nonetheless, these programs have not been as effective as one might have hoped. One reason is that they include an "implicit tax" on any income the poor may earn. When a poor family earns another $1,000 of income, it may consequently have to give up, say, $800 of welfare benefits it receives from the government. (Sometimes it's more than this, sometimes less.) This $800 is called an 80% "implicit tax," because, from the point of view of the poor, it's as though they had $800 of their additional $1,000 of income "taxed away." If they only get $200 net benefit when they go out and earn $1,000, why bother? It is critical that you understand this concept of an implicit tax, and why a high rate of this tax weakens the incentive of the poor to work. For some families in our present welfare system, this implicit tax has been very high indeed—in some instances approaching, or even exceeding, 100%. In such cases, the poor who earn another $1,000 will lose $1,000 of welfare payments from the government. Their income doesn't increase at all; they have no monetary incentive to get a job.

What Are the Proposals to Replace the Present Welfare System?

A guaranteed minimum income (GMI) Under this program, shown in Figure 37-3 in the textbook, the government would guarantee a family a minimum income of, say, $10,000. Any shortfall in the family's earnings would be covered by a payment from the government. The problem with this policy is that it has a built-in 100% implicit tax that leaves no incentive for the poor to go to work. If they do, and earn another $1,000, their welfare payments from the government are reduced by this same amount. It doesn't matter whether they earn $5,000 or $6,000. Their income is fixed by the government at a $10,000 level. So they don't benefit at all when they earn that $1,000 more. Ensure that you fully understand this scheme in Figure 37-3 in the textbook, before you proceed to the more complicated proposal for a negative income tax in Figure 37-5 in the text.

A negative income tax (NIT) This proposal also provides the poor with a guaranteed minimum income; but in addition it provides them with an incentive to go out and earn income on their own. Their implicit tax in this program can be set at, say, 50% (rather than the 100% implicit tax in the GMI proposal above). Thus a family that earns another $1,000 of income has its payments from the government reduced by only $500. It therefore gets a net benefit of $500, which provides it with an incentive to work. Note that the "income-after-subsidy" line CA that was completely flat in Figure 37-3 in the textbook—and therefore provided no incentive to work—has now been replaced by the upward-sloping line CQ in Figure 37-5 in the textbook. Since some of the benefit from increased income can now be kept—it is no longer all lost—there is an incentive to go to work.

If, as its proponents recommend, the negative income tax were to replace the entire inconsistent set of present welfare policies, it would provide another benefit. It would be more equitable because all the poor would be treated alike; all would face the same minimum income, and the same implicit tax. However, this policy would not be problem-free. Like any other antipoverty program, it could not simultaneously achieve the three desirable but conflicting goals of (1) providing an acceptable minimum income for everyone, (2) preserving the incentive for people to work, and (3) keeping costs down. As an example of how these goals may conflict, suppose the government decides to achieve the first goal by raising the minimum income level from $10,000 to $12,000. This will shift the "income after" line CQH in Figure 37-5 in the textbook up by $2,000 throughout its whole length, thus increasing the gray "subsidy gap" that the government must fill. Thus this measure may conflict with objective (3) of keeping costs down.

Unfortunately, the results of experiments in Denver and Seattle suggest that in practice the negative income tax doesn't work as well as many economists had hoped. In fact, compared with even the present welfare system, the incentive it provides for the poor to go to work is disappointing. It also seems to cause an increase in marital breakdown. Why these adverse effects arise is not clearly understood. Perhaps it is because the subjects of these experiments had their options—such as quitting work—clearly explained to them.

The disappointment in these experimental results has led some to suggest the alternative of a wage subsidy that would provide financial assistance to the poor by increasing their wages. Because it would increase the reward for work (the wage rate), it is hoped that this scheme might provide a stronger work incentive. Its main drawback is that it would remove any guaranteed minimum income, and thus would provide no assistance to those individuals who, because of age or disability, cannot work to support themselves. Accordingly, some method would have to be devised to "tag" such people, so that they could qualify for special government support. While such a system would be necessary, it would be far from foolproof. One problem is that some of the able-bodied who did not want to work would try fraudulently to have themselves tagged as disabled.

Concluding Remarks

So far, in analyzing our present welfare system and the GMI and NIT proposals to replace it, the focus has been on the cost of a welfare system, in terms of the reduced incentive to work by the recipients of welfare. But there is another cost as well—the cost of raising the taxes from the general public to finance the welfare expenditure. There is evidence that there is about a 25% to 35% loss when taxes are raised, because *those who are taxed* respond in such a way as to keep their taxes down, and reduce efficiency in the process. Make sure—in Figure 37-4 in the text—that you can clearly distinguish between these two costs—that is, the perverse incentives imposed on the public that has to *pay* for welfare payments, and the disincentive to work of the poor who *receive* the welfare payments.

Important Terms: Match the Columns

Match the term in the first column with the corresponding phrase in the second column. But before you do so, write out your own definition of the term in the first column.

_____ 1. Poverty
_____ 2. Poverty line
_____ 3. Jobs Training Partnership Act (JTPA)
_____ 4. Equal Pay Act (1963)
_____ 5. Civil Rights Act (1964)
_____ 6. Social security
_____ 7. The Work Incentive Program (WIN)
_____ 8. Aid to Families with Dependent Children (AFDC)
_____ 9. Food stamps
_____ 10. Public housing
_____ 11. Implicit tax
_____ 12. Culture of poverty
_____ 13. Guaranteed minimum income

a. The identification of those who, because of age or disability, are unable to earn an income, and therefore deserve special support from the government
b. A program that provides medical services for the poor
c. A proposed government program to ensure that no one receives less than a specified amount of income
d. A program under which the federal government pays local governments to clear slums, build houses, and rent these houses to low-income tenants
e. The amount of welfare payments lost by a family that earns another dollar of income
f. A proposal for the government to provide the funds for increasing the wages of low-income earners

_____ **14.** Negative income tax
_____ **15.** Tagging
_____ **16.** Wage subsidy
_____ **17.** Medicare
_____ **18.** Medicaid

g. An income equal to 3 times the minimum cost of an adequate diet

h. Vouchers that provide food for the poor

i. A program that guarantees everyone a minimum income and provides a work incentive by allowing people to retain part of any income they earn

j. A program that provides medical services for the elderly

k. A program that subsidizes the training and employment of people on welfare, and also makes it possible for parents to take jobs by providing day-care facilities for children

l. A program to which employers and employees contribute, with benefits paid out to the retired or disabled

m. A program that provides for welfare payments to families not headed by an able-bodied male

n. The dependence of welfare recipients upon welfare payments

o. A government program providing retraining and relocation assistance

p. The legislation that requires that women be paid the same as men engaged in the same work

q. The legislation outlawing discrimination in hiring, firing, and other employment practices

r. Inadequate income to buy the necessities of life

True-False

T F **1.** By 1984, only 1 American family in 20 was below the poverty line.
T F **2.** There is a larger number of poor blacks in the United States than poor whites.
T F **3.** The poor are located in the lower left-hand corner of the Lorenz curve.
T F **4.** Anyone who eats a diet below the requirements of minimum nutrition is defined to be below the poverty line.
T F **5.** The poverty line is not adjusted over time to take account of inflation, because inflation is not the problem.
T F **6.** The Work Incentive Program was established to subsidize the training and employment of welfare recipients.
T F **7.** Because the poor can qualify for several government welfare programs, they are sometimes able to raise themselves not only to the poverty line, but above it.
T F **8.** Transfer programs such as food stamps relieve the symptoms of poverty rather than attacking its causes.
T F **9.** Under a guaranteed minimum income, all Americans would receive the same income after taxes and subsidies.
T F **10.** The implicit tax in a welfare system is the sum of the benefits lost divided by the additional earned income.

Multiple Choice

1. It becomes impossible to lift all Americans out of poverty, if we define it as:
   a. the bottom half of the U.S. income distribution
   b. any income less than $10,000
   c. the bottom tenth of the U.S. income distribution
   d. (a) or (c)
   e. (b) or (c)

2. Select the correct word below to put in the blank in this sentence: It is _____ better to attack the causes of poverty than its symptoms.
   a. always
   b. usually
   c. seldom
   d. almost never
   e. never

3. By 1983, the percentage of Americans living below the poverty line was about:
   a. 21%
   b. 13%
   c. 10%
   d. 5%
   e. 1%

4. The program that is most important in maintaining U.S. income is:
   a. social security
   b. Aid to Families with Dependent Children
   c. unemployment insurance
   d. food stamps
   e. medicaid

5. Allowing Americans a tax deduction for interest payments on mortgages on their homes:
   a. subsidizes those who own homes
   b. subsidizes those who do not own homes
   c. penalizes those who own homes
   d. subsidizes all Americans
   e. penalizes all Americans

6. Which of the following government programs is designed to attack the causes of poverty?
   a. Work Incentives Program (WIN)
   b. social security

c. food stamps

d. public housing

e. Aid to Families with Dependent Children

7. A guaranteed minimum income would result in:

a. greater equity and greater efficiency

b. less equity and greater efficiency

c. less equity with no change in efficiency

d. less equity and lower efficiency

e. greater equity and lower efficiency

8. The income-maintenance program that would provide the poor with the largest incentive to work is one in which the "income-after-subsidy" line:

a. has zero slope

b. has a slope close to zero

c. has a slope of 15°

d. has a slope of 20°

e. has a slope of 35°

9. The maximum implicit tax on any family facing the set of U.S. welfare policies is:

a. 50%   d. 100%

b. 80%   e. more than 100%

c. just under 100%

10. If a family living in government subsidized housing is required to pay 25% of its income in rent, then for this reason alone it is facing an implicit tax of:

a. zero   d. 100%

b. 25%   e. 125%

c. 75%

11. A welfare program that pays you $5,000 if you earn nothing and $4,500 if you earn $2,000 has an implicit tax of:

a. zero   d. 50%

b. 25%   e. 105%

c. 40%

12. Experiments suggest that providing people with easy access to, and complete information about, welfare payments:

a. reduces their incentive to work

b. increases their incentive to work

c. leaves their incentive to work unchanged

d. doesn't affect the incentive to work of the poor, but raises it for middle-income families

e. doesn't affect the incentive to work of the poor, but lowers it for middle-income families

13. Which of the following should offer the least work incentive to the very poor?

a. no taxes or subsidies

b. the present welfare system

c. a negative income tax

d. a wage subsidy scheme

e. a guaranteed minimum income

14. With a negative income tax, an increase in the implicit tax rate will:

a. increase the slope of the income-after-tax line

b. decrease the slope of that line

c. leave the slope of that line unchanged

d. raise the point where the income-after-tax line intersects the vertical axis

15. Suppose that a negative income tax is set up with the minimum income set at $8,000, and the implicit tax rate set at 50%. In this case, a subsidy would be paid by the government:

a. to no one

b. only to those earning less than $4,000

c. only to those earning less than $8,000

d. only to those earning less than $12,000

e. only to those earning less than $16,000

Exercise

Consider the four following tax-subsidy programs:

a. Every family earning less than $5,000 receives enough subsidy to give it an income of $5,000 after taxes and subsidies. On every dollar earned over $5,000, a family must pay a 20% tax.

b. Every family receives a subsidy of $5,000, but then pays a 50% tax on every dollar earned.

c. Every family receives a subsidy of $3,000, but then pays a tax of 30% on every dollar earned.

d. Every family receives a subsidy of $3,000, but then pays a tax of 50% on every dollar earned.

In Figure 37-1 plot the line for each program showing how a family's income after taxes and subsidies is related to its income before taxes and subsidies. For each program, indicate in Table 37-1 the marginal tax rates on income earned above $5,000.

FIGURE 37-1

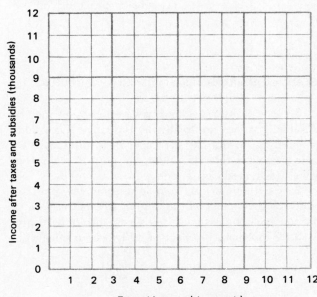

Table 37-1

Program	Marginal tax rate on income earned above $5,000
A	
B	
C	
D	

Suppose that the distribution of earned income (before taxes and subsidies) in the economy is given by Table 37-2.

Table 37-2

Annual income before taxes and transfers (thousands of dollars)	0	3	5	6	10	15	20	50
Number of families earning this income	1	2	4	4	3	2	1	1

In Table 37-3 fill in the net tax (i.e., tax minus subsidy) paid to each family under each of the programs.

Table 37-3

Income (in thousands)		0	3	5	6	10	15	20	50
Net tax of each	A								
family under	B								
program:	C								
	D								

In Table 37-4 show the total net taxes collected—that is, total taxes collected minus total subsidy paid. Assume that, regardless of the tax-subsidy program that is imposed, there is no change in the incentive of work and therefore the earned income of each family. In other words, the income distribution in Table 37-2 doesn't change, regardless of the tax-subsidy program.

Table 37-4

Programs	Total net taxes
A	
B	
C	
D	

Essay Questions

1. "Social insurance and welfare programs may be desirable, but they are totally unproductive. They don't add anything to the nation's capacity to produce." Do you agree with this statement, or not? Explain your answer. (Use medicaid as one of your examples.)

2. Use a numerical example to show why poverty, defined as the income of the bottom 10% of the population, is a meaningless and useless measure of hardship.

3. If the main ill effect of AFDC is to encourage fathers to leave home so their families can qualify for welfare, what do you think of maintaining the program but disqualifying any family whose father has abandoned them?

4. If the government gave equivalent cash transfers instead of food stamps and other types of assistance in kind, would the recipients be better off? Why? Would their children be better off? Why does the government provide assistance in kind?

Answers

Important Terms: 1 r 2 g 3 o 4 p 5 q 6 l 7 k 8 m 9 h 10 d 11 e 12 n 13 c 14 i 15 a 16 f 17 j 18 b

True-False: 1 F 2 F 3 T 4 F 5 F 6 T 7 T 8 T 9 F 10 T

Multiple Choice: 1 d 2 b 3 b 4 a 5 a 6 a 7 e 8 e 9 e 10 b 11 b 12 a 13 e 14 b 15 e

Exercise:

Figure 37-1 completed:

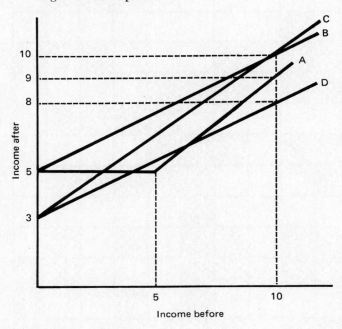

FIGURE 37-1

Table 37-1 completed:

20%
50%
30%
50%

Table 37-3 completed:

−5,000	−2,000	0	200	1,000	2,000	3,000	9,000
−5,000	−3,500	−2,500	−2,000	0	2,500	5,000	20,000
−3,000	−2,100	−1,500	−1,200	0	1,500	3,000	12,000
−3,000	−1,500	− 500	0	2,000	4,500	7,000	22,000

Table 37-4 completed:

10,800
0
0
36,000

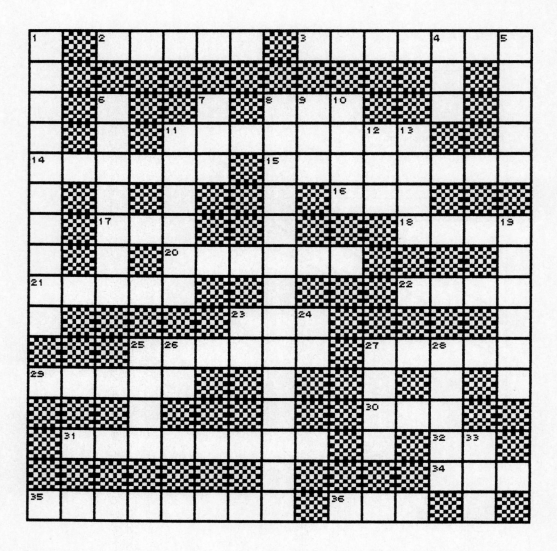

Across

2, 3. education and training are examples of this
8. during a recession, there is a _____ in output
11. program to provide medical services to the elderly
14, 15. this program has been one of the principal reasons for the decline in poverty in the United States
16. an export of Sri Lanka
17. a hard wood
18. strikebreaker
20. fairness
21. assume; take as given
22. an anti-poverty program (abbrev.)
23. a major South American city (abbrev.)
25, 27. a way of illustrating inequality
29. major producer of aluminum
30. tool for cutting wood
31. program to provide medical services to the needy
32. see, behold
34. a form of international reserve created by the International Monetary Fund (abbrev.)
35, 36. a way to discourage pollution

Down

1. an anti-poverty program (2 words)
4. a source of revenue for the government
5, 19. this illustrates the idea that something is lost when income is transferred
6. labor, land, and capital are _____ of production
7. snakelike fish
8. one of the causes of poverty
9. frozen water
10. agreement
11. an institution that brings buyers and sellers together
12. regret
13. long periods of time
23. regarding
24. the land of Dorothy's dreams
25. one of the factors of production
26. above, and supported by
27. expense
28. philosopher who suggested that people should disregard their present positions, in order to judge the best distribution of income
33. lyric poem

CHAPTER 38

MARXISM AND MARXIST ECONOMIES

MAJOR PURPOSE

Historically, the most influential criticism of the capitalistic, free-enterprise system was that set out by Karl Marx. He charged that this system distributes income in an unfair way because it provides income to owners of capital—that is, to "capitalists." In this chapter, we examine Marx's criticism in detail and his proposed alternative: a revolution followed by a socialist state in which capital would be owned by the state on behalf of all the people. We then describe three important socialist experiments—those in the Soviet Union, Yugoslavia, and China. In the Soviet example, the focus is on the practical difficulties encountered in putting socialism into practice. In the other two examples, the focus is on what happens when a socialist state starts to introduce elements of free enterprise. In the Chinese case, this is a particularly interesting issue because there are signs that such changes are revitalizing the economy. And a rapidly growing economy of that enormous potential size could pose a serious economic challenge to the more stagnant Soviet economy.

Learning Objectives

After you have studied this chapter in the textbook and the study guide, you should be able to:

Describe the labor theory of value, and the subsistence theory of wages

Explain Marx's concepts of surplus value and the exploitation of the working class

Define and clearly distinguish between socialism and communism

State two predictions of Marx that have not been verified by history

Criticize both the theory and practice of socialism

Explain how capital is raised for investment purposes in a socialist state

Describe the problems associated with central planning

Explain why there is typically less innovation in a socialist state than in a free-enterprise economy

Explain the problems the Soviets face in setting production targets in their 5-year plans

Describe the "second economy" in the Soviet Union

Describe the problems facing the consumer in an economy that is not closely oriented to the marketplace

Compare the Soviets' disguised unemployment with our overt unemployment

Compare the Soviets' suppressed inflation with our inflation

Explain to what degree the Soviets have succeeded in equalizing incomes, and the problems they have encountered because of the increasing importance of human capital

Compare the Soviet and Yugoslavian economic systems, explaining the advantages and disadvantages of the Yugoslavs' market-oriented socialism

Describe the ways in which the government still exerts a great deal of centralized control over the Yugoslavian economy

Describe the recent attempts to make the Chinese economy more closely oriented to the market

Explain why there is a conflict between equity and efficiency even in a socialist economy

HIGHLIGHTS OF CHAPTER

This chapter can be broken down into three broad topics: (1) Marx's criticism of a free-enterprise system and the socialist-communist system he proposed, (2) the application of Marxism in the Soviet Union, and (3) the more market-oriented application of Marxism in Yugoslavia and China.

Marxism

Marxism is based on (1) the labor theory of value, and (2) the subsistence theory of wages. It claims that there is a class struggle in which workers (the "proletariat") are exploited by the capitalists (the "bourgeoisie" who own the capital equipment and other means of production). Instead of enjoying all the fruits of their labor, the workers receive just enough to subsist, with the rest going in the form of "surplus value" to the capitalists. According to Marx, the only way of resolving this class struggle is a revolution in which workers forcibly seize the ownership of physical capital from their exploiters. They then set up a socialist state in which there is a dictatorship of the proletariat and capital is owned by the state. In turn this is followed by a communist system in which the state has withered away, and capital and other forms of property are owned by the community as a whole.

One criticism of Marxist theory is that its predictions have not been borne out by history: (1) The dictatorship of the proletariat, rather than withering away, has remained powerful in Marxist states, and (2) under capitalism, workers have enjoyed rising real income rather than the increasing misery predicted by Marx.

Another criticism of Marxist theory is that if capitalists are eliminated, some other way must be found to generate physical capital for investment. The Marxist solution is to generate capital by taxation—in particular, heavy taxes on consumer goods—rather than by personal saving. However, this raises three problems: (1) Taxes (forced saving) may be more burdensome than voluntary saving; (2) when governments invest the funds they have raised, they typically lack the inventiveness of private capitalists; and (3) some substitute must be found for the profit motive as a means of allocating capital among different industries.

The concept of profit raises an important issue in the debate between capitalism and Marxism. Supporters of Marxism and capitalism alike generally agree that monopoly profits should not go unchecked. Supporters of capitalism argue that this can be done through government regulation under a basically capitalist system. Marxists argue that regulation is ineffective because big business interests are so powerful that they end up controlling their own regulators. A capitalist response to this criticism is that big business does indeed have power; and so does the government. But this is better than having all of the power in the hands of the government—as happens in a communist state.

The Soviet System

Two important features of the Soviet system are: (1) Most physical capital is owned by the state rather than by private individuals, and (2) the decisions on how much of each good to produce and how much to invest in each industry are not made by market forces, but are instead made by a central government planning agency (Gosplan) in its 5-year plans. These plans set yearly production targets, or quotas, for each industry and—in even more detail—for each plant. There are three major problems with central planning of this sort:

1. It is difficult for the government to determine a set of consistent output quotas. For example, the right output for the steel industry depends on the output of those industries that use steel, such as machinery and autos. But at the same time, the right output for the *machinery* industry depends on the output of those industries that use machinery, such as *steel*. How do you solve for the output of either steel or machinery when each depends on the other? The answer is that it is not easy. Although there are mathematical techniques for solving such problems, it is seldom possible for a planning agency to get the quotas just right. Consequently, bottlenecks—such as a shortage of steel—are common in the Soviet Union.

2. Consumers' wants tend to be ignored in the Soviet system. When steel is in short supply, it goes to produce bridges or machinery, not refrigerators for consumers. Thus consumer goods are in chronic short supply, and this leads to the long lineups that are a feature of Soviet life. Another reason the Soviet consumer is short-changed is that each production manager tends to concentrate on satisfying a quota rather than on producing the types of goods that consumers want. (For more on the plight of the Soviet consumer, see Box 38-1 in the textbook).

3. It is not clear that the Soviet degree of central planning could be made to work without a repressive Soviet-style political dictatorship. Marxists reply that our freedom is enjoyed only by the rich and powerful. And they point to one apparent advantage of central planning: It produces very little measured unemployment. However, critics point out that if someone is working to produce unwanted goods this really constitutes "disguised" unemployment.

The 5-year plans of the Soviet Union have emphasized rapid growth. For example, during the 1960s, the real rate of Soviet growth was 6% to 10%, which far exceeded the growth rate in the United States. However, the reason for this was not that the Soviet Union has a better system for generating growth. Instead it was due to the fact that investment in the Soviet Union has run about 30% of GNP, compared to 15% in the United States. When one compares the Soviet Union with a country like Japan that also invests this high a percentage of its GNP, Soviet growth does not compare favorably. Moreover, despite the heavy diversion of its GNP into investment, Soviet growth has recently become particularly disappointing; it has fallen close to zero.

Market-Oriented Socialism in Yugoslavia and China

In Yugoslavia, as in the Soviet Union, the state owns most of the physical capital. But production decisions are much less centralized in Yugoslavia. Firms there are operated by workers, who elect a manager. This manager, like the manager of a capitalist enterprise, attempts to maximize profits, which are then distributed to the workers.

However, the government still exerts a great deal of centralized control over the economy:

1. Although most firms are allowed to change their prices, they can do so only within fixed limits.
2. As in the Soviet Union, the government diverts about one-third of GNP into investment.

3. The allocation of this investment into different sectors of the economy is also determined by the central government.
4. The government sets out 5-year plans, as in the Soviet Union (although these plans are not strictly enforced).

There have been three special problems with the Yugoslav system;

1. Some of the "worker-enterprises" have a monopoly position. In socialist debate, it has been assumed that such an enterprise would not be able to exploit its monopoly power in a socialist system. However, that is not the case. Managers have exploited a monopoly position by restricting their output and thus raising their price.
2. There is not enough incentive to create new firms. Thus many existing firms do not face the threat of competition.
3. Because workers share in profits, workers in profitable enterprises earn more than workers in unprofitable enterprises. The result is the sort of income inequality that Marx was trying to eliminate. Thus the attempt to make the economy more efficient by introducing profit-sharing incentives for the labor force has also made the distribution of income less equal. Even in a socialist society, there is a conflict between efficiency and equity.

Yugoslavia is not the only market-oriented socialist economy. Some other communist countries—in particular China and Hungary—have also been moving in this direction. Incentives to increase production have worked so well in Chinese agriculture that they have been extended to industry as well. In both these sectors of the economy, the result has been substantially higher production levels. It will be interesting to watch what sort of challenge a revitalized Chinese economy may pose for the relatively stagnant Soviet economy.

Important Terms: Matching the Columns

Match the term in the first column with the corresponding phrase in the second column. But before you do so, write out your own definition of the term in the first column.

_____ **1.** Capitalism
_____ **2.** Socialism
_____ **3.** Communism
_____ **4.** Labor theory of value
_____ **5.** Subsistence wage theory
_____ **6.** Surplus value
_____ **7.** Gosplan
_____ **8.** 5-year plan
_____ **9.** Proletariat

a. The Marxist term for the working class
b. The situation that exists if people are employed, but in useless tasks
c. In Marxist theory, the ideal system in which all means of production and other forms of property are owned by the community as a whole and the central government has "withered away"
d. An economic system in which most physical capital is privately owned

_____ **10.** Bourgeoisie
_____ **11.** Dictatorship of the proletariat
_____ **12.** Disguised unemployment

e. A plan that sets up production and investment targets for each industry
f. The theory that, in a capitalist economy, workers' wages can never rise, except temporarily, above a socially defined subsistence level
g. The transitory stage, according to Marx, that follows the workers' revolution, before the government withers away and the ideal state of communism is achieved
h. An economic system in which physical capital and other means of production, such as land, are owned by the state
i. The Marxist term for the capitalist class
j. The difference, according to Marx, between the total value of output (all of which "belongs" to labor) and the wages actually received by labor
k. The theory that the value of any good is determined solely by the amount of labor that goes into producing it, including the labor embodied in the capital used to produce the good
l. The central planning agency in the Soviet Union

True-False

T F   **1.** According to Marx, labor receives a socially defined subsistence income barely sufficient to meet the workers' basic needs.
T F   **2.** According to Marxist theory, a communist society is one in which the state has withered away.
T F   **3.** A major reason why it has been difficult to control the abuse of personal power in the Soviet Union is that there are no free elections in which the public can remove the party in power and replace it with another.
T F   **4.** Marx believed that the labor time spent on producing machinery and the income earned by capitalists on that machinery were both surplus value.
T F   **5.** According to Marx, economic history was a story of the proletariat exploiting the bourgeoisie in a class struggle.
T F   **6.** Marx spent a great deal of time discussing how, in his communist society, conflicts would be resolved by groups with conflicting interests.
T F   **7.** Compared to a free-enterprise system, the Soviet planning system has led to a much more efficient use of inputs.
T F   **8.** The decaying czarist regime in Russia was overthrown in 1917 by Lenin and his group of communist revolutionaries.
T F   **9.** Many workers in the Soviet Union (as well as in the United States) have become capitalists, in the sense that they have accumulated substantial quantities of human capital.
T F   **10.** In Yugoslavia workers get higher wages if their firm earns more profits.
T F   **11.** Between 1980 and 1985, the Chinese economy was made less sensitive to market pressures.

Multiple Choice

1. Marx's analysis was based on:
   a. the labor theory of value
   b. the theory that wages tended towards their socially-defined subsistence level
   c. the marginal productivity theory of wages
   d. (a) and (b)
   e. (a) and (c)
2. Marx's recommended system for production and income distribution was:
   a. from each according to his need; to each according to his ability
   b. from each according to his ability; to each according to his need
   c. from each according to his ability; to each according to his wants
   d. from each, and to each, according to his ability
   e. from each, and to each, according to his need

3. Marx believed that once a communist society was established:
   a. power would corrupt, and absolute power would corrupt absolutely
   b. power would corrupt, but absolute power would provide freedom
   c. the power of the state would increase, but the power of any individual would decrease
   d. the power of the state and all individuals would increase
   e. the state would wither away
4. Marx charged that capitalism was unfair because of its:
   a. income payments to capitalists; he recommended having ownership of capital by the state
   b. income payments to capitalists; he recommended taxing capitalists' income more heavily
   c. inadequate income payments to capitalists; he rec-

ommended the transfer of some labor income to capitalists
   d. low income payments to highly skilled workers; he recommended paying skilled workers more
   e. high income payments to highly skilled workers; he recommended paying highly skilled workers less
5. Marx argued that:
   a. surplus value goes to labor under a capitalist system
   b. surplus value goes to capital under a capitalist system
   c. surplus value goes to capital under a communist system
   d. deficit value goes to capital under a communist system
   e. deficit value goes to capital under a capitalist system
6. In Marxist countries, communism refers to:
   a. a period of violent class struggle
   b. a transitional period leading to socialism
   c. a period in which the means of production (capital equipment, etc.) are owned by the state
   d. a period in which the means of production are owned by the community as a whole
   e. a period in which there is a dictatorship
7. According to sympathetic critics, one of the most significant weaknesses of any Marxist system is that it:
   a. provides enormous political power to its leaders, but inadequate means of controlling them
   b. provides its leaders with enormous political power, but inadequate economic power to do the job
   c. provides its leaders with enormous political power, but inadequate income
   d. provides its leaders with enormous political power, but inadequate financial power to do the job
   e. cannot provide employment opportunities
8. Human capital is owned by:
   a. the state in a capitalist system
   b. the state in a communist system
   c. the employing firm in a communist system
   d. the employing firm in a capitalist system
   e. neither the state nor the employing firm in either system
9. The Soviet Union has:
   a. more officially measured inflation than the United States, but less disguised unemployment
   b. less officially measured inflation than the United States, but more disguised unemployment
   c. more officially measured unemployment and inflation than the United States
   d. less disguised unemployment and officially measured inflation than the United States
   e. about the same officially measured inflation as the United States but less disguised unemployment
10. In the Soviet Union:
   a. vast accumulations of money can be passed on to future generations, just as in the United States
   b. vast accumulations of money cannot be passed on to future generations, nor can human capital
   c. vast accumulations of money cannot be passed on to future generations, but human capital can be

   d. both kinds of wealth can be passed on
   e. neither kind of wealth can be passed on
11. The savings necessary to finance the expansion of automobile factories:
   a. is provided voluntarily in our system. (Those whose incomes are low are not required to save at all.)
   b. is provided voluntarily in the Soviet Union
   c. is "forced saving" in the Soviet Union. (It is paid in taxes to the government by all the public, whether or not they wish to save.)
   d. (a) and (b)
   e. (a) and (c)
12. The Soviet system of political dictatorship:
   a. is not consistent with Marx's views
   b. is consistent with Marx's views that the overthrow of capitalism would be followed by a dictatorship
   c. makes it more difficult for central planners to impose their authority
   d. makes it more difficult to divert resources from consumer goods to heavy industry
   e. is supported by all Marxists in other countries
13. In the Soviet system:
   a. the state owns most productive assets
   b. prices are determined largely by a central planning agency
   c. consumers choose from a relatively narrow selection of goods
   d. preference in production is given to heavy industry over consumer goods
   e. all of the above
14. Bottlenecks arise in the Soviet Union because:
   a. of the problems of setting up a completely consistent system of production quotas
   b. workers receive all the income
   c. there is no disguised unemployment
   d. investment is a smaller percentage of GNP than in the United States
   e. the inflation rate is higher than in the United States
15. Compared to the Soviets, the Yugoslavs face:
   a. a less serious problem of overt unemployment, but a more serious problem of disguised unemployment
   b. a more serious problem of overt unemployment, but a less serious problem of disguised unemployment
   c. the same problem of overt unemployment, but a less serious problem of disguised unemployment
   d. a more serious problem with both forms of unemployment
   e. a less serious problem with both forms of unemployment
16. Between 1980 and 1985, the Chinese government moved:
   a. from the Cultural Revolution to the Great Leap Forward
   b. toward more orthodox Marxism
   c. away from more orthodox Marxism to the Great Leap Forward
   d. away from more orthodox Marxism toward Stalinism
   e. toward a greater degree of free enterprise

Exercises

1. Marx contended that in a free-enterprise system [workers, capitalists] exploit [workers, capitalists] by acquiring the surplus value—that is, the difference between _____. Marx's solution was a [violent, nonviolent] revolution in which the [proletariat, bourgeoisie] would seize the property of the [proletariat, bourgeoisie]. A [communist, socialist] system would then follow in which there would be a [democratic government, dictatorship] of the [bourgeoisie, proletariat] and property would be owned by the [community as a whole, state]. Eventually, this would pave the way for a [communist, socialist] system in which the state would [wither away, further consolidate its political power] and all property would be owned by the [community as a whole, state].

2. In the Soviet Union, investment is largely financed by [forced, voluntary] saving in the form of [taxation, subsidization] of [consumer, producer] goods. This investment represents about _____ % of GNP, with the big surprise being that this investment has recently generated such a [high, low] rate of growth. Central planning of investment and production levels is undertaken in the Soviet Union by _____. No matter how complicated the mathematical techniques, miscalculations in the targets occur, and these lead to [excess supply, bottlenecks]. In such circumstances, it is [producers, consumers] who do without. This group is also at a disadvantage because decisions on the models, styles, sizes, etc., of what should be produced are not determined by the [marketplace, hired managers] but instead by the [marketplace, hired managers]. In contrast, Yugoslavia and China have taken important steps to ensure that decisions will be made more by [market pressures, hired managers] and less by [market pressures, hired managers].

In the Soviet Union, the problem of inequality [has, has not] been solved, in large part because [workers, capitalists] have been investing in [physical, human] capital which [can, cannot] be owned by the state.

Essay Questions

1. "A communist society inevitably follows a socialist dictatorship of the proletariat." Explain the degree to which you agree or disagree.

2. What are the problems facing Soviet planners that do not arise in our system?

3. It was often argued in the 1960s that Soviet growth exceeded that of the United States because the Soviets were playing "catch-up ball." Growth is easier in a less advanced economy because it's easier to copy technology than to develop it. Explain why you agree or disagree with this view.

4. "The growth of the labor union movement has severely damaged the credibility of Marxist theory in two respects: First, it has played a role in invalidating one of Marx's predictions. Second, events in Poland in the early 1980s made it clear that a socialist government does not necessarily represent the interests of the working class." Explain why you agree or disagree.

5. Describe what is, in your view, the ideal organization of society. Try to ensure that the system you suggest would work in practice as well as in theory.

6. The textbook makes the point that, while Soviet-style planning reduces measured unemployment, it often replaces this with disguised unemployment. Likewise, the Soviets do not appear to suffer as seriously from inflation as we do. In what sense do you think that the Soviets have also replaced measured inflation with a less obvious kind? (Hint: Is the value of your money really constant if prices remain the same but bottlenecks make goods harder to find?)

7. Can the labor theory of value explain why land has value? Why oil deposits have value? (You may wish to review the discussion in Chapter 35 of how land and resource values are determined.)

8. What do you think the practical problems are in defining a "subsistence wage"? (Hint: Do you think the problems of defining a poverty line in Chapter 36 apply here as well?)

9. Suppose you are a noncommunist politician in an African state. For the last 20 years the communist members of your parliament have been recommending a switch to a Soviet-type system because it offers a more rapid growth rate. What is your view?

Answers

Important Terms: 1 d 2 h 3 c 4 k 5 f 6 j 7 l 8 e 9 a 10 i 11 g 12 b
True-False: 1 T 2 T 3 T 4 F 5 F 6 F 7 F 8 F 9 T 10 T 11 F
Multiple Choice: 1 d 2 b 3 e 4 a 5 b 6 d 7 a 8 e 9 b 10 c 11 e 12 b 13 e 14 a 15 b 16 e
Exercises: 1. capitalists, workers, what labor creates and what it is paid, violent, proletariat, bourgeoisie, socialist, dictatorship, proletariat, state, communist, wither away, community as a whole. 2. forced, taxation, consumer, 30%, low, Gosplan, bottlenecks, consumers, marketplace, hired managers, market pressures, hired managers, has not, workers, human, cannot.

ANSWERS TO
CROSSWORD PUZZLES

CHAPTER 1

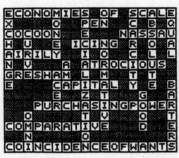

CHAPTER 3

CHAPTER 5

CHAPTER 7

CHAPTER 9

CHAPTER 11

CHAPTER 13

CHAPTER 15

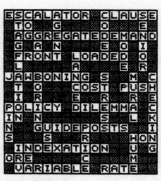

CHAPTER 17

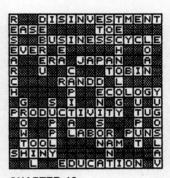

CHAPTER 18

CHAPTER 19

CHAPTER 21

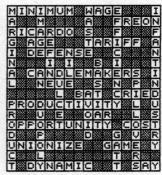

CHAPTER 27

CHAPTER 33

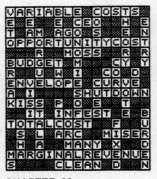

CHAPTER 23

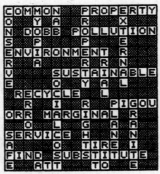

CHAPTER 29

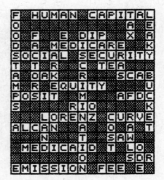

CHAPTER 35

CHAPTER 25

CHAPTER 31

CHAPTER 37